'WISDOM AND GREATNESS IN ONE PLACE'

'Wisdom and Greatness in One Place'

The Alexandrian Trader Moses ben Judah and his Circle

Dotan Arad and Esther-Miriam Wagner

https://www.openbookpublishers.com

All external links were active at the time of publication unless otherwise stated and have been archived via the Internet Archive Wayback Machine at https://archive.org/web

Any digital material and resources associated with this volume will be available at https://doi.org/10.11647/OBP.0352#resources

Semitic Languages and Cultures 37

ISSN (print): 2632-6906
ISSN (digital): 2632-6914

ISBN Paperback: 978-1-80511-070-5
ISBN Hardback: 978-1-80511-071-2
ISBN Digital (PDF): 978-1-80511-072-9

DOI: 10.11647/OBP.0352

Cover image: Georg Braun and Frans Hogenberg, *Map of Alexandria* (1575), Metropolitan Museum of Art, https://commons.wikimedia.org/wiki/File:Map_of_Alexandria_MET_L.2009.33.07.jpg
Cover design: Jeevanjot Kaur Nagpal

The fonts used in this volume are Charis SIL, Scheherazade New and SBL Hebrew.

CONTENTS

ACKNOWLEDGEMENTS

The idea of this book was conceived in a pub during a friendly conversation in a tiny pub in Cambridge around 2010. We discussed the low availability of Judaeo-Arabic texts from the late Middle Ages for research and decided to join forces in attempting to tackle a challenging task: publishing a corpus of dozens of documents stored in the Bodleian Library, identified by the shelfmark Heb. C.72. While some scholars were aware of this collection of documents and a few individual letters from it had even been published, no comprehensive research had been undertaken, leaving these faded and torn fragments in obscurity.

As with many collaborative volumes, it took a good number of years, sweat, and blood for this book to finally manifest and we are enormously grateful to Prof. Geoffrey Khan and Dr Aaron Hornkohl for accepting us into the Cambridge Semitic Languages and Cultures series.

The University of Cambridge and Open Book Publishers have been inspirational publishers to work with, and our thanks go to Paul Moore in particular.

Many colleagues helped to bring this book about, and our heartfelt appreciation goes to Dr Amir Ashur, Prof. Benjamin Arbel, Prof. Charles Burnett, Dr Mike Carr, Prof. Michael Cooperson, Prof. Mordechai A. Friedman, Dr Renard Gluzman, Dr Yehoshua Granat, Dr Dan Grinberger, Prof. Joseph Hacker, Prof. Judith Henschke, Dr Nathan Hofer, Dr Rebecca Jefferson, Prof. Geoffrey Khan, Dr Ruth Lamdan, Dr Hagai Pely, Dr Christopher Wright, and Dr Liran Yadgar. Special thanks to Dr Anne Burberry for her meticulous work in proofreading the book and preparing it for printing.

We thank the Faculty of Asian and Middle Eastern Studies, Cambridge, for providing the greater part of the funding for publication of this volume. We are also grateful for the financial and administrative support from the Woolf Institute, Cambridge, and financial assistance from the department of Jewish History and contemporary Jewry, Bar Ilan University, our employers who enabled us to complete work on this volume. The Bodleian Library Oxford provided a most wonderful atmosphere to study the manuscripts, surrounded by equally interested manuscript scholars, while the Woolf Institute and a sunny corner office gave us the inspiration for an intensive week of work and a last push to complete the final version.

May this book further scholarship on fifteenth-century Jewish Alexandria and beyond, and illuminate the life and work of our eponymous Moses b. Judah.

INTRODUCTION

1.0. The Collection and Its Importance

For a historian and a linguist/philologist to write a shared volume is an endeavour rarely undertaken. Yet with the corpus presented in this volume, two intriguing aspects of research come together. On the one hand, the sources come from a time and place from which few sources have emerged and about which little is known, making it a prime focus for new avenues of historical investigation. On the other hand, from a linguistic point of view, the Judaeo-Arabic correspondence of the corpus is a true rarity—with only a handful of other comparable letters extant—offering a unique opportunity to undertake a synchronic linguistic description of fifteenth-century utilitarian prose. The two authors, applying their different skill sets, have thus surveyed, transcribed, and translated the sources together, and analysed them from both historical and linguistic points of view.

In the introduction to his great series, *History of the Jews in Egypt and Syria under the Rule of the Mamlūks*, Eliyahu Ashtor (1944; 1951; 1970) described the main problem facing the historian of this period: the lack of sources. In comparison to the Fāṭimid and Ayyubid periods, from which many thousands of documents are extant in the Cairo Genizah, little remains from the Mamlūk period. Only 74 documents were published by Ashtor in his study: in comparison, the mercantile letters of the eleventh century published by Moshe Gil (1997) alone number more than 900. A few further documents from the Mamlūk period were published by Mann (1931), Assaf (1946), Goitein (1953; 1984), Mark Cohen (1984; 1986; 2005b), and others. In the last decades, some more Hebrew documents from the late Mamlūk period have been published by Abraham David (most in David 2013; 2016). However, the series by Ashtor, almost 50 years after its publication, remains the basic introduction to the history of the Jews under the Mamlūks[1] and the main collection of Judaeo-Arabic letters from this period accessible to readers. The present book, therefore, with its new sources and angles of investigation, contributes substantially to both the historical and the linguistic research on the Mamlūk period.

Our corpus is also unique because of the region it relates to. The majority of Egyptian Genizah documents from this period concern Cairo and Fusṭāṭ. Our book puts the community of Alexandria at the centre of its discussions. It provides new data on the social and religious life of the city and sheds particular light on its Jewish elite. Most previous research on the Jewish communities of the Mamlūk period has focused on two major cities: Cairo (including Old Cairo/Fusṭāṭ) and Jerusalem. The former is documented through the Genizah materials, and the latter well documented from a variety of other sources, including letters, pilgrims' diaries, Mamlūk historiography, and records from the Sharia court of the city. Some data on other Jewish communities, such as Damascus, Aleppo, and Hebron, have been preserved in Muslim and Christian sources, as well as Christian pilgrims' dia-

[1] For an updated short introduction to the history of the Jews in this period, see Mazor (2021).

ries and European archives. Our information on Alexandria, however, remains very limited. Its Jewish community was relatively small in comparison with those of Cairo or Damascus. Lacking in prominent rabbinic figures, it had little influence on the spiritual life of eastern Jewry. Alexandria was, however, the gate to the west. It was a vibrant centre of trade: people, goods, books, and ideas arrived in its port and had great influence on its social and cultural life. The port of Alexandria was often the first Mamlūk territory onto which Maghribian, Ashkenazi, Italian, and Spanish Jews (including *conversos*) stepped after their long voyages. Its Jewish (and non-Jewish) population may have been comparatively small, but it still had a vivid communal life. Unlike conservative Cairo, it had taverns run by Christians and Jews to entertain sailors and other foreigners, which were also frequented by the local population (Christ 2012, 167–84). The new picture of this community presented in this book may typify similar medium-sized communities along the eastern Mediterranean, especially other port cities, such as Tyre or Tripoli.

At the heart of this book stands a unique collection of manuscripts from the Bodleian Library in Oxford, Bodl. MS Heb. c. 72. Despite attempts to trace the history of their acquisition with the help of Bodleian librarians, we have not been able to determine how the materials came to Oxford. The manuscripts' classmark is not included in the Neubauer and Cowley catalogues nor among those of the typescript Bodleian handlist, and thus they must have been purchased at a much later date, probably between

1910 and 1920,[2] a fact supported by the high number in the Heb. c. classmark range. The traces of caked mud on some of the fragments might indicate burial in a grave, but, as suggested by a number of scholars who have inspected the fragments, they may also have been used in the binding of books—based on how some of the fragments were cut, possible traces of glue in the mud caking, and other traces in the margins of fragments. Although the fragments can now be found itemised on the Friedberg Genizah website (www.genizah.org), and are tightly connected through personalities mentioned in the Genizah documents (as well as in documents from this period from the Cairo Community Archive), they certainly did not come from the Ben Ezra Synagogue. Instead, they must have been part of a different collection or archive, but how this collection came to be used in the bindings of books is not at all clear.

All the documents in the Bodleian collection appear to have a connection to Moses b. Judah, a fifteenth-century community leader, bibliophile, and scholar. Most of the documents are letters addressed to him, or to the leaders of the Alexandrian community, of whom Moses was the most prominent. The collection also includes a legal document, which gives illuminating insights into social life in Alexandria in that period. In this volume we have divided the documents into two groups: those that refer mainly to communal affairs, marked as C (= communal documents), and those that are personal to Moses b. Judah and his circle, marked as P (= private letters). The division between the two categories

---

[2] We would like to thank Dr Rebecca Jefferson for this estimate.

is sometimes a question of balance. Certain letters contain both public and personal matters.[3] But in most cases the difference between the two genres is clear.

The collection also includes literary sources, which can be dated to the fifteenth century. The connection between the letters and the literary sources is not entirely self-explanatory. Nevertheless, as we shall show later, there is enough evidence to link the corpora together. We therefore suggest that these fragments came from Moses' own library and reflect his intellectual taste (for further discussion, see §2.5).

To the materials of the Bodleian collection, we have added a few documents from the library of the Jewish Theological Seminary in New York that relate to Moses and his circle.

Our fascination with the sources sustained us through the difficulties of being two researchers based in different countries preparing a volume together. The richness of the material, centred as it is on a particular person in a specific time and place, makes this corpus of fragments very precious. This distinguishes it from other sources, such as the Genizah fragments. Although the Genizah has an abundance of autographs by certain writers, such as the hundreds of legal documents composed by the court

---

[3] This is also the situation in Genizah documents from the Classical Genizah period. For example, a letter by the Alexandrian leader Yeshuʿah b. Joseph, written around 1060, contains both public matters (the ransom of captives and more) and trade affairs (Bodl. MS Heb. b. 3/16). This letter was published by Gil (1997, IV: no. 671) and again by Frenkel (2006, no. 1).

scribes Hillel b. Eli and Ḥalfon b. Manasseh, in addition to fragments of literary works copied by those two authors and complemented by some personal correspondence, it would be difficult to trace what books Hillel and Ḥalfon may have owned or worked with in the course of their intellectual pursuits. In the Bodleian corpus, however, a range of letters on various topics open up both the public and private worlds of Moses b. Judah—his position in the community, mercantile activities, and intellectual interests. From book orders to descriptions of evenings with wine and good food, the letters paint a lively picture of the man, his social environment, circle of friends, eating and drinking habits, and great love of books.

2.0. Historical Background of the Documents

As noted above, we have made a division of the documents in our corpus into those concerned with communal affairs, on the one hand, and those pertaining to Moses b. Judah's intellectual and mercantile circle, on the other. The letters in both sections contain rich historical data. We cannot discuss all the subjects mentioned in the documents but will attempt to provide a general survey of the main historical issues that they touch upon. Further information can be found in the commentary following the transcription and translation of each document and literary text, including mention of notable linguistic features (a summary of the linguistic phenomena found in the letters is provided separately in §III.2.12).

The first section includes letters written by the heads of the Jews in the Mamlūk Sultanate, the Negidim. Most of the Negidim's letters in our corpus deal with communal affairs in Alexandria. Other letters relate to the payment of the poll tax, the leadership of the community, and the immigration of *conversos*, i.e., converted Jews from the Iberian Peninsula, mentioned by Moses b. Judah's associates. This group of letters is complemented by a unique deed from the year 1481, written by the local leaders of the community of Alexandria, which also sheds light on communal life in the city. The unique corpus, supplemented by other sources, allows us for the first time to attempt in this introduction to provide a comprehensive discussion of the community of Alexandria in the Mamlūk period (§2.1). The new data on the late Negidim justify an update of the discussion on the Nagidate in the fifteenth century, based on our corpus and other selected documents from the Genizah and the Cairo Community Archive (§2.2).

The second section of our corpus is dedicated to the letters sent to Moses b. Judah by his associates and the agents of his commercial network. The letters deal with many different subjects, which are discussed in the commentary following each letter, but two main topics appear again and again: commodities bought and sold by his agents and books that they purchased. To illustrate the background to this world of Egyptian Jewish traders, we examine the main processes of international trade on the eastern shores of the Mediterranean and some of its Jewish protagonists (§2.3). This is followed by an analysis of the data on the main protagonist of this book, Moses b. Judah (§2.4).

The third section contains fragments of diverse literary works from varying textual genres. These fragments were preserved together with Moses' archive of correspondence in bindings, and we believe there is a high probability that they came from his library. This assumption is supported by various pieces of corroborating evidence. For example, the literary letter Bodl. MS Heb. c. 72/2 + 24 is visually very similar to the rest of the correspondence; all the fragments can be dated to roughly the same time period on the basis of codicological analysis; details of some of the preserved literary works are discussed in the correspondence; and, finally, the torn pieces of the same letters (e.g., Bodl. MS Heb. c. 72/21 + 40 + 30 and Bodl. MS Heb. c. 72/35–36) contain the two dominant colourations of the collection—a reddish-brown and a beige hue—which can be found in all the fragments.

Through identification of the literary fragments, and the various books purchased for him by his agents, we have tried to reconstruct the contents of Moses' library (§2.5). This reconstruction not only teaches us about Moses himself and his place as a local scholar, but also fills in the larger picture of the literary tastes of the Jewish elite and intelligentsia in the Mamlūk state as a whole.

2.1. The Jewish Community of Alexandria

Our corpus sheds new light on the communal life of Alexandria's Jews in the late Mamlūk period. The Jewish community of Alexandria is one of the communities of the diaspora with the longest continuous history, from the Hellenistic period until the twentieth century. Indeed, it is even possible that they lived in the same area of the city from Late Antiquity until the Middle Ages (Frenkel 2006, 36).

In the Hellenistic and early Roman period, Alexandria was one of the most important communities of the Jewish diaspora, and many well-known and influential works, such as the Septuagint and Philo's works, were composed there. Rabbinic sources describe the community and its fabled synagogue with much admiration (e.g., t. Sukkah 4.4). The 'Golden Age' of the community came to an end in 117 CE, after its destruction by the Emperor Trajan (Traianus), following the Jewish rebellion of that year.[4] In the late Roman and Byzantine periods, a small Jewish presence persisted in the city, as shown in papyrus finds, but the community never recovered the glory and power of former times.[5]

The Muslim conquerors of Egypt established their new centre at Fusṭāṭ. The lack of sources on Egyptian Jews from the early Islamic period does not allow us to gauge the status of Alexandria among other communities in Palestine and Egypt at that time. Nevertheless, as the data on Egyptian Jewry becomes richer, thanks to the Genizah materials, from the eleventh century onwards, it is clear that Fusṭāṭ was by this time already the leading

---

[4] ומי החריבה? טרוגיינוס הרשע 'and who demolished it? Trajan the tyrant' (y. Sukkah 5.1).

[5] For archaeological remains of the Jewish presence in Alexandria in the Hellenistic, Roman, and Byzantine periods, see Horbury and Noy (1992). On the disruption of the Jewish community of Alexandria after the rebellion, and the rise of the Christian community in its stead, see Modrzejewski (1995, 161–231).

community in Egypt. Evidence from Genizah materials leads to the conclusion that culture and tradition in Alexandria were a little different from Cairo,[6] but systematic research to elaborate this has not yet been undertaken.

The community of Alexandria, in the Fāṭimid period as well as in later periods, mostly relied on the political and spiritual power of the Jewish elite in Fusṭāṭ and, as that faded from the end of the eleventh century onwards, increasingly in Cairo. The Jews of Alexandria had their local leaders, but none of them had authority over other communities in Egypt.

The history of the Alexandrian community in the Fāṭimid period (969–1171) has been discussed comprehensively by Frenkel (2006; 2020).[7] She examines the roles of the local leaders, their education, the strategies they employed for building their political power, their relations with the Cairene centre, and more. The core of the book is a collection of biographies of the leading members of the community. Frenkel shows that this leadership was subject to outside forces. Throughout most of the eleventh century, Alexandria was under the authority of the Palestinian Yeshivah, located in Jerusalem. With the decline of the Palestinian Gaonate, and the turmoil in the Holy Land caused by the Seljūq invasions, the last third of the eleventh century saw the Jews

---

[6] S. D. Goitein draws attention to this in several places; see, for example, Goitein (1988, 82, 249).

[7] A reference to the revised and updated English edition (2020) of the Hebrew original (2006) has been added for the benefit of the English reader. However, the English version does not include an edition of the 100 Judaeo-Arabic letters that appear in the Hebrew version.

of Egypt look closer to home for their governance, with the rise of a new type of leadership in Cairo, the *Riʾāsat al-Yahūd*.[8] The *Raʾīs al-Yahūd* 'Head of the Jews', who was permanently entitled Nagid in Hebrew, was the official leader of the Jews in Syria, Palestine, and Egypt. During the late Fāṭimid period, the Nagidate was held by members of Geonic families who had settled in Egypt and some powerful local families.

The Jewish community of Alexandria was in this period divided along religious lines into two groups: Rabbanites and Karaites.[9] The Rabbanites themselves were divided into two groups based on origin: the 'Palestinians', who comprised the more ancient factions of Jewish Egyptian society, and the 'Babylonians', i.e., later arrivals from Iraq and Persia. Each group had its own rites, such as liturgical versions and halakhic traditions. This division also shaped social life in Alexandria. The members of each group had their own synagogue.[10] The eleventh century also saw

---

[8] This shift was discussed extensively by Cohen (1980). Shulamit Sela (1994) offered a new model. She argued that the authority of the head of the Yeshivah was limited only to the Rabbanites and tried to trace the position of 'head of the Jews' in earlier periods. Marina Rustow (2008, 67–108) criticised Sela's arguments and presented a revised version of Cohen's model. For a brief summary of the debate, see Arad (2023, 55–57). See also hereinafter, n. 47.

[9] There is not much research on the Karaites in Alexandria in the Fāṭimid period. See Goitein (1988, 365); Bareket (2003, 244); Rustow (2008, 282, 341–42).

[10] On the two synagogues in Alexandria, see Goitein (1962b, 37–38, 131; 1971, index volume); Frenkel (2006, 41–42).

the creation of a distinct group in Egypt, comprised of immigrants from North Africa, the Maghribians.[11] The Maghribīs, predominantly traders with a strong sense of collective identity, tried to maintain themselves as a distinctive body and, for instance, paid their taxes directly to the Muslim authorities, even as the leaders of the city objected to such practices (Frenkel 2006, 77–79; see also Goitein 1971, 67; Ben-Sasson 1987, 66). Such a complicated mosaic of Jewish society (Palestinians, Babylonians, Maghribians, Karaites) was not unique to Alexandria, of course, but also characterised the community of Fusṭāṭ/Cairo and other Egyptian communities (Bareket 1999, 4–21).

2.1.1. The Ayyubid Period

In the Ayyubid period (1171–1250), the Nagidate was mainly in the control of Maimonides (1138–1204)[12] and his descendants, against a background of continuous conflict with the Palestinian Geonim in Egypt over who would wield authority.[13] The Maimonidean dynasty established a different type of leadership, which expressed itself in less hierarchical order and high involvement

---

[11] On the Maghribians in Alexandria in the eleventh century, see Mann (1931, 369); Goitein (1962b, 77); Frenkel (2006, 86–91).

[12] Maimonides himself was a head of the Jews but, unlike his descendants, did not bear the title *nagid*.

[13] Mordechai A. Friedman has published several studies on the tension between Maimonides and his son Abraham on the one hand, and the Geonim of the ha-Shishi ('the Sixth') family and other leading Palestinian figures in Fusṭāṭ on the other. See Friedman (1996; 1999; 2005; 2016a). On Maimonides' conflicts, also see Ben-Sasson et al. (1991).

of the Nagid in the daily management of the communities. The leaders of the Maimonidean family continued to lead Egyptian Jewry until the beginning of the fifteenth century. Following the termination of this dynasty, a new stage began in the Nagidate, which will be discussed in detail later.

As with the immigration of Babylonians and Maghribis in earlier periods, the Ayyubid period saw a sharp rise in the migration of French Jews to Egypt and the integration of their leading scholars into the local leadership (Goitein 1980, 338–43; Kanaforgel 1986; Reiner 1988, 50–80; Cuffel 1999). Jews from other Christian lands also increasingly settled in Egypt. Frenkel describes in detail some of the personalities who arrived and became local leaders in Alexandria, such as R. Pinḥas (Frenkel 2006, 121–27), R. Anatolī (Frenkel 2006, 128–33), and R. Samuel b. Jacob (Frenkel 2006, 133–36). Some of them found it difficult to attain status in public life, due to their foreignness, lack of language skills, and ignorance of local customs, while others learnt Arabic quickly and succeeded in integrating well into the milieu of Egyptian rabbis.

The changes brought about by this foreign influx were short-lived. The French immigrants did not retain their separate identity into the Mamlūk period. It appears they assimilated into local Jewish society, and we lose sight of a distinct group of French Jews in the documentary record. Document C.6, for example, contains the names of the 'Seven Town Elders' of Alexandria. Only one of them has a western European nickname, Mūsā

Faranjī, but it seems he was a Spanish newcomer, and not a descendant of the French families who arrived in the thirteenth century.[14]

Other social processes in Egypt were longer-lived and influenced economic life until the end of the Mamlūk period and even later, notably the settlement of Christian traders in Egypt. The Crusades renewed the connections between Western Europe and the East. Salaḥ al-Dīn recognised the economic advantages of trade with the West contributing to the Egyptian market, and he gave permission for traders from the Italian maritime republics to settle in Alexandria. Similarly, Jewish traders in the islands and on the eastern shores of the Mediterranean built strong relations with Italian, Catalan, French, and other foreign merchants. These relations are reflected in many of the documents in our corpus.

2.1.2. The Mamlūk Period

At the beginning of the thirteenth century, the celebrated poet and translator Judah al-Ḥarīzī made a long tour through the communities of the Near East. His impressions were recorded in many poems, in Arabic and Hebrew, and in one of them that al-Ḥarīzī dedicated to the community of Alexandria, he glorified the religious devotion of the local Jews and praised it in vivid language (Al-Ḥarīzī, Kitāb al-Durar, 119–20 [Arabic], 81*–82* [English]):

---

[14] Another elder is al-Siqillī, i.e., 'the Sicilian' (his personal name has not been preserved), but the Sicilian Jews had a separate culture, which was deeply connected to the Jewish Arabic-speaking world.

As for the inhabitants of Alexandria, they are possessed of intelligent souls and pure deeds. I have seen no comparable congregation holding so fast to the rope of religion and obedience, performing acts of kindness according to their means, I declared about them:

وطايفةٍ حوت إسكندريّة

Within Alexandria's precincts there is a congregation,

لها همم أنارت كوكبيّه

Who shine in the galaxy through their aspiration.

خلا ئقهم مفضلة أبيّه

Their manners are noble and of elevation,

وتشملها نفوس جوهريّه

Of which only essential souls are in possession.

مواردهم لواردها نديّه

Their springs shower the visitor with water,

وفي يدهم إيادٍ عسجديّه

And their hands extend gifts of gold.

فكم شيمٍ لديهم حاتميّه

Numerous are their qualities worthy of Hatim,

يؤيدها عزائم صارميّه

Upheld by determined resolves.

شمائلهم شمائل عنبريّه

Their qualities are pure amber,

تدير بها العلى كاسا سميّه

In which dignity, as a noble goblet, resolves.

... تحقر ساهريّه

Their [...] would confound the nightly stars,

وعزمتهم تفلّ ال.....يّه

Their resolve blunt [the sharpened sword].

Yet an Ayyubid-period panegyric, as interesting as it may be, cannot really help us delve into the main characters and developments that occurred among the Alexandrian Jews of the Mamlūk period (1250–1517). The sources on Alexandria's Jews in the Fāṭimid and Ayyubid periods are relatively rich, and many of them have been published (a hundred documents by Frenkel alone, and more by other scholars). The poverty of Genizah sources concerning Alexandrian Jews in the Mamlūk period, on the other hand, stands out. There are some exceptions, and a few documents related to Alexandria in this period have been published by Ashtor in his book *History of the Jews in Egypt and Syria under the Rule of the Mamlūks*.[15] Two (TS 6J2.1 and TS 16.287) were dated by him to the beginning of the fifteenth century (Ashtor 1970, 100–5), but Goitein (1971–1973, 68–69) has clearly shown that they were written 200 years earlier than that. Our knowledge of the Alexandrian community in the Mamlūk period is thus very limited. Such sparse and isolated sources in the published works do not allow us to produce even a partial picture of the social and communal institutions of the local Jews in that period.

It is clear, then, that the documents that we are presenting for the first time in this book will provide a vital contribution to our understanding of the communal and intellectual life of Alexandrian Jews in the late Middle Ages. They are particularly rich for the second half of the fifteenth century and provide an essential complement to the previously known literary and historical

---

[15] For example, Bodl. Heb. d. 68/101 (Ashtor 1970, 10–12). See hereinafter, §2.1.4.

sources. Together, these enable us to sketch the full panorama of life in fifteenth-century Alexandria.

In contrast to the Fāṭimid period, which was a 'golden era' in the history of the Jews of Alexandria, largely due to the comfortable economic conditions and the broad autonomy given by the government, the Mamlūk period was a time of relative decline and stagnation.[16] The intensity of this decline was not so drastic as depicted by Arab historians in the Mamlūk period, but its existence cannot be denied (see Ayalon 1993). Economic freedom of action was damaged as a result of the process of monopolisation of some sectors by the Mamlūk emirs, and by heavy taxation. The economic decline grew stronger in the late Mamlūk period, because of the exploitation of new routes to India and the Far East that bypassed Egypt, and the European conquests in the New World, which radically eroded Alexandria's status as a central storehouse for far-eastern merchandise.

Like other Jewish communities under Mamlūk rule, the Jews of Alexandria suffered from a worsening of attitudes towards non-Muslim inhabitants of the city, both at the hands of their Muslim neighbours and from government officials, leading to increasing oppression and harassment. For example, an Arabic source reporting on an attack on Christian and Jewish homes in Alexandria, probably during the reign of *sulṭān* Qalāwūn (1279–

---

[16] For a general survey of Alexandria in the Mamlūk period, see Labib (1978, 134–37); Frenkel (2014). The term 'decline' and the phenomenon of 'declinism' has been much debated since Herman's (1997) discussion of decline in Western history. For an examination of the term in the Mamlūk period, see Hofer (2017).

1290), describes rioters destroying the residences of non-Muslims, under the claim that the houses had been built illegally higher than Muslims' houses (Ashtor 1944, 92).

Some Jews sought to alleviate their lot by converting to Islam, as was common too among Christians.[17] Conversion opened the door for *ḏimmīs* (Jewish and Christian non-Muslims) to achieve high rank in the Mamlūk administration without attracting hatred and suspicion from their colleagues or the *ʿulamāʾ* (the Muslim religious scholarly elite). One of the most well-known converts of the Mamlūk period was a Jew from Alexandria, Saʿīd ibn Ḥasan, who became a Muslim in the month of Shaʿbān 697 H (May 1298). After an attempt to arrange a public dispute with Christian and Jewish scholars in front of the *sulṭān*, he emigrated to Damascus, where he wrote (in 1320) a polemical work against the *ḏimmīs* (el-Leithy 2005, 283–88).

In general, it can be said that, although the Jews of Alexandria experienced harassment from their Muslim compatriots from time to time, their status was better than that of the local Copts and foreign Christians, whose reputation in the eyes of the Muslims was far worse and who consequently lived under continuous threat. Christians, especially foreigners, were suspected of cooperating with the Mamlūks' enemies. Symon Semeonis, for example, an Irish traveller who arrived in Alexandria in 1323, describes the immediate and insulting harassment that he and his friend experienced on arrival in the port. They were stoned by

---

[17] Conversion was in this period more common among the Copts than among the Jews. On conversion among the Copts in the Mamlūk period, see Little (1976); el-Leithy (2005).

passers-by, and their luggage was confiscated for checking. The officials in the gate of the city broke the images of the saints brought by the pilgrims and called them "dogs and most vile pigs," while some local Christians, who wanted to flatter the officials, cried out (Esposito 1960, 47–49):

> These individuals are surely spies and their arrival here will bring us no good. Let them be expelled in shame from the city and let them return to the countries of the Christians or idolaters whence they came.

Jews were usually exempted from such unpleasant treatment. Though they experienced hatred and disrespect (Semeonis, for example, reported that the Muslims called the Jews "dogs"[18]), they mostly led their lives without disturbance.

2.1.3. Demography and Society

The Alexandrian Jewish community experienced a demographic decline in the Mamlūk period, due to general social developments in the Mamlūk sultanate,[19] as well as to local events such

---

[18] "The ribdals called all the western Christians *Franks* [in the Latin Origin: *Frangy*], the Greeks *Rūmi*, and the Jacobites or Christians of the Girdle *Nysrany*… and the Jews are *Lihud* [*al-Yahūd*] or also *Kelb*, that is dogs [Judeos autem *Lihud*, et alio nomine *Kelb*, id est canes]" (Esposito 1960, 55). The Catholic traveller did not mention a similar negative nickname for the Christian groups, which may also reflect a certain European anti-Semitic bias.

[19] The decline was caused by many factors, such as plagues, droughts, and wars, but the most prominent factor was the Black Death. There is no accurate information on the number of the dead in Egypt during it,

as the war between the Mamlūks and Peter I, king of Cyprus. His crusade against the Mamlūks led to the destruction of the city in 1365. The Cypriot forces took thousands of captives with them when they withdrew, some of them Jews.[20]

The decline of Alexandria's Jewish community in the late Mamlūk period is reflected in stark numerical terms by some witnesses. Benjamin of Tudela, the famous twelfth-century traveller, reported 3,000 Jews living in the city. The reliability of Benjamin's account is problematic for various reasons, one of which is its doubtful authenticity (see, e.g., Ashtor 1967–1968, 11). Even if we take his narrative and numbers at face value, however, it is unclear whether his numbers refer to single individuals, to taxpayers, or to families, and it is possible that he numbered different communities by different methods in his account (Ashtor 1967–1968). Some historians have argued that Benjamin's estimate for the number of Alexandria's Jews, even if it reflects the number of individuals only, must be exaggerated (Ashtor 1967–1968, 12; Goitein 1962b, 78). A similar number, however, was given by another traveller, Meshullam of Voltera, some three hundred years later. In 1481 he visited Alexandria and reported that he heard from the elders that their community had diminished in the last generation (Yaari 1948, 48):

---

but the common estimation is about a third of the population. See Wiet (1962); Dols (1977; 1981); Irwin (1986, 134–38).

[20] On this invasion, its background, and its results, see Edbury (1991, 153–54, 161–69, 178–79); Christie (2014, 102).

> And there are Jews who remember that in their time four thousand Jews were there [= in Alexandria], but now they are diminished like the bulls of the holiday.

The last phrase is important for understanding the perception of the community that the Jews of the city held. The term "the bulls of the holiday" refers to the seventy bulls that were sacrificed for the festival of Sukkot in the period when the Temple still stood. On the first day of Sukkot, the priests sacrificed 13 bulls, on the second day, 12 bulls, etc., until the last day of the festival, when only seven bulls remained for sacrifice. In rabbinic sources, the seventy bulls are a symbol of something that is in a state of decline. The Talmud explains *Bet Shammai*'s opinion that a man has to light the candles of Hanukkah in declining order (eight on the first day, seven on the second day, etc.) with the words: "like the bulls of the holiday" (b. Shabbat 21b). The Jewish elders of Alexandria, hence, understood their community as being in a permanent process of diminution.

Meshullam mentioned that at the time of his visit there were circa 60 Jewish households in the city. We do not know the size of the average Jewish family of those days, but we can estimate that there were in his time approximately 300 Jews in all. Yet the numbers continued to dwindle. Seven years later, the famous Italian scholar, R. Obadiah of Bertinoro, visited the city. In a letter composed in 1488, he stated that he found in Alexandria just 25 Jewish householders (Adler 1930, 222; Hartom and David 1997, 50). Ashtor (1951, 429) suggested that the huge gap between the two reports can be explained by the assumption that Meshullam included the Jews in the environs of Alexandria, while Obadiah referred only to the urban population of the city.

The fifteenth century, therefore, must be judged as a period of demographic decline in Alexandria, and in Egypt overall. This process occurred not only among the Rabbanite Jews but also among other groups. Karaites lived in Alexandria in the Fāṭimid period,[21] but in the Mamlūk period they probably decreased in number, like other communities in the city. There is some evidence for a Karaite presence in Alexandria during the Mamlūk period. For example, Israel b. Samuel ha-Dayyan, a Karaite sage who was active in the early Mamlūk period, mentioned in his calendrical work, *ʿinyan ha-ʿibur*, the Karaites "who settle close to the Land of Israel, the communities of Cairo, Alexandria, which is Noʾ Amon, Damascus, Aleppo, which is Aram Ṣoba, and Aram Naharayim (probably Hit, Iraq)" (MS Jerusalem, National Library 28° 6864, 80a). The Karaite poet Moses b. Samuel, who lived in the middle of the fourteenth century, and converted to Islam before returning to Judaism (see Zawanowska 2010), mentioned in his *diwān* a Karaite named Jacob the cantor who lived in Alexandria (Mann 1935, 249–50). The fifteenth-century Karaite physician Moses b. Abraham b. Saʿadiah was born in Alexandria and later moved to Cairo (Ashtor 1951, 553–54). In his description of the city (1323–1324), Semeonis included a detailed survey of the diverse sects, and mentioned among them Karaite Jews, but it is

---

[21] For example, the twelfth-century Karaite poet Moses b. Abraham Darʿī probably lived in Alexandria for a while (he later moved to Cairo). See Yeshaya (2011, 51–52 n. 17).

not clear if he was referring to Alexandria specifically or to the Mamlūk territories in general.[22]

As described above, the community suffered a continuous decline in the Mamlūk period, and in the 1480s there was probably not a single Karaite family left in the city (Ashtor 1951, 112). The same fate befell the local Samaritan community: in the fifteenth century it ceased to exist (Schur 1992, 110; Arad 2017a, 259). This process furthered the consolidation of the Rabbanite Jewish community of the city. While Cairo suffered from a conflict between the Rabbanites and the Karaites, as evidenced by a difficult dispute in 1465,[23] the Rabbanite community of Alexandria was free from such tensions.

In the fifteenth century, the social mosaic of the Alexandrian community changed again. While the Karaites disappeared, European Jews arrived. A continuous wave of Jewish immigrants started arriving in the East, and some of them settled in the city.

---

[22] "Some are called in Hebrew *Rabanym*, who keep the law according to the glosses of the teachers; others are known as *Caraym*, who observe the law according to the letter" (Esposito 1960, 55). Later, when he described the dress of the Jews in Alexandria, he mentioned only Rabbanite Jews (Esposito 1960, 59). However, in his description of Cairo, where there was undoubtedly a steady Karaite community, he said: "Men and Women of practically every tribe and nation and language under the sun are to be found in Cairo, and the population is in all respects similar to that of Alexandria" (Esposito 1960, 75). For an updated survey on the Karaites in Alexandria in the Mamlūk period, see Arad (2023).

[23] On this conflict, see Hirschfeld (1906); Brinner (1999); Rustow (2007); Arad (2013, 106–7).

Most of them came from Spain and Portugal. European Jews in Alexandria are mentioned in Genizah documents and in our corpus. For example, Joseph Castro, a typical Sephardi name, is mentioned in the letters (P.5.b; C.5). Three other people—Mūsa (C.6), Jacob (C.1.a; C.2), and his brother Isaac (C.2)—are referred to as *Faransī* (פרנשי). In this period, in a Jewish context, this Arabic term usually refers to Iberian emigrants. Other nicknames testifying to European origins are *Siqillī* (C.5; C.6), *Mayurqīnī* (from Majorca; P.7), and *Qarqashūnī* or *Qarqasonī* (which name may indicate an origin from Carcassonne, Provence; P.4.f). This trend is well documented not only in Jewish, but also in European, sources. For example, an archival document from Florence testifies that in 1422 a Jewish dragoman named Abraham served the Florentine traders in the port. Inter alia, he translated for them a privilege given to them by *sulṭān* al-Ashraf Barsbay (Ashtor 1951, 111). Diego de Mérida, a Spanish traveller, visited Alexandria in 1511 and mentioned a Jewish shoemaker from Spain he met there (Ashtor 1951, 445).[24] Another element that became established in the Jewish societies of Egypt and Palestine during the fifteenth century was immigrants from the Maghreb (Hacker 2000; Arad 2014). Some of them were autochthonous, Arabic-speaking Jews, while others were originally Sephardi refugees who spent a certain period in the Maghreb before continuing their journey eastward. Here again, some of them found

---

[24] On R. Joseph Iskandarānī, probably an Iberian emigrant, see hereinafter, §2.1.5.

Alexandria an appropriate place to settle and were integrated into the local trade and administration.[25]

The presence of foreign Jews from the Iberian Peninsula and the Maghreb grew stronger in the first decades of the sixteenth century, and the Alexandrian community consequently experienced a period of revival.[26] The community remained relatively small, however, and never returned to the size or status of its ancient glory.

2.1.4. Leadership

Sources from the Ayyubid period show that the local leadership in Alexandria was in the hands of a collective group of leaders, which included the *Muqaddam*, the judge (*dayyan*) and a council of 'elders', honourable persons of respectable families. The elders took an important part in the leadership. For example, when Moses Maimonides was asked for a communal ruling which forbade a particular slaughterer to continue in his work, the ruling was accepted by the *dayyan* of Alexandria together with a group from "the elders of the community" (Maimonides, *Responsa*, §173). Another question delivered to Maimonides from Alexandria mentioned that in 1180 "the elders of the community" arranged fundraising events "day and night" to collect money to ransom a captive (Maimonides, *Responsa*, §452). R. Abraham, the son of Maimonides, was asked for a ruling that was accepted in June 1135

---

[25] For example, see Duran, *ha-Tashbeṣ*, III:66 (Maghrebi Jews in Alexandria in 1422).

[26] On the community of Alexandria at the beginning of the Ottoman period, see Winter (1983, 13–16).

by "the *dayyan* with an assembly of elders" (Abraham Maimonides, *Responsa,* §106). In a deed from 1253, "the elders of the Alexandria community who are living in her" (זקני קהל נא אמון אלמקימין בהא) gave permission to El'azar b. Solomon to be supported by the communal *waqf.*[27] The elders appear alone in the document. It seems that the council of the elders was considered the authoritative body for control and management of the endowments of the community.

The scarcity of legal documents from Alexandria from the Mamlūk period makes it difficult to understand the nature of the position of *dayyan* in this period. Nevertheless, a unique source mentions the situation in Alexandria: a letter in Hebrew and Judaeo-Arabic, kept in the Russian National Library in St Petersburg (RNL Evr. II A 1683, published in Arad 2023). The letter was sent by Moses b. Samuel the physician, a Karaite leader, "to R. David b. Moses, *dayyan* of the Rabbanite congregation in Alexandria" (אלי ר' דוד בן מושי דין אלג'מאעה אלרבנים בתגר אלאסכנדריה). Undated, it is nevertheless datable to the second half of the fourteenth century. However, the meaning of "*dayyan*" here is not clear. The writer blames the addressee for behaving unjustly towards the Karaites and for discriminating against them in favour of the Rabbanites: "The oppressed are the Karaites alone" (כי העשוקים הם בני מקרא לבד). The writer criticises David b. Moses for placing a heavy burden on the Karaites' shoulders: "All of them are one nation and have one [= the same] law. Why

---

[27] Bodl. Heb. d. 68/101, published by Ashtor (1970, 10–12) and again by Gil (1976, 477–78). The reading by Gil is more accurate; see Blau (1980a, 216).

would you place on them [a yoke] heavier than that decreed by the fathers?" (כי הכל עם אחד וחקה אחת להם[28] ולמה תוסיף עליהם יותר מאשר תקנו האבות). It seems therefore that the term *dayyan* here does not refer to a judge according to Jewish law, but rather to a 'secular' position, and that the "heavy yoke" (כובד העול) described here refers to the taxes owed to the government. David b. Moses was undoubtedly the head of the local Rabbanite community but was simultaneously responsible for all the Alexandrian congregations. He was probably an official appointee (possibly called in Arabic terms *Shayḵ al-Yahūd*[29]) who was responsible for the collection of taxes from the Jews—Rabbanites and Karaites alike—and was blamed for dividing the burden unfairly between the two communities.

This model of collective leadership continued in particular circumstances throughout the Mamlūk period. Document C.6 in our corpus testifies that the authority in Alexandria, at least in certain fields, was still exercised by a council of elders. The deed declares that "on the thirtieth day of the holy month of Nissan, 5241 of the creation [1481 CE]… the [upright] elders, the 'Seven Good Men of the Town'" gathered to administer the inheritance of a dead person.

The elders' authority was not limited to financial affairs, as they were considered generally responsible for overseeing communal life as the highest authority in that field. After receiving a

---

[28] Following Num. 15.15.

[29] On the *Shayḵ al-Yahūd* in the Mamlūk and early Ottoman periods, see Arad (2013, 159–63); Arad (2021, 73–75). On the sixteenth century, see Cohen (1982, 43–45); Singer (1994, 35–36).

report from one of the Alexandrian leaders on a lack of discipline among the members of the community, the Nagid wrote a strong letter in response to the community and warned them that they must obey the 'Seven Elders of the Town': "Whoever disobeys them regarding the value of the financial obligations... they should judge this as 'stealing from many'..." (C.1.a/22–23). On another issue in his letter, he warned again: "Anyone who does not obey them, they should take him to court" (C.1.a/27). In a third exhortation, he ordered: "They should do what (the elders) choose in this matter" (C.1.a/46; see also ll. 31, 45).

The function of the *dayyan* is mentioned neither in the Nagid's letter, nor in the deed mentioned above, nor in other documents in the corpus. The only *dayyan* mentioned in the corpus is not local but lived in Syracuse (P.6). It may be that, because of the reduced size of the community, the town did not hire a judge, and legal issues were determined by the *dayyan* of Cairo. On the other hand, we have to be careful with an *argumentum ex silentio*, and it is still possible that a judge held a position in the community, regularly or ad hoc.

The conclusion that arises from our corpus regarding the Jewish leadership in Alexandria is that its character was somewhat amorphous and there was no official head of the community.[30] Some members of elite families exercised authority, but

---

[30] Compare Frenkel's (2006, 206) conclusion: הציפיה למצוא בכל תקופה מנהיג אחד מוכר ורשמי, המנהל את ענייני הקהילה, נתבררה כמופרכת... כוח השלטון באלכסנדריה לא היה מרוכז בידיו של מנהיג בודד אלא בוזר על פני שכבה שלמה של עילית מנהיגה.

none of them had superiority over their colleagues. The prominence of Moses b. Judah in this group of local leaders is undoubted, but he probably held no official appointment from the Nagid or the community.

2.1.5. Intellectual Life

The collected biographies presented by Frenkel (2006) help us to understand the similarities and differences between the Alexandrian Jewish elite of the Fāṭimid and Ayyubid periods on the one hand, and that of the late Mamlūk period, as reflected in our corpus, on the other. Some traits are very similar, such as their involvement in international trade, their high level of education, and their close ties with the Nagid. But the comparison also reveals a difference in the intellectual worlds of the two groups.

While the figures that appear in Frenkel's book were engrossed in talmudic commentaries, halakhic monographs of the Geonim, and also scientific literature, mainly medicine (Frenkel 2006, 216–20), Moses b. Judah does not seem to have shared these passions—though he was interested in other areas of Jewish intellectuality, such as kabbalistic literature. However, one field was of importance to both the Alexandrian elite of the Fāṭimid and Ayyubid periods and that of the fifteenth century: commentaries on the Hebrew Bible.

Further differences can be observed in the field of literature. The Alexandrian Jewish leaders of the earlier periods showed a deep love for Hebrew poetry: writing their own poetry, copying the works of other poets, and generally showing an appreciation for the art (see Frenkel 2006, 220–21), as reflected in the huge excitement generated by the visit of the great Spanish Hebrew poet Judah ha-Levi.[31] Those of the later period did not preoccupy themselves, it seems, with poetry, nor show the same fondness for it. In their letters, as presented in this book, they do not quote any recognisable poetry, nor refer to poets and poems. We have no evidence to suggest that Moses b. Judah, who wanted to purchase a large array of books for his library, tried to buy any *dīwān* of poetry. Yet, Moses and his colleagues displayed interest in other, more practical, literary genres, such as exemplar letters in highly poetic Hebrew.

Some of the members of Moses b. Judah's circle did have intellectual ambitions. They valued fine books and dedicated financial resources towards buying them. Some of them had a deep knowledge of the traditional Jewish sources, such as Nathan Sholal and the anonymous sage who wrote letter P.9. But these figures did not live in Alexandria. So, what do we know about the rabbinic milieu in Alexandria itself during the Mamlūk period?

Except for the sages of the Maimonidean dynasty, there are few known scholars who lived in Egypt during the Mamlūk period. The famous commentator and lexicographer Tanḥum b. Joseph ha-Yerushalmi (d. 1291) lived, at least at the end of his life, in Fusṭāṭ (see, e.g., Shy 1997; Chiesa 2008). His son, the poet

[31] The events surrounding ha-Levi's visit to Egypt, the poems written during his visit, and his relations with the local prominent Jewish figures are discussed extensively by Gil and Fleischer (2001); Scheindlin (2008); Yahalom (2008, 75–123); Goitein and Friedman (2013); and Granat (2018).

Joseph b. Tanḥum, also lived in Egypt.[32] In the last decades of Mamlūk rule, several prominent scholars, most of them of Sephardi origin, were active in Egypt, among them David ibn Zimra (see Goldman 1970), Nissīm Bivas, Joseph Korkos, and others. All probably lived in Cairo.

The number of scholars who were active in Alexandria is significantly lower. A unique testimony concerning an Alexandrian intellectual in the second half of the thirteenth century was preserved in Elʿazar b. Matityah ha-Dani's super-commentary on Ibn Ezra's Torah commentary. Elʿazar was probably of French origin and settled in Palestine, but spent an unknown period of time in Egypt. In Alexandria he met a local scholar named Ṣadōq b. Elishamaʿ b. Shemaʿyah and studied with him.[33] We have no evidence of a single prominent scholar active in Alexandria in the fourteenth century. At the end of the fifteenth century, Joseph, probably a Sephardi refugee from Spain, settled in the city. The seventeenth-century historian Joseph Sambarī (or Samkarī) introduced him in these words: "R. Joseph, of 'the Scribe' family, the elder, a Sephardi immigrant. He was a great physician and settled in Alexandria. Later he arrived here, in Cairo."[34] In Cairo

---

[32] The date of his death is unknown, but it seems that he was still alive in 1330; see Nave (1970, 60); Dishon (2005, 15).

[33] קבלתי מפי חכם מנא אמון שמו צדוק בן אלישמע בן שמעיה (MS Vatican, Biblioteca Apostolica ebr. 54, 32b). On Elʿazar b. Matityah, see David (1990–1991).

[34] הר' יוסף מבית הסופר הזקן מיוצאי ספרד והיה רופא מובהק ונתיישב באסכנדריא ואחר כך בא פה מצרים (Shtober 1994, 200).

he was given the nickname Iskandarānī. Joseph Iskandarānī's descendants were the leaders of the Mustaʿribs, the local Arabic-speaking Jews in Cairo, during the sixteenth century and the first half of the seventeenth century.[35] Sambarī, whose monumental work *Divre Yosef* was the first history of the rabbinic elite in Egypt from the early Muslim period to his own time, mentions few scholars in Alexandria during the Ottoman period, and none at all during the Mamlūk period.

Information on intellectual life in Alexandria in the Mamlūk period is limited. In the circle of the Nagid, probably in Cairo, an educational institution called *Yeshivatah shel Torah* 'the Academy of the Torah' existed during the Mamlūk period. The term *Yeshivatah shel Torah* appears in documents from the tenure of David ha-Nagid I (1222–1300), in the middle of the thirteenth century,[36] until the end of the tenure of David ha-Nagid II,[37] at the beginning of the fifteenth century.[38] There are no details in the sources on the character of the institution. No institution

---

[35] On the Iskandarānī (or Skandārī) family and its scholars, see Ben-Simeon (1908, 5a–7a); Shtober (1994, 200–1); Arad (2011, 54–56).

[36] For example: TS NS J 165; Goitein (1965, 248–49). On the academy in the fourteenth century, see Goitein (1984, 101).

[37] The dates of his birth and death are unknown. However, it is clear that in 1409, he was still alive, because he is mentioned in a letter from that year. See Mann (1931, 431–34); Ashtor (1951, 27–30); Fenton (2003, 18). On these documents, see also Arad (2013, 186 n. 16).

[38] MS Mosseri V 206; Mann (1931, 429–31). For discussion of this institution, see Arad (2013, 300–2).

equivalent to the Cairene academy existed in Alexandria. Nevertheless, we can assume that the local scholars in Alexandria had a *Midrash,* an unofficial framework for gathering and studying, as was common in urban communities in the Mamlūk and early Ottoman periods.[39] This would probably have met inside one of the synagogues in the city.

Some information on the intellectual atmosphere of Alexandria during the Mamlūk period can be gleaned from the books that were copied in the city during that period. They reflect local scholars' interest in different aspects of Jewish written culture.[40] In Alexandria in 1327, Isaac b. Yefet the cantor copied the Judaeo-Arabic commentary of Tanḥum ha-Yerushalmi on Ecclesiastes.[41] Half a century later, in 1383, a compendium of David Qimḥi's *The Book of Roots* (*Sefer ha-Shorashim*) was copied in the

[39] For a wider discussion on the *Midrash* in the Mamlūk and early Ottoman periods, see Arad (2013, 293–99). See also our discussion hereinafter, §2.4.

[40] Of course, biblical and liturgical books were copied as well; for example, Abraham b. Solomon finished copying a Pentateuch with vowels (only a few fragments of Deuteronomy were preserved) on 29 March 1347, in Alexandria (MS St Petersburg, RNL Evr. II B 901; see colophon on f. 13a).

[41] נגמר פירוש ר' תנחום על ספר קהלת ביום שביעי מחדש מרחשון שנת חמשת אלפין ותמנין ושבעה שנין ליצירה במדינת נא אמון האל יזכה הקורא בו לבנין הארמון בזכות אב המון 'The Commentary of R. Tanḥum on Ecclesiastes was finished on 7th of Marḥeshvan, 5087 of the Creation, in the city of No' Amon (Alexandria). The reader of it will be granted the establishment of the palace (i.e., the temple), in favour of the father of multitude (Abraham)' (MS London, BL Or. 5063, 218a).

city by Joseph b. Jacob the teacher (*ha-melammed*), for the use of Samuel b. Joseph b. Saʿadiah, perhaps a local scholar.[42] In 1426, a copy of *Torat ha-Minḥah*, an anthology of *midrashim* (rabbinic sermons) composed by Jacob Siqillī, was copied in Alexandria by Meʾir b. Elʿazar Abān[!] Ḥesed (אבאן חסד).[43] A decade later, two manuscripts were copied in the city by Joshua b. Judah the physician. The first contains some super-commentaries on Ibn Ezra and kabbalistic works,[44] and the second contains other works on Kabbalah.[45]

Moses b. Judah showed continuity in his intellectual interests. All the genres above—midrashic literature, Bible commentary, Hebrew grammar, and Kabbalah—are well represented in his library, as will be discussed in more detail below.

---

[42] MS Oxford, Bodl. 1482 (Hunt. 292). See the long colophon on 237b–238a, 239a–239b.

[43] MS St Petersburg, Institute of Oriental Studies of the Russian Academy B 210. See colophon on 363b.

[44] MS Vatican, Biblioteca Apostolica ebr. 103. The manuscript was copied in ה'קצ"ו (1435/6). See colophon on 59a.

[45] MS Paris, Bibliothèque Nationale heb. 853, 38–138. The scribe finished his work on 10 January 1437 (see colophon on 79a–79b). See details hereinafter, n. 142. Another manuscript that may perhaps have been copied in Alexandria in the Mamlūk period is a Hebrew–Yiddish dictionary of the Pentateuch, copied in September 1513 (MS Hamburg, State and University Library Cod. Hebr. 137). It was copied "here in Alessandra the capital" (פה אלסנדרא הבירה), but it is more reasonable to assume that the name אלסנדרא refers to Alessandria in Italy than to Alexandria in Egypt.

2.2. The Nagidate of Egypt in the Fifteenth Century

In official Arabic documents, the recognised leader of the Jewish community in Egypt was called *Raʾīs al-Yahūd* 'the Head of the Jews' from the Fāṭimid period onward. The Jewish residents themselves called their leader Nagid.[46] The earliest origins of the title and its role are a big question among researchers and there have been, and remain, some major disagreements. While the researchers of the nineteenth and early twentieth century thought this position, including its Hebrew title Nagid, was established close to the beginning of the Fāṭimid caliphate, Shelomo Dov Goitein and his disciple Mark Cohen claimed that it emerged only in the last third of the eleventh century. However, Shulamit Sela and Elinor Bareket have tried to substantiate the traditional view.[47] In any case, it seems that all scholars agree that the Hebrew term Nagid was not in permanent use for this position, no matter when it was established, before the beginning of the thirteenth century. Maimonides, for example, who undoubtedly served as *Raʾīs al-Yahūd*, was not called Nagid. Only from 1213 CE, during the leadership of his son, Abraham (d. 1237), did it become a permanent Hebrew title of the *Raʾīs*, which persisted in

---

[46] *Nagid* in biblical Hebrew means, mainly, 'leader' or 'prince'. See Brown, Driver, and Briggs (1953, 671); Koehler and Baumgartner (1995, 667). The term was in use in different regions in the Middle Ages, such as Spain, North Africa, and Egypt, and referred to several leadership positions.

[47] See Mann (1920, 251–55); Ayalon (1939); Goitein (1953–54; 1971, 23–40); Cohen (1980, 3–42); Sela (1994); Bareket (2004); Shtober (2005); Rustow (2008, 100–8).

use until the end of the Nagidate in the aftermath of the Ottoman conquest of Egypt in 1517.

The Negidim were glorified with a large number of attributions and praises in Genizah documents. One of the most frequent of the epithets bestowed upon the Nagid in documents is 'the Mordechai of our time' (מרדכי הזמן).[48] It expresses the concept of the Nagid as defender of his community and its interests before the *sulṭān*, emulating Mordechai's actions in the Persian court.

The Nagidate simultaneously symbolised honorific and pragmatic concepts. On the one hand, it represented the dreams and wishes of the Jewish congregation. Any sort of Jewish self-government was a source of pride. The biblical term Nagid, which was associated in the public consciousness with glorious kings such as David (1 Sam. 13.14; 25.30; 2 Sam. 6.21; 7.8), Solomon (1 Kgs 1.35), and Hezekiah (2 Kgs 20.5), conveys the greatness they saw in this office. But on the other hand, the Jewish congregation also had a more mundane understanding of the role of this office. In contrast to some other medieval Jewish leaders,

---

[48] This title follows equivalent attributions used within Muslim society, for example, *Iskandar al-zamān*; see Mayer (1938, 166). For 'the Mordechai of our time', see documents related to David ha-Nagid, Maimonides' grandson (TS 16.76; TS 16.355; TS 6J9.10; TS 13J4.13), and to his son, Abraham (TS 12.406; TS 20.10; TS Misc. 28.26). Such attributions are also used to refer to the last Negidim, who were not part of the Maimonidean dynasty: ʿAmram (CUL Or. 1080J208; TS 12.573) and Joseph (TS 12.815).

most of the Negidim had no claim to Davidic family[49] or other noble family,[50] and no symbolic value that could be used to enforce their authority. The Jewish people understood the limits of the Nagid's power and were aware of his weak position and dependence on the Muslim rulers—but hoped, at least, that their leader would use his connections inside the governor's court to save them from plots and calamity.

The Nagid was considered by the Muslim governors to be the representative of the three Jewish sects: Rabbanites, Karaites, and Samaritans (see Sela 1994). Nevertheless, supremacy was given to the Rabbanite Jews, and the office of the Nagidate was, at least in the Mamlūk period, in Rabbanite hands only. Templates of documents intended for clerks in the Mamlūk state contain copies of the official appointments of the Negidim. These documents detail their duties and rights. Among the duties was the regular transfer of the poll tax imposed on the Jewish community to the treasury of the sultanate, as well as ensuring the Jews' compliance with the *ḏimmī* laws. Among the Nagid's privileges were the appointment of certain religious functionaries

---

[49] On the status of the descendants of King David in Jewish medieval society, see Franklin (2012). The only *Ra'īs al-Yahūd* who claimed Davidic origin was David b. Daniel, who was active in Egypt and Palestine in the 1080s and early 1090s. He did not use the term Nagid, but rather the terms *Nasi* (exilarch), *Rosh golah* (head of the diaspora), or *Rosh galuyut kol Israel* (head of all Israel's diasporas). Concerning him, see Gil (1979); Cohen (1980, 178–212); Franklin (2012, 118–19, 123–26).

[50] However, the Negidim of the thirteenth and fourteenth centuries gained prestige thanks to their respected origin as Maimonides' descendants.

(judge, cantor, slaughterer, etc.) in the Jewish communities throughout the Mamlūk state, responsibility over marriage and divorce within his congregation, and the right to excommunicate those who refused to accept his authority (see Gottheil 1907; Bosworth 1972).

Officially, the authority of the Nagid extended over all the Mamlūk territories. Indeed, for at least some of the Mamlūk period, the office of a vice-Nagid existed, who was responsible for Syria and Palestine. Similar deputy offices, as mentioned in Arabic sources, were held by the Christian Patriarchs in the Mamlūk state (Gottheil 1907, 534; Mayer 1938, 165). There is no information on the vice-Nagid in Hebrew sources until the beginning of the fifteenth century, when some sources confirm a vice-Nagid living in Jerusalem, who was subordinate to the Nagid in Cairo (Hacker 1980, 127–28; David 1980). It seems that the authority of the vice-Nagid was limited to Jerusalem only, while the communities in the north of Palestine and in Syria were subordinate directly to the Nagid in Egypt. Despite the existence of the vice-Nagid in Jerusalem, the Nagid himself also visited the city from time to time to demonstrate his authority.[51]

Several suggestions have been made in the relevant literature to illuminate fundamental questions about the Nagidate: the origin of the office (see n. 47), the time of its demise,[52] the identities of those who served as Negidim, and the accurate time of

---

[51] As testified by R. Isaac Abravanel; see below, §2.2.7.

[52] In the past, researchers accepted Joseph Sambari's chronicle, which mentions Negidim also during the sixteenth century (see, for example, Hirschberg 1974, 586, 589), but today it is common to date the end of

their tenures.[53] The following section will focus on the Nagidate during the fifteenth century. First, we will briefly survey the Negidim of the first half of the fifteenth century, and afterwards, we will focus on the last four Negidim, two of whom, Solomon b. Joseph and Nathan Sholal, are well represented in our corpus.

2.2.1. The Negidim of the First Half of the Fifteenth Century

In the early fifteenth century, a dramatic change occurred in the institution of the Nagidate. After the death of R. David II,[54] the last descendant of Maimonides in that office,[55] the Maimonidean dynasty exited the public stage. From then on, the office was no longer transferred as an inheritance from father to son (or other relatives) for longer than two generations, leading to a period of instability. This instability is reflected in the fact that over the course of more than two hundred years, from the time of R. Abraham Maimonides (who began serving as Nagid shortly after his father's death in 1204) to the end of the (second) tenure of R. David II, just six people served as Negidim in Egypt, while in the

---

the Nagidate to 1517, following the Ottoman conquest of Egypt; see David (1972).

[53] For example, the question of the tenure of Maimonides as head of the Jews, and the time he served in this office, caused significant dispute in the field. For an updated discussion, see Friedman (2005).

[54] The year of his death is unknown, but it is clear that it was not before 1409; see discussion above, n. 37.

[55] Concerning R. David ha-Nagid (the Second), see Mann (1931, 418–28); Goitein (1953). On his works, see §2.5.

fifty years after, about four, and perhaps more, served in this office.

Our knowledge of those decades is very limited. We cannot accurately determine the length of the Negidim’s tenures, and we are not even sure as to their actual number. In 1422 a Nagid called Simon is mentioned (Duran, *Ha-Tashbeṣ*, III, §66; Mann 1931, 428), but we do not know if he was appointed to the office right after David II, or whether there was an anonymous Nagid between them. Recently, a new individual, Isaac al-Fāsī, has been identified by Arad (2013, 89–90) as having held the office of the Nagidate. A *Sijill* document from the Muslim court of Cairo (Cairo Community Archive, no. 31) tells us that in 825/1422, Isaac b. Joshua b. Samuel, the Maghribian who came from Fez, “the head of the Jewish congregations in Egypt,”[56] came to the court and sued a member of the Jewish community for illegally taking over an estate belonging to the community endowment. In the same year, the aforementioned Isaac established an endowment of his own in a well-known alley in Cairo[57] “for the poor of the Rabbanites Jews who live in Cairo and Fusṭāṭ.”[58]

The presence of two Negidim in the same year (1422) opens the gate to many hypotheses. Did Simon die and Isaac take his

---

[56] الرايس اسحق ابن يوشع ابن شمويل اليهودي المغربي الفاسي رايس طوائف اليهود بالديار المصرية.

[57] The real estate was near the Venetians’ neighbourhood, adjacent to the ‘Seven Halls’ alley, a well-known alley mentioned in many Arabic documents.

[58] على فقراء اليهود الربانيين المقيمين بالقاهرة والفسطاط (Cairo Community Archive, no. 42).

place (or the other way round)? Was one of them removed from his office and the other replaced him?[59]

Eliyahu Ashtor (1951, 84–86) concluded that, in roughly the same period, a Nagid called Joseph b. Obadiah was active (see Neubauer 1886, no. 629), but the existence of a Nagid with such a name is very doubtful (Richler 1981). Joseph Hacker (1985, 246–47) suggested that in 1433 someone called ʿAmram served as Nagid and he probably had relations with the Jews of Italy.[60] The next information on the Nagidate is from 1438. An Arabic chronicler mentions that in this year the *sulṭān* appointed a Jew from Alexandria to be Nagid, but the representatives of the Jewish congregation expressed their dissatisfaction in front of one of the emirs, and he called the new Nagid, took away his signs of honour and insulted him (Ashtor 1951, 86). Such dissatisfaction with the Nagid occurred again four years later, when the Jewish congregation submitted a petition to the *sulṭān*, with serious accusations against their leader, ʿAbd al-Laṭīf.[61] They argued that "he undermined the principles of their religion and

---

[59] The Hebrew document concerning Simon is from 11 Iyyar 5182 (= 12 May 1422). The Arabic documents concerning Isaac are not accessible today, so we cannot check the date. We can only determine the year (825 H) according to the catalogue of the archive.

[60] A Nagid called ʿAmram also served in the seventies and the eighties of the fourteenth century, and it is not clear if they are different individuals or not. For another uncertain figure in the Nagidate of the fifteenth century, see hereinafter, n. 147.

[61] Cohen (1984, 444 n. 52) suggests identifying the anonymous *Nagid* in the event of 1438 with ʿAbd al-Laṭīf.

matters having to do with their faith,”[62] and accused him of exploitation, despotism, erroneous judgment of the Jewish law, and more. They requested to have him removed from office.

This event heralds a new period in the history of the Nagidate. The information about the Negidim becomes much richer, and we can feel on firmer ground. In the last sixty years of the Nagidate, their tenure was more relaxed and tranquil. We have no further reports of efforts to remove a Nagid from office, and the Negidim seem more powerful. In this period, two pairs of related Negidim served in office. The first was a father and son, and the second an uncle and nephew.

2.2.2. Joseph and Solomon: A Father and Son in the Nagidate

In the 1450s and 1460s, the head of the Jews was Joseph b. Ḵalīfa. He is mentioned in a deed from 29 May 1458 as “Joseph the great Nagid,”[63] and his name also occurs in other sources.[64] A letter sent to Nathan Sholal (TS 10J24.3 + CUL Or. 1080J174) mentions that, in the time of Joseph ha-Nagid, a man brought

---

[62] אכרב קואעד מלתהום ואמור דינהם (TS AS 150.3; translation by Cohen 1984, 432).

[63] יהוסף הנגיד הגדול (TS 8.195, published by Ashtor 1970, 108–9). Ashtor’s reading is not accurate in some cases. For example, in l. 7, Ashtor reads בו לכלל הסכמות, but it ought to be לבו לכלל החכמות ‘his heart for all the sciences’. We found the continuation of this torn deed (TS Ar. 50.43), but the end of it is still missing. On the verso is a deed in Judaeo-Arabic from 1459.

[64] For example, in an undated torn *ketubbah* (TS 12.815, published by Ashtor 1970, 109–10).

cheese that had not undergone supervision for *kashrut* to Egypt and lied that he bought it from Jews. Joseph punished him and forced him to sell the cheese to gentiles.

Our knowledge of Joseph ha-Nagid is limited. One episode of his public activities is known in detail, however, thanks to an anonymous Judaeo-Arabic story called "The story about the Europeans who became Karaites."[65] According to this tale, a group of *conversos* Jews arrived in Egypt from the Iberian Peninsula in 1459. They wanted to return to the Jewish faith but preferred to adopt the Karaite path rather than the Rabbanite. In September 1465, Joseph heard that this group of *conversos* was going to fast on Yom-Kippur according to the Karaite calendar. Furthermore, he was informed that the Iberian newcomers did not eat the meat of the Cairene Rabbanites. Joseph called on their leader, David, and blamed him: "You are not eating our food and you are walking a different path from us!"[66] When David admitted that they did not eat the Rabbanites' meat because they followed the Karaite *halakhah*, which forbids eating the tail fat of sheep, the Nagid

---

[65] קצה אלאפרנג' אלד'י דכלו בדת בני מקרא (MS London, BL Or. 2358, 73–83). On this text, see the references in n. 23 above. Another source regarding Joseph ha-Nagid is an Arabic legal document dated 1466 (to be published by Arad in press b).

[66] איצ'א אנכם מא בתאכלו מן אכלנא ואנכם מאשיין עלי טריקה ג'יר טריקתנא (BL Or. 2358, 74b): *ṭarīqa* also means 'a religious group or school', like the Sufī orders, etc. It could therefore be translated as: 'you are following a school different from ours'.

told him angrily: "This is a path of heresy, and you are Karaites!"[67] The Karaites took fright at the Nagid's reaction and went to the Muslim court, requesting a fatwa that would allow a Rabbanite to become a Karaite, and vice versa. While the Ḥanafī, the Mālikī, and the Ḥanbalī judges ruled to permit the request, the Shāfiʿī judge thought it was forbidden and stated that, if a Karaite or a Rabbanite wanted to leave his group, he must become a Muslim. In the meantime, the Nagid convened a meeting in his home, in the presence of representatives of the two sides, but they did not succeed in reconciling. Finally, the Karaites bribed the *sulṭān*'s son, and his servants forced Joseph to come to the house of the Mālikī judge. The judge put Joseph ha-Nagid and one of his associates in gaol for three days and ruled that every Jew could join the other group, and that anyone trying to interfere with a Jew joining the group he liked would pay a fine of 1,000 *ashrafī* to the Sultanate treasury.

Our information on the Nagid's son, Solomon ha-Nagid, is limited too. We can learn some information on his family from a levirate agreement of 1482 preserved in the Genizah. This deed informs us that his wife's name was Faraj. After Solomon's death, his brother Yeshuʿah (ישועה) married Solomon's widow, according to the law of levirate marriage. Yeshuʿah already had a wife and was obliged to divide his nights between them: "He will

---

67 פאג׳אבה אלנגיד הד׳א דרך מינות ואנתם קראיין.

equalise between the two wives. One night for this one, and one night for that one."[68]

For Solomon's activities as Nagid, we have a special source. Meshullam of Voltera, the Italian traveller and banker, met him in 1481, and described his administration (Adler 1907, 172):

> The *sulṭān* has placed over the Jews, the Karaites, and the Samaritans, a Jewish lord, rich and learned and much honoured. His name is R. Solomon b. Joseph.[69] He is native to this country and his father was also Nagid and the *sulṭān*'s physician. The Nagid has power over the Jews in all of the *sulṭān*'s dominions; both in criminal and civil matters his word cannot be contradicted.[70]

Meshullam also reported that Solomon ha-Nagid had four judges in his court. The names of the judges look very distorted, probably because the Italian copyist was not familiar with Judaeo-Arabic names and nicknames, and hence corrupted their copying.[71] Meshullam also said that Solomon had, in addition to the four

---

[68] אנה יסוי בין אלזוגתין לילה לדי ולילה לדי. TS 13J4.16, published by Ashtor (1970, 112–15) and again by Friedman (1986, 148–51). See also Goitein (1960, 95; 1983, 307).

[69] The Hebrew original adds here: נ"ע [= נוחו עדן], והוא עשיר ונכבד מאד 'may he [i.e., Joseph] rest in peace. And he [i.e., Solomon] is rich and very venerable'.

[70] In the original: והמלך שם על היהודים ועל הקראים ועל השומרונים נגיד יהודי, אדם נכבד וטוב ויודע [ספר], שמו ר' שלמה ב"ר יוסף נ"ע, והוא עשיר ונכבד מאד, והוא מהארצות ההם, ואביו היה ג"כ נגיד, והיה רופא מהסולדאנו. וממשלת הנגיד היא בכל מדינות המלך ובכל מלכותו על היהודים, הן בדיני נפשות הן בדיני ממונות, ועל דבריו אין להשיב (Yaari 1948, 57).

[71] The corruption of the Hebrew original became worse in Adler's English edition.

judges, two scribes. The first was Judah b. Arikha (יהודה בן אריכה).[72] The second was David, who is named, in the only manuscript of Meshullam's work, as אלחמר. If this version is reliable, perhaps David was a donkey driver (حَمَّار) before he became a scribe, but this option looks implausible. It may be more probable to assume that the name here, like other Arabic names in the text, has been corrupted. We can perhaps suppose, therefore, that the original name of the scribe was דוד א' שמס, the very same David ibn Shams, the Nagid's scribe, who wrote many of the letters in our corpus. Meshullam added interesting details on the Nagid's government. According to him, the Nagid had a prison for punishing members of his congregation.

Meshullam described the reception he received from Solomon ha-Nagid (Adler 1907, 172–73):

> [The Nagid] showed me very much honour… And so from that day onwards I was forced to sit next to the Nagid in the Synagogue, between him and the Judges, and was also forced to eat with him very many times; and seeing that he honoured me in the presence of all the Jews they all honoured me also… and not only this but the Nagid made me find favour in the eyes of the *sulṭān*'s great dragoman who is called Tagri Vardi,[73] and is of Jewish descent.[74]

---

[72] In Adler's edition it is distorted to 'Judah Aruba'.

[73] This has to be Tağrī Birdī (تغري بردي).

[74] The argument that Tağrī Birdī was of Jewish origin is not supported by Muslim sources but mentioned by some Christian pilgrims. Other pilgrims said he was originally Christian. Ashtor (1951, 530–40) argued that he was a Jew who converted to Christianity in Spain and tried to come back to Judaism in the east but was forced to convert to Islam. In

This description illustrates well the considerable prestige of the Nagid and the excellent relations he had with the *sulṭān* and the Mamlūk elite. With this in mind, against this courtly background, we can perhaps better understand the authoritative and decisive language that Solomon employs in our corpus. Not many letters from Solomon are preserved, but they shed a certain light on his activity as Nagid. However, the scarcity of letters from him preserved in the Genizah, in comparison with the greater number of letters from Nathan and Isaac Sholal, his heirs on the throne of the Nagidate, may reflect that his public activity was much less than that of his successors.

2.2.3. Nathan (Jonathan) Sholal

In contrast to Joseph and Solomon, who were natives of Egypt, the next two Negidim were of foreign origin. The Sholal family's rise to power in the last decades of the Mamlūk regime indicates the strengthening of the Maghribian Jews as a dominant element in the Jewish society of Egypt and the Holy Land, a process of which we saw first signs in the Nagidate of Isaac al-Fāsī. The family had not settled in the Maghreb for a long period. Their origin was the Iberian Peninsula, but after the pogroms in Spain in 1391, they emigrated to North Africa.

---

the original: והנגיד וכבדני במאד מאד באופן כי מהיום ההוא והלאה הוכרחתי לישב אצלו בבית הכנסת בינו ובין השופטים, והוכרחתי לאכול עמו כמה וכמה פעמים ובהיות כי מעלתו כבד אותי לעיני כל ישראל, כולם היו מכבדים אותי ולא די זה שנתנני לחן בעיני הטורצימאנו הגדול מהסולדאנו, נק' טאגריוורדי, שהוא מזרע יהודים כמו שאמרתי (Yaari 1948, 57–58).

The name שולאל is usually pronounced and spelled as 'Sholal' by scholars, but there is some evidence suggesting it may have been pronounced as 'Sholel'.[75] In documents from Majorca, members of the family are referred to by the form שוליל (in Hebrew) or *Xulel* (in Catalan; Arxiu del Regne de Mallorca 122; mic. 8460 in IMHM; see Baer 1929, 340–41). The form שוליל appears in other sources[76] and reflects the way the name was pronounced. Other evidence for this pronunciation can be found in a letter by Abraham, the son of Isaac Sholal, the last Nagid. The writer signed at the end of the letter (TS 13J20.30): מקווה רחמי האל 'waiting for God's mercy' אברהם כהן שלאל. Using a rhyme with the writer's name was a very common literary ornament in this period,[77] and the use of the word האל as a rhyme could thus prove the pronunciation of the family name. However, for reasons of consistency, we shall continue to follow the common spelling.

Unlike his predecessors in the Nagidate, the biographical details of Nathan[78] are well known, thanks to a unique family list,

---

[75] Another option is to read it as 'Solel', due to the custom among Iberian Jews of representing ש as *s* (for example: שאלוניקי 'Salonica', קאשטרו 'Castro', etc.). We thank Dr Ruth Lamdan for this comment.

[76] For example, Nathan is mentioned in a chronicle on the expulsion from Spain of his contemporary, the kabbalist R. Abraham b. Eliezer ha-Levi, as ר׳ נתן הכהן שוליל; see Avila, *Keter Torah*, Introduction (ad loc.).

[77] For example: R. Ḥayyim Capusi: ה׳ ניסי חיים כפוסי; R. Joseph ibn Ṣayāḥ/Ṣīʾaḥ: ועצמותיו כטל אורות כדשא יפריח יוסף בן לא״א נב״ת אברהם ן׳ ציאח (see more examples of his signatures in Arad 2008, 136); R. Simon ibn Ḥabib: מגור מסביב שמעון בן חביב.

[78] In some sources he is called יהונתן (Jonathan). It appears that he used both names, but the more frequent name is Nathan.

preserved—in his handwriting—in a copy of the Pentateuch belonging to him found in the synagogue of Jobar, a village near Damascus (today, part of the city). In this list, he gave the date of his birth: "I was born, I—Nathan ha-Kohen Sholal—[in the] year of 5197 from the creation of the world, equivalent to 1437 CE, on 18 Av, may God turn it to be good, equivalent to 20 July, on the Sabbath."[79] In his youth he lived in the Maghreb, probably in Tlemcen, where his father Saʿadiah served as a rabbi (see Ashtor 1951, 449–50; David 1988a, 375). Later he moved to Genoa, and after a while emigrated to Palestine and settled in Jerusalem. In 1482 or 1483 he moved to Cairo, where he lived for the rest of his life; in 1484 he was appointed Nagid. He had seven children: Saʿadiah (b. 1461), Ephraim (b. 1463), Abraham (1465–1482), Dulce (a girl, b. 1467), Masʿūda (a girl, born in Genoa in 1469), Simḥah (a girl, born in Jerusalem in 1471), and Isaac (b. 1474).

Nathan is the best documented among the Negidim of the fifteenth century. At least seven letters sent to him,[80] and three

---

[79] נולדתי אני נתן הכהן שולאל ש׳[נת] הקצ״ז לב״ע [= לבריאת עולם] והיא ש׳ אלף תל״ז למנין הנוצרים י״ח בחו׳ אב יה״ל [= יהפכהו ה׳ לטובה] והוא כ׳ ביולי ביום שבת. The list was published by Toledano (1907). Ashtor (1951, 449 n. 10) wrote that Nathan was wrong, and the Christian date ought to be 13 July 1437, but Nathan was in fact right. 18 Av 5197 was indeed 20 July 1437.

[80] TS 16.216, published by Ashtor (1970, 115–19); ENA 2740.2; CUL Or. 1080J246; TS 18J5.7; ENA 3307.12, published by David (1988a); CUL Or. 1080J174 + TS 10J24.3, one of the fragments of which was published by Assaf (1946, 194–95), before David (1999, 304–7) found the second half of it and republished the whole letter; TS Misc. 28.166,

letters by him (T-S NS 167.16–17, P.2, and C.2), are preserved in the Genizah. He is also mentioned in a few *ketubbot* and other deeds from the 1490s,[81] as well as in some other Genizah documents.

2.2.4. Nathan in Jerusalem

Nathan arrived in Jerusalem not later than 1471. The city had two distinctive features that differentiated it from other cities in the eastern Mediterranean in that period—its multicultural Jewish society and the high proportion of scholars in the community. The social composition of Jerusalem in the late fifteenth century was very diverse: in addition to the native Jews, who were still the majority in the community, there were also Ashkenazi, Sephardi, Italian, and Maghribian Jews, as well as a tiny group of Karaites. Nathan was one of the outstanding figures among the Maghribians,[82] and he also played an important part in the circle

---

an unpublished letter in Judaeo-Arabic. We aim to discuss this letter on another occasion.

[81] 1492—TS Misc. 28.71, published by Ashtor (1970, 119–20); ENA 3616.3, published by David (1988a, 400); 1495—TS 8J6.19, published by Ashtor (1970, 121); 1499—Bodl. MS 2875.3, published by Assaf (1946, 187–88). He is also mentioned in a torn deed (TS 10J13.25, published by David 1988a, 398–99). David suggested that it was written in the summer of רמ״ט (1489), but because it cites a previous deed written in Tammuz 5249 (בראש חדש תמוז שנת הרמ״ט ליצירה), i.e., 1489 CE, it is reasonable to assume that the later deed is from the next year (ר״ן) at the earliest.

[82] On the Maghribian Jews in Jerusalem in the fifteenth century, see Hacker (2000).

of the scholars within the community. Meshullam of Voltera met him in Jerusalem in 1481. In a travelogue, after describing the official Jewish leadership of the city, Meshullam described a group he called *Maskilim*: והמשכילים שבהם הם: ר׳ שלון[!] אשכנזי, והוא רב, ר׳ נתן והוא רב, ושלשה או ארבעה רבנים אחרים אשר לא ידעתי את שמותם. ‘The *Maskilim* of them are: R. Shalom[83] Ashkenazi, he is a rabbi; R. Nathan, he is a rabbi; and there are three or four other rabbis, whose names I do not know’ (Yaari 1948, 77).[84] It is plausible to assume that Nathan here is R. Nathan Sholal. The title *Maskil* ‘educated, learned’, as has been explained by Elchanan Reiner (1992, 28), applies to a scholar who has no official position in the community. Nathan himself uses this term in his letter to describe a group of scholars, probably from Jerusalem (TS NS 167.16r, l. 35, published in Glick et al. 2014, 973–85). Other sources show that Shalom Ashkenazi, as well as other Jerusalemite scholars of foreign origin (Ashkenazi, Sephardi, and also Maghribian), had close contacts with Nathan, both during his time in Jerusalem and after his departure. Although he was an Arabic speaker and belonged to a cultural group—the Maghribians—

[83] Meshullam’s work was preserved in only one manuscript (MS Florence, Biblioteca Laurenziana Plut. II.44, 39v). The spelling here is שלון ‘Shalon’, but it is probably a scribal error, or reflects a unique pronunciation of ‘Shalom’.

[84] The text of the description of the Jewish leadership in Jerusalem in Meshullam’s travelogue is very problematic. For a reliable edition, see Reiner (1992, 37). For comparison of all the scholarly renderings of the text, see Arad (2013, 342–43).

that shared many characteristics with the native local community, he did not integrate into the local elite, but found his place in a circle of foreign scholars instead. This distancing of himself from the established leadership led to substantial conflict between him and them, and ultimately to his departure from the city.

In 1474, a few years after Nathan’s arrival in the city, a crisis occurred in the Jerusalemite community. As a result of Muslim religious zeal, the old (and only) synagogue in Jerusalem was destroyed by a Muslim mob. The *sulṭān*, Qaytbay (1468–1496), was angered by the act of vandalism and published an order that gave the Jews permission to re-establish the building.[85] The cost of the construction was very high, and the community treasurers were forced to borrow large sums to cover it. For many years afterwards, the management of the community was marked by hopeless attempts to find sources of funding for the dwindling treasury. The leaders of the community, who were called *zeqenim* ‘elders’, resorted to extreme measures. They imposed heavy taxes, took over the properties of deceased community members who had no direct heirs, and sold the community’s *heqdesh* properties, including holy books and Torah scrolls that had been donated for the public’s use. Obadiah of Bertinoro, the Mishnah commentator, described it in these terms (Adler 1930, 229):

---

[85] The events were described by the Jerusalemite Qadi Ibn ʿUbayya, who played a part in them; see Goitein (1948–1949). Another description of the events was written by the contemporary Qadi and historian Mujīr al-Dīn; see *al-Uns al-Jalīl*, 300–14. See also Ashtor (1951, 401–15); Luz (2004; 2014, 209–11).

> The Jewish Nagid who has his residence in Cairo is appointed over all the Jews who are under the dominion of the King of Egypt; he has all the power of a king and can punish and imprison those who act in opposition to his decrees; he appoints the *dayyanim* (judges) in every community. The present prince lived formerly for a long time in Jerusalem but was obliged to leave it on account of the Elders, the calumniators, and informers who were there. He is called R. Nathan ha-Cohen, is rich, wise, pious, old and is a native of Barbary. When I came to Cairo he showed me much honour... and tried to dissuade me altogether from going to Jerusalem on account of the informers there; all scholars and rabbis formerly in Jerusalem left the city in haste in order to preserve their lives from the oppressions of the Elders... these grey-haired criminals went so far as to sell all the scrolls of the law with their covers, the curtains, the pomegranates,[86] and all the sacred appurtenances that were in Jerusalem, to Gentiles, who were to carry them away into foreign lands... The Nagid told me he could not well put a stop to this because he feared that the Elders would speak evil against all the Jews to the King.

Nathan and the other foreign scholars rejected the policy of the *zeqenim* but could not induce them to adopt another course. As a result, the tension between the scholars and the *zeqenim* became intolerable and they escaped from the city. Nathan emigrated to Egypt, and others moved to Gaza and Damascus later, probably in 1483. The main source for the steps taken by the *zeqenim* is the letters of Obadiah of Bertinoro. Obadiah arrived in Jerusalem in 1488 and was not an eyewitness to the events. His description was based mainly on what he heard from

---

[86] Ornaments of metal for the Torah scroll.

Nathan when they met in Cairo. Scholars who accept Obadiah's account have described the *zeqenim* in highly critical terms as abusing their congregation.[87] Subsequent research has conveyed a different picture, seeking to explain the extreme policy of the *zeqenim* from their point of view.[88]

It is impossible to know how Nathan's career might have developed had he remained in Jerusalem, but it is clear that his forced emigration to Egypt led to him attaining the highest position of Jewish leadership in the east—the Nagidate.

2.2.5. Nathan as a Scholar

Although Nathan is mentioned by scholars of his time as a talmudic scholar, we do not know much about his intellectual world or his methodology for studying or dispensing halakhic decisions, except from two responsa (discussed below). Nonetheless, we can learn something about his ideological leanings, such as his objection to philosophy, as reported by R. Obadiah of Bertinoro in his itinerary (Hartom and David 1997, 70–71):

> ובמצרים בא אחד מארץ המערב והתחיל להיות פורה רוש[89] ולדבר בפילוסופיאה ודחפו הנגיד בשתי ידיים
>
> Someone arrived in Egypt/Cairo from the Maghreb and started to be '[a root that] beareth gall', and to speak on philosophy, and the Nagid 'pushed him with two hands'.[90]

---

[87] See David (2013, 3–23), based on a previous article, David (1979).

[88] See Rozen (1981, 78–79); Reiner (1992, 41–52). For summary and additional discussion, see Arad (2013, 169–71).

[89] In the Masoretic Text: פֹּרֶה רֹאשׁ (Deut. 29.17).

[90] This passage is missing in Adler's (1930) edition.

R. Obadiah used the phrase דחפו בשתי ידיים ('pushed him with both hands') as an allusion to the talmudic story that describes the rejection of Jesus by the circle of sages. Jesus' teacher, according to this source, was Joshua b. Peraḥiah, שדחפו לישוע הנוצרי בשתי ידיים 'who pushed Jesus of Nazareth with both hands' (b. Soṭah 47a; Sanhedrin 107b).[91] In using this allusion, Obadiah suggested that Nathan considered philosophy a heresy, just like Christianity, but, cleverly, he perhaps hinted at his own differing opinion: the Talmud criticised the harsh attitude of R. Joshua toward Jesus, and concluded: לעולם תהא שמאל דוחה וימין מקרבת 'Always let the left hand thrust away and the right hand draw near'.

Nathan therefore shrank from philosophy, but like his associate, Moses b. Judah, he showed a deep interest in philosophy's spiritual rival—the Kabbalah. The Escorial Library preserves a manuscript that includes a few works on the subject of Kabbalah, such as a super-commentary on Nachmanides' secrets in his commentary on the Pentateuch, *Zohar*, and other works. The copyist lived in Tlemcen, where Nathan spent his youth, and finished his task on 27 February 1468. On the last page (MS Escorial G-1-15, 132b), the scribe specified the name of the requester of the copy, והוא להבחור... ר' נתן שולל, and Nathan also signed his name at the end of the manuscript. The manuscript later reached Isaac Sholal, his successor in the Nagidate, and after his death it was sold by the trustee of Isaac's son Abraham to the famous sage R. David ibn Zimra.

---

[91] This saying was erased in most printed editions by the Catholic censors.

Another kabbalistic work (by R. ʿAzriel of Gerona) was copied by one of Nathan's associates, who mentioned the Nagid in a letter appended to the copy (MS New York, JTS 2331).

A Hebrew letter to Nathan, sent from Jerusalem to Cairo, helps us reconstruct his library:

> Concerning the books, know that we found them among your books scattered here and there, and we collected them, until four of them were left in our hands, which are: (Babylonian) Talmud (tractate) Ketubot; commentary on Psalms in Arabic; and commentary on (Mishnah, tractate) Avot of R. Israel ben Israel,[92] also in Arabic.[93]

In his objection to philosophy, Nathan rejected a major part of Judaeo-Arabic literature, but he was interested in other genres, such as Bible and talmudic commentaries.

No works by Nathan are known and only two *teshuvot* (responsa) of his have been identified. The first will be discussed below. The second (TS NS 167.17), which deals with family affairs, has been published recently (Glick et al. 2014, 973–85).[94] It concerns a divorced man who remarried and vowed to his new wife that he would not have any sexual relations with his first

---

[92] R. Israel Israeli. His father's name was actually Joseph. He lived in Spain in the second half of the thirteenth century and the beginning of the fourteenth century. On his commentary on Avot, see Ilan (2006).

[93] CUL Or. 1080J246: ומענין הספרים, דע אדוני שמצאנו אותם בין ספריך מפוזרים זה בכאן, וזה בכאן, ולקטנו אותם, עד שנשארו לנו מהם ד׳, והם גמר כתובות, ופי'[רוש] תלים בלשון הגרי ופי'[רוש] אבות לר׳ ישראל בן ישראל ג״כ בלשון הגרי. The fourth book was probably another part of the commentary on tractate Avot. See CUL Or. 1080J246, verso, l. 22; David (1988a, 401).

[94] The identification of the author was first offered by Arad (2013, 195).

wife. After a while he divorced his second wife too and wanted to return to the first. Nathan in his responsum harshly criticises the anonymous *dayyan* who released the man from his oath, and gives advice to the addressees, scholars who were from his close circle, on how to deal with the *dayyan*.

Besides producing responsa, Nathan also taught disciples. We do not know much about his activity as a teacher, but we can identify at least one of his pupils, R. Samuel b. Moses ibn Ḥakīm (also known as Ibn Ḥāqān), a remarkable halakhic scholar of the first half of the sixteenth century in Egypt. Thanks to him, we learn some interesting details about the private life of his teacher. In a responsum concerning the question of whether Rabbanite Jews can marry Karaites, Samuel mentions that many Karaite families 'converted' to Rabbanite Judaism in Egypt, and no one refused to marry them. But, he added (Assaf 1946, 228–29):

> The truth is that my teacher, the rabbi, the Nagid, our rabbi, the honourable rabbi Jonathan ha-Kohen Sholal, may he rest in peace, when his first wife died… he was offered a virgin in marriage, a Kohen's daughter, rich and noble, of those families but he did not want to take her. I was young then, and I did not have the courage to ask him the reason for this.[95]

---

[95] האמת כי מורי הרב הנגיד רבינו כמוהר״ר יונתן הכהן שלאל זלה״ה כשמתה אשתו הראשונה... שדכו לו בתולה אחת כהנת עשירה ומיוחסת מאותן המשפחות ולא אבה לקחתה... ואני הייתי רך בשנים ולא היה לי לב לשאול ממנו פתרון הדבר. R. Samuel, who permitted marriage to Karaites, explained that his teacher Nathan thought there was no problem with an ordinary Jew marrying a Karaite woman, and the halakhic problem related only to *Kohanim*. Various

2.2.6. Nathan's Activity as Nagid: The Supervision of Endowments

As Nagid, Nathan was responsible for many community activities, principally acting as a judge, appointing *dayyanim* and local leaders over their communities, representing the Jewish minority's interests in the *sulṭān*'s palace, and being formally responsible for the taxes paid by the Jews. A full description of Nathan's administrative policy as Nagid is beyond the goals of the present book, which looks at his intellectual world. The relatively large number of preserved documents concerning him, in comparison to the other Negidim, could, however, be used for a wide and detailed analysis of his leadership. As an example, we shall look at one area of his public activity, the supervision of endowments.

One of the obligations of the Nagid was the management of the *waqf* houses and lands of the Jewish community. A few *waqf* deeds from the years 892 H (1487), 893 H (1488), and 899 H (1493/1494), during the tenure of Nathan, have been preserved (Cairo Community Archive, nos 47, 51, 62, 97). All the properties were located on the same street as the synagogue in the Jewish neighbourhood of Cairo. Some of them had been donated by Moses Abū Shaʿara, an associate of Nathan Sholal.[96] In a *waqf* deed

---

scholarly literature has been written on the controversy about marriage to Karaites in Egypt. See a summary in Arad (2013, 103–5).

[96] There is no access to the archive today, so it is impossible to check if the Nagid is mentioned in these documents, but it is reasonable to assume he appears there, as the supervisor of those properties. On Abū Shaʿara's close contacts with Nathan, see TS 10J24.3 + CUL Or. 1080J174. For more details on him, see commentary on letter P.3.g.

signed in 888 H (1483/1484), on the eve of Nathan's rise to power, it is said that the woman who donated the property—"Sarah the Rabbanite Jew"—intended its income for the Jewish poor in Jerusalem, and that she chose the Nagid as the manager of the house. The manager of the *waqf* is described as "the one who will be the head of Jews," but no name is mentioned.[97] The reason for this is probably because this *waqf* was founded in the interim period between the death of the preceding Nagid, Solomon b. Joseph (1482), and the appointment of Nathan. In a later *waqf* deed, his successor, Isaac Sholal, is mentioned: this deed, for a *waqf* of a plot of land near the old synagogue in Cairo[98] established by Moses Abū Shaʿara in 914 H (1508/1509; Cairo Community Archive, no. 61), records that it was produced in the presence of Isaac the Nagid.[99]

Our corpus sheds new light on Nathan's activities as the man responsible for the pious foundations in the Jewish communities. In a letter from our corpus (C.2), Nathan issues an order to Moses b. Judah: "(regarding) R. Shalom ben Zaytūn, may God save him, get from him the two florins he has for the pious foundations' treasury, and give it to the same R. Ḥayyim, may God save him, who is mentioned before: if he receives it, it is as if I myself had received it." In asking him to transfer the *waqf* donation to his direct representative R. Ḥayyim, Nathan is assuring Moses that his responsibility for it will thereby be ended, as it

97 اوقفته على الفقراء والمساكين اليهود المقيمين بالقدس الشريف, وجعلت النظر عليه لمن يكون رئيسا على اليهود.

98 بخط زويلة بجوار كنيسة الربانيين بدرب الكنيس.

99 وقد صدرت هذه الوقفية بحضرة الرئيس اسحق ابن ابراهيم رائس طوائف اليهود بالقاهرة.

will be as if he had given it to Nathan himself, and if the money should subsequently get lost, he will bear no guilt.

More information on Nathan's involvement in the management of the *waqf* properties is displayed in a torn Hebrew letter, probably from the time of Nathan's Nagidate.[100] The writer reports that two scholars, R. Shmuel and R. Abraham, had asked him to pass on certain objects, perhaps sacred books or artefacts of the *heqdesh*. By his account, he answered (MS Mosseri V 344.1):

> Here indeed I am to fulfil the Nagid's order, and all the objects are ready before you, as well as what I have in my possession, until not even a penny remains of it... Hereby I say, if you want to take it with you to Egypt (or: Cairo), do it, and if you want to keep it in any place you wish—do not tell me where it is, because I am also sending a letter, with a sworn statement, to his Excellency the Nagid, to remove the burden from me, because I have enough sorrow in pursuit of my livelihood. I was continually worried about their safe-keeping, and I did not find a place (for them) as appropriate and suitable as I would have wished... I wrote to the honourable rabbi Samuel, may God save him, that because he is able... he must do with the *Heqdesh*'s objects what seems (correct) to him.[101]

---

[100] However, it could be also from the time of Isaac Sholal.

[101] הנני הנני להשלים מאמר הנגיד והנה כל הכלים מזומנים לפניכם וגם כל מה שבידי עד שלא ישאר ממנו פרוטה מזה ומזה... ועוד אמרתי אם תרצו להוליכו עמכם למצרים עשו, ואם תרצו לשומרו באי זה מקום שתרצו לא תאמרו לי איפה הוא, כי אני ג"כ שלחתי כתב בשבועה לנגיד יר"ה [= ירום הודו] להשליך מעלי המשא, כי די לי צערי לבקש פרנסתי, שבכל שעה נצטערתי על שמירתם ולא מצאתי מקום ראוי והגון כרצוני...

In fulfilling the Nagid's order (מאמר הנגיד) concerning the *heqdesh* objects that were in his possession, the writer expressed his worries about the responsibility of keeping such precious objects safe and made clear that he was actually glad of the opportunity to give them to the emissaries of the Nagid and free himself from this burden.

These sources show the last Negidim taking a close interest in the administration of the Jewish pious foundations.

2.2.7. Nathan's Status within Jewish Consciousness in the Medieval World

The Negidim's legal authority only extended over the Jews of the Mamlūk state, but they also projected a powerful image into the consciousness of the Jewry of the medieval world at large. They did not claim to be of Davidic origin, like the Babylonian exilarchs, and their Torah scholarship was not highly regarded, but as mentioned above, they were considered a manner of 'Jewish royalty' during the long and difficult exile.

R. Isaac Abravanel (1437–1508), the famous commentator and statesman, deals in his composition *Yeshuʿot Meshiḥo* 'The salvation of His anointed' with the talmudic saying: "The son of David cannot appear ere the two ruling houses in Israel shall have come to an end, viz., the Exilarchate in Babylon and the Patriarchate in Palestine" (b. Sanhedrin 38a).[102] This saying was used in

---

[כ]ת[ב]תי לכמה"ר שמואל [יצ"ו] שהואיל ויש לו יכולת... ש[יע]שה מהכלים של הקדש מה [שיר]אה לו.

[102] On the original context of this quotation, see Neusner (1969, 107–18, esp. 109). This saying is attributed to the sons of R. Ḥiyya, i.e., to

Christian–Jewish polemic as a proof that the Messiah, i.e., Jesus, had already come in ancient times. Abravanel defended the Jewish position by stating that the Exilarchate was in existence until only 150 years before his own time, and that the Patriarchate in Palestine was still in existence. Due to political circumstances, the Patriarchate had moved to Cairo, the Mamlūk capital, but it was a direct continuation, in Abravanel's eyes, of the ancient Patriarchate (Abravanel, Yeshuʿot Meshiḥo, II, p. 21b):

> Indeed, the Patriarch in Palestine is the Nagid, who still rules today in Egypt (or: Cairo); since the palace of this state's king is in Egypt, the Patriarch emigrated from Jerusalem to sit there, close to the authorities, but he often comes to Jerusalem to give judgment.[103]

Abravanel finished writing his book in the kingdom of Naples in 1498, so we can be quite sure that he was referring here to Nathan in particular, who was ruling then. Abravanel adopted this unique example of Jewish self-government in the east as a useful weapon in the Jewish–Catholic controversy then raging in western and central Europe.

Unlike his predecessors, Nathan was recognised as a notable scholar and considered an inseparable member of the Jewish

---

the late Parthian period. Our information on the Exilarchate in the Parthian period is very limited. On the Exilarchate in the Sassanian period, see Herman (2012). On the Exilarchate under Muslim rule, see Gil (2004, 83–116).

103 ואמנ'[ם] הנשיא שבא"י הלא הוא הנגיד שעד היום עומד במצרי'[ם] כי להיות בית מקדש מלך הארץ ההיא במצרי'[ם] נעתק הנשיא מירושלי'[ם] לשבת שם קרוב למלכות ופעמי'[ם] רבות עולה לירושלי'[ם] לשפוט. For a discussion of Abravanel's words, see David (1980, 329).

'Republic of Scholars' of his time. He combined political power and intellectual strength, which the Jewish scholars of his generation, and the next generation, respected highly. An expression of his status among contemporary scholars can be found in his involvement in the controversy over the status of the family of Shemaryah of Thessaloniki (שמריה שלוניקאו). Negative rumours had spread about this family, who were probably Byzantine-Jewish, following a forbidden marriage, and some scholars decided it was therefore forbidden according to the *halakhah* to marry any members of the family. The controversy continued for a long time, and famous rabbinic figures were involved in it, such as Joseph Kolon, the Italian arbiter (d. 1480), and Moses del Medigo from Crete.

Nathan Sholal was asked to express his viewpoint on the matter. He gave the decisive opinion that it was forbidden to slander the family members and thought the rumour baseless. His responsum reveals his character as a tough, self-confident arbiter, who felt he had almost unlimited authority in his hands. His sharp words testify to his unique status as both halakhic scholar and political leader at the same time (Ha-Levi, *Zeqan Aharon*, §1, 2b):

> I am imposing a decree of exclusion, banishment, and excommunication[104] on anyone who expresses this false slander… whoever has spoken improperly [against the family]

---

[104] *Ḥerem* and *Niduy* are two levels of excommunication, with *Ḥerem* considered more severe. The exact details of the differences between these two sanctions are not agreed upon among rabbinic commentators. For a detailed survey, see Zevin (1983, s.v. Ḥerem, 326–43). *Shamatta* (or in the common pronunciation, *shamta*) is an Aramaic word meaning

> and does not repent, his blood will be on his own head (דמו בראשו) to accept in his 248 organs[105] that which we are imposing upon him… I trust that they will accept our words in this hour without me needing to continue to punish further… anyone who wants to give honour to the Land of Israel, for which I am responsible, and accept the burden of its kingdom of Heaven, even if he does not accept the burden of its secular kingdom, must obey our decision. And whoever will not obey of his free will, will obey unwillingly, because we will be assisted by Heaven.[106]

Nathan here recruits the prestige of the land of Israel to ensure obedience to his halakhic opinion and resolve the ugly dispute. Like Abravanel, he did not see himself first of all as a leader of Egyptian Jewry but as the exclusive ruler of Palestinian Jewry, and this was the principal element in the reputation of his position. His words about the two kingdoms are somewhat cryptic, but we may perhaps interpret them in this way: the Nagidate obtained its power from the *sulṭān*. All the Jews in the Mamlūk

‘ban, excommunication’ (Sokoloff 2002, 1163). On the different grounds for imposing a *Ḥerem/Niduy* sanction, see Leibson (1975). In the medieval halakhic literature, the difference between these three terms is blurred, and it is very common to mention all of them together, sometimes by the acronym נח"ש (*Niduy, Ḥerem, Shamta*).

[105] In the talmudic tradition, there are 248 organs in a man’s body (m. Ohalot 1.8), while the woman’s body has 252 organs (b. Bechorot 45a).

[106] אני גוזר בגזרת חרם ונדוי ושמתא על כל מי שיוציא עוד זה הלעז השקר... ומי שלא דבר נכונה ואינו חוזר בו דמו בראשו לקבל ברמ״ח אבריו מה שגזרנו עליו... ובוטח אני בהן שישאו פנינו בדבר הזה בשע׳[ה] הזו מבלי שאוסיף להעניש יות׳[ר].. וכל מאן דבעי למעבד יקרא לארץ ישראל דאנן עלה ומקבל עול מלכותא דרקיע דידה אף אם אינו מקבל עול מלכות׳[א] דארעא דידה חזי ליה לקבל גזירתין ומי שלא יקבל ברצונו יקבל בעל כרחו שמן השמיים יסייעונו.

state were obliged to obey the Nagid according to the official sultanic decree. Nathan was aware of the fact that, officially, he had no legal claim to authority over the Jews outside the Mamlūk state ("Even if he does not accept the burden of its secular kingdom").[107] A Jew in Istanbul, Crete, or Venice had no obligation to obey him, because he was subordinated to other rule, but Nathan demanded he accept the spiritual supremacy of Jerusalem, and as a result, accept his authority, as the exclusive representative of the real kingdom, "the kingdom of Heaven" of Jerusalem.

2.2.8. The Sholal Family: An Epilogue

Nathan served as Nagid for 18 years. His death is described in the aforementioned family list, which adds some interesting details on his burial:

> My master, the honourable rabbi Nathan ha-Kohen Sholal, was summoned to the heavenly academy (נתבקש לישיבה של מעלה) on Monday night, two hours before sunset, 39 for the counting (of the *ʿOmer*), that is 24 of *Iyyar* (5)262 of the Creation (= 12 May 1502), and he served in the authority of the Nagidate 18 years, and was buried between the Nagid, the honourable rabbi Joseph and the physician ʿAbd al-Walī, and around the three of them a stone fence.

According to this apparently reliable testimony, Nathan was buried in Cairo. But what became of his grave? R. Jacob Berav (1474–1546), the famed Sephardi scholar, mentions in his responsa (Berav, *Responsa*, §38):

---

[107] The location of the inquirers is not known, but it is clear they did not live in the Mamlūk state. See Ashtor (1951, 452 n. 20).

> In the time of the Nagid R. Isaac Sholal, may he rest in peace, when I was in Egypt,[108] we discussed this affair, because the notable, the honourable rabbi Nathan Sholal, did not order that he should be brought to the land of Israel. Our decision was to bring him, and that is what was done, and he was brought.

Seemingly, we have here testimony that Nathan's remains were removed for burial in Palestine, probably in Jerusalem. But researchers disagree in interpreting this source. Nathan is not mentioned here as is usual as 'Nagid', just as "the honourable rabbi," so that leaves open the possibility that Jacob Berav is referring to another Nathan Sholal, some relative of the Nagid. Further evidence will be required before the matter can be settled.

After Nathan's death, his office was inherited by his nephew and brother-in-law, Isaac Sholal, a figure who has been illuminated by several studies, mainly by Abraham David (1988a; 1999; 2016, 223–48). Isaac acquired an important position in the spiritual life of the Jews in the twilight of Mamlūk rule. Like his uncle Nathan, he was honoured by the local scholars in Egypt, Palestine, and Syria, and was considered their patron. He financially supported scholars in several Yeshivot in Safed,[109] Jerusalem,[110] and elsewhere, and controlled their activity. He produced

[108] R. Jacob Berav emigrated later to Safed.

[109] See, for example, the letter of the sages of Safed to Isaac: MS Washington, Freer Gallery of Art 50, published by Gottheil and Worrell (1927, 246–65) and again in corrected version by David (2016, 313–24).

[110] See, for example, the letter of R. Joseph Kolon from Jerusalem (probably the grandson of the aforementioned Joseph Kolon) to Cairo: ולפחות

some *taqqanot* (communal rulings), including one that released scholars from paying taxes (in 1509), according to talmudic rule.

After the Ottoman conquest of Egypt in 1517, the position of the Nagidate was abolished, and Isaac emigrated to Jerusalem, where he died on the sixth or seventh of November 1524. A court record from 1546 documented a lawsuit involving his son, Abraham. The Muslim scribe wrote that his father Isaac was known by two nicknames: 'Sholal' (شلال) and 'the Nagid' (Cohen and Simon-Pikali 1993, 360). Isaac's family members played an important part in the activity of the Jewish leadership in Jerusalem during the sixteenth century, as is clear from the *Sijill* documents of the Muslim court in Jerusalem. The most prominent person among them was Solomon b. Moses (Salamūn ibn Mūsā) Sholal, who is mentioned in the *Sijill* documents as one of the elders (*shuyūḵ*) of the Jewish community of Jerusalem from 1555 to 1575 (Cohen Amnon 1984, 40; Cohen and Simon-Pikali 1993, index s.v. סלמון בן מוסא שלאל). Solomon succeeded his father, Moses b. Ḥayyim Sholal, who was also one of its elders.[111] However,

---

אני צריך [...] נ׳ דו׳ לשנה, ואדוננו הנגיד יר״ה שולח לי כ״ד 'I need at least [...] 50 ducats per year, and our master, the exalted Nagid sends me 24' (MS London, BL Or. 5561A.5, published by David 1987, 234–36). On Isaac's patronage of the scholars of Jerusalem, see also David (2016, 235–48).

[111] See, for example, Cohen and Simon-Pikali (1993, 98–103). In this long discussion, which was held in the Muslim court on 28 June 1560, the Muslim scribe mentions that among the local Jewish dignitaries were "Moses b. Ḥayyim Sholal and his son Salamūn" (موسى بن خييم شلال وولده سلمون). The discussion dealt with the right of the Jews to bury their dead in a certain area on the Mount of Olives. For a photograph of the

it seems that their impact was local, and they had no significant influence on Jewish life elsewhere in the Ottoman Empire. Thus, the institution of the Nagidate came to an end. Jewish political power now moved from Cairo to Istanbul, where wealthy Jewish courtiers acted as lobbyists for their people’s interests. The main change regarding Jewish autonomy between the Mamlūk period and the Ottoman period was the absence of official leadership for the Ottoman Jews. While the Nagid represented the Jews in front of the Mamlūk *sulṭān*, the Ottoman Jews had no official leader who had authority over all the Jews in the Empire. Such a position began to exist (in part) only in the nineteenth century, with the position of the *Ḥakham Bashe* (Chief Rabbi; see Hacker 1984). Another important shift pertained to the status of the judicial system. The Nagid had official responsibility for this system and had the right to appoint judges in the sultanate. In contrast, in the Ottoman period, the courts were afforded no official recognition by the Muslim governors of the Jews in the Ottoman Empire (see Hacker 1994). The end of the Nagidate therefore opened a new page in the history of the Jews of the Orient.

2.3. Trade in the Eastern Mediterranean in the Fifteenth Century

No discussion of the period would be complete without giving some background on the nature of mercantile activity in the eastern Mediterranean at this time. Trade in the Mediterranean ports

---

original long Arabic text, see Cohen and Simon-Pikali (1993, between p. 84 and p. 85, three pages of photographs, without pagination).

was rich and diverse, and was carried out by many different actors, representing many nations and cultures. There is accordingly a large body of scholarly literature on this topic, of which the works of Roser Salicru I Lluch and David Abulafia are perhaps the most comprehensive. In this introduction, we shall describe some of the main processes driving trade and emphasise some points crucial to understanding Jewish participation in international trade in this period, as background to the texts featured in our corpus.[112]

From the documents of the Classical Genizah period, we know that Egypt had a substantial middle class of Jewish merchants, who traded around the Mediterranean, down the Red Sea, and along the coast of the Indian Ocean.[113] The increasing domination of Mediterranean trade by Italian city-states in the eleventh century, and the arrival of the Crusaders in the eastern littoral, forced changes, which—coupled with a shift in attitude towards the status of Jews within the Islamic realms—ultimately

---

[112] On commerce in the Mamlūk period, there is a huge body of literature. Excepting the collected volumes of Ashtor's articles (1969; 1978; 1983; 1986; 1992), see, for example, Wiet (1955); Fischel (1958); Wansbrough (1965); Darrāj (1963); Imamuddin (1980); Arbel (1988); Abulafia (1988; 1994); Allouche (1994); Lev (2002); Pedani Fabris (2002); Meloy (2003); Berkey (2004); Sennoune (2004); Valérian (2004; 2005); Christ (2012).

[113] Among the important works on the Jewish mediteranean merchants in the Fāṭimid and Ayyubid periods are Goitein (1967, 148–352); Goitein (1973); Aodeh (1992); Gil (2004, 615–721); Goitein and Friedman (2008); Ackerman-Lieberman (2014); Cohen (2017).

culminated in the erosion of existing Jewish mercantile structures by the Mamlūk period. Instead, powerful merchant and aristocratic families monopolised most of the trade, forcing out the Jewish middle class and leaving behind only a much smaller group of Jewish traders who had no share in the Indian Ocean trade and only limited contacts in the Mediterranean, trading in a limited range of goods. The same happened to Jews working in Egyptian industries: once-flourishing economic sectors such as the Jewish sugar industry were taken over by Mamlūk aristocracy, and Jewish middle-class industrialists disappeared (Ashtor 1983, VIII:85–86). This economic downturn in the Jewish community coincided, but not coincidentally, with a period when relatively few documents were deposited in the Genizah, and we thus have little first-hand information about the Jewish communities of Egypt and the Levant in this period. This decline in the Jewish role in international trade was a part of, and magnified by, the general economic decline in the east in this period (see, e.g., Cahen 1970).[114]

By the fifteenth century, a new mercantile Jewish class had established itself in Egypt, consisting mostly of Jews originating from Christian lands, such as Crete, Italy, and Catalonia. Christian traders from these places are well represented in our corpus, in addition to their Jewish colleagues, such as Elijah b. Elyaqim of Crete, who was probably of Jewish-Greek origin (Romaniote; see P.5.a and P.5.b). The trade between the Aegean Islands and Alexandria was predominantly in the hands of indigenous Greeks

---

[114] For criticism of the concept of 'decline', see n. 16 above.

from the Venetian colonies, many of whom were Jewish (Christ 2012, 96).

Catalan traders were a great force in early fifteenth-century Mediterranean trade, active in Rhodes and in Alexandria, and often in competition with the Venetians. The trader Biagio Dolphin, for example, complained in the early fifteenth century that “no spices were left in Alexandria since the arrival of a Catalan merchant fleet” (Christ 2012, 233). This flourishing Catalan influence appears to have waned in the second half of the fifteenth century. Ferrer (2012, 43) points out that there were an average of five voyages per year between 1442 and 1462, and although there is still information about voyages to Alexandria towards the end of the fifteenth century, they became infrequent. The German pilgrim Felix Faber found the Catalans’ *funduq* in Alexandria virtually deserted in 1483.

Local intermediaries were crucial for the Venetians in Alexandria, as most of them knew no Arabic. They often relied on Jewish interpreters. Christ (2012, 94, 149) describes various Jewish dragomans in early fifteenth century Alexandria. One called Obeit (Obed), probably from the Jewish merchants’ milieu of Crete, was prominent in Alexandria and acted as translator for the Venetian consul. Another, Saim, was from Seville, raised in Jerusalem, and acted as the *sulṭān*’s chief dragoman. Other Jewish dragomans bore names such as Abraham and Moses.

Letter P.5.b mentions the supply of wine and cheese from Crete to the Alexandrian market. Jacoby (1999, 58) gives an account of the Mediterranean cheese trade, and of cheese from Crete in particular. He describes how the cheese trade is attested from the twelfth century onwards and appears to have grown in the course of the fourteenth century. Some interesting evidence about Cretan cheese in Egypt appears in a document written in Alexandria in the middle of the twelfth century (during the Nagidate of Samuel b. Ḥananiah). The cheese had apparently been sent with a letter from the Jewish judge in Crete, who confirmed it was produced according to the *halakhah* (CUL MS Or.2116.10, formerly MS Christ's College, Cambridge, Abrahams Coll. 10; published by Frenkel 2006, 254–55). In the fifteenth century, Crete's main exports to Alexandria were wine, cheese, honey, and wax (Frenkel 2006, 59).

Letter P.6 also touches on the import of kosher cheese into Egypt, but it is not clear where the cheese in question came from. The writer, Isaac Bayt ʿAṭṭān, was in Syracuse when the letter was composed, and this is probably where his Catalan business associate, Bernard, was also located at the time of writing, and where the wares were bought under the advice of Isaac, but it also possible that the commodities had originated elsewhere. It is, in any case, remarkable that Christian traders were bringing kosher cheese with them to Egypt to sell, but it presumably speaks to the demand that must have existed from the large Jewish community there. This document sheds light also on the cooperation between Jewish and Christian merchants. Moses b. Judah was requested in the letter to assist Bernard with acclimatising to the local trade of Alexandria.

Cretan wine was famous and imported all over in the fifteenth century, including to England, Venice, Constantinople, and Alexandria (Jacoby 1987, 49). Jews in Crete were involved in all stages of the production of kosher wine, including the manufacture of wooden barrels for storage.[115] In Muslim countries in particular, where production of wine was severely curtailed or non-existent, there was high demand in Jewish communities for kosher wines. Cretan Jewish traders imported not only kosher but also non-kosher wine into Egypt, and often also traded in cheese (Jacoby 1987).

Christ (2012, 167–84) states that the wine trade was not completely forbidden, and that there were taverns in Alexandria that served wine to foreign and local Christians, and also to Muslim locals. These taverns were tolerated in Alexandria, as a port town, but not in Cairo. The taverns were, however, often considered a nuisance not only by Muslim authorities but also by Christian merchants, since they attracted unsavoury clientele. On occasion, the Muslim authorities cracked down on the trade in wine, yet this was usually limited to Cairo. When 300 barrels of alcoholic beverages were poured away in Alexandria in 1419, this was not done on orders of government officials, but by an anti-European mob, instigated by Sufi leaders, who pillaged the dwellings of European and local merchants.

The importation of kosher wine by Jewish merchants served not just the Jewish community, but also occasionally Christians. In one case, sixty barrels of wine were delivered directly to a Venetian tavern-owner (Christ 2012, 172).

Many of the Jewish traders in Sicily came from Tunisia (Ashtor 1979, 223–24), which was perhaps the origin of the

---

[115] On the Jewish practices of wine production in place on the island, see Arbel (2008).

writer of letter P.6. So suggests the linguistic and codicological evidence, although Ashtor also points out that the ethnic composition of Palermitan Jewry resulted in Maghrebian Arabic being taken up as the vernacular of the Jewish community.[116] Sicily also attracted a large number of Catalan traders, among them many Jews, with continuous immigration throughout the fifteenth century. The high percentage of Jewish Catalans was perhaps what prompted the writer of letter P.6 to specify that the Catalan trader was a Christian.

The wares mentioned in the mercantile correspondence from within Egypt, such as the letters sent by Ṣedaqa Nis, comprise very different commodities: ammoniac, spices such as pepper, nutmeg, and cloves, paper, borax, brazilwood, and various textiles.

We hope that the mercantile details in our corpus will provide a rich and interesting resource for future research, and that it will stimulate further study of the economic circumstances of late fifteenth-century Egypt.

2.4. Moses b. Judah

The corpus of letters and documents published here appears to have originated from the personal archive of Moses b. Judah. Our sources on him, beyond the evidence gleaned from our corpus, are very poor. Nevertheless, we have a description of him from

[116] On the Arabic spoken by the Sicilian Jews, see Tirosh-Becker (1990). For more references, see Arad (2009, 102 n. 4).

Obadiah of Bertinoro, who was his guest[117] in February 1488 (Adler 1930, 220–21):

> We reached Alexandria on the 14th of Shebat (= 5 February 1488), tired and weary. Here God gave us favour in the eyes of a generous man who was very much beloved even by the Arabs, by name R. Moses Grasso, dragoman to the Venetians. He came to meet us and released us from the hands of the Arabs who sit in the gate and plunder foreign Jews at their pleasure. He took me in his house, and there I had to remain while I stayed in Alexandria. I read with him in a book in Cabbala, which he had in his possession, for he dearly loved this science. By thus reading with him I found favour in his sight, and we became friends. On the Sabbath he gave a dinner, to which he invited the Sephardi who had come with me; his two sons were also there when he brought me into the dining-room… R. Moses brought us confectionery, fresh ginger, dates, raisins, almonds, and confectionery of coriander seeds; a glass of wine is drunk with each kind. Then followed raisin wine, which was very good, then malmsey wine from Candia,[118] and again native wine. I drank with them and was exhilarated.[119]

---

[117] As a port city, and the main gateway to Egypt, Alexandria attracted many scholars who visited the city. The local residents considered hosting them an honour. On the hosting of prominent scholars, such as Daniel b. ʿAzariah and Moses b. Joseph ibn Kashkīl, by the Alexandrian leader Yeshuʿah b. Joseph, see Frenkel (2006, 58–59, 71–73). On Judah ha-Levi's visit, see above, n. 31.

[118] מלוושיאה די קנדיאה (Malvasia di Candia).

[119] "Exhilarated" is Adler's euphemistic translation. In the Hebrew original, we find the baser ושכרתי עמו 'I got drunk with him'. For a critical Hebrew edition, see Hartom and David (1997, 48–49).

In this vital scene we can find some of the basic characteristics of Moses: his high social status and prestige in the eyes of his fellow Jews— an appreciation shared "even by the Arabs"—his wealth, generosity, and desire for attaining wisdom. Moses shaped his home as a salon for gathering and learning. His solicitation of the Italian scholar, almost forcing him to stay at his house and pressing him to study Kabbalah with him, speaks to an overriding, perhaps even overbearing, love of learning.[120]

Although Obadiah did not mention the name of Moses' father (Judah), the identification of his host with our Moses can be assumed quite certainly.[121] The wealth of Moses, his central position among the Jewish community of Alexandria, his connections with the Italian merchants, his interest in Kabbalah—all of those are plainly on display in our corpus and support this identification. The best proof of the link between our corpus and the Obadiah of Bertinoro source is a letter from David ibn Shams (P.3.b), where Moses is called "his honourable highness and sanctity, our master and rabbi, Moses the dragoman." He is also described as having the same profession in the Arabic address of another letter

[120] Again, Adler's translation in this context is a little gentle compared with the original text: "He took me in his house, and there I had to remain while I stayed in Alexandria." The original shows R. Obadiah did not like the idea but was forced to stay: והביאני אל ביתו ולא יכולתי להמלט ולצאת מביתו כל ימי היותי שם 'He took me into his house, and I could not escape and leave his house during all the days I stayed there'.

[121] This assumption was offered first by Benayahu (1984, 259) and is supported by Hacker (2000, 575).

(P.3.a): "to be given to the *muʿallim* Mūsā b. Judah the dragoman."[122] The possibility that two Jewish dragomans, both called Moses and sharing common character traits, were active in Alexandria in the 1480s seems unlikely. Moses is described here as the dragoman of the Venetian consulate in Alexandria. Obadiah mentioned in his travelogue the four European consulates in the city, three of them of Italian city-states: Venice, Genoa, and Ancona (the fourth was the Catalan consulate).[123] The Venetian traders were the most prominent in the commerce between Italy and the east.[124] Moses' role as the dragoman of the Venetian consul and the mediator between the foreign traders and the local market gave him a central position in urban life, and an ability to influence the Jews' status in society and in the local economy.

David ibn Shams also mentions that Moses' evident wealth was accompanied by generosity and virtue: "His table is full of all the best, which is similar to the falling of the Manna…[125] His good virtues are flowing." And David's phrases display even more aspects of his patron, such as his connections with the Muslim

---

[122] In the original: يسلم ليدالمعلم موسي بن يهودة الترجمان.

[123] ושם היום ארבעה קונצולי מארצות הנוצרים, וויניציאני ויינוווסי וקטאלאני ואנקוניטאני (Hartom and David 1997, 51).

[124] On the Venetian traders in the east, see Ashtor (1974, 5–53; 1976, 533–86); Arbel (1988, 227–88).

[125] The writer alludes here to the description of the wealth of R. Judah the Patriarch: "Antoninus [Caesar] and R. [Judah the Patriarch], from whose table neither lettuce, nor radish, nor cucumber was ever absent either in summer or winter" (b. ʿAvodah Zarah 11a). R. Judah the Patriarch became a symbol of 'the rich sage' in Jewish literature, as is reflected also in this book's title.

governors: "Beloved by kings, friend of princes."[126] We do not have clear proof for close contact between him and the *sulṭān*, but the word "princes" undoubtedly refers to his connections with the Mamlūk emirs. From our sources in their current state, we cannot determine which political offices Moses held, if any. We do not know if he had, for instance, any administrative position, in addition to serving as the dragoman of the Venetian consul. Nevertheless, it is clear that his wealth, his connections, and his social status enabled him to achieve free access to the governor. He could use this power as a lobbyist for the interests of the Jewish community. This facet of his character is portrayed in a letter (C.2) sent to him by the Nagid, Nathan Sholal, who praised Moses as "the honourable, the respectable, the generous among Israel, who stands in the breach (העומד בפרץ) for the congregation of Jekuth[iel]."[127] The biblical expression 'stand in the breach'[128] occurs in some documents from the Classical Genizah period (e.g., TS 13J15.7; TS Misc. 35.45; Bodl. MS Heb.c.28.15), but is

[126] אהוב המלכים. ידיד הנסיכים.

[127] "The congregation of Jekuthiel" (עדת יקותיאל) is a literary nickname for the people of Israel. It is also an allusion to the addressee, which is based on the *derasha* of the talmudic sages on the name 'Jekuthiel'. R. Simon b. Pazzi once introduced an exposition of the Book of Chronicles as follows: "All thy words are one, and we know how to find their inner meaning. [It is written], 'And his wife the Jewess bore Jered… and Jekuthiel… and these are the sons of Bithya the daughter of Pharaoh' (1 Chron. 4.18)… 'Jekuthiel, because Israel trusted in God (*qivu la'El*) in his days' (b. Megillah 13a)."

[128] Cf. Ezek. 22.30 and, in particular, Ps. 106.23, where it is Moses standing in the breach.

a frequent phrase in the late Mamlūk period (e.g., TS 20.149; CUL Or. 1080J216; TS 10J12.29; ENA NS 31.30; letter C.2 in our corpus).[129] It denotes the efforts of a leader to defend his people from the harassment of the authorities. For example, at the end of the Aleppo Maḥzor (1527), there is a collection of *piyyuṭim* for *Berit Milah* (circumcision). One of them is dedicated to an honourable man called Joseph.[130] The poet praises him as one who "stands in the breach within a 'terrible'[131] congregation" (*Maḥzor Aram Ṣoba* [The Aleppo Prayerbook], 748b).[132]

Moses' official position in the Jewish leadership of Alexandria is not clear. Was he the *Shayḵ al-Yahūd* of the city, a representative of his community before the rulers and responsible for their tax payment? Or was he one of the *shuyūḵ*, the elders' council of the community? We cannot answer this question at present. The only official title we know he carried was 'head of the cantors' (ראש החזנים), given to him by the Nagid (C.1a). However, his

---

[129] See also this expression in a poem written by Joseph ha-Levi Nūʾās, published in Arad (2013, 372). On Nūʾās, see Beeri (1999).

[130] For multiple usages of the song, the copyist wrote in its title, "for whom a child was born to him, and his name is Joseph," but of course originally the song was written for a specific Joseph, whom we cannot identify.

[131] איומה is a common term of praise for the Jewish nation, following Song 6.10: "Who is this that looks forth like the dawn, fair as the moon, bright as the sun, terrible as an army with banners?"

[132] On this song, see also Arad (2013, 182). It is impossible to date this *piyyuṭ* exactly, but it seems that it is from the Ayyubid or the Mamlūk period. Some of the *piyyuṭim* in this corpus were clearly written in that time; see Elizur (2008, 109–17).

high status within the local Jewish leadership is without doubt. The fact that the letter by Solomon ha-Nagid (C.1a), which was addressed "to the entire holy, praiseworthy, and glorious community of Alexandria," was kept specifically in his personal archive proves his key position in the local elite and implies that Moses himself was, in fact, the addressee of the letter.

Although some of the letters in the corpus discuss communal matters, in which Moses was asked to intervene for their resolution, most of them deal with his private affairs. By 'private affairs' we mean all issues that were part of his diversified medieval Mediterranean world: trade, taxation, social connections, spiritual life, family, etc. The letters reflect first and foremost his business activity. He is portrayed as a talented merchant who managed to weave a commercial network in the Mediterranean ports. He also used his experience and linguistic skills to help European merchants establish themselves in local Mamlūk commerce. His skills and reputation were famous. One of his associates told him that (P.4.d):

> They told me they are very satisfied with your activities, and their desire is that you would always stand in their store, especially in the time of the boats, and that you would serve them heart and soul, not just to meet each other, and that they would benefit your honour at any time, and will give support to you today and tomorrow.

In a further letter (P.6), another colleague of Moses wrote to him:

> I inform you that one of the Catalan Christians will come to you... We want you to support him somewhat, for your and his benefit: this Christian inquired about someone in Alexandria who is (his) equal, to support (him) in the

> market place, and in other things. I told him: there is someone in (Alexandria), his name is R. Moses. He is an agent and equal (to you) in every regard.

Moses built, therefore, a commercial network, sometimes temporary and sometimes permanent, with Jewish colleagues, foreign Christian merchants, and even local Muslim traders.[133]

The most prevalent theme in these letters is the desire to buy. In a number of letters his associates inform him about commodities and merchandise: weights, prices, quality, availability, means of transfer, etc. Such traders' letters are very common in the Genizah collections. As in some letters from the classical Genizah period, the material commodities and the books appear side by side with no differentiation, perhaps because they were considered, inter alia, a valuable commodity. The two kinds of goods are intertwined and represent the diverse faces of Moses b. Judah.

Moses' correspondents regularly inform him about books. Moses appears in the letters as a real bibliophile, being remarkably selective and demanding. He wanted to have in his library only the finest books, written on high-quality paper or vellum, in clear and professional handwriting. For example, Elijah b. Elyaqim wrote to him (P.5.a):

> Your honour wrote to me that you have received the books, and you wrote also that the (scribe's) handwriting of the book of *Torat ha'Adam* is not [beautiful] in your honour's eyes, and that there is difference between it and (the quality of) the paper I have sent to your honour from Candia.

---

[133] For example, Badr al-Dīn al-Maṣrī (the Cairene) and Muhammad (P.4.c).

Elijah apologised and tried to convince Moses that he had done everything possible to obtain good manuscripts for his patron. The tone of apology is common in many letters. Another writer, Isaac Bayt ʿAṭṭān, apologises for the delay in the delivery of the books he promised to send (P.6): "I inform you that the books that I promised to buy for you—I did not have time to write them for you, but those which I promised to you—I am making haste so that they will arrive at yours (soon)."

But the purchase of books could have served other aims besides filling Moses' own library. Books were a sought-after consumer product.[134] It is possible, therefore, that Moses was a trader in books, as well as other merchandise. Nevertheless, due to some sources describing him as a local learned man, we can assume that at least some of the books he purchased were intended for his own use.

We can also assume that Moses' home was a centre of attraction for the Jewish elite in Alexandria. In the absence of public libraries in Jewish society in those days, the private libraries of wealthy members of the community served for study, alongside the collections of books held in *Midrashim* (communal centres for study and prayer).[135]

---

[134] On books as a commodity in the Mamlūk period, see Behrens-Abouseif (2019). Behrens-Abouseif discusses the production of books and the formation and management of libraries in Cairo and describes the book market in the sultanate.

[135] On the *Midrashim* as libraries in the Sephardi communities, see Hacker (2010).

2.5. Moses b. Judah's Library

Given the difficulty of determining the exact purpose of each book mentioned in the documents of the corpus—for personal use or for sale—we use here the term 'library' in its broadest sense, i.e., the entirety of the books held by Moses, whether for a long period or only briefly.

The fact that both letters (C + P) and literary fragments (W) of our corpus come from bindings and share common features reinforces the suggestion that they originate from a common source. It seems that the binding process was carried out in Alexandria, where Moses' archive was kept. Some links connect the two genres of documents. For example, Moses mentions in his letter (P.1/v20, 23) "the work" (החבור), a term that refers to the *Mishne Torah*, and leaves of the *Mishne Torah* are preserved in the corpus (W.2.a + W.2.b). One of his associates mentions "(the) Four Former Prophets and their commentary" (P.7/15–16), and a leaf from Qimḥi's commentary on Kings is included in our corpus (W.3). Another associate mentions in his letter (P.10/218a/15–16) "samples of letters" (מליצות), and some examples of this genre are indeed preserved in the corpus (C.7; W.14). Nevertheless, given the current limited knowledge of these documents' history and how they arrived in Oxford, the exact character of the connections between the letters and the literary fragments remains an open question.

The library of Moses b. Judah has not been preserved, nor do we have a list of its full content. We can therefore only guess which genres were represented in it, how many books were held there, whether it included early printed books (incunabula), etc.

Nevertheless, the names of books mentioned in the letters to and from Moses, and the few folios of Hebrew books apparently preserved with Moses’ archive, can give us a general impression as to his areas of interest and afford a glimpse of the intellectual horizons of the eastern Jewish elite in the late Middle Ages.

The list of the books Moses held, or, alternatively, wanted to purchase, is quite diverse. It includes canonical literature such as the Bible (Torah, Esther, Psalms); rabbinic literature; and a selection of medieval works, such as biblical commentaries, Talmud commentaries, *halakhah*, linguistics, history (*Josippon*), ethical literature (*Musar*), philosophy, and Kabbalah. Most of these works come from the same cultural area, the Spanish–Provençal cultural zone, including works of Nachmanides (*Torat ha-ʾAdam*; Pentateuch commentary), Jonah Gerondi (*Sefer ha-Yirʾah*), ʿAzriel of Gerona (commentary on the *Ten Sefirot*), David Qimḥi (commentary on the book of Kings), and Joseph Elbo (*The Book of Principles*). There are no Ashkenazic works in the corpus, though there is one book that was copied by an Ashkenazi scribe (W.2.a + W.2.b).

It is very difficult to determine what Moses’ favourite field was, as we have to make do with apparently random remnants from, and testimonies to, his library. Nevertheless, we suggest that his library reflects changes that had occurred in the intellectual fashions of the period: philosophy was leaving the stage and a new school of thought was replacing it, the Kabbalah.

Only one work in classical Jewish philosophy is documented in our corpus: *The Book of Principles* by Joseph Elbo (ca 1380–1444). Ṣuriel Dayyan, one of Moses’ associates, informed

Moses that he bought a copy of it for him (P.7). It is also worth noting that, in one of the letters addressed to Moses (P. 9), Maimonides' opinions in *The Guide of the Perplexed* are discussed.

Moses' library contained another philosophical work, the *Tajrīd al-ḥaqāʾiq*, but this work is not a 'natural member' of the family of Jewish philosophical thought. The *Tajrīd al-ḥaqāʾiq al-naẓariyya wa-talk̲īṣ al-maqāṣid al-nafsāniyya* (*Abstract of Speculative Truths and Extract of Ethical Aims*) is a wide-ranging treatise in Judaeo-Arabic written by David b. Joshua, the last Nagid from the Maimonidean family.[136] It is a lengthy work on philosophical and ethical issues, which Paul Fenton, the leading researcher of R. David's literary legacy, called "the last important composition in Judaeo-Arabic philosophy" (Fenton 2003, 19). In the first part, the author engages in a discussion of subjects such as prophecy, miracles, and the eternity of the soul. In the second part, he shows the path towards becoming a perfect man in the light of Sufi ideas. As this suggests, the book is based on a mixture of ideas and sources, including contemporary philosophy (*The Guide of the Perplexed*, Ibn Sīnā), Sufi literature, and Kabbalah.[137] R. David relies on Maimonides' theology, but interprets it in Sufi terms.

---

[136] The descendants of Maimonides left behind a rich literary estate—part of which is still only preserved in manuscripts—which was influenced deeply by the Sufi tradition. On Abraham Maimonides and his writings, see Russ-Fishbane (2015). On his writings and those of the other figures in the Maimonidean dynasty, see Fenton (2003). For a shorter English version, see Fenton (1991). Fenton (1987; 2006) also published some of David b. Joshua's works.

[137] For a description of this composition, its manuscripts, and Genizah fragments, see Fenton (1984, 2–8).

In this trend, he follows his ancestors' approach. One of the central characteristics of the Maimonidean School is the adherence to Maimonides' legacy, in *halakhah* as well as philosophy, and the concurrent adoption of the main ideas of Sufi mysticism. This surprising shift in the Maimonidean family's thought has fascinated researchers, who have turned to various different explanations.[138] Thus, R. David's composition is a kind of mystical treatise replete with philosophical terminology, and it cannot be considered a direct continuation of rational Jewish philosophy.[139]

The book is mentioned in a letter sent to Moses, probably by his associate David ibn Shams, which says (P.3.f):

> Concerning the *Tajrīd al-Ḥaqāʾiq*, we inform the master that I obtained for you the first part on *diwān* paper, which someone had copied for me a while ago. It was not completed; some things had remained (uncopied). The servant is currently having it amended. They should take it from him and complete it for you on my order. If it is delayed, it will go out in its (present) state.

As mentioned above, the book is divided into two parts. David bought the second part of this composition for Moses too,

---

[138] These include the Hassidic influence of R. Abraham Maimonides' father-in-law on R. Abraham, the strengthening of the Sufi orders in Ayyubid and Mamlūk Egypt, the weakening of philosophical studies in the Muslim world in that period, etc.

[139] Note Fenton's (1984, 7) judgement: "A cursory glance over the contents of these manuscripts will suffice to indicate the ethical and philosophical preoccupations of the author which are thoroughly imbued with Maimonidean ideology tainted with Neoplatonic and Sufi coloring."

copied by a different scribe: "As for the second part, I own one (written) in the hand of R. ʿAmram. If you prefer, I shall send it to you" (P.3.f). We have no additional information about this ʿAmram.

In comparison to philosophy (and Judaeo-Sufi literature), the Kabbalah apparently occupied a greater part of Moses b. Judah's book collection. Kabbalah was an attractive and popular field of study in Egypt and North Africa in this period.[140] In the fourteenth century, R. David II was using kabbalistic motifs in his works (Fenton 2000, 20).[141] In the 1430s, a scribe copying some kabbalistic works in Alexandria wrote in his colophon (MS Paris, Bibliothèque Nationale heb. 853.3, 79a–79b): "This book has been finished. I wrote this book for myself in Alexandria on the shore of the Great Sea. It was finished during the night of 24th of Ṭevet, 5197 of the Creation (= 10 January 1437), Joshua b. Judah the physician, may he rest in peace."[142] We cited above Oba-

---

[140] Hacker (2000, 597–600). Our knowledge of the study of Kabbalah in Palestine in the Mamlūk period is very limited. On kabbalistic manuscripts that were copied in Jerusalem at the end of the fourteenth century, see Allony (1984, 13).

[141] On the possibility that David II's father, R. Joshua, refers (with a negative attitude) to the study of Kabbalah in public, see our online article: Arad and Wagner (2013).

[142] נשלם זה הספר וכתבתי אני לעצמי זה הספר באסכנדריה דעל כף ימה רבה ונשלם שלישי בחדש טבת בליל כד שנת הקצ"ז ליצירה יהושע בר' יהודה הרופא נ"ע. The manuscript contains some kabbalistic anthologies, such as *Shomer Miṣvah* by Abraham Abulafia. This scribe also copied *Sefer ha-Yiḥud* by

diah of Bertinoro's testimony concerning Moses b. Judah's interest in books of Kabbalah. This interest is also reflected in the letters. In the only letter sent *from* Moses that is preserved in our hands (P.1), he asks the author to check if someone (the letter is torn here) "could… give me the book of the *Zohar*." A few lines after that, he asks again: "inform me, could he take out the anthology of the *Zohar*, which he mentioned, from the one that holds it, or not?"

Despite the fundamental research of Gershom Scholem and his school on this most important work of Jewish mysticism, many questions about the *Zohar* remain. Recent research has turned to the process of the creation of the *Zohar* in its final structure. Judah Liebes (1993, 85–138, 194–227) has examined how and by whom the *Zohar* was written and concluded that it was composed by a group of scholars (including Moses de Leon, who was formerly considered to be the exclusive author) in Spain. Boaz Huss (2015) has discussed how the idea of the *Zohar* as a specific book was developed and shown that its final structure only formed in the sixteenth century with its first printed editions (Mantua 1557 and Cremona 1558). Ronit Meroz (e.g., 2007; 2018) has looked at unknown zoharic passages, those not included in the standard printed editions. Our letter makes a small contribution to these questions. Moses wrote in the pre-printing period of the evolution of the *Zohar*. There are no two identical

---

Asher b. David, the grandson of the famous Abraham b. David of Posquières (MS Vatican, Bibliotheca Apostolica ebr. 103). See Beit-Arié, Sirat, and Glatzer (1986, II: no. 73; III: no. 32); Hacker (2000, 598).

manuscripts of the *Zohar*. Every manuscript contains different divisions and a unique anthology of zoharic passages, and only the printers determined the final shape of the book. The letter points to a copy of a collection of zoharic texts in the last quarter of the fifteenth century and strengthens the impression that the *Zohar* as a complete and defined text, i.e., with an authoritative version, had not yet appeared, at least in Moses' intellectual environment.

Another pseudepigraphic kabbalistic book Moses wanted to purchase is *ha-Qanah*. Ṣuriel Dayyan told him about a copy of this book, which he then tried to purchase (P.7/23; see also P.1/32). The origins of this important work, which contains a spiritual commentary on the 613 commandments, are mysterious. It was written at or shortly after the end of the thirteenth century and the identity of the author is unclear. Gershom Scholem and others thought it was written in Spain, but today Byzantium is commonly accepted as its place of composition (see Ta-Shma 1980, 56–63).[143] Only a few manuscripts of *ha-Qanah* written before the sixteenth century have been preserved, all from the cultural milieu of Byzantine Jewry (such as MS Vatican, Bibliotheca Apostolica ebr. 198, which was copied in 1478). The book was unknown, presumably, outside this cultural sphere before the sixteenth century.[144] We do not have clear details of where Moses got his own copy of *ha-Qanah*, but it probably arrived from a Jewish centre in the Maghreb: Ṣuriel Dayyan, the writer of the letter who informed Moses b. Judah about the book,

---

[143] For comprehensive research on *ha-Qanah,* see Oron (1980); Pely (2008).

[144] We want to thank Dr Hagai Pely who helped us to clarify this point.

ran businesses in Tripoli and Tunis. If so, this gives a clue as to the circulation of this kabbalistic work outside the Judaeo-Byzantine world. Furthermore, it supports Joseph Hacker's explanation of the route by which the Kabbalah was transmitted into Egypt in the late Mamlūk period. In his discussion of Kabbalah study in fifteenth-century Egypt, Hacker (2000, 598–99) pointed to two sources from which kabbalistic manuscripts arrived in Egypt: Spain, and the Maghreb. There is an alternative, however. In another letter in our corpus, P.6, a trader called Ṣuriel is mentioned, who reached Rhodes, Modon, and other communities in this area. If he can be identified as the Ṣuriel Dayyan mentioned before, this would raise the possibility that Ṣuriel purchased *ha-Qanah* in Greece or in one of the Mediterranean island communities (such as Candia, Crete), which were the main sources for Moses' library.[145] If this second possibility is correct, it might shed light on the diverse ways in which the Kabbalah arrived in Egypt in the late Mamlūk period.

Moses also asked his correspondents to purchase for him one of the important compositions of the Gerona Kabbalistic School—*Shaʿar ha-Shoʾel* (*The Gate/Section of the Questioner*), a

---

[145] On manuscripts of the Kabbalah that were copied in the Byzantine area, see Riegler (2010, 75–90). Riegler assembles there 29 manuscripts copied in the Mediterranean islands between 1324 and 1538. Thirteen of them are works of philosophy, and five have kabbalistic content.

commentary on the *Ten Sefirot*[146] by R. ʿAzriel of Gerona. His associate described his efforts to him in a letter (P.10):

> Your honour commanded me, my brother, to copy for him the commentary on the Sefirot, i.e., the questions that arrived from Alexandria to our beloved, the loyal and pious, his honourable highness and sanctity, our teacher R. David Shemesh, may God save him. After that I looked for and found another version in the hands of the educated scholar R. Obadiah, descendant of R. David ha-Nagid. We compared them [to each other] and we saw that the one I have copied there has an advantage over the other, in that what appears to be an addition to the other, is written after the samples of letters.

In other words, the writer told Moses that he had found two copies of this work, and had compared them, weighing them critically against each other. He then copied the passages that were missing in the version he had originally copied for his master. This testimony shows that at least two versions of this kabbalistic work were known in Egypt at the time, and both were held by men associated with the Nagidate: David Shemesh (or: Shams), the Nagidate's scribe, and R. Obadiah, a descendant either of the last Nagid of the Maimonidean family, David, or another Nagid, less well-known, but called David too.[147]

---

[146] On the genre of commentary on the *Ten Sefirot*, which was popular in kabbalistic literature, see Oron (2014, 212–29). See also Abrams (2013, 7–63).

[147] גזע ר' דוד הנגיד 'descendant of R. David ha-Nagid'. The terminology of the Hebrew original is not clear. Secondly, the identification of this "David ha-Nagid" here is complicated. See commentary on letter P.10/13.

BODL. MS HEB. C. 72

PART I: DOCUMENTS

C: COMMUNAL DOCUMENTS
THE PUBLIC AFFAIRS OF ALEXANDRIA

Contents

C.1.a: Letter from Solomon b. Joseph ha-Nagid to the Community of Alexandria

Bodl. MS Heb. c. 72/21 + Bodl. MS Heb. c. 72/40 + Bodl. MS Heb. c. 72/30

General Introduction

This is a letter from the Nagid, copied by his scribe, David ibn Shams, to the community of Alexandria. The fact that the letter was saved in Moses b. Judah's archive reflects his high position in the community and indicates that he was actually the addressee of the letter. The community of Alexandria was experiencing inner conflict due to criticism of the activities of the *Zeqenim* (the Seven Town Elders), especially pertaining to financial decisions. The Nagid backs the local leadership and warns the members of the community against disobedience of the *Zeqenim*, and also gives instructions about how to arrange the cantorship in the synagogue. The letter was written close to the Day of Atonement, but the year is unknown.

Physical Description

Fragment 21: 28.4 × 13.9; paper; 1 leaf; 27 lines + marginalia (recto); 1 line + marginalia (verso); torn, holes, red-brown stains, a distinctive wormhole.

Fragment 40: 6.5 × 13.8; paper; 1 leaf; 8 lines + marginalia (recto; verso is blank); torn, holes, beige stains.

Fragment 30: 18.4 × 13.7; paper; 1 leaf; 19 lines (recto; verso is blank); torn, holes, red-brown stains.

 https://doi.org/10.11647/OBP.0352.01

Transcription

Recto

1. בשמׄא רחמׄנא וחנׄנא לקׄי בינׄו עמׄי עשׄו[1]
2. בשרתי צדק בקהל וכו' הנה אל ישועתי אבטח ולא
3. ושאבתם מים בששון וכו' לי"י[2] הישועה על עמך
4. הנה לא ינום ולא וכו' ישראל נושע בי"י תשועת
5. וצדיקים ישמחו וכו' אשריכם זורעי על כל
6. ואמרתם כה לחי וכו' י"י עוז לעמו יתן י"י יברך
7. שלמה בכ"ר יוסף זלה"ה[3]
8. שלומות רבות וישועות קרובות וברכות טובות כעדר קצובות
9. אשה לאחותה משולבות מלפני שוכן ערבות לאל[פים] ולרבבות
10. כמרחבי מרומות וכעמקי תהומות עם ברכת אברהם זקן בא
11. בימים וזכות נעקד כשה תמים ותומת יושב אוהלים וחקיק
12. דמותו במרומים כולם יהיו נזר ועטרת וצניף ותפארת גפן
13. אדרת לתהלה לשם ולתפארת לכלל הקהל הקדוש המשובח
14. המפואר קהל נאאמון המלא חכמות כרמון בתורה הטהורה
15. עדה נבחרה אלופי המשרה עם י"י נקרא ישמרם וינצרם האל
16. העוטה כשלמה אורה ויצילם מכל זעם וצרה ויהיו תחת צל
17. וסתרה ליהודים היתה אורה אנ"ס[4]
18. יחיט אלי עלם אלמכׄאדים בעד אלסלאם אלתאם אלשאפי עלי כל אחד
19. מן אלקהל במפרדה הי"ב[5] באן חצׄר אלינא ה"ר יעקב פרנשיל י"ל ואנה[י]

---

[1] = לישועתך קויתי י"י; בעזרת י"י נעשה ונצליח; עזרי מעם י"י עֹשה שמים וארץ.

[2] = לה' ('To the LORD').

[3] = זכרונו לחיי העולם הבא.

[4] = אמן נצח סלה.

[5] = השם יברכם.

20. לנא באן אלמכאדים פי חצר בליג' בסבב אלעונש אלדי אטלקנאה קבל
21. תאריכה עלי כל מן יכ̇אלף שבעה טובי העיר פי מא ירוה בכ̇וף
22. אללה תע' ללקהל ויכ̇אלפה° פי מתל דלך ופי מן יועצא עליהם פי
23. וזן אלמג̇ארם אלדי תחף אלקהל כל וקת בוקתה ויסתחלו גזל רבים
24. וי[..] ג[..]הו עליהם פי תרבחהם כ̇[..]ת̇א̇ לק[.. ...]א עלי אלעונש ולם
25. יעלמו בית דין ולם יוצל ל[... ... ... אל]עונש ויציר כל מן
26. [...]מתעדי מעה פת̇דל עלייה עלי אנני אתית להם העונש
27. ואעדקה [ב]שבעה טובי העיר ואיי מן כאלפהם יפעלו פיה אלמשפט
28. [...]
29. [.... ....] פכאן גמיע דלך עלי כאטרכ[ם אלכרי]ם וקד
30. אגבת למ̇ יעקוב אלי סואלה והתרתי העונש ללק[הל ...]ה ואעדקת
31. אלאמר בשבעה טובי העיר בשרט אן יכון להם אלטאיע ואלעאצי לנא
32. והאדה אלאמר יבקא מתעלק בדמתהם מא לם יכברונא במן יעציהם
33. תם אן בלג'נא אן אלחזנים וחידין ולם ענדהם מן יסאעדהם וכל אחדא
34. ביתעפף ען אלתפלה ואלסדר ויציר אלקהל נע ונד מן ג'יר רת̇בה
35. והאדה קט מא סמענאה ען קהל נא אמון אלי' פי האדה אלאיאם
36. פמן גמיע אלקהל[ות ...]יתעלמו אלרתבה ואלקעדה מן ענדכם
37. פלמא בלגנא דלך קצדנא אן נזידכם מחאסן ז[..]ל ונלזמהם ב[אמו]ר
38. תפעלוהא תצירו עלי קאעדה גמילה מע צפה אלכואלד פאערפכם
39. באן נובת אלמ̇ מוסי מעאני יכון מעה מוסי א̇ אבו אלחסן וקדרנא
40. מעה דלך ונובת יעקוב חנך יכון אכיה אלמ̇ יוסף י"ל ראש החזנים
41. ויסתמר אכוה מעה ונובת עפיף אלדבאח יכון אלמ̇ מוסי א̇ יהודה
42. ראש החזנים ויכון עפיף מסתמר מעה ויציר כל אחדא מסתמר
43. פי נובתה ואלזמנא אלמ̇ יוסף חנך ואלמ̇ מוסי מעאני ואלמ̇ מוסי א̇ יהודה
44. אן יכונו ראשי החזנים ומא דונהם אלדי דכרנאהם אעלאה ואיי מן
45. אכתארוה אלשבעה טובי העיר בעד דלך אן יסאעד פי אלחזון ליציר
46. להם דרבה פי דלך פיפעלו מא יכ̇תארוה בהאדה מא אלזמנאכם בה
47. ומן לא יקבל דלך יחצ̇ר אלינא ילחן בחג̇תה וננצ̇ר פי אחואלה תם

48. אערף אלמכאדים באן אלמ̇ שמואל י"ל ארסל יתשכא לנא מן גהה נפסה
49. כון אנה מכסור אלכאטר ליס לה קלב אן יחצ̇ר פי בית הכנסת מע
50. אלקהל כמא כאן וכצוצא אדא כאן לבסה חזאיני פיסתחי אן יקעד
51. פי אלמגלס עלי האדה אלצפה פארסל יטלב מנא התרה ואנה יג̇לס
52. אלמדרש בבית הכנסת הגדולה ואמא בבית הכנסת [הקטנה]
53. יג̇לס פי מוצ̇ע אן יכתאר ואג̇זנא לה דלך̇ ואג̇בנאה אלי סואלה
54. והתרתי לו העונש פיכון דלך̇ עלי כאטרכם אלכרים השם ינחם לבבו
55. ולבבכם בביאת הגואל ובניין אריאל וכו' ותבושרו במחילה וסליחה וכפרה

Margin

ויקיים עליכם מקרא שכתו[ב כי] ביום הז[ה ....] אמן וכן יהי רצון

Verso

מן ענד אדוננו הנגיד י"ל לקהל נא אמון השם יהיה בעזרכם

Translation

Recto

1. In the name of the merciful, the gracious. I wait for your deliverance, O Lord (Gen. 49.18). In the name of God we will do and succeed. My help comes from the Lord, maker of heaven and earth (Ps. 121.2).
2. I proclaimed [Your] righteousness in [a great] congregation (Ps. 40.10), etc. Behold the God who gives me triumph, I am confident, [unafraid] (Isa. 12.2).
3. Joyfully shall you draw water [from the fountains of triumph] (Isa. 12.3), etc. Deliverance is the Lord's, [Your blessing be] upon Your people (Ps. 3.9).

4. Behold, [the guardian of Israel] neither slumbers nor [sleeps] (Ps. 121.4), etc. But Israel has won through the LORD, triumph [everlasting] (Isa. 45.17).
5. But the righteous shall rejoice (Ps. 68.4), etc. Happy shall you be who sow by all [waters] (Isa. 32.20).
6. Say: To life (1 Sam. 25.6), etc. May the LORD grant strength to His people, may the LORD bestow [on His people wellbeing] (Ps. 29.11).
7. Solomon, the son of the honourable rabbi Joseph, God rest his soul in the world to come.
8. A lot of peace and salvations soon and good blessings like a flock of ewes all shaped alike
9. combined one with the other (see Exod. 21.17), in front of those who abode upon the skies (see Ps. 68.5), for thousands and tens of thousands
10. as the wide skies and the deep depths, with the blessing of Abraham, the elder
11. well stricken in age (Gen. 24.1), and the right of the one bound like a lamb without blemish (= Isaac) and the completeness of the one sitting in tents (= Jacob; see Gen. 25.27), and his image
12. engraves in heaven. All of them will be a crown and a garland and a diadem and a beauty (see Isa. 62.3), and a stately
13. vine (Ezek. 17.8) in praise, and in name, and in glory (Deut. 26.19), for the entire holy, praiseworthy
14. and glorious community of Alexandria, which is filled like a pomegranate with wisdom of the pure Torah,

15. chosen assembly, the heads of the authority, those who are called 'the people of the LORD', God will save and keep them, the LORD who
16. covers himself with light as with a garment (see Ps. 104.2), and will save them from every rage and trouble, and they will be under his shadow
17. and his shelter, the Jews had light (Est. 8.16). Amen, forever.
18. (This letter) brings to the knowledge of the honourable addressees, after complete and honest greetings to every single one
19. of the community especially, may God bless them, that R. Jacob Faransil(?), may he live forever, presented himself and he informed
20. us that the masters are in serious distress concerning the penalty that we imposed before
21. this time (today) on anyone who would not obey the Seven Elders of the Town, concerning what they will rule in fear
22. of God exalted for the community and who would contradict (them) like that. Whoever will disobey against them regarding
23. the value of the financial obligations, which the community … every time and time again, they should judge this as 'stealing from many'
24. […] on them […] in their profits […] of the fine. They did not
25. inform the *Bet Din*, and it was not brought to [… … … …] the fine. Everyone who will

26. [...] transgresses the law with him, you should call upon him provided that I gave them the fine.
27. He should give it over to the Seven Town Elders. Anyone who does not obey them, they should take him to court.
28. [...]
29. [...] and all this should be to your [honourable] knowledge. I already
30. replied to M. Jacob, to his question. I released the fine for the [community...] and passed
31. the matter on to the Seven Elders of the Community with the condition that they should deal with the obedient and the rebellious for us.
32. This matter remains in their responsibility as long as they do not inform us who rebels against them.
33. Then it reached us that the cantors are on their own, with no one to support them. Everyone
34. is withdrawing from prayer and from the *seder*, leaving the community vagabond, without any order (or: ritual[6]).
35. This is only what we have heard from the community of Alexandria today(?)[7] these days,
36. and from all the communities [...] they should know the order (or: ritual) and the seating among them
37. After we received this, we wanted to give you good advice [...]. We need in these [matters]

---

[6] See Blau (2006, 238).

[7] The meaning of 'אלי is not clear. Perhaps it is an abbreviation of *al-yawm* 'today', but it could also be an abbreviated attribute describing Alexandria.

38. that you arrange them in a beautiful manner together with the upper row. I inform you
39. concerning the rotation (of public address) of M. Mūsā Maʿānī, together with him will be Mūsā b. Abū l-Ḥasan. We prepared
40. this with him. (Concerning) the rotation of Jacob Ḥunak: his brother M. Joseph, may he live forever, will be the head of the cantors,
41. and his brother will remain with him. The rotation of ʿAfīf the butcher will be M. Mūsā b. Judah,
42. head of cantors. ʿAfīf will remain with him. Everyone should remain
43. in their rotation. We compelled M. Joseph Ḥunak, M. Mūsā Maʿānī, and M. Mūsā b. Judah
44. that they should be heads of cantors, and no one else except for those we mentioned above, and anyone
45. chosen by the Seven Town Elders. After that he should support the cantorship, to establish
46. for them a method in this matter. They should do what (the elders) choose in this matter. We did not compel you concerning it.
47. Anyone who does not accept this should present himself to us to explain his need, and we will look into their affairs. Then
48. I inform the masters that M. Samuel, may he live forever, sent to complain to us on his own behalf,
49. because he is exhausted of mind. He does not have the heart to present himself in the synagogue together with

50. the community like he used to. In particular as his clothes are that of mourning, so he would be ashamed if he were to sit
51. in the seat on that bench. He sent to ask from us for permission and that he would sit
52. in the *Midrash* (section) in the big synagogue. Concerning the small synagogue,
53. he will sit in a place he chooses. We granted him that, and we replied to his question.
54. I released him from the fine. All this should be to your honourable knowledge. May the Name comfort his heart
55. and your hearts by bringing the redemption and rebuilding *Ariel* (= Jerusalem) etc. May you be notified (that you got the) pardon, forgiveness, and atonement (of God).

Margin

(God) will manifest unto you the verse that says: "[For] on this day [atonement shall be made for you to cleanse you of all your sins]." Amen, and may it be (God's) will.

Verso

From our lord the Nagid, may he live forever, to the community of Alexandria, may the Name be your assistance.

Commentary

Line 1:
"In the name of the merciful, the gracious." The collocation רחמנא וחננא is taken from the Aramaic translation of Exod. 34.1 (רחום וחנון). It appears also in the form בשמך רחמנא וחננא 'In **your**

name, the merciful, the gracious' (for example, Bodl. Heb. d. 54/19). In earlier periods, the typical motto was בשמך רחמנא. This last form, which was very common, is discussed by Mark Cohen (2007, 22–23), who calls it "the Jewish Basmala." In at least one letter, we found an even shorter version, which includes only one word: בשמא (T-S 8J17.6.; the letter is from 1236).

"In the name of God we will do and succeed." Unlike the other phrases, this is not a biblical phrase but a traditional blessing (maybe following Ps. 1.3). The first line in this letter is written in larger letters, which are marked by triangles of dots, while the following five lines also mark the biblical quotations with double strokes above the words. This appears to be a pragmatic way of following the halakhic commandment to rule writing material when biblical quotations are given.[8] In letters written on paper, where ruling is more difficult than on parchment, dots are used to fulfil the commandment of ruling and achieve a separation from ordinary text.

Lines 8–12:

Compare Bodl. MS 2806, Heb. b. 3/31: שלום שלום ממרומים וברכות עצומות כנחלי ימים וברכת אברהם זקן בא בימים ויצחק שנעקד כשה תמים ויעקב שעשה מטעמים עם שאר הברכות [שבעשרים] וארבעה ספרים יחולו על ראש כ"ר שמואל...

Line 8:

"Like a flock of ewes all shaped alike." According to Song 4.2: "Thy teeth are like a flock of ewes all shaped alike, which are

---

[8] See, for example, Maimonides, *Mishne Torah*, *Hilkhot Sefer Torah* 7.16, which requires ruling when more than three words are cited.

come up from the washing." The author refers here mainly to the end of the phrase: "whereof all are paired, and none faileth among them" (Song 4.2), which indicates that all of the community's members are righteous people.

Line 11:
"And his image engraves in heaven." This expression is based on a *midrash* that says that the image of Jacob's face is engraved on the chair of God (see Gen. Rabbah 82.2).

Line 20:
"Which we imposed." The author uses here the *pluralis majestatis*, as the head of the Jews.

Line 21:
"The Seven Good Men of the Town." See commentary on C.6/8.

"Concerning what they will rule in fear of God." The writer emphasises that the *Zeqenim* are making decisions justly and honestly, with no personal interests.

Line 23:
"Stealing from many." This is a strong accusation. The sages considered this sin a grave one and noted that it is difficult to atone for because the sinner does not know to whom to give back the money (see, e.g., t. Bava Qama 10.8). Maimonides created a list of 24 cases of which repentance is very difficult, and says: "Among these are five [transgressions], for which it is impossible for the person who commits them to repent completely. They are sins between man and man, concerning which it is impossible to know the person whom one sinned against in order to return

(what is owed him) or ask for his forgiveness" (see his examples, *Mishne Torah, Hilkhot Teshuvah,* 4.3).

Line 31:
"They should deal with the obedient and the rebellious for us." The hierarchy that is reflected here is circular. The Nagid is backing the local leaders and approving their communal and legal decisions, while the local leaders are constructing the Nagid's power in the public mind by focussing punctiliously on his status and his glory, by giving gestures of honour, directing letters and questions to the Nagid's office, and punishing rebels against the Nagid's authority.

Line 33 and onwards:
The Nagid is here dealing with problems relating to public prayer in Alexandria. He obtains the legitimacy to take care of these affairs not just from the Jewish representatives who elected him, but also from the Muslim government, who saw him as the chief supervisor of the religious life of the Jewish minority in the Mamlūk state. This was one of his basic duties in the eyes of the Mamlūk authorities.

Line 34:
It is not clear which *Seder* is mentioned here. Maybe it is *Seder al-Tawḥīd,* a philosophic text on the monotheistic faith, interweaved in a special liturgical corpus for the first day of Nisan, which was left as a remnant from the antique Palestinian order. This order has been described well by Fleischer (1968; 1999). We have some very late manuscripts of this order (e.g., MS Paris, AIU IV C 24; CUL Add. 1531), and it has even been published, in Alexandria in 1887, but Fleischer did not find evidence for it having

been read in the late Middle Ages. The present authors, however, have discussed a letter of R. Joshua the Nagid,[9] from the middle of the fourteenth century, which mentions this liturgical order (Arad and Wagner 2013). R. Joshua criticised a preacher in Fusṭāṭ, that "when he teaches the order of oneness (צדר תוחיד)... he is not understanding its meaning," and here we find a mention of what is apparently the same text again, in a letter of Solomon the Nagid.

Line 39:
"Mūsā Maʿānī." See commentary on C.6/10.

Line 40:
"Jacob Ḥunak." This family (Ḥunak or Ḥunayk) appears in documents from the late Mamlūk period and the early Ottoman period. Members of the family continued to participate in the leadership of the communities in the early Ottoman Period. David Ḥunayk was one of the leaders of the Mustaʿribs in Cairo in the late sixteenth and early seventeenth centuries (ENA NS 1.57; ENA NS 29.11; Mosseri VII 32.1, published by Arad 2011, 63–65; see especially the discussion in 63 n. 215). One of the *heqdesh* houses of the Mustaʿrib community in Cairo in that period was called "the house of Ḥunayk" (בית חונייך, CUL Or. 1080J253), maybe after the renter who lived there, Elijah Ḥunayk (see ENA NS 7.14).

Line 41:
"ʿAfīf." This can maybe be identified as ʿAfīf the cantor (עפיף אלחזן), who is mentioned in a list of payments, probably from the second half of the fifteenth century (ENA 2348.3). ʿAfīf was a

[9] A draft in MS Mosseri IV 85 and a final scribal copy in TS 12.608.

common name among Egyptian Jewry in the late Mamlūk and early Ottoman period. ʿAfīf was a butcher. The combination of cantor and butcher was very popular (see Arad 2013, 260–61).

Line 42:
"Head of cantors." The cantors cooperated to some extent in a guild, which was under the supervision of the head of cantors. We do not have accurate information on his duties and rights. In a Karaite document in Judaeo-Arabic from Cairo, dated to 1575 (MS St Petersburg, RNL Evr. Ar. II 1378, published by Arad 2016, 26–30), the term 'the big cantor' or 'chief Cantor' (חזן כביר) occurs, which may refer to a parallel position among the Karaites.

Line 45:
The Hebrew term *ḥizzun* (חִזּוּן) appears also in rabbinic texts from the early Ottoman period (Ibn Zimra, *Responsa*, VI, §2078; Ṣahalon, *Responsa*, §104). It was also used among the Karaites in that period (see, e.g., MS St Petersburg, RNL Evr. Ar. II 1378).

Line 55:
"May you be notified (that you got the) pardon, forgiveness and atonement (of God)." This blessing is still used by Yemenite Jews today. The custom is that one says to his friend: תבושר במחילה וסליחה וכפרה, and the other replies to him: ואתה תבושר במחילה וסליחה וכפרה. The roots of this blessing are ancient. In an anonymous liturgical text for the Day of Atonement, written by a poet from the land of Israel around the sixth century, the following line appears: יום יבושרו השבים במחילה סליחה וכפרה מאלהים 'A day in which those who repent will be notified of pardon, forgiveness, and atonement from God' (CUL Or. 1081 2.69).

C.1.b: Letter from the Nagid (Probably Solomon b. Joseph) to the Community of Alexandria

Bodl. MS Heb. c. 72/28 + Bodl. MS Heb. c. 72/17bis + Bodl. MS Heb. c. 72/41

General Description

This letter, written by the scribe David ibn Shams for the Nagid, was sent as an answer to a letter received from the community of Alexandria (see l. 8). The letter is not preserved completely. Its left side and the beginning and the end of it are still missing. Some of its contents therefore remain enigmatic. The letter is preserved in two main fragments: lines 1–5 in Bodl. MS Heb. c. 72/28 and lines 6–21 in c. 72/41. We thought at first that there was not an immediate continuation between these two fragments; however, we fortunately succeeded in identifying a third fragment (Bodl. MS Heb. c. 72/17bis), which is a mirror-copy of the letter, made while the two fragments were still combined. In this copy, lines 3–21 are preserved, and prove that there is no missing part between the two fragments. The mirror script in the third fragment also helped us to improve our reading of some words. In the letter, the Nagid refers to a person of the community who does not obey the leadership (l. 12), and falsely portrays himself as a poor man in need of support, without justification (l. 14, see commentary). He could cause danger or financial damage to the community by spreading calumny to the authorities. It may be assumed that, in the missing part of the letter, the Nagid

 https://doi.org/10.11647/OBP.0352.02

guided the leaders of the community as to how to deal with this person.

Physical Description

Fragment 28: 4.8 × 7.5; paper; 1 leaf; 6 lines (recto; verso is blank); torn, holes, rubbed, beige stains.

Fragment 41: 15.9 × 7.7; paper; 1 leaf; 16 lines (recto; verso is blank); torn, holes, rubbed, beige stains.

Transcription

1. [הקהל הק]דוש המפוא[ר ...]
2. [...] קהל נא אמון [... ... ... השם]
3. יהיה בעזרם וישמיד צורר[ם...]
4. וישמרם צורם ויאיר אורם [...]
5. יחיט אלי עלם אלמכאדים הי"ב [...]
6. אלמכאדים[1] ותאמלנאהא וס[...]
7. ושכרנא אללה תע' עלי בקא[הם ...]
8. אמא מא דכרוה אלמכאדים [...]
9. אלבלד פאן מא תסבבנא ל[...]
10. אן ראגענא ענכם מראד ע[...]
11. מן אלתערץ' אליכם ומא חאט[ר ...]
12. בתאעכם פאנה עצי עלי אל[...]
13. אלתרבה ג̇מיעהא וספר אלדי [...]
14. ואולאדה ועמל נפסה פקיר ו[...]
15. ואלחכאם מא להם ג'רץ̇ אלא [...]
16. אסראר ויתו̇גה באלמסרות [...]

---

[1] Fragment Bodl. MS Heb.c.72.41 starts here in l. 7.

17. אנה אמת כאן מצׄ֯ר אנה מ[...]
18. אקל מן כמסין אשרפי וכאן [...]
19. אלקאצׄי נצׄר אלכאץ בחצׄור אל[...]
20. ויוסף חנך ומוסי מעאני ואב[רהים ...]
21. ודכר אן כל ואחד מ[ן] האדה [...]

Translation

1. [...] the holy and glorious [community ...]
2. [...] the community of Alexandria [... ... ... may the Name]
3. be their assistance and destroy [their] enemy [...]
4. And may God save them and illuminate their light [...]
5. It should be to the knowledge of the masters, may God bless them [...]
6. the masters. We considered it and [...]
7. We thanked God exalted for [their] well-being [...]
8. Concerning what the masters mentioned [...]
9. the city. If you do not cause us[2] to [...]
10. that we return on your behalf the desired [...]
11. from opposing you. He did not [guard ...]
12. of yours. He disobeyed the [...]
13. of the cemetery (or: the dust), all of it. He travelled [...]
14. his children. He pretended to be a beggar. [...]
15. and the arbiters only had the intention to [...]
16. secrets. He would turn to calumny (to the Muslim authority) [...]
17. that it is true. He was forced to [...]

---

[2] See Blau (2006, 284).

18. less than 50 *ashrafī* dinars. It was [...]
19. The Qāḍī viewed the special (case) in presence of the [...]
20. as well as Joseph Ḥunak, Moses Maʿānī, and Ab[raham ...]
21. He mentioned that every single one of this [...]

Commentary

Lines 1–2:

For these praises, see C.1.a/13–14.

Line 2:

For the completion [השם] יהיה בעזרם, see C.1.a, verso.

Line 12:

"He disobeyed the..." The matter is unclear. Maybe it is related to the matter discussed in C.1.a (see ll. 22, 31–32).

Line 14:

"He pretended to be." For עמל נפסה in this meaning, see Blau (2006, 459). It is not clear what the intention of this man was. One option is that he introduced himself as a poor man and deceived the people by pretending that he needed support. Another option is that *faqīr* here means an ascetic, who behaved like a Sufi dervish, and caused people to believe that he was a holy man worthy of support, according to the values of both Muslim and Jewish societies. The Nagid, it seems, wanted to warn the community about the lies of this particular individual.

Line 16:

מסרות 'calumny' appears to be a loanword from the Hebrew root מס"ר 'to betray someone to the authorities, to inform against'. See, for example, TS 8J17.33.

Line 20:

Joseph Ḥunak and Moses Maʿānī were appointed as the heads of the cantors in Alexandria, beside Moses b. Judah (see C.1.a). On the family of Ḥunak, see commentary there on l. 40.

C.1.c: Mirror Copy of Letter C.1.a

Bodl. MS Heb. c. 72/53

General Description

A 'copy' of letter C.1.a in mirror script, i.e., excess of ink transferred from one page to another. Although the three fragments Bodl. MS Heb. c. 72/21 + 40 + 30 were all written in the same hand, we could at first not prove that they were in fact from the same letter, and what their original order was. The discovery of this copy confirmed our arrangement of the three fragments constituting letter C.1.a. The transfer of ink must have happened due to close contact between the two pages, before letter C.1.a was torn into three pieces.

Physical Description

28.5 × 19.7; paper; 1 leaf; 26 lines of mirrored script (verso; recto is blank); torn, holes, red-brown stains; unusual blue-grey paper.

 https://doi.org/10.11647/OBP.0352.03

C.1.d: Mirror Copy of a Missing Letter to the Community of Alexandria, Probably from Solomon b. Joseph ha-Nagid

Bodl. MS Heb. c. 72/14bis

General Description

A ‘copy’ of the beginning of a missing letter by the Nagid, in the handwriting of his scribe David ibn Shams, to the community of Alexandria. The letter has only been preserved in mirror script on the verso of another letter. The beginning of the Nagid's letter preserved here was written in Hebrew, but the letter itself was probably composed in Judaeo-Arabic.

Physical Description

Dimensions are as P.5.b (Bodl. MS Heb. c. 72/14). The mirror script can be found on the right-hand side of verso. Only a small part of the beginning of the letter is mirrored, showing how it was folded over while being stored in close contact with P.5.b, when the ink transfer happened.

Transcription

1. בשמׄא רחמׄנא וחנׄנא [לקׄי בינׄו עמׄי עשׄו(?)][1]
2. הנה לא ינום ולא ישן שומר
3. אשריך ישראל מי כמוך עם
4. ברוכים אתם [לי"י עושה שמים]

---

[1] = לישועתך קויתי י"י; בעזרת י"י נעשה ונצליח; עזרי מעם י"י עֹשה שמים וארץ.

 https://doi.org/10.11647/OBP.0352.04

5. ואמרתם כה לחי ו[אתה שלום]
6. י"י עוז לעמו יתן י"י [יברך את]

Translation

1. In the name of the merciful, the gracious. [I wait for your deliverance, O LORD (Gen. 49.18). In the name of God we will do and succeed. My help comes from the LORD, maker of heaven and earth (Ps. 121.2)(?)[2]]
2. Behold, the guardian [of Israel] neither slumbers nor sleeps (Ps. 121.4)
3. Blessed are you Israel! Who is like you, a people [saved by the LORD] (Deut. 33.29)
4. May you be blessed [by the LORD, the maker of heaven] (Ps. 115.15)
5. Say to him: Long life to you! [Good health to you] (1 Sam. 25.6)
6. May the LORD grant strength to His people, may the LORD [bestow on His people wellbeing] (Ps. 29.11).

Commentary

Lines 1–6:

These verses look like standard blessings, but they can teach us important information about the addressees of the letter, even though we cannot learn anything about its content. In the title we stated that this letter was addressed to the community of Alexandria from the Nagid. What is the justification for this conclusion?

---

[2] The completion here is doubtful.

The letter is written in the handwriting of David ibn Shams. David starts another public letter on behalf of the Nagid (C.1.a) in a very similar way, with a list of verses of blessings, but he also uses the same format in the beginning of two private letters to Moses b. Judah (P.3.b; P.3.c). All the four letters by David have the same framework: They open with an identical Aramaic motto, בשמא רחמנא וחננא 'In the name of the merciful and the gracious', and finish with the verse "May the LORD give strength to his people" (Ps. 29.11). However, a careful reading reveals the different character of the letters.

Table 1: Comparison of opening blessings of letters written by David ibn Shams

C.1.d (72/14bis)	C.1.a (72/21 + 40 + 30)	P.3.b (72/20)	P.3.c (72/22)	
בשמ֯א רחמ֯נא וחנ֯נא [לק֯י בינ֯ו עמ֯י עש֯ו(?)]	בשמ֯א רחמ֯נא וחנ֯נא לק֯י בינ֯ו עמ֯י עש֯ו	בשמ֯א רחמ֯נא וחנ֯נא ל֯ק֯י	בשמ֯א רחמ֯נא וחנ֯נא	1
הנה לא ינום ולא ישן...	בשרתי צדק... הנה אל ישועתי אבטח...	אני לדודי ודודי לי...	כי שמש מגן י"י אלהים...	2
אשריך ישראל...	ושאבתם מים בששון... לי"י הישועה על עמך...	שלום רב לאוהבי תורתיך...	ומצא חן ושכל טוב...	3
ברוכים אתם לי"י...	הנה לא ינום... ישראל נושע בי"י...	והתענג על י"י...	בורא ניב שפתים...	4
ואמרתם כה לחי ואתה שלום...	וצדיקים ישמחו... אשריכם זורעי על כל	ואמרתם כה לחי ואתה שלום...	ואמרתם כה לחי ואתה שלום...	5
י"י עוז לעמו יתן...	ואמרתם כה לחי... י"י עוז לעמו יתן...	והאיש משה עניו מאד...	י"י עוז לעמו יתן...	6
		שמר תם וראה ישר...		7
		י"י עוז לעמו יתן...		8

In letter C.1.a, most of the verses speak in the plural (e.g., ושאבתם... וצדיקים ישמחו... אשריכם...). Some of them refer explicitly to "(the people of) Israel" (e.g., הנה לא ינום ולא יישן שומר ישראל; ישראל נושע בי"י...) or to "your people" (לי"י הישועה על עמך...), which is appropriate for a public letter. The first verse even contains the word קהל (בשרתי צדק בקהל רב...), which was a synonym in Medieval Hebrew for 'a community'. In contrast, letters P.3.b and P.3.c lack this feature, and the verses cited at the beginning of them speak in the singular. The verse "Say as follows: 'To life'. Greetings to you and to your household" (1 Sam. 25.6) starts in the plural (ואמרתם) and finishes in the singular (ואתה שלום), and therefore fits both kinds of letters, public and private. In addition, letter P.3.b exhibits an explicitly intimate character. David uses the verse "I am my beloved's, and my beloved is mine" (Song 6.3), which was interpreted in the classic Jewish commentaries as a metaphor for the relationship between God and the nation of Israel, but here it expresses the love between the two friends, Moses and David. In the initial verses, this letter also contains a clear allusion to Moses himself, by the quotation "Now the man Moses was very meek" (Num. 12.3).

Letter C.1.d displays the same characteristics as letter C.1.a. It also contains verses that speak in the plural, and the two first verses refer explicitly to the people of Israel. In the light of this fact, it is clear that letter C.1.d was written to a certain community. Its presence in the Archive of Moses b. Judah and the similarity of its initial verses to those of letter C.1.a lead us to the conclusion that it was written by the Nagid, probably Solomon b. Joseph, and addressed to the Alexandrian community.

C.2: Letter from Nathan Sholal ha-Nagid to Moses b. Judah

Bodl. MS Heb. c. 72/17

After 1483

General Introduction

The Nagid sends the addressee different requests concerning financial affairs within the Alexandrian community, directed to Moses as its leader, and as a man who has the reputation and power in his hands to implement his authority over the members of the community.

This letter was published by David (1988). There are some differences between his and our reading.

Physical Description

21.9 × 15.2; paper; 1 leaf; 30 lines + 2 marginalia lines (recto); 1 line + 21 lines of mirrored script (verso); torn, holes, beige stains; a distinctive wormhole.

Transcription

Recto

1. לק"י[1]
2. שלו' שלו' וכו'
3. ואתה שלו' וכו'
4. בורא ניב וכו'

---

[1] = לישועתך קויתי י"י.

 https://doi.org/10.11647/OBP.0352.05

5. אשרי אדם   וכו'
6. יי"י עז לעמו וכו'
7. נתן כהן אמת
8. שלומות רבות לאלפים ולרבבות ונחמות כתובות וברכות חתומות י[בואו(?)]
9. ויחולו על ראש היקר החשוב הנדיב בישראל העומד בפרץ לעדת יקות[יאל כב']
10. גדו' קדו'[2] ר' משה י"ל[3] בכ"ר יהודה נ"ע ישמרו שוכן עלילה ישימו לשם ול[תהלה]
11. אחר דרישת השלום יודע למעלתך כשיעמוד אליך מוביל כתבנו ז[ה]
12. אשר שמו ר' חיים י"ל בן פורת שתתן לו כל החפצים שתחת ידך ש[ל]
13. היתומים ואל תעכב מהם שום חפץ וגם כל מה שיש מהחפצים ש[ל]
14. היתומים הנזכרים ביד בני אדם אחרים שתשתדל בחסדך על זה
15. הדבר וכל מי שתחת ידו מאלו החפצים שיתקבצו כולם ותתן אותם
16. לזה הנכבד הנזכר ואל תניח מי שיעכב על ידו בשום ענין כי הו[א]
17. נחפז ללכת במהרה ואל תטריחנו לכתוב על זה פעמים רבות
18. והשתדל בזה הדבר מאד עד שיקבל זה הנכבד כל החפצים משל[ם]
19. ואין להאריך על מעלתך כי אם בשלומך ובשלום כל הקהל כאחד ושל[ום]
20. גם אודיעך שר' אברהם בחליץ היה עליו לר' אברהם בן חסאן נ"ע ששה פרחים
21. וחמשה מאידי והיה כתוב עליו שטר חוב בערכאותיהם ושלח אותו השט[ר]
22. בחייו עם ר' יעקב פרנשי נ"ע לבקש ממנו החוב הנזכר ואחר שמת ר' יעקב
23. ור' אברהם בן חסאן שלחו לי מירושלם ת"ו לפי שהיו לי מעות על [ר'] אברהם
24. הנזכר ואמרו לי תקבל זה מחובך ותעשה חסד עם היתומים והאלמנה

---

[2] = כבוד גדולת קדושת.

[3] = יחי לעד.

25. ואני שלחתי לו ונתן לי ר' יצחק פרנשי יצ"ו[4] השטר שהיה [ביד] אחיו והראה אותו [אל(?)]
26. ר' צדקה ניס ועם כל זה כפר ואמ' עד שיקיימו אותו כדי להפסד[5] ליתומי[ם]
27. ענין הקייום ובקש מר' צדקה הנזכר שיעשה פשרה בארבעה פרחים וביו[תר]
28. מעט ואני לא רציתי ועתה אם הוא מודה ישלם החוב הנזכר ואם הוא כופר
29. ישבע שבועה בתורה בנקיטת חפץ לפני ב"ד[6] ויכתבו השבועה וישלחו אותה
30. אלי ואחר כך יזמן האל מה שיהיה אחר כך ושלום לכם ולכל הקה[ל] בי[ח]ד ושלו'

Margin

1. ר' שלום בן זיתון יצ"ו תקבל ממנו השני פרחים שבידו לקודש ותתן אותם לזה ר'
2. חיים הנזכר יצ"ו ומה שהגיעו הגיעני

Verso

יגיע ליד מה"ר[7] משה בכ"ר יהודה נ"ע   מאת אדונ'ו הנגיד יצ"ו

Translation

Recto

1. I wait for Thy salvation, O LORD (Gen. 49.18).
2. Peace, Peace, etc. (Isa. 59.17).
3. And peace be both unto thee, etc. (1 Sam. 25.6).
4. createth the fruit [of the lips], etc. (Isa. 59.17).

---

[4] = ישמרהו צורו ויחייהו.

[5] Should be: להפסיד.

[6] = בית דין.

[7] = מורנו הרב.

5. Happy is the man, etc.[8]
6. May the LORD [give] strength to his people, etc. (Ps. 29.11).
7. Nathan Cohen Truth
8. Much peace, thousands and tens thousands, and written condolences, and 'signed' blessings [shall come(?)]
9. and carry out upon the head of the honourable, the respectable, the generous among Israel, who stands in the breach for the congregation of Jekuth[iel, the honourable]
10. great and holy, R. Moses, may he live forever, the son of the honourable rabbi Judah, his soul rest in Eden, shall be saved by him who has great exploits, and he will make him to be a name [and a glory] (following Zeph. 3.20).
11. After inquiring about the wellbeing (of you), your honour shall be informed that, when [this] carrier of our letter will arrive to you,
12. whose name is R. Ḥayyim, may he live forever, ben Porat, give him all the objects [of the] orphans, which you hold (as deposit),
13. and do not leave in your hands any object, and also all the objects [of]
14. those orphans which are held by another people, make an effort, by your grace, for this
15. matter, and everyone who holds one of those objects (should take care that) all of them will be collected. Give them

[8] It is difficult to determine which verse exactly the author is quoting (it could be Pss 32.2, 84.6, 84.13; Prov. 3.13, 8.34, 28.14).

16. to that honourable (man) mentioned before (= R. Ḥayyim b. Porat). Do not let anyone disturb him in any form, because he is
17. in a hurry to go quickly. Do not bother him to write about it many times.
18. Make a big effort in this matter, until that honourable (man) will get all the objects entirely.
19. There is no need to extend (this letter) for your honour, just (wishing) you peace and (wishing) the whole community peace, each and every one, and peace (will be).
20. I inform you also that R. Abraham Baḥliṣ was in debt to R. Abraham ben Ḥassān, his soul rest in Eden, by six florins
21. And five *muʾayyidī,* and a deed of debt was written against him, (which was made out) according to their (Muslim) law, and he (= Abraham b. Ḥassān) sent that deed
22. while he was still alive with R. Jacob Faransī, his soul rest in Eden, to demand him (to repay) this debt. After R. Jacob died
23. and R. Abraham ben Ḥassān (also died), they sent to me from Jerusalem, may it be rebuilt and established, because that I had (a claim) of money on [R.] Abraham
24. who is mentioned before. I had been told: "Get this (as a re-payment) of your debt and do a grace to the orphans and the widow."
25. So, I sent to him, and R. Isaac Faransī, may God save him, gave me the deed, which was in the hands of his brother, and he showed it [to(?)] R. Ṣedaqah Nis,[9]

---

[9] According to the completion we suggested above: והראה אותו [אל] ר' צדקה ניס.

26. but nevertheless, he denied and said (he will not pay) until it [=the deed] will be ratified, aiming to cause loss to the orphans
27. from the ratification matter. He asked R. Ṣedaqah, who is mentioned before, to make a compromise of four florins and little [more(?)]
28. but I did not want (this). Now, if he admits, he will pay that debt, and if he denies,
29. he must swear on a Torah (scroll), by raising an object in front of the *Bet Din* (the Jewish court), and (the Judges) shall write the oath and send it
30. to me, and after that God will determine what will happen. Peace be upon you and upon all the community [together], and peace (will be).

Margin

1. (regarding) R. Shalom ben Zaytūn, may God save him, get from him the two florins he has for the pious foundations' treasury, and give it to the same R.
2. Ḥayyim, may God save him, who is mentioned before: if he receives it, it is as if I myself had received it.

Verso

To be given to our master Rabbi Moses, the son of the honourable rabbi Judah, his soul rest in Eden. From our master, the Nagid, may God save him.

Commentary

Recto

Line 6:
"Nathan Cohen Truth." 'Truth' is the official motto of Nathan as Nagid; see letter P.2/1.

Line 7:
"Written condolences." i.e., the condolences that were written in the books of the prophets.

Line 8:
"Who stands in the breach for the congregation of Jekuthiel." A clue to Nathan's contacts with the Mamlūk emirs and his ability to promote the interests of the Jewish community in the *sulṭān*'s palace. Jekuthiel is a rabbinic nickname for Moses, following 1 Chron. 4.18 (see b. Megillah 13a), and 'the congregation of Jekuthiel' is a literary nickname for the people of Israel. The image here is based on the description of Moses in Ps. 106.23: "Therefore He said that He would destroy them, had not Moses, His chosen one, stood before Him in the breach, to turn away His wrath from destroying them." The phrase עומד בפרץ as an adjective for an honourable man appears also among the Karaites, for example: יקר הל'[וי] אשר היה עומד בפרץ לפני אחיו בית ישראל 'Yakar the Levite, who was standing in the breach, for his brothers, the house of Israel' (RNL Evr. Ar. I 1464, 19v., published by Mann 1935, 283).

Line 10:
"Shall be saved by him who has great exploits." This is a problematic phrase, literally 'lives in an exploit'. Maybe it is an error

and should be שוכן עלייה (who lives in the heavens). עלייה is literally 'attic', but appears in literary texts with the meaning 'heaven'. See, for example, Ps. 104.3.

Lines 11–17:
Moses served here as a custodian (אפוטרופוס) of orphans. According to Jewish law, the local court of every Jewish community should take care of orphans and appoint a custodian over their property.

Line 11:
"Ben Porat." This name, following Gen. 49.22, is probably a family name or permanent nickname. It could be also a Hebrew form of the Arabic name Ibn Furāt.

Lines 19–29:
The details here are not clear enough to be sure, but the situation seems to be as follows: Abraham Baḥliṣ (see commentary on l. 19) owed Abraham b. Ḥassān a certain amount of money. B. Ḥassān sent a messenger, R. Jacob Faransī (or: Faranjī) to collect the debt, but he did not succeed. In the meantime, the messenger and the owner of the debt had died. The Nagid was trying here to take care of the debt, for the benefit of the orphans and the widow, but Baḥliṣ refused to pay, and demanded to confirm the debt deed's validity in court—but this process created a loss for the orphans because the deed was made out in front of a Muslim court, according to Sharia law. Validation of it cost money. Baḥliṣ offered an alternative—to pay a reduced amount of the debt. The Nagid refused to accept either option, to avoid wasting the orphans' money. The Nagid now asked Moses to use his authority to force Baḥliṣ to choose one of two options: to pay the debt or

to swear in front of the Jewish court of Alexandria that he did not owe money to the orphans and the widow. An oath was a sacral ritual in those days. People believed that if they lied, a punishment would come down on them from Heaven, so forcing Baḥliṣ to swear was an efficient way of encouraging him to settle the debt.

Line 19:
"Baḥliṣ." This is a rare name. Compare Samuel Baḥliṣ, who is mentioned in a Judaeo-Arabic letter from this period (TS AS 152.65). Perhaps the name should be pronounced: *bū ḥaliṣ*. This is a Maghribian name and would indicate that Abraham was of North-African origin.

Line 21:
פרנשי (i.e., *faranjī, ifranjī;* 'European') is very common nickname in Egypt in the late Mamlūk period and reflects the copious immigration of Jews from Western Europe, mainly Spain (even before the expulsion of 1492) to the Mamlūk state in the fifteenth century. Jacob Faransī is also mentioned in a letter from Ṣedaqah Nis to Nathan Sholal (TS 10J24.3 + CUL Or. 1080J174) and could be identified as יעקב פרנשה who is mentioned in a Judaeo-Arabic letter (TS NS 304.45).

Margin

Lines 1–2:
The addressee is asked to accept the donation of Shalom b. Zaytūn to the endowment treasury (*waqf*) and to give it to the Nagid's messenger.

Line 1:
"Shalom b. Zaytūn." Zaytūn means 'olives'. He was also, probably, of North-African origin. Concerning him, see David (1988, 407 n. 10).

"Pious foundations treasury." The Nagid here uses the Hebrew term *qodesh.* For this term, see Goitein (1971, 99–100); Gil (1976, 3).

Line 2:
"If he receives it, it is as if I myself had received it." See Arad (2013, 193).

C.3: Letter from David ibn Shams to Moses b. Judah

Bodl. MS Heb. c. 72/44

General Introduction

In this letter, published by Arad (2018), David informs Moses b. Judah that he has fulfilled his mission regarding Moses' wife and her sister, who were probably staying in Cairo at that time. He also relayed that the Nagid (probably Solomon b. Joseph) and his elders' council discussed the communal problems in Alexandria, decided how to react, and called the scribe, probably to write an official letter from the Nagid's office to the community of Alexandria. This proves that David was not the Nagid's only scribe. David added that a messenger was on his way to Alexandria and asked Moses to arrange a fundraising appeal for him.

The letter is written in the conservative style, i.e., orientated towards Classical Judaeo-Arabic norms, which marks all the letters of David ibn Shams.

We want to thank Prof. Mordechai A. Friedman for his notes on this document.

Physical Description

14.1 × 11.3; paper; 1 leaf; 16 lines (recto; verso is blank); torn, holes, red-brown stains.

 https://doi.org/10.11647/OBP.0352.06

Transcription

1. [...]מה אלכרי[מה] באן וצלת [... ... אל]מכדו' ופהמת [...]
2. [... ושכרת(?) אל]לה תע' עלי [צ]חת מגאז אלמכדו' אמא מא דכרה [אלמכדו']
3. [... מן ג]הת בית אלמכדו' פאגתמע אלממ' עליהא ועלי אכתהא וכלמתהם
4. [...] פיה כפאיה ואטאעו אלאכׄתין עלי מא קררנאה מעהם
5. [...] מא רסמת וצברנאהם אלי סלך אלעאם ווגדׄנאהם מחמّלין מן אלנאס
6. [... א]ל[ז]איד ואלנאקץ ומא עליהם אצׄר מן אלפצׄוללייה פזולנא
7. [...] מן דהנהם פיכון דלךּ עלי עלם אלמכדו' ואמא מן גהת אלמשאר
8. [...] ומא קד חצל לךּ מעה פבלגׄת אלאמר ללנגיד וללגׄמאעה ואתפקו
9. [...] ורסאל שליח ~~אליס~~ אלי אלסופר יחצׄר בה ונבצר צׄרר אלקהל ומא
10. [... נק]ררה נזילה ענהם פאן אלסמאיע כתיר מנךּ ומן גׄירךּ פאלמכדו'
11. [... תנ]צׄרה עלי אלשליח ותסאעדה עלי מקצודה ומהמא וצל אליה
12. [...] ללנגיד וללקהל ואערפךּ אנה עני אין לאל ידו והו בר טובים
13. [...] תעלם דלךּ פלא תכלוה יחצׄר אלי מגׄבור אלכאטר עואיד פצׄלכם
14. [... ולא ת]כליה יחצׄר אלי באלסופר פאן חצׄורה פיה מצלחה לכם גאית̈ מّא[1] יכון
15. [...] עלי עלמךּ אלכרים תם בעד אלסלאם אלתאם עלי אלמכדו' ועלי
16. [... ועלי אלא]צחאב ואלמחבין כל ואחד באסמה ושלום

Translation

1. [... It should be to your] honourable (knowledge) that the [note of the] master arrived and I understood [its contents]
2. [... and I thank] God exalted for the good state of the master's passage. Regarding what [the master] mentioned

[1] The *mem* was marked with *shaddah*. For this rare phenomenon, see Arad (2018, 180 n. 71).

3. [...] regarding the master's wife, the servant met up with her and her sister, and I talked to them
4. [...] in it in enough quantity. The two sisters obeyed what we decided for them.
5. [...] what I sent,[2] and we asked them for patience until the end of the year. We found them dependent on the public('s support).
6. [...] more or less,[3] and the more harmful from the officiousness. We stopped
7. [...] from their mind. This should be to the knowledge of the master. Concerning the implied (above)
8. [...] and that what happened to you with him. I relayed the matter to the Nagid and the council, and they agreed
9. [...] and sending a messenger to the scribe to be present with him. We see the damage in the community and what
10. [... we] decide to remove it (or: him) from them. The rumours are many, from you and others. The master
11. [... you will] see it from the messenger. You should assist him (to fulfil) his intention. Whatever arrives to him
12. [... forward it] to the Nagid and to the community. I inform you that he is poor, (and) "does not have the power" (see Gen. 31.29). He is from a good family.
13. [...] You should know this. Let him only present himself (in a) satisfied (state), by virtue of your grace.

---

[2] Or: you sent, or: you commanded (see Friedman 2016b, 863).

[3] See Friedman (2016b, 239).

14. [… do not] let him come without the scribe. Indeed, his presence would be of advantage for you, as much as possible.
15. [… it should be] to your honourable knowledge. Now complete greetings to you and to
16. [… to the] friends and to the beloved ones, every single one in his name. Peace (will be).

Commentary

Line 8:

"I relayed the matter to the Nagid and the council." It appears that the term 'the council' means here 'the council of the elders'.[4] The Nagid was not an autocrat. A council of 'elders' worked with him and helped him to implement his policies. This pattern of leadership was evident already in the fourteenth century: in the time of R. Joshua b. Abraham the Nagid, R. Jacob of Hebron, a poet, addressed a letter sent to Cairo as follows: הנגידים החכמים התמימים... כבוד גדולת קדושת מרינו ורבינו רבי יהושוע נין הנגידים וחביריו הזקנים ההגונים והקהל [הי]קרים (TS 24.63). Jacob considered the leadership in Cairo to be a group of Negidim, led by R. Joshua, and surrounding him 'his friends, the elders'. The writer placed R. Joshua and the elders on the same level. Our information on the patterns of leadership of the Nagidate in the fifteenth century is very limited, but there is evidence that this pattern continued at least until the time of the Negidim of the Sholal family. In his travelogue, Meshullam of Voltera mentioned, at the beginning of

---

[4] Compare the letter of Joshua ha-Nagid: "the council of the elders may they be blessed" (ג'מאעת אלזקנים ברוכים יהיו, Bodl. Heb. e. 98/68, published by Goitein 1984, 94–95).

the 1480s, a group of notables around the Nagid Solomon b. Joseph, probably the same Nagid mentioned here in this letter. Meshullam called them שופטים. The term שופט (literally: judge), refers in Meshullam's writing not just to judges but also to the leaders of the community, the 'elders'. For a discussion of this, see Reiner (1992, 38 n. 49) and Arad (2013, 79 n. 74).

Line 12:
For the term עני בן טובים, see t. Pe'a 4.10. Frenkel understood the term בני טובים in the Genizah letters as refering to the elite families of the Jewish society (Frenkel 2006, 209–10). Mention of בן טובים / בר טובים 'from a good family' is very common in recommendation letters in the Genizah. For discussion, see Cohen (2005a, 67–70).

C.4: Letter from Elijah Qarqūsa to Moses b. Judah

Bodl. MS Heb. c. 72/35–36

General Description

This letter from Elijah Qarqūsa to Moses b. Judah is written in a highly unusual script and orthography, making it very difficult to decipher and understand. The author seems unfamiliar with Hebrew script and Judaeo-Arabic spelling conventions, but his spelling reveals a familiarity with Arabic script (for a fuller linguistic analysis, see §III.2.12). The letter is mainly concerned with mercantile matters and property affairs. Most intriguing is the mention of *conversos*, Jewish newcomers from Spain.

Physical Description

Both fragments come from the same letter, which was cut in the middle of a line. The two fragments show different colourings, beige and red-brown, which suggest they were kept under different conditions at some point, but the wormholes of 36 mirror those of 35, which indicates that they were perhaps kept together with the lower part (36) folded over. The lower part (36) also contains mirrored script, which the upper part does not.

Fragment 35: 23.8 × 19.9; paper; 1 leaf; 27 lines (recto); 16 lines + marginalia (verso); torn, holes, red-brown stains; wormholes mirror those in 36.

Fragment 36: 5.9 × 20.1; paper; 1 leaf; 6 lines (recto); 3 lines of marginalia + various lines of mirrored script (verso); torn, holes, beige stains; wormholes mirror those in 35.

 https://doi.org/10.11647/OBP.0352.07

Transcription

Recto

1. [ב]עד אלסל[אם ... ...] יא סידי ומ[ול]א[י] ואלדי
2. [מעל]מי מוסה אׄ יהודה מיני אני' אלייא קרקוסה
3. [... ...] ומסלים עלי' חצׄארתד אלשריף [... ...]
4. נעלמיךׄ באן מוסי' נקולוו ג'א פלוס אב[י]
5. וגׄבני רבאייעי ופיהי' קמוסיין ואחד סגיר
6. ואחיד כׄביר וטרח. ואנתו בעאריפׄ[...]
7. באן הו עלי' תלתי' ומשתיין ראחו אלמושתיין
8. וראח אלקמוס סגיר ואנתי תסאל עליהם [...]
9. לא ירוחו ואני' עת[ית] לעזיז מיאה [... ...]
10. אלקמוסיין ואת[..]תי וקולתו אש תגי תנפוד להי'
11. ראטליין זיית עלי' אלעיד וחכׄיית אלמסאד יד
12. אלמׄ ~~דאוד~~ דוד מא עריפת [נ"ית] אש היי' מארדוך
13. יכד אנהום מין יד וכילך חיים יר'שלימי' יתאתיי
14. בכול שי יארוח
15. ואסעי' נרגאביך באן תסלימלי עלי' סת סתית
16. כׄתיר כׄתיר ותאעתי' מינביהאת בכׄתיר כׄתיר
17. וקולהי' וחק הוולאי אלחרופׄ אפרחת להי'
18. מתל לו כאנית אוכתי אללה תע' יפרח אליה
19. יביקי הו להי' ויגעלו וליד אלחייה אמין [...]
20. [.] בזכות גמיע אנביאים וצדיקים כולהי'
21. ובזכות סיידיני' שמואל הרמאתי וקולהי' באן
22. אלחׄ הרון אכאת מינו 6 מיידי' תגליק אלכׄרי'
23. וכתוב אגׄאר ג'דיד ואתבקי כרייתהי'
24. שהר ונופץ אכאת מינהי' [..]רא אלו[..]
25. הו פאריגי' עליש אנג'ית קא[. ... .]

26. הו[1] ברסום [... ... ...]
27. [... ... ...] תג'י מר[.]את[.] אנכאן הוי'
28. [י]רתגיהי' ידיליךׄ כׄראהי' 144 אשהר ואנכׄאן הוי'
29. לא ירידהי' אני' אמי' נסכון אוולי חתי נכריהי'
30. אל מ' יוסף אלכאדים קאלי באן אנתו בעמלי כתאב
31. קולתלו אמי' יסכונהי' אוולי' אלאנוסים
32. אנכאנו פי אלקעה ואנא גיד מׄ אילו כדאד(?)

Verso

1. יסקונו פיהי' אלאנוסים מא נסאכנו פיהי'
2. יהוד ושלום ועאד נקוליך באן ר' שלומה
3. תרפוני' קאלי באן בעד אל[...] אלעיד [...]
4. ~~אלק~~ אלכתאב פרוג ואלקופא בתע א זביב
5. ליסעי' מא אנבעאת שיין וזביב אליוסרפי(?)
6. ב 100 ב 150 אלקנטאר בילכׄתיר 400 ואלכ[...]
7. אלדי תיבעת תיתליבני אבי חלפני באן [כול]
8. מא נכריגהום מין ידי לא כאני אבשוש
9. כיףׄ אני' נג'י אסכנדריי' נג'יבו פי ידי
10. ואסעי' נרגאביך באן תסלימלי עליי'
11. סתיתי' וסלמלי עלי' אלמׄ שמואל ומראתו וסלמ[לי]
12. עלי' כאלתי שרה אום עזיז ואסלמלי עלי'
13. אלמׄ כאדר ועלי' אלמׄ עבדון וסלימלי כתיר
14. עלי' אלמׄ דויד אללה תע' יחייה ומליך אל[..]
15. ויג'על פיהום ברכאת אלייהו הנאבי
16. אוכתיב יום ב' ה' ניסאן שנת ה'ר'מ'ה'

---

[1] Here fragment Bodl. MS Heb. c. 72/36 starts.

Margin

1. יצאל [אלכת]אב ליד [...]
2. מוס[ה אֿ יהודה]
3. לס[כנדרייא]

Translation

Recto

1. After (extending) greetings […], O my master [and lord], my father,
2. and my master Mūsā b. Judah, from me, Elijah Qarqūsa.
3. […], to be given to your honourable majesty […]
4. I inform you that Messer(?) Nicolo brought money of my father
5. and he brought me a box(?), in it (were) two gowns, one small,
6. one big, and kerchiefs. You should know(?)
7. that he has […] three and […] The […] sold.
8. The small gowns (also) sold. You ask about them […]
9. They are not selling. I gave to ʿAzīz 100 […]
10. two gowns […]. I said: When(?) you arrive, you should send to them
11. two *raṭls* of olive oil for the holiday. I received the ropes (or: palm tree fibres) by the hand of
12. M. David, I did not know what it is. Mardūḵ
13. understands that they are from the hand of your agent Ḥayyim Yerushalmi. May it be sold
14. at whatever price.

15. Now I would like you to greet from me Sitt Sutayt
16. very much. You should give many, many regards.
17. Her words, indeed, those letters—I was glad for her
18. as if she was my sister. May God exalted make him happy.
19. May he remain (a support) for her. May he give him a son. Amen. [...]
20. For the merit of all the prophets and righteous men, all of them,
21. and the merit of our master Samuel ha-Ramati. Her saying (was) that
22. the *ḥaver* Harūn, I took from him six *mu'ayyadī*, which forecloses the hire.
23. You should draw up a new letting (contract). It remained on its hire
24. a month and a half. I took from her [...]
25. He is finishing up everything. I saved [...]
26. It is intended for [... ... ...]
27. [... ... ...] you should come [...]. If he
28. requests it, he should suggest to you its hire for 144 months. If he
29. does not want it, my intention is surely to live (there) at first until I hire it out.
30. M. Joseph, the beadle, told me that you are busy with (drawing up) a document.
31. I told him that surely he can live (there) at first. If the *conversos*
32. are in the apartment, I am fine (with that). M. Elijah(?) [...]

Verso

1. (While) the *conversos* will live in it, we will not rent out to
2. any Jews (there). Peace (will be). Also, I tell you that R. Solomon
3. Tarfūnī told me that after the [...] of the holiday [...]
4. the letter: A pullet and [...] basket of(?) raisins
5. Now, nothing has been sold. Yusrafi(?) raisins are
6. 100 to 150 per *qinṭār*, for more than 400. The [...]
7. which you should send, will be demanded from me. My father was insistent that [everything]
8. I will let out of my hands will not be [safe(?)].
9. When I am going to Alexandria, I will bring it in my (own) hands.
10. Now I would like you to greet for me
11. my Sutayt. Greet for me M. Samuel and his wife. Greet [for me]
12. my maternal aunt Sarah Umm ʿAzzīz. Greet for me
13. M. Ḵādir and M. ʿAbdūn. Give many greetings for me
14. to M. David, may God keep him alive, and Malik the [...].
15. May the blessings of Elijah the prophet be upon them.
16. I am writing on Monday, 5th Nissan 5245 (of the Era of Creation = 30 May 1485 CE).

Margin

1. [This letter] should arrive to the hand of [... ...]
2. Mūsā [b. Judah]
3. to Alex[andria]

Commentary

Recto

Line 2:
"Elijah Qarqūsa." He is probably a relative of Mardūḵ Qarqūsa, the writer of letter P.8. Another possible reading of the word is סרקוסה (Syracuse). If that reading is correct, it means that Elijah was of Sicilian origin (from Syracuse), or Spanish origin (from Saragossa).

Line 4:
"Messer(?) Nicolo." The reading and the interpretation are not certain. We understood it as a personal name (Nicolo), with a title such as the Italian Messer (M.) preceding. A trader called Nicolo is mentioned in letter P.7/18, 30. Another option is to understand this word as the Arabic word *naqūlu*, i.e., 'I inform you that Mūsā—we said to him that my father's money arrived'.

Line 12:
"Mardūḵ." This can probably be identified as Mardūḵ Qarqūsa; see letter P.8.

Line 13:
"Ḥayyim Yerushalmi." Maybe this is Ḥayyim b. Porat, who is mentioned in letter C.2.

Line 21:
"And thanks to our master Samuel ha-Ramati." The emphasis on Samuel above all other prophets demonstrates the importance of his personage in the Jewish thought of the Mamlūk period. The

grave attributed to Samuel, located north of Jerusalem, was considered a major sacred site from the Crusader period onwards. It seems that, in the Mamlūk period, it was the most significant place among the holy sites in Palestine. Many sources document the prayers at the site, and the system of delivering donations of money, oil, and more to the sanctuary around the grave (see, e.g., Ashtor 1970, 125–27; Arad 2012, 460). As Reiner (1992, 52–63, esp. 59–61) proved, the sanctuary was one of the main sources of income for the community of Jerusalem. For a wider discussion, see Arad (in press a).

Recto, line 21–Verso, line 2:
In these lines the writer discusses the hiring of real estate in Alexandria. The whole meaning of his words is not clear, due to the bad condition of the manuscript. Nevertheless, it seems that this apartment (or those apartments) was not the private estate of Moses; rather, it was part of the community *heqdesh* (endowment). The rent fees of those estates were one of the main sources of income for the community.

Line 30:
"M. Joseph, the beadle." Concerning this person, see also letter P.8/18. This is probably Joseph b. Barukh, the beadle of the Alexandrian synagogue, whom Meshullam of Volterra met during his visit to the city in June 1481 (Yaari 1948, 49).

Line 31:
"The *conversos*." Jews who had previously converted to Christianity in the Iberian Peninsula started to arrive in Egypt in significant numbers in the fifteenth century, seeking a secure place to return to their original Jewish religion. In 1465, a huge scandal

happened in Cairo, when Joseph the Nagid revealed that a group of newcomer *conversos* had joined the Karaites instead of the Rabbanites (on this event, see Hirschfeld 1906; Brinner 1999; Rustow 2007; see also above, 43–44). On the immigration of Iberian Jews (including *conversos*) to the east in the fifteenth century, see Hacker (1985). It seems that the community of Alexandria took care of the newcomers and let them live in the *heqdesh* apartments, which were probably rented out at a low price.

Verso

Line 3:
"R. Solomon Tarfūnī." A Hebrew letter by a man of this name, who can probably be identified with our Solomon Tarfūnī here, is kept in the Mosseri collection (Mosseri II 188.1).

Line 15:
"May the blessings of Elijah the prophet be upon them." The prophet Elijah enjoyed a special reverence among the Alexandrian Jews, as reflected in local legends about his appearance in the old synagogue of Alexandria, which was called after his name. For discussion, see Arad (in press a).

C.5: Letter from a Certain Hārūn to Moses b. Judah

Bodl. MS Heb. c. 72/38

General Introduction

This letter was probably written in 1485 CE. The writer was most likely living in Sicily or spent a period there for his commercial affairs (see l. 12). It contains additional lines in the margin written in the handwriting of David ibn Shams. The verso is in a similar hand to the recto, but appears to have been written at a different stage.

The letter is written in a comparatively conservative style, with a few post-classical Judaeo-Arabic spelling conventions, such as the spelling of Classical Arabic *tāʾ marbūṭa* with *tav* and the inconsistent spelling of the /a/ sound, not following the prescriptive spelling norms of Classical Arabic. Classical Arabic *ʾalif maqṣūra* spelled with *yāʾ* usually receives a stroke above the *yāʾ*, apparently in an effort to mark its reading as an /a/ sound—as in, for example, תעאלי' in l. 7 and עלי' in l. 12—thus displaying familiarity with Arabic-script spelling conventions.

Physical Description

20.1 × 15.5; paper; 1 leaf; 22 lines + marginalia (recto); 12 lines (verso); verso is written inversely in relation to recto; holes, rubbed, red-brown stains.

 https://doi.org/10.11647/OBP.0352.08

Transcription

Recto

1. בורא ניב שפתים וגו' ואמרתם כה לחי וגו'
2. והאיש משה ענו וגו' ברוך תהיה מכל וגו'
3. יתן לך כלבבך וגו' ימלא י"י כל משאלותיך וגו'
4. י"י עוז לעמו יתן וגו'
5. סלאם אללה תעאלי' ורחמתה וברכתה עלי אל אך אלעזיז הדרת ר' משה
6. מגן עדן לא ינשה אן אלממ' הרון משתאק פלמכדום כתיר ו[מנתצר]
7. לגואבכם אללה תעאלי' יסמענא ענכם אכבאר סארא ויחיה על לבך [...]
8. חמודיך מידיו אנ"ס וינהי לעלמה אל כרים אן עואיד אל מכדום אל גמילה
9. אן יחיל אלמכדום אלממ' באל ג̇אליה עלי אולאד אל קמאט ויתעאל עדא
10. ירסלהא פאלמכדום מצי מן אל סנה תסעת שהור ומא ארסל שי פמן
11. צדקתכם ואחסאנכם חסב עואידכם אלכרימה תרסלו אלגאליה צחב[ה] חד
12. תקא או תחילונא עלי' חדא פי אלמדינה לאן אל צרורה דאעיה לדלך
13. ולא תסאל מא אל ממ' פיה מן אלצ̇יקה ואל תראסים בסבב אלבאקי
14. פלא תחרג אל ממ' לכתאב אכר תא[...] והדא כלה בסבב אלאדלאל עלי
15. צדקאתכם ואן אל ממ' ירסל לך אל וצול צחבת מן תרסל מעה אלפלוס
16. בעד אלסלאם עלי' אלמכדום ועלי' אלמעלם סלימאן כראת ועלי' אל
17. מעלם נגיב י"ל ועלי ג̇מיע אלג̇מאעה כלה מגדולם ועד קטנם בי[1]
18. ושלומך יגדל ויחיט לעלם אלמכדום אן מתוג̇ה ללתגר צחבת
19. ר̇ יוסף קשתרו י"ל שבץ יסמי שלמה סקלי וזן אלממ' ענה אלג̇אליה
20. פתם אנה אעטאני מנהא סת אנצאף ואתאכר ענ"ה סתה ותלתין נצ[ף]
21. פצה פאעלם אנך לא תמכנה ~~לא~~ לספר חתי' אנה יזן אל סתה ותלת[ין]
22. נצף

---

[1] = (?)ברוכים יהיו.

Margin

1. אלממ' מחבךׄ דוד ס"ט כתיר אלאשתיאק אלׄי צדקאתכם אלכרימה וקד וצל פצׄל אלמכדו' עלי יד ר'
2. יעקב א' אלנגיד ואלדי וצל אלכרקה אלזרקה ואל ארבע באלאת אלורק ואכד מני ½ 10 נצף פצׄה ולם
3. ערפת תפציל מא עומל פאלמכדו' ירסל לנא אלגׄואב מפצל ותסאעד אלש' הרון עלי מקאצדה פאנה
4. פי צׄרורה כבירה [... ... ...]

Verso

1. ויא ר' משה מן פצלך וחינאנך ואצל ללתגר אל מחרוס שכׄץ אסמה מוסי' אבן
2. מרזוקה אל מזאבי ללממ' ענדה באקי גאלׄי[ה סנ]ת תסע יׄז נצף וגאליה הדא
3. אל סנה אתנין וארבעין נצף אלגמלה תסעה וכמסין נצף וקאלו אהל ביתה
4. אנה מא יסאפר סוי' לאסכנדריאה ויכד ללמדינה פתם מן קאל אנה ראיח
5. ללגרב פמן פצלךׄ ואחסאנךׄ וצדקאתךׄ כראמה לשם ית' לא תמכנה לספר
6. אלגרב אלׄי' אן תאכד מנה אל תסעה וכמסין נצף פצׄה לאן אלממ' וזנהא
7. ענה ואלמכדום יעלם אן אלממ' מא פי חאלה שיי ולו דרית אנה יסאפר
8. רסמת עליה ומא כליתה יסאפר חתי' יזן אל מבלג אלמדכור ואן כאן
9. מא יזן ללמכדום אלמבלג אלמדכור ואלא עוק עליה אלבאב ונחנא
10. אסתדנא סיידנא אלנגיד יצ"ו פי הדא אלאמר עוׄץ אלעונש ואלמכדום
11. יכׄלי כ"ר צדקה ניס י"ל יסאעדה פי דל אמר עלי לסאן סיידנא אלנגיד י"ל
12. ושלומך יגדל לעד ולא ידל ושלום

Translation

Recto

1. [The LORD that] creates the fruit of the lips, etc. (Isa. 57.19). Say: To life, etc. (1 Sam. 25.6).

2. Now the man Moses was [very] meek, etc. (Num 12.3). You shall be blessed above all [peoples], etc. (Deut. 7.14).
3. May he grant you your heart's desire, etc. (Ps. 20.5). May the LORD fulfil all your petitions, etc. (Ps. 20.6).
4. May the LORD give strength to his people, etc. (Ps. 29.11).
5. The peace of God exalted (be upon you), and his mercy, and blessing, to the magnificent brother, his majesty R. Moses.
6. He will not be forgotten from Paradise. The servant Hārūn is longing for the master very much. [He awaits]
7. your answer. May God exalted let us hear happy news from you. May (God) give
8. your [...] sons (literally: loved ones) life from his hands on your heart, Amen, forever. (The servant) would like to bring to his honourable knowledge, that (with) your profits being so handsome,
9. he should give a bill of exchange to the servant for the (payment of the) poll-tax for the children of al-Qammāṭ and support in their livelihood.
10. He should send it. As for the master, nine months of the year have passed, and he has not sent anything. From
11. your benevolence and your kindness, on the basis of your honourable custom, you should send the poll-tax with[2] a
12. trustworthy person, or you should give us a bill of exchange via someone in Palermo because of the urgent necessity in this (matter).

---

[2] See Blau (2006, 363).

13. Do not ask about (the trouble) the servant is in because of poverty and dire straits (or: the curfew[3]) on behalf of the remainder.
14. Do not force the servant (to write) another letter [...]. This is all because of (me) trusting
15. your generosity. The servant will send the receipt to you with whoever you send the money by,
16. after (wishing) greetings to the master and to *Muʿallim* Sulaymān Karāt, and to
17. *Muʿallim* Najīb, may he live forever, and to the whole community, big and small, may they be blessed(?).
18. Your well-being may be increased. The master should know that someone is heading for the port (or: to Alexandria) with
19. R. Joseph Castro, may he live forever. He is called Solomon al-Siqillī. The servant paid the poll-tax for him.
20. He gave me six half-dinars of it, but I am still owed thirty-six silver half-dinars by him.
21. I instruct you that you do not let him travel until he pays those thirty-six
22. half-dinars.

Margin

1. The servant your friend David (has) much longing for your honourable generosity. The present of the master just arrived by the hand of R.

---

[3] See Ashtor (1951, 297 n. 21).

2. Jacob son of the Nagid, who brought the green cloth and the four bales of paper. He took from me the ten and a half silver half-dinars. I did not
3. know the details of what was done. The master should send to us the reply in detail. You should assist *Shaykh* Harūn in his undertakings, because he is
4. in great need [... ... ...]

Verso

1. O R. Moses, by your grace and mercy. About to arrive to the fortified port is someone called Mūsā b.
2. Marzūqa, the gutters maker. He owes the servant the rest of the poll-tax of year nine, seventeen half-dinars, and the poll-tax of this
3. year, forty-two half-dinars, together fifty-nine half-dinars. His family said
4. that he is travelling via Alexandria heading towards Palermo. Then someone said that he is heading
5. for the West, so please by your grace, kindness and fairness, for the name (of God) exalted, only let him travel
6. to the West after taking from him those fifty-nine half-dinars of silver. Because the servant paid them
7. on his behalf, and the master knows that the servant currently has nothing at all. If you learn that he is travelling,
8. write about him and do not let him travel unless he pays the mentioned sum. If
9. he does not pay the mentioned sum to the master, block him from the door. We

10. will petition our master, the Nagid, may God save him, regarding this matter for compensation of the fine. The master
11. should let the honourable rabbi Ṣedaqah Nis, may he live forever, assist him in the matter according to the decree of our master the Nagid, may he live forever.
12. May your well-being be great for eternity and never cease. Peace (will be).

Commentary

Recto

Line 6:

The blessing contains a nice rhyme *Moshe–Yinashe*. Similar rhymes can be found in a *piyyuṭ* from Morocco, recited before reading the 'Song of the Sea' (Exod. 15) in the Torah: אשירה כשירת משה, שיר לא יינשה, אז ישיר משה, את דברי השירה, and also in the introduction of R. Moses Isserles (Kraków, d. 1572) to his well-known halakhic work *Darke Moshe*: בחבור זה הנקרא דרכי משה, אשר לעולם לא ינשה.

In פלמכדום, *fī* and the article form a union, with long ī spelled defectively and *ʾalif* omitted. This is rare in the Classical period but appears to occur more often in Mamlūk/early Ottoman letters (see Wagner 2010, 66).

Line 8:

חמודיך. This word proves that Moses had more than one child.

Line 9:

קמאט. The writer started to write wrongly קא but then fixed the א to מ. קמאט was a common nickname in the period, and occurs for example in names such as: עבדאללה קמאט and שמואל קמאט (Bodl. [2834.36] MS Heb. b. 13/56, from ca the fourteenth century); אולאד עבדאללה אלקמאט 'the sons of ʿAbdallah Qammāṭ', who appear in TS K 15.18, an accounts list dated 1647 of the Seleucid era (1335/6 CE); דוד קמאט (TS J1.34, TS AS 145.45, ca second half of fifteenth century); סעיד קמאט (BL Or. 10578 N1, fifteenth or early sixteenth century). A *qammāṭ* is a 'rope-maker', according to Lane (1863–1893, 2565). Dozy (1881, 406) defines this term as a *revendeur des moutons* 'retailer of sheep', while Blau (2006, 564) has 'retailer'.

Line 12:

תקא spelling for ثقة. In עלי חדא we find traces of the accusative ending attached to colloquial חד 'one'. אלמדינה is Palermo.

Line 13:

תראסים 'curfew' is a typical term in late Mamlūk letters (see Ashtor 1951, 516 n. 37).

Line 15:

Tāʾ marbūṭa is spelled with *tav* in צחבת.

Line 16:

כראת. The meaning of this name is not clear yet. Maybe he or one of his ancestors was a leek seller (كُرَّاث). Sulaymān Karāt was one of the notables in Alexandria. The gathering described in C.6 was held in his house. His Hebrew name would have been שלמה. His son, שמואל בר כ"ר שלמה נ"ע ידיע כראת, is mentioned in a will of his wife ʿAziza from 1495 CE (ENA N-S 47.12). Another family member, Judah Karāt, is mentioned in a payments list from approximately the beginning of the sixteenth century (BL Or. 10578 N1).

Line 18:
"the port (or: Alexandria)." *Thaġr* is 'a port city', but also serves as a common nickname for Alexandria.

Margin

Line 2:
"Jacob son of the Nagid." In 1484, Nathan Sholal started his tenure as Nagid, but it is impossible to identify Jacob as one of his sons. We have a detailed personal list of Nathan's children (see Introduction, §2.2.3), and the name Jacob is not mentioned among the names. The exact date of the appointment of Nathan is unknown, and this letter was probably written before he started in his position. It is reasonable to assume that Jacob was the son of Solomon b. Joseph, the Nagid, who died not later than 1482.

Verso

Line 2:
"Year 9" could designate 879 H (= 1474/5 CE) but is more likely 889 H (= 1484 CE), i.e., the letter was written in 890 H (= 1485 CE).

In [ה]דא, the writer obviously first wrote the colloquial pronoun *da*, and then corrected it to the Classical Arabic pronoun *hāḏā* in an attempt to standardise or elevate the register of the language.

Line 7:
The double spelling in שיי may reflect the form *shuyay/shuyay*, as the writer does not use the double spelling of *yāʾ* in similar examples, such as שי in l. 10.

C.6: Voucher for Collection of a Will by the Leaders of the Community of Alexandria

Bodl. MS Heb. c. 72/31 + Bodl. MS Heb. c. 72/33 + Bodl. MS Heb. c. 72/34

General Introduction

This text consists of three fragments of a deed, written in the court of Alexandria on 8 April 1481, in Aramaic, Hebrew, and Judaeo-Arabic, concerning the administration of an inheritance by the Alexandrian leaders.[1] This deed contains important testimony on communal life in Alexandria in the early 1480s. The document teaches us that the community was being led by seven 'elders', all mentioned in the deed. The most surprising detail in the document is that one of the seven leaders of the community was a woman. In light of the absence of women in leadership in medieval Jewry, this information is unique and has special importance. The manner in which this woman, Shaqra, is described in the document, however, points to the exceptionality of her circumstances. In contrast to all the other leaders, who are described by their origin or by their profession, she is the only one among the seven identified by mention of her relatives: her father, and also her husband. We can assume that the scribe could not give her an independent status and presented her as subjected

[1] On the management of inheritance by the Alexandrian leaders in the Fāṭimid and Ayyubid period, see Frenkel (2006, 188–89).

 https://doi.org/10.11647/OBP.0352.09

to the males in her life. Moreover, it is possible that she was considered a representative of her dead husband, who was perhaps one of the elders himself.

The deed is fragmented and torn. Probably, after the elders (or the judges of the court) transferred the money of the deceased to the orphans and other heirs, they ripped it to shreds to avoid future claims. Unfortunately, not all of the fragments were preserved and therefore the content of the deed is not entirely clear. All we can say on its content is that it deals with a last will, written in Jerusalem and having arrived in Alexandria. The leaders of the community, the seven 'elders', were appointed as custodians of the orphans' property and gathered together to discuss (or to confirm) the will.

Moses b. Judah is not included here as one of the leaders who took care of the will, but the fact that this deed, which is not related to him or to his family, was preserved in his archive, testifies again to his high social status and his involvement in the local leadership. We know from earlier periods that people felt it was safe to keep their private archives in the houses of the community leaders (Frenkel 2006, 194). It is possible, therefore, that the heirs chose to store the document in Moses' house. The letter was published by Arad (2018).

Physical Description

Fragment 31: 14.2 × 8.2; paper; 1 leaf; 19 lines (recto); various lines (verso); torn, holes, red-brown stains; jottings on verso may have been used as index.

Fragment 33: 8.9 × 6.4; paper; 1 leaf; 14 lines (recto); jotting (verso); torn, holes, red-brown stains.

Fragment 34: 5.7 × 6.5; paper; 1 leaf; 6 lines (recto; verso is blank); torn, holes, red-brown stains.

Transcription

72.31 in black; 72.33 in blue; 72.34 in red

1. בש' רח'[2]
2. וחנ'[3]
3. שהדותא דהות באנפנא אנ[ן ס]הדי דחתומות ידנא
4. לתתא סוף שטר שוברא דא [מה] הוה ביום שלשים לחדש
5. ניסן המקדש[4] שנת הרמ"א ליצ[יר]ה למנינא דרגילנא לממני
6. ביה הכא במדינת נא אמון ד[על כ]יף ימא רבא מותבה
7. חצ̊רו פי בית אלמו' אלמע' סלימ[אן] כראת ס"ט זקני [היו]שר[5]
8. שבעה טובי העיר והם אלמו' [אלמע'] סלימאן ס"ט ואלמו' אלמע'
9. מוסי פרנשי ס"ט ואלמו' אלמע' נ[...] אלסקלי ס"ט ואלמו' אלמע'
10. מוסי מעאני ס"ט ואלמו' אלמע' יו[סף] צבאג ס"ט ואלמו' אלמע'
11. מוסי בּ נעאמה ס"ט ואלאמראה [סת אלא]מל שקרה א'[6] אלש' יוסף
12. אלבריקי נ"ע אלדי בעלה או זוגה[א אלש'] יעקוב סהלאן נ"ע אפטרופסים
13. עלי גמיע מתרוכה בצוואה [...]תהא מן ידהא בבט

---

[2] = בשמא רחמנא (compare C.1.a; C.1.d; P.3.b and P.3.c).

[3] = וחננא .

[4] Read: המקודש.

[5] The phrase אלקהל אלגליל וזקני היושר can be found in TS 8J5.25, l. 12, which dates to 1261 CE.

[6] = אבנה׳.

14. ר' יום טוב סופר ב"ד[7] שלירוש[לים] תוב"ב[8] והם בחאל אלצחה
15. ואלטוע וגואז אלאמר לא מק[הורין] ולא מגבורין ולא סאהוי[ן]
16. ולא גלאטנין ולא ענדהם שי [מן] גמיע מפסדאת אלשהאדה
17. אלא בלב שלם ונפש חפצה וד[עה] נכונה מיושבת ואשהדו
18. עלי אנפסהם אלכרימה שב[עה] טובי העיר אלמד' אנהם
19. [...] ללהקדש גמל[ה ......] בלגהא [...... עש]ר סהם מן א[...]
20. [........................ ... ...]גר[...]

Translation

1. In your name, the merciful
2. and the gracious.
3. A testimony was made in front of us, the witnesses whose signatures
4. are in the end of this deed of voucher: [what] happened on the thirtieth day of the month of
5. holy *Nissan*, 5241 to the creation (= 8 April 1481 CE), according to the calendar we use (lit. in accordance with the counting method we are accustomed to count)
6. here in the city of *No' Amon* (= Alexandria), which is settled [on the] Great Sea's shore
7. presented in the house of M. Sulaymān Karāt, may his end be good, the [upright] elders,
8. the 'Seven Good Men of the Town': M. Sulaymān, may his end be good, and M.

---

[7] = בית דין.

[8] = תיבנה ותיכונן במהרה בימינו.

9. Mūsā Faransī, may his end be good, and M. N[…][9] al-Siqillī, may his end be good, and M.
10. Mūsā Maʿāni, may his end be good, and M. Jo[seph] Ṣabbāġ,[10] may his end be good, and M.
11. Mūsā Nuʿāma, may his end be good, and the woman [Sitt al-ʾA]mal Shaqra, the daughter of *Shaykh* Joseph
12. al-Brīkī,[11] may his soul rest in Eden, who was the wife of [*Shaykh*] Jacob Sahlān, may his soul rest in Eden, (all of them are) custodians
13. on all his bequest, according to a will that [originates] from her own, in her possession, in the handwriting of
14. R. Yom Ṭov, the scribe of the court of Jerusalem, may she be rebuilt and be established soon in our days, while they are healthy
15. and obedient, and have legal claim, and they are not [doing it unwillingly], and they are not forced and not inadvertent
16. and are not deceived and they have nothing [from] all the things which would invalidate the testimony
17. but (they are) wholehearted and have free will and they are sober and self-possessed. They testified
18. for their honourable selves in front of the 'Seven Good Men of the town', the aforementioned, that they
19. […] to the endowment (treasury) all of […] its sum [……] […]teen parts from 20. […]

---

[9] Presumably, 'Nissim' or 'Nāṣir' or 'Najīb'.

[10] 'The dyer'.

[11] Probably a manufacturer (or seller) of *brīk* (بريك), a pastry dish known in Tunisia.

Commentary

Line 6:

"On the Great Sea's shore." 'ha-Yam ha-Gadol' (Heb.) or 'Yama Rabba' (Aram.; = the Great Sea) is the common name in the Bible and in the sages' literature for the Mediterranean Sea.

Line 7:

The meaning of Karāt is unclear. He also appears in letter C.5. See commentary on C.5/16.

Line 8:

"The Seven Good Men of the Town." A talmudic term (see b. Megillah 26b) which designates people who acted as representatives of the town in communal matters. The number of the people in this body was not always precisely seven. A leadership of seven elders appears more than 100 years later in Cairo, in the Mustaʿrib community (see Hacker 2011; Arad 2013, 173).

"M. Sulaymān." This is without a doubt Sulaymān Karāt who was mentioned before.

Line 9:

"Faransī." See commentary on letter C.2/21. Mūsā Faransī is probably משה ידיע פרנשי, who is mentioned in a will from 1495 (ENA NS 47.12). His wife's name was ʿAzīza daughter of Elʿazar. It is also possible to identify him with the sage R. Moses b. Shem-Ṭov al-Faranjī (משה ב"ר שם טוב אלפראנג'י), who is mentioned in a letter from the sages of Safed to the sages of Jerusalem in 1503 (MS Jerusalem, National Library 8° 2001).

"N[...] al-Siqillī." He or one of his ancestors came from Sicily. Sometimes this nickname refers in particular to people from

Palermo, one of the most central cities in the island (see Goitein 1973, 317 n. 3). Sicily was under Spanish rule in this period and after the expulsion decree of 1492 there was a huge wave of immigration from Sicily to the east, including Egypt, but a presence of Sicilian Jews in Egypt is already documented in the Fāṭimid period. Sicilian Jewish traders settled in Egypt and North Africa as a result of the well-developed trade between those centres (the documents on Sicily and Sicilian Jews from the classical Genizah period were assembled by Ben Sasson et al. 1991). Jews of Sicilian origin appear also in documents from the Mamlūk period: Abī l-Ḥasan al-Siqillī is mentioned in a list of donations from the winter of 1335 (TS K 15.18); Shabbetay al-Siqillī is mentioned in a deed in Judaeo-Arabic written in Cairo in 1383/4 (MS Philadelphia, Annenberg Institute in Pennsylvania University, Halper 349); another Shabbetay from Sicily, called al-Masīnī, that is to say from Messina in Sicily, is mentioned in a deed from 1492 written in the Nagid's court in Cairo (ENA 3616.3); ישועה פאמפלו סקלי is mentioned in a payments list, probably from Cairo, from approximately the beginning of the sixteenth century (TS AS 152.11); Jacob al-Siqillī and Samuel al-Siqillī are mentioned in undated payments lists from the Mamlūk period (TS J 1.60; TS K 15.75). In a deed of purchase from a Rabbanite Jew by a Karaite Jew in Cairo in 1368, a house called "the house of the Sicilian" is mentioned (Richards 1972, 114–15). For a dowry list of a Sicilian bride from the fifteenth century, see TS 12.12.

Line 10:

"Maʿānī." The name indicates that he or one of his ancestors came from *Maʿān* (معان) in southern Jordan. This nickname appears in

Genizah letters from the thirteenth century (Breslavi 1954, 207), but there is no clear evidence for a Jewish community in *Maʿān* in the fifteenth century. On Jews in Jordan during the Mamlūk and early Ottoman periods, see Breslavi (1954); Arad (2013, 25–26).

Line 11:
"[Sitt al-ʾA]mal." If this completion is right, the meaning of this nickname is 'the lady of hope'. She also had a personal name, Shaqra. As Ashtor (1951, 333) noted, women in eastern Jewish society in the Mamlūk period usually had only Arabic names, while the men bore also Hebrew names. This assumption needs further investigation—there is always the possibility that this has to do with modesty concepts. Writing down the Hebrew names of women may have been a taboo, thus leading to the preservation of only their Arabic nicknames in the records.

Line 14:
"R. Yom Ṭov." Rabbi Yom Ṭov b. Joseph ibn Emmanuel, the scribe, was a scholar of Iberian origin and is known from various sources, including Genizah documents (e.g., TS NS 99.66 [1483 CE]; TS 16.260). On his father, R. Joseph, who was a judge in Jerusalem in the 1460s, see Hacker (1984, 29–31).

C.7: Sample Letter, Based on a Letter to the Community of Cairo

Bodl. MS Heb. c. 72/48–49

General Introduction

This is a template and guidance for how to write letters in high poetic Hebrew. Perhaps it is a page from a bigger collection of samples of letters. Such a book was in some places called an *ʾIgron* (from *ʾiggeret*, a letter). Although this is only a template, which has never been sent, it is an important historical source, because it is based on a real letter (or letters). The original letter on which at least part of this text was based was sent to the community of Cairo, as it says in f1/13: "the community of Cairo, that he who dwells in heaven may save them." Another clue that the original letter was sent to Cairo is the praise in f1/v16: "who princely see the king's face, who are highest in the kingdom." This description fits well the Jewish clerks who worked in the Mamlūk administration and had relatively free access to the *sulṭān*'s palace in Cairo as well as to the emirs. It is possible, therefore, that Moses' scribe, or one of his associates, took a copy of a letter that was sent from Alexandria to Cairo, and re-used it for this purpose.

The first part of this text (f1/2–v17) is a general opening of a communal letter. The writer gives respect first of all to the sages of the community (f1/v7), but mentions also other classes in the community. The Nagid is not mentioned here at all. We can only assume that he was mentioned in the original letter but was omitted here to allow the text to be adapted for any other community.

 https://doi.org/10.11647/OBP.0352.10

The second part of the text (f1/v19–end) provides guidance as to how to write a letter of request for a donation. For further discussion, see Arad (2020).

Physical Description

19.7 × 28.4 (15.1 one leaf); paper; 2 leaves (bifolium); 22–24 lines + marginalia; torn, holes, red-brown stains.

Transcription

Folio 49 Verso

1. סדר הלצה לרבים
2. [אליכם אי]שים אקרא עדה קדושה נבחרה עם [...........]
3. [.........] יו"י עיני העדה אצילי ישורון חסידי הדור חמדת
4. [.........] לובשי צדקה כשרין[1] למודי יו"י לוחמי מלחמות
5. [.........] המשרה טהורי הגוף טובי מפעל טורי מרגליות
6. [..............] נוטרי(?) מצות וחוקים יחידי טהרה ידידי עליון ישרי
7. [... ב]עלי השם כבודי נאמנה כוללי חוקים נאמני הארץ
8. מביני חכמות מלומדי מלחמות מואסי בצע מעשקות
9. נוחלי פנינים נחלי השוע אשר על מימיהם צדקה נזרעת הנדיבות סנהדרי הזמן סוללי דרך
10. [...] דרך סוחרי צדקות סופרי זכיות פדויי יו"י פלילי התורה דמיוני מלאכי השרת קדושי
11. הארץ רודפי השלום שומרי מזוזות שוחרי רצון שומעי צעקת
12. דלים תמימי דרך תוחלת אב המון נחלת עקוד תולעת יעקוב
13. קהל מצרים ישמרם שוכן שמים [ורו]מה האד'רים בגלותם
14. האבירים בתהלתם ברוכי יו"י בשמותם למשפחותם לבית
15. אבותם גאולי מפעלותם דגלי צבאותם הישרים בליבותם

---

[1] Read: *ka-shiryon.*

16. ותיקי צדקותם זכי ישרותם חוסן ישועתם טובי עין במתנו'[2]
17. יודעי בינה לעתותם כאשר צוו בתעודותם להאמיר
18. ולהחמיר בקדושתם מוסרי נפשם על טהרתם נוחלי
19. מוסר מזימ'תם סוחרי תורתם עומדים על משמרותם
20. פאירי מגבעותם מלבישים לאביונים כסותם צמח יו"י לצבי
21. מפלאותם קדומי תהל'תם ראשי איומתם ש'אבי מי תשועתם
22. תולי עין למחיש גאולתם הכוכבים במסלותם נהרי נחלי דבש
23. חמאתם [...] הנקראים בשם זכיותם ונודעים ביופי מעלותם
24. נדב'תם סותם וצדק'תם[3] כסותם ופתיחת ידיהם חומותם

Margin

1. [......] אבירי קדומה אדירי החכמה בקיי(!)[4] המוסר בוחרי תושיה בחוני החכ[מה]
2. [... הדעת ... חו]סן ישועות גבירי אמונת עתים גלילי התבונות דוברי מישרים י[...]
3. [......................]די שם טוב זועמי רשע

Folio 48 Recto

1. ופזור נדבותם יסוד ארמנותם והחזקת יד טובתם מבצר
2. משענותם חמדת הקלות[5] הקדושות הנפוצים עד אר[צו(?)]ת נפ[וצות(?)]
3. הנחוצים לקבל טוב שכר פזורי מוצא ומערב מחמן ב[פאת]
4. צפון ובפאת תימן הדרים ~~בארצות~~ במדברות אויביהם הגרים בארץ [לא]
5. להם בארמנות פרא יסעיר ובמארב ארבע חיות עד יעיר ד[...]

---

[2] = במתנותם.

[3] The scribe wrongly wrote וצדקדתם and corrected it by adding a *vav* above the line, without deleting the extra *dalet*.

[4] Read: בקיאי.

[5] Should be: הקהלות.

6. אהבת עולם לעורר מאמר נשלם וחסד יו"י מעולם ועד עו[לם]
7. עליהם וצדקתו אליהם והמון רחמיו מהם ובהם החכמים ה[גדולים(?)]
8. והשרים הנסגלים והזקינים האצילים ~~והב~~ והישי[ש]ים הנד[גלים]
9. והבחורים המגודלים אשר שם הטוב להם כצללים ובי[...]
10. אל נכללים כל תהלה נוחלים ומנחילים אשר נטעם יו"י כא[רזים מכבי(?)]
11. חימה המבעירה מאוילים ושדים להם כמגדלים הגדול[ים ...]
12. הגדולים רבי הפעלים ראשי החיילים יחכה יו"י לרחמם [...]
13. ולהרימם וי[ק]ום לחננם כזוהר הרקיע להשימם להו[שיבם]
14. באהלים כימי מועד במקומם ועל מבועי מים ל׳הלם ב[...]
15. פדויים לעלות להר צבי קדש המרומם והלכו גאולים [...]
16. העצומם[6] הם הרואים פני המלך בנסיכות היושבים ראש[ונה]
17. במלכות שומרכם בל ינום ועזרכם בל יישן ומן ה[דא ...]
18. יתכלם עלי אלמעני אלמטלוב ואן כאן אמר צדקה פיקו[ל]
19. תחלת כל דבר להודות ולהלל צור ישעכם אשר השא[ירכם]
20. לפליטת מעון קדוש יאמר לכם היותם מעוז לד[ל]
21. לאביון מסעד למטי יד להחזיק יד עני ואביון ומ[טה][7]
22. יד הרוגי זמן רשע צורר אדירים ועויין גבירים ומ[כה(?)]
23. חורים ומחליש גבורים ומוריש עשירים ירוע כביר[ים]

Folio 48 Verso

1. [ול]א יחון נשוא פנים ולא ירחם כל נבונים פתע פתאום
2. [...]צון[8] יגזורו[9] וחצות לילה יגועשו עם ויעבורו ולזאת המכה
3. [מקדם(?) ה]וכנה מדת החסד שהיא מצות הצדקה להציל

---

[6] Read: העצומים.

[7] Or in plural: ומ[טי]. Cf. Folio 49 recto, l. 5.

[8] It is hard to complete this word. [ל]צון or [ר]צון is not possible, and the letter before the *ṣadi* could be *ḥet* or *vav*.

[9] Maybe this is a scribal error and it should be: יגזור. See translation.

4. [גז(?)]ול ולמלט עשוק ולהיות לו מחסה ומסתור ~~למל~~
5. [ל]מלוט מחמס מלכודתו ומרשת מכמרתו זה עני
6. [ייק]רא[10] להושיט לו שרביט הרחמים וחיה ודל משויע[11]
7. [יי]ענה[12] ב[טו]ב מענה כן כן[13] צוה לו ~~ה~~מלך מלכי המלכים על יד נאמן
8. [ביתו רא]ש הנביאי~~ו~~ם[14] אדון הנסיכים כי[15] ימוך אחיך והחזקת בו נסמך וחי עמך
9. [לע]שות לו כל דברו על תלו די מחסורו אשר יחסר
10. [לו] לפי כבודו ויקרו ולא נעלם מיקרכם אתם שרי הקדש
11. [כל א]שר פירשו מאורי העולם במצוה זו וכמה היא חביבה
12. [לפ]ני המקום ועוצם חיבתה ואם כל פה לפניכם נאלם
13. [...] כל סתום ועמום[16] ממכם(!) לא נעלם כי אתם עיני ~~הע~~
14. [הע]דה(?) ומעיני התעודה ומקור החכמה שרים
15. [לפ]ניכם במלים עצרו[17] וחכמים יגידו כי תפארת עזמו
16. [א]תם אבל שלא לכלות ספר אגרת מענין סדרוהו
17. [ח]כמי דתינו בדבריהם היקרים להתברך ולא להזכיר
18. [אל]א להזהיר למעלתכם כי הכל תוצאות תמצית מימי נחליכם
19. [ה]מפיצים חוצה ומאתכם תורה תצא ודבר השם שמור

---

[10] Or: [נק]רא.

[11] Read: משווע.

[12] Or: [ת]ענה.

[13] Should be: כי כן. It seems that the scribe corrected the first כן to כי.

[14] ראש נביאיו was fixed to ראש הנביאים.

[15] In the Masoretic text: וכי.

[16] Following Ezek. 28.3.

[17] Following Job 29.9.

20. [ב]פיכם אמת כגודל חסדיכם דינו לכף זכות ולמען
21. [נו]שא טורים אלו דברי צעירי משרתיכם לפני כבודכם
22. [הגדו(?)]ל ונישא וגבה מאוד אולי ייטיב אלהינו אחרית[נו][18]

Folio 49 Recto

1. על [.........]ש עליו בחסדי מנעמיכם ידוע לפני מ[עלתכם]
2. שמ[ידות(?)[19] החס]ד הם עשר כנחקק בפסוק כי אני יו"י עש[ה חסד][20]
3. מ[שפט וצד]קה בארץ כי באלה חפצתי נאום יו"י [...][21]
4. מ[.........] בגלותינו ונשאר לנו מעט מז[ער(?)[22]]
5. ולחמול על דל ולהלוות מטי יד בתורת ח[סד ...]
6. שחייב אתה לה‎לוותו[23] ואינו לרצון מלווה [...]
7. שהוא בתורת חיוב לא תיהיה(!) לו כנושה [לא תשימון]
8. עליו וכל הענין עד שברחמים בראתי עו[למי אם אתה]
9. מרחם עליו גם אני ארחמך מן השמים ומחיבת
10. זאת המצוה לפני השם אמרה בסיני ובערבות מואב ש[נאמר]
11. כי יהיה בך אביון לא תקפוץ את ידך מליתן לו ולא תאמ[ץ]

---

[18] Or: [אחרית[ו.

[19] Or: [שמ[עלות], שמ[דרגות.

[20] The Masoretic text also has here: עֹשֶׂה חֶסֶד (without *vav* in the participle).

[21] Jer. 9.23.

[22] Following Isa. 10.25; 16.14; 29.17.

[23] The letter *he* was at first written above the word in its correct place (after the first *lamed*), but the script was unclear, so the scribe rewrote the letter above the double *vav*.

12. את לבבך מלדבר עליו לאחרים <כדאמרינן א'ר' אבהו אמר משה לפני הקב"ה
ר' שלעולם[24] במה תרים[25] קרנן שלישראל אמר לו בכי תשא[26]>[27] שאל
פילסוף(!) אחד את ר'[28]
13. גמליאל מאי קרא ולא ירע לבבך בתתך כלום יש לך אדם
14. שמפזר נכסיו ולא ירע לבבו אמר לו אם יאמר לך
15. אדם הלויני בלא ערב תלויהו אמור(!)[29] לו לאו ואם נתן לך ערב
16. נאמן תלויהו אמר לו הין והדברים קל וחומר ומה
17. אם כשעריבו[30] בשר ודם אתה מלויהו וכשעריבו מי
18. שאמר והיה העולם לכל(!)[31] שכן וכן הוא אמור(!)[32] מלוה יו"י
19. חונן דל וכתיב והיה מעשה הצדקה שלום להודיע
20. למעלתכם כי מוביל כתבינו ~~פלו~~'[33] אירעוהו מאורעות
21. רבות ועתה עם הקדש זרעו לכם וגו' אולי יוכל הועיל

---

[24] = ריבונו שלעולם.

[25] In manuscripts and in the Vilna printed version: תרום (b. Bava Batra 10b).

[26] At the end of the sentence, the writer added שאל 'asked' to mark the continuation in the text.

[27] The addition given in < > brackets was written in the margin.

[28] = רבן.

[29] Should be: אמר.

[30] It seems that the copyist at first read this word from the copy that was in front of him as כשעירבו 'when he mixed it', and wrote this form, and then corrected it to כשעריבו (= כשערבו) in *plene scriptum/ketiv male*; likewise, at the end of the line, he first wrote וכשעירבו and then corrected it to וכשעריבו.

[31] Should be: לא כל.

[32] Should be: אומר.

[33] = פלוני.

22. לכסות מערומיו ולהכין צדה לדרך פעמיו ולחמו ומימיו
23. ותחשב זאת לכם לצדקה ותכתב לדור אחרון [...] לכ[ם(?)]

Translation

Folio 49 Verso

1. A sample of a letter to a public audience.
2. [To you O m]en I call (Prov. 8.4), a chosen holy congregation, the nation […]
3. […] God, the eyes of the congregation (following Num. 15.24), the notables of *Jeshurun*, the pious people of this generation, the desire of […]
4. [… They] put on righteousness as a breastplate (following Isa. 59.17), study (the law of) God (following Isa. 54.13), fight the wars of
5. […] government (following Isa. 9.6), have a pure body, act well, (they are like) columns of gems
6. […] (those who) [save] commandments and laws, rare in their purity, friends of the Most High (see Deut. 32.8; 1 Sam. 2.22; Isa. 14.14), straight
7. […] men of renown (following Gen. 6.4), those who are great in the Torah, those who (fulfil) all the laws, the trustees (or: the loyal) of the land
8. Those who understand wisdom, expert in wars (following Song 3.8), despise the gain of oppressions (following Isa. 33.15),
9. inherit pearls, like rivers of generosity, on their water charity is sown (following Isa. 32.20; Hos. 10.12), the Sanhedrin of this time, pave a way (following Isa. 57.14),

10. [...] a way, going around doing charity, count (or: write) the good deeds, who were freed by God (following Isa. 35.10), the Judges of the Torah, similar to the [ministering] angels, the holy men
11. upon earth (following Ps. 16.3), seek the peace (following Ps. 34.15; m. Avot 1.12), keep the doorposts (following Prov. 8.34), seek the will (of God), listen to the shouting
12. of the poor (following Job 34.28), those whose way is blameless (Ps. 119.1), they are the hope of the father of a multitude (of nations [Gen. 17.4–5]; = Abraham), the inheritance of the bound (= Isaac), the worm of Jacob (Isa. 41.14),
13. the community of Cairo, may he who dwells in heaven and on high save them which are mighty in their exile,
14. distinguished in their glory, blessed by God, (all of them) in accordance with their name, their family and their
15. clan,[34] redeemed by their actions, the flags of their armies, those who are upright in their hearts (following Ps. 125.4),
16. devoted in their charities, pure in their uprightness, and in the strength of their salvation (following Isa. 33.6), generous (literally: have a good eye; following Prov. 22.9) in their giving,
17. understand their time (following 1 Chron. 12.33), according to what they were obliged by their (dual) Torah,[35] for raising
18. and adding restrictions for their holiness, they are devoted [to keeping] their purity, inherit

---

[34] "by their clans and families" is a repeated phrase in Numbers.

[35] The written law and the oral law.

19. the lesson of their wisdoms, 'merchants' of their Torah (see Prov. 3.14), stand on their position,
20. (with) their magnificent head covering they dress the poor in their clothes,[36] their wonderful acts are like "the branch of God which shall be beautiful" (Isa. 4.2),
21. their glory is ancient, the heads of their people, draw water of their salvation (following Isa. 12.3),
22. wait for the one who hastens their redemption, stars in their orbit (following Judg. 5.24), rivers of streams of sweet (literally: honey)
23. butter, [...] those who are called after the reputation of their purity (or: their good deeds) and are known for the beauty of their virtues;
24. their donations are their garment, and their charities are their clothes, and the opening of their hands is their wall,

Margin

1. The heroes of the ancient (Torah), the strong persons of wisdom, those who are proficient of the lessons, choosers of the knowledge, prominent of intelligence,
2. [... of knowledge, ... of the rich store] of salvation, nobles of the stability of the time (following Isa. 33.6), rods of sagacity, who speak what is right (following Isa. 33.15), [...]
3. [.................... those who ...] good reputation, who seethe with anger.

---

[36] Or, if we read *pe'ure* (פאורי): 'stand on their position wearing their magnificent head coverings'.

Folio 48 Recto

1. and the good giving of their contributions is the foundation of their palaces, and their support of the hand (of the needy) is the fortress
2. which they rely on. The (most) desirable (community) among the holy communities, which are spread [unto the far lands(?)]
3. who will get quickly their good reward, who spread in the east and west, [in the] north [side]
4. and the south side, who live in their enemies' ~~lands~~ deserts, who dwell (or: who are strangers) in a land [that is not]
5. theirs (following Gen. 15.13), in palaces where an onager goes wild, and in the ambush of the four animals, till (God) will arouse [...]
6. his everlasting love (Jer. 31.2), to arouse the completed saying "the grace of the God is from everlasting to everlasting" (Ps. 103.17)
7. upon them, and his charity (or: righteousness) to them (see Ps. 103.17), and his great mercy to them. Among them, the [great(?)] scholars,
8. and the precious princes, and the noble elders, and the [seniors] who are festooned [with banners],
9. and the 'full grown' youth (following Ps. 144.12), who have a good reputation like shadows and among (or: in) the [...]
10. of God they are included, inherit and bequeath (m. Bava Batra 8.1) all the glory, those who are planted by God [as cedars] (following Num. 24.6), [extinguish]

11. (God's) anger which burns by the fool, and their breasts are like tall towers (following Song 8.10)
12. the great […], men of actions (following 2 Sam. 23.20), head of the forces, God is waiting to have mercy on them [and to …]
13. and to lift them up, and He will arise and show favour (see Ps. 102.14) to them, and to make them (bright) like the brightness of the sky (Dan. 12.3), to [settle them]
14. in tents like festival days in their place, and to guide them on springs of water […]
15. They will ascend, as redeemed captives, to the venerable and beautiful holy mountain (i.e., the Temple Mount) (Dan. 11.45). The redeemed will walk (Isa. 35.19)
16. [in the] huge […], who princely see the king's face, who are highest (literally: who sit first)
17. in the kingdom (Est. 1.14). Your guard will not sleep, and your supporter will not slumber (following Ps. 121.4). From [this point …]
18. he has to speak on the wanted issue. If it is a matter of charity he shall say:
19. The first thing is to thank and praise the rock of your salvation (following 2 Sam. 22.47), who [left you]
20. as a (surviving) remnant (in His) [Holy] dwelling.[37] You should be called Holy (following Isa. 4.3), (because) you have been a refuge for the destitute (Isa. 25.4), a […]

---

[37] See commentary.

21. to the needy, a backrest to the impoverished, to support the poor and the needy and the [impoverished],
22. those who died by the evil destiny (literally: time), who hates the strong persons, and is hostile to the nobles, and who [beats(?)]
23. the highborn, and weakens the heroes, and makes the rich poor, who will collapse the strong ones (Job 34.24)

Folio 48 Verso

1. and will not have mercy on the honourable (following Deut. 28.50; Lam. 4.16), and will not pity the clever ones. Suddenly
2. [...] they decree,[38] and at midnight the people are shaken and they pass away (Job 34.20). For that trouble
3. the virtue of grace was [formerly(?)] prepared, which is the commandment of *Ṣedaqah* (charity), to save
4. [one who was robbed(?)] and to rescue the oppressed,[39] and to be a shelter and refuge for him,
5. to extricate him from his injustice trap and from his fishing net. This poor man
6. will be called to hold out the sceptre of mercy to him, so that he may live (following Est. 4.11), a needy man who is begging (following Ps. 72.12; Job 29.12)

---

[38] In accordance with our suggestion that there is a scribal error here and the word should be יגזור, one can translate it as ‘he (i.e., the destiny) decrees’.

[39] For the collocation of ‘oppressed’ and ‘robbed’, see Deut. 28.29.

7. [will be answered(?)] with a [good] response, because this is what the king of the kings of the kings ordered for him (following Est. 3.2) by his trustee (see Num. 12.7),
8. [the head] of the prophets, the master of the princes: “If your brother becomes poor... you shall support him,” for he will be provided, “and he shall live with you” (Lev. 25.35),
9. [to do] for him everything completely, for his need in whatever he lacks (Deut. 15.18),
10. according to his honour and prestige. It is not forgotten from your honour, you, the princes of holiness,
11. [all that] was interpreted by the lights of the world about this commandment (= charity) and how much it is beloved
12. [in front] of God, and its great affection. Although every mouth be dumbfounded in front of you
13. [...] every incomprehensible and dark (thing) is not hidden from you (following Ezek. 28.3), because you are the eyes of
14. [the congregation(?)] (following Num. 15.24) and the springs of Torah,[40] and the origin of wisdom, princes
15. refrained from talking (following Job 29.9)[41] [in front] of you, and sages will say (Job 15.18) you are the glory of their strength (following Ps. 89.18).
16. However, to avoid filling up (this) letter on a matter which was (already) compiled
17. by the sages of our religion in their honourable sayings, which spread blessing, and (I do) not (want) to remind

---

[40] See commentary for another option.

[41] See also Job 4.2 (וַעְצֹר בְּמִלִּין מִי יוּכָל ‘But who can withhold himself from speaking?!’).

18. [but] rather to encourage your honour, because all (my words) are coming from the best of your river's waters,
19. which is scattered abroad (following Prov. 5.16). The (saying of) Torah will go out from you (following Isa. 51.4), and the saying of the Name is kept
20. [in] your mouth. Vindicate (this poor man), for
21. [those who carry] those columns. This is what your youngest servants say in front of your honour
22. which is intensely [great(?)] and exalted and high. May God make [our] (or: [his], i.e., the poor man's) end good (following Deut. 8.16)

Folio 49 Recto

1. on [……] upon him in your pleasant graces. It is known to [your honour]
2. that [the virtues of grace(?)] are ten, as it written in the verse "I am God [(1) who practises (2) grace,]
3. [(3) justice, (4) and righteousness] (5) in the earth. (6) For (7) in these things (8) I delight, (9) declares (10) God" (Jer. 9.23) […]
4. [……….] in our exile, [very(?)] little is left to us […]
5. to have mercy on the poor, and to lend to the impoverished as [a grace …]
6. that you must lend to him, and it is not according to the lender's will […]
7. which is an obligation, "you shall not be like a moneylender to him [neither shall you lay]

8. upon him (interest)" (Exod. 22.24), etc., till "because I created [my world] with mercy" (Mekhilta de-Rabbi Ishmael, *Kaspa*, §187). [If you]
9. pity him, I will also pity you from heaven (see also t. Bava Qama 9.30; y. Bava Qama 8.7). Because of the affection of this
10. commandment in front of the Name, he said it (twice), in Sinai and in the plains of Moab, [as it is written:]
11. "'If among you (one of your brothers)[42] should become poor… you shall not shut your hand'—for not giving him, and 'you shall not harden
12. your heart'[43]—for not speaking (for the benefit) of him to others" (Midrash Tan'aim, Deut. 15.7) <as we say: "Rabbi Abahu said: Moses addressed himself to the Holy One, blessed be He, saying: 'Sovereign of the Universe, wherewith shall the horn of Israel be exalted?' He replied, 'when you will lift up' (Exod. 30.12; b. Bava Batra 10b).>"[44] One philosopher asked Rabban
13. Gamliel: what is the meaning of the verse "and your heart shall not be grudging when you give" (Deut. 15.10)? Is there anyone who
14. spends his property and his heart is not grudged? (Rabban Gamliel) said to him: If someone will tell you,

---

[42] These words (מֵאַחַד אַחֶיךָ) are not quoted by the copyist.

[43] The order of the two instructions here is opposite to that found in the verse: לֹא תְאַמֵּץ אֶת לְבָבְךָ—מלדבר עליו לאחרים. וְלֹא תִקְפֹּץ אֶת יָדְךָ—מליתן לו.

[44] The sentence between the angular brackets was written in the margin.

15. lend to me without a guarantor, would you lend to him? (The philosopher) told him: No. (Rabban Gamliel said:) And if he is giving you a faithful guarantor,
16. would you lend to him? (The philosopher) told him: Yes. *Argumentum a fortiori* (*qal va-ḥomer*). If,
17. when he has a human (*basar va-dam*; literally: of flesh and blood) guarantor, you lend to him, then when he has as a guarantor who
18. spoke and the world was made, all the more so! It is also said: “Whoever is generous to the poor,
19. lends to God” (Prov. 19.12), and it is written: “And the effect of righteousness will be peace” (Isa. 32.17). It should be known
20. to your honour that the carrier of our letter, ~~so-and-so~~, [...] many troubles happened to him.
21. Now, the holy people (following Isa. 62.2), “sow for yourselves (righteousness)” (Hos. 10.12), etc. Maybe it could help
22. for covering his nakedness and for preparing provision for his legs’ journey (following Gen. 42.25 + Ps. 85.14), and his bread and water (following Exod. 23.25).
23. It shall be considered for you as a charity (following Gen. 15.6; Ps. 106.31), and shall be written for the [last] generation (following Ps. 102.19) [... to you(?)]

Commentary

Folio 49 Verso

Line 3:
"The eyes of the congregation." In the Talmuds, the sages attributed the title *e'ne ha-edah* to the High Court (b. Horayot, 5a–5b), or its head (y. Horayot 1.4), or to the sages in general (b. Bava Batra 4a).

"Jeshurun." A common poetic name for the people of Israel, following Deut. 32.15; 33.5; 33.26; Isa. 44.2.

Line 4:
All the adjectives here start with *lamed.* The writer uses this poetic technique hereinafter too: in l. 5 (*ṭeṭ*), l. 6 (*yod*), and ll. 7–10 (*kaf, mem, nun, samekh, pe,* without *lamed* and *'ayin*). Ll. 10–11 are organised according to the sequence *resh–shin–tav,* and then in l. 11 three consecutive adjectives start with *shin,* and in l. 12 two adjectives start with *tav.*

Line 5:
"Columns of gems." We translated according to the assumption that *turim* is a Hebrew word (see Exod. 39.10). If it is Aramaic, the expression should be translated as 'mountains of gems'.

Line 7:
"The honour of the Torah." The translation here depends on the understanding that *ne'emanah* is the Torah, following Ps. 19.8.

Line 9:
"Inherit pearls." Pearls (*peninim*) here is a nickname for the Torah, following Prov. 3.15.

הנדיבות: The scribe probably intended to delete the word *ha-nedivut* but forgot to do it. Another option is that the expression *naḥale ha-shoʿa* in the upper line is a suggestion of an alternative version (נחלי הנדיבות/נחלי השוע). For *shoʿa* as a synonym of *nadiv*, see Isa. 32.5.

Line 11:
"Keep the doorposts." The writer describes the addressees as diligent people who pass the door of God's house (in the post-Temple period, the synagogue or the *Bet Midrash*) early in the morning.

Line 13:
[ורו]מה. The proposed completion is based on the meaning of *roma*, a word probably invented by the early poets, which is a synonym of 'sky, heaven'. It appears in the early *piyyuṭim* many times in the expression שוכן רומה (maybe following Isa. 57.15).

Lines 13–22:
The praises are organised in alphabetical order.

Line 17:
"According to what they were obliged by their (dual) Torah." See commentary on P.3.b/17.

Line 21:
"The heads of their people." *Ayummah* is a nickname for the people of Israel (following Song 6.4, 10).

Line 24:
סותם. From *sut* (סות), a garment, following Gen. 49.11.

Margin

Lines 1–2:
The metaphors here convey the profound understanding of the Oral Law demonstrated by the addressees. The six words of Isa. 33.6 (אֱמוּנַת עִתֶּיךָ חֹסֶן יְשׁוּעֹת חָכְמַת וָדָעַת) are a symbol of the six orders of the Mishnah (see b. Shabbat 31a).

Folio 48 Recto

Line 3:
"Spread in the east and west." We understood *moṣa* in the expression *pezure moṣa* (פזורי מוצא) as a synonym for 'east', in accordance with Ps. 19.7. The word מחמן (*miḥman*?), which is a rhyme for *teman*, is perhaps a poetic variant of *ḥama* (sun), influenced by the form *ḥaman*. *Ḥammanim* (חַמָּנִים) is mentioned a few times in the Bible (e.g., 2 Chron. 14.4) and usually interpreted as an object of idolatry for sun worshippers. *Maʿarav miḥman* should therefore be interpreted as 'where the sun (*miḥman*) is setting (*maʿarav*)'.

Line 4:
"Their enemies' deserts." The writer first wrote 'lands' (*araṣot*) and then corrected it to 'deserts' (*midbarot*). This may reflect his will to decorate the image with the characters of the archetypal world of Ishmael (see commentary on l. 5), who is connected closely with the desert (see Gen. 16.7–16; 21.14–21). For a wider discussion on these lines and the social history that is reflected here, see Arad (2020).

"A land that is not theirs." This quotation refers to Egypt (see Gen. 15.13), where the addressees are living.

Line 5:
"In a palace where an onager goes wild, and in the ambush of the four animals." The onager (*pere*) is a symbol for Ishmael and the Muslims, following Gen. 16.12. It reflects the fact that the writer and the theoretical addressees are living under Islamic rule. The four animals are a reference to the prophecy of Daniel 7 about the four animals, i.e., the four kingdoms that will rule the world. Ll. 4–5 are intended to describe the difficulties of the people of Israel as a small minority under the world's strong forces (Islam and Christianity).

בארמנות פרא. This expression is influenced by Isa. 32.14 (כִּי אַרְמוֹן נֻטָּשׁ, הֲמוֹן עִיר עֻזָּב; עֹפֶל וָבַחַן הָיָה בְעַד מְעָרוֹת, עַד עוֹלָם מְשׂוֹשׂ פְּרָאִים, מִרְעֵה עֲדָרִים).

Line 8:
השרים הנסגלים. *Nisgalim* is probably an adjective from *segulah*.

Line 9:
"A good reputation like shadows." The metaphor here is based either on the nature of the shadow as an element that accompanies one constantly, or on the view that the addressees' good reputation is like a *ḥuppah* above their heads to protect them from damage (see Isa. 4.6). In the Bible, the shadow sometimes has positive symbolic meaning. It is considered a source of protection (Isa. 4.6; 25.4; Jon. 4.5–6) and symbolises divine providence, e.g., "God is your shade on your right hand" (Ps. 121.5). It seems that this positive association was in the writer's mind when he created the expression under discussion. It may be also that he is referring to Num. 14.9. *Rashi* in his commentary explains that the shadow mentioned there is a symbol of the righteous (thanks to

Rafi Moses, Iddo Roth, Shmuel Polacheck, and Ariel Samuel for their ideas).

Line 11:
"Their breasts are like tall towers." This expression looks strange, but the writer did not intend a visual description of the addressees here, but refers to an 'archetype body', which he knew from the canonical sources. The biblical quotation in the background, "I am a wall, and my breasts are like towers" (Song 8.10), was interpreted by the sages as a reference to Abraham (Gen. Rabbah 39.3); Ḥananiah, Misha'el, and 'Azariah (Gen. Rabbah 39.3); and the sages themselves (b. Bava Batra 7b–8a), but the most reasonable association here is the *midrash* which explains this metaphor with respect to Moses and Aaron (Song Rabbah 4). Teaching Torah to the students is compared there to breastfeeding.

Lines 17–18:
"From this point speak... he shall say." This is the only Arabic sentence in the text.

Lines 19–20:
The phrasing here is very complicated. It seems that the word קדוש belongs to both the preceding and the following phrase (מעון קדוש\קדוש יאמר). All the phrasing here is influenced by Isa. 4.3. However, specific collocations are inspired by other verses. ויש[אירכם] לפליטת מעון is following Gen. 32.9 and the biblical term שארית הפליטה (1 Chron. 4.43; see also Ezra 9.14–15). מעון קדוש is following Deut. 21.15; Jer. 25.30; Zech. 2.17. קדוש יאמר לכם is following Isa. 4.3.

Line 21:

למטי יד. See Lev. 25.25.

Lines 22–23:

Medieval people did not blame the government or society as responsible for the problem of poverty. They saw poverty as a natural law (see Deut. 15.11: "For there will never cease to be poor in the land"). That which was responsible for human suffering was 'time, destiny'. These lines (with f2/1–2) describe it in a graphic, even demonic, way as the "evil time."

Folio 48 Verso

Line 2:

The aim of the writer is to declare that the economic situation of the poor is not an inevitable destiny but can change surprisingly.

Line 7:

"The king of the kings of the kings." The title 'king of the kings' was known in the ancient Middle East (in ancient Assyria: *šar šarrāni*; in Persia: *shahanshah)* and appears in Aramaic form *(melekh malkhaya)* in the Bible (Dan. 2.37; Ezra 7.12). The term 'king of the kings of the kings' was developed in Hebrew to describe God as one step above the human kings and it is a typical nickname for him in rabbinic literature.

"Trustee." A nickname of Moses known from Num. 12.7. רועה נאמן (Heb.) or רעיא מהימנא (Aram.) 'loyal shepherd' is a common nickname for Moses in rabbinic literature. The Aramaic form gave its name to one of the sections of the *Zohar, Ra'aya mehemna*.

Line 10:
"According to his honour and glory." See b. Ketubot 67b; *Mishne Torah, Hilkhot Matnot ʿAniyim* 7.2.

Line 13:
"The eyes of the congregation." The sages understood this expression as a reference to the High Court (see b. Horayot 5b) or to the sages as a whole (b. Bava Batra 4a). The original expression (*ʿene ha-ʿedah u-maʿayne ha-teʿudah)* has a nice rhyme and tone.

Line 14:
"Springs of the Torah." The translation reflects the reading *u-maʿayne*. Another option is to read *u-meʿayne,* that is to say, 'those who study the Torah deeply', but the first option looks to be the right reading, due to the parallelism *maʿayan–maqor*. One of the meanings of *maqor* is 'a spring of water' (see, for example, Jer. 2.13; 17.13); *Teʿudah* is probably a nickname for the Torah, in accordance with Isa. 8.16.

Lines 17–18:
"Not to remind but rather to encourage." The writer here uses the Hebrew expression wrongly. In medieval and early modern rabbinic sources, the expression *eni ke-mazhir ela ke-mazkir* 'I am not warning, rather I am reminding' appears.

Folio 49 Recto

Lines 2–3:
The commentary here is based on Jer. 9.23 and attributes symbolic meaning to the numbers of the last sentence ("practises grace... declares God"). The exact content of the commentary is unclear. We did not find this commentary in the literature of the

sages or in medieval works. We can find some similarity to this commentary in a talmudic commentary (b. Bava Batra 9b):

> R. Isaac also said: "He who gives a small coin to a poor man obtains six blessings, and he who addresses him with words of comfort obtains eleven blessings." "He who gives a small coin to a poor man obtains six blessings"—as it is written, "Is it not to share your bread with the hungry?" (Isa. 58.7) etc.... "He who addresses to him comforting words obtains eleven blessings"—as it is written, "if you pour yourself out for the hungry" (Isa. 58.10) etc....

However, in the talmudic source, each clause in the verse is counted,[45] whereas here each word is counted separately.[46]

Lines 7–8:

"Etc." The writer perhaps means that you should copy also Exod. 22.25–26 and then add the Mekhilta de-Rabbi Ishmael (tractate

---

[45] Six blessings: (1) Then shall your light break forth like the dawn, (2) and your healing shall spring up speedily; (3) your righteousness shall go before you; (4) the glory of God shall be your rear guard. (5) Then you shall call, and God will answer; (6) you shall cry, and he will say, "Here I am" (Isa. 58.8–9).

Eleven blessings: (1) Then shall your light rise in the darkness; (2) and your gloom be as the noonday, (3) and God will guide you continually (4) and satisfy your desire in scorched places (5) and make your bones strong; (6) and you shall be like a watered garden, (7) like a spring of water, whose waters do not fail; (8) and your ancient ruins shall be rebuilt; (9) you shall raise up the foundations of many generations; (10) you shall be called the repairer of the breach, (11) the restorer of streets to dwell in (Isa. 58.10–12).

[46] (1) עושה (2) חסד (3) משפט (4) וצדקה (5) בארץ (6) כי (7) באלה (8) חפצתי (9) נאום (10) יו"י.

Kaspa, §187): "…I shall hear; for I am gracious, because I created my world with mercy."

Lines 8–9:

Compare: "he who pities the poor, the Holy One, blessed be he, pities him" (Midrash Sekhel Ṭov, Gen. 19). A similar saying, not limited to the poor but referring to all men, is mentioned in the Babylonian Talmud: "he who pities the creatures (*beriyot,* persons) is being pitied from heaven" (b. Shabbat 151b). See also t. Bava Qama 9.30; y. Bava Qama 8.7.

Line 12:

The verse כי תשא את ראש בני ישראל should be translated as 'When you take the census of the people of Israel' (ESV), but R. Abahu interprets the word תשא literally ('lift up'), in order to say that God advised Moses that the thing which could lift up the status of his people is giving charity (the verse continues: "then each shall give a ransom for his life", i.e., the half-shekel donation of each of the Israelites).

Lines 12–19:

A commentary from Midrash Tana'im (Deut. 15). Some other dialogues between a 'philosopher' and Rabban Gamliel are mentioned in the talmudic literature; see, for example, b. ʿAvodah Zarah 54b; Gen. Rabbah 1.12; Derekh Ereṣ Rabbah 5.

P: PRIVATE LETTERS

MOSES B. JUDAH'S CIRCLE

Contents

6. Letter from Isaac Bayt ʿAṭṭān to Moses b. Judah
   Bodl. MS Heb. c. 72/18
7. Letter from Ṣuriel Dayyan to Moses b. Judah
   Bodl. MS Heb. c. 72/23
8. Letter from Mardūḵ Qarqūsa to Israel ʿAṭāʾīn and Yeraḥmiel ʿAṭāʾīn
   Bodl. MS Heb. c. 72/37
9. Letter from an Anonymous Scholar to Moses b. Judah
   Bodl. MS Heb. c. 72/2 + 72.24
10. Letter from an Anonymous Writer to Moses b. Judah
    JTS MS 2331, 217b–218a
11. Letter from an Anonymous Writer to a Certain Yedidiah
    Bodl. MS Heb. c. 72/50
12. Letter from an Anonymous Writer
    Bodl. MS Heb. c. 72/54

P.1: Letter from Moses b. Judah (?) to Saʿīd ibn Muhaḏḏab

MS ENA 4101.6A

18 April 1489

General Introduction

The letter, written in Hebrew, deals mainly with issues concerning Moses' library. Moses mentions several books he wants to purchase or to sell and asks the addressee to take care of some new manuscript-copying projects for him. He also discusses some business matters.

This letter was first published by Jacob Mann (1926, 305–8). Hacker (2000, 577 n. 19) made a list of corrections to Mann's publication and concluded that this letter is ready for a re-edition (מן הראוי להוציא איגרת זו מחדש). Mann did not offer an identification of the author. Although Moses b. Judah's name is not mentioned explicitly, the identification of him as the author (as offered by Hacker 2000, 577 n. 20) seems reasonable. However, Hacker did not identify the addressee.[1]

Physical Description

28 × 11; paper; 1 leaf; 36 lines (recto); 32 lines + marginalia (verso); torn, rubbed.

---

[1] He suggested cautiously that the addressee was Nathan Sholal.

 https://doi.org/10.11647/OBP.0352.11

Transcription

Recto

1. מעאמי"ל[2]
2. אלוף העדה ומעיניו תורת אלהיו בלבו
3. לא זזה מבין עיניו חרד ליום שעוברים
4. בו בני אדם כבני מרון הוא מתלמידיו
5. שלאהרן במעשים נאים ומשובחים וכשר'ן
6. על מצחו תמיד הענוה והיראה לזכרון
7. יהי אלהיך בעזרך ויאר פניו אליך המקיף
8. בפרטי סתריך[3] ואל תהי תפלת הדיוט
9. קלה בעניך אחי ואהובי אחרי דרישת שלום נפשך
10. היקרה בעיני אלהים ואדם כשעור הראוי
11. למע' תורתך באתי להגיד תשוקתי
12. הגדולה למע' חסדך עלי יגמלך השם
13. חן וחסד ורחמים ועתה אדוני וקציני
14. הגיעני כתבך הבהיר כשמש מזהיר
15. ושמחתי בו שמחה שלימה שכבודך וכל
16. אנשיך בגדר הבריאות כן יהיה תמיד
17. שנשמע עליכם רוב שלומות וכבר
18. שמענו שהגיע כ"ר יצחק שולל לרשיד ואני כבר
19. כתבתי למע' שני כתבים קודם לזה אחד
20. מרשיד עם הספן ואחד על ידי כ"ר צדקה
21. ניס יצ"ו ובקשתי ממעלתך שתשלח לי
22. רבי[ע] אמה בגד משי מזה המין שבכתב

---

[2] = מגני על אלהים מושיע ישרי לב (Ps. 7.11).

[3] Mann reads incorrectly: בפרשי סהריך, and tries to explain this phrase, but our reading is certain.

23. וזה הענין לא פחות ולא 'תר וכבר שלחתי
24. בכתב אחר חתיכה אחרת מזאת בחסדך
25. תשלחנה לי במהרה עם הקודם כי אני צריך
26. אליה קודם המועד וגם ה' ארטאל חלוה
27. [ת]שלח [ביד] כ"ר דוד הסופר ובנו כ"ר מאיר בעד
28. [... ... ...] ל[י] כי[4] אני שלחתי לך
29. [... ... ...] להעתיק ל[...[5]]
30. [... ... ...] מאוד[6] לס' קנא בחסדך
31. [... ... ... לפ]ניהם שירצה אחד מהם
32. [... ... ...] שכר כמו
33. [... ... ...] כתיבת אבות[7] ל[ר'] ישראל שלהם
34. [... ... ...] הס'[8] להעתיק[ו]

Verso

1. [... ... ...] לא ימנעו ממני [...]
2. [... ... ... מ]קשיה ובחסדך ר'
3. [... ... ...] הכחל ששאלתו מאת
4. [... ... ... ותודי]עני אם לקח שום פשרה(?)
5. [... ... ...] אם יוכל לתת לי ס' הזוהר
6. [... ... ...] אם לא וגם תודיעני אם
7. [... ... ...]ם כתיב שיש לו בקלף
8. [... ... ...] תראהו אם הוא מרחיב פירוש

---

[4] Mann reads the last two words as: [ת]הלים, but this is very doubtful.

[5] Maybe: לכ"ר (= לכבוד רבי).

[6] Mann reads here: בחור.

[7] The text is blurred, and the reading is doubtful. Hacker read: כתיבת אב [...] שלהם.

[8] = הספר.

9. בתרגום שלו תראהו לר' צדקה אם תרגום
10. רב יוסף תתפשר עמו ותקנהו לי ותודיעני
11. אם יכולהו להוציא הלקוטים שלזוהר שאמר
12. לי ממי שהוא תחת ידו אם לא וגם תודיעני
13. אם גבה כבודך הנשאר מהדמים שלאשתיואן
14. מהיהודי שהוא עם השמש ותודיע למרדוך
15. שלא יתן לאשת השמש בעד אשתי רק י"ו
16. נצף לא יותר ותודיעני אם לקח כ"ר אברהם
17. אלשויך הנשאר מן אלאשתיואן אם לא ובחסדך
18. תסייע מרדוך לקחת מר' ישועה נשאדרי
19. או פרח זהב או הספרים ותודיעהו
20. שיקח מר' צדקה ד' ספרים מהחבור וימכרם
21. וימכור שאר הספרים שיש לו משלי וגם
22. כבודך לא תמכור פי' תלים פחות מג' דוכת
23. וג' ספרים מהחבור דוכת לא פחות ופי'
24. איוב עשרה מאי' או ט' ותזכר המזכרת
25. שהנחתי למעלתך תעשה מה שיש בה
26. כפי היכולת ומענין הצמוקים כבר כתבת[י]
27. למע' שבאה ספינה טעונה ועדין לא הוריד[וה]
28. ולא עשו שער וגם בזה היום באה ספינה
29. טעונה צמוקים ושעוה ועורות וכשיורידו
30. ויתחילו למכור נודיע לכבודך ותפרוש שלומי[ם]
31. לאחי ר' מאיר ואביו ר' דוד הסופר יצ"ו וגם כ"ר
32. חנניה יצ"ו חתנך וכל הנלוים אליך לשרתך

Margin

1. כנפשך החשובה המליאה תורה ומצות וכשרון וכנפש הנרצע לעבדותך הכותב
2. בסדר קדושים תהיו כ"ג לספירה שנת ונתתי מטר אר[צכם]

Below

1. [...] אללה תע' ליד אלמו' אלח' סעיד יצ["ו י]ד[י]ע
2. א' מהדב

Translation

Recto

1. My shield is God Most High, who saves the upright in heart (Ps. 7.11).
2. The leader of the congregation, and its spring; the law of his God is in his heart (Ps. 37.31)
3. and does not remove from against his eyes; (he) fears from the day that
4. people pass (before God) like sheep; he is among the pupils
5. of Aaron as he has good and praiseworthy deeds and aptitude;
6. humility and fear (of God) are always on his forehead (Exod. 28.38) for remembrance.
7. May God be with your help, and make his face to shine upon you (Num. 6.25), he who knows
8. your hidden things in detail. Do not consider a prayer of a layman
9. unvalued in your mind (b. Megillah 15a).[9] My brother, my beloved, after greetings of your soul,
10. which is respected in the sight of God and man (Prov. 3.4), in appropriate measure
11. for your honourable Torah, I come to express my great desire

---

[9] There (in all manuscripts and printed editions): ברכת and not תפלת.

12. for your honourable grace upon me. The Name will pay you
13. charm and grace and mercy. Now, my master and commander,
14. your letter, which is bright like the shiny sun, has arrived to me
15. and I was happy about it in complete happiness, (to hear) that your honour and all
16. your people are in good health, let it be like that forever,
17. that we will hear about you great peace. We already
18. heard that the honourable rabbi Isaac Sholal arrived in Rosetta. I already
19. wrote two letters to your honour before that: one
20. from Rosetta with the sailor, and the other one by the honourable rabbi Ṣedaqah
21. Nis, may God save him, and I asked your honour to send me
22. a quarter cubit of a silk cloth, from this kind which (is mentioned) in the letter.
23. This is the matter, no less, no more. I have already sent
24. with another letter a different piece of it. Please
25. send it to me quickly with the first (person), because I need
26. it before the holiday, and also 5 *raṭl* of *ḥalwa*.
27. Send it with the honourable rabbi David the scribe and his son, the honourable rabbi Meʾir, in return for
28. [...] to [me], because I sent you
29. [...] to copy for [the honourable rabbi(?)...]
30. [...] very much for the book of Qanah. Please
31. [... in front of them(?)], that one of them will want
32. [...] payment, like

33. […] copying their (tractate)[10] of Avot of [R.] Israel
34. […] to copy the book

Verso

1. […] he would not prevent me […]
2. […] Please R.
3. […] the *kuḥl* (= kohl) which you asked (or: borrowed) from
4. [… inform] me did he take any […]
5. […] could he give me the book of the *Zohar*
6. […] or not. Inform me also does
7. […] *Ketiv* which he has on vellum
8. […] look at it and see if he interprets at length
9. in his translation. Show it to R. Ṣedaqah. If it is the translation
10. of Rav Joseph, compromise with him (on price) and buy it for me. Inform me
11. if he could take out the anthology of the *Zohar*, which he mentioned
12. to me, from the one that holds it, or not. Also inform me
13. if your honour collected what remained from the money of the Black Spleenwort
14. from the Jew who is (staying) with the beadle. Tell Marduḵ
15. to give the beadle's wife, for my wife, only 16
16. half-dinars, no more. Inform me, did the honourable rabbi Abraham
17. al-Shuwayḵ take which remained from the Black Spleenwort, or not. Please

---

[10] Or: their copy of the (tractate).

18. help Marduḵ to take from R. Yeshuʿah Nushādirī
19. a golden florin or the books, and inform him
20. that he has to take from R. Ṣedaqah four books from the Work (of Maimonides) and sell them.
21. He should also sell the other books of mine he holds. Also,
22. your honour, do not sell the commentary on Psalms for less than three ducats
23. and three books from the Work for one ducat, no less, and the commentary
24. on Job for ten *muʾayyadī* or nine. Remember the reminder
25. I left to your honour. Do what is in it
26. as well as you could. Concerning the raisins: I already wrote
27. to your honour that a loaded ship has arrived, and [it] did not unload yet
28. and the price(?) was not determined, and also today a ship has arrived
29. with a cargo of raisins and wax and leathers. When they will unload (it)
30. and start to sell (it), we will inform your honour. Please send greetings
31. to my brother R. Meʾīr, and to his father, R. David the scribe, may God save him, and also to the honourable rabbi
32. Ḥananya your son-in-law, may God save him, and all those who accompany you for serving you.[11]

[11] For another option for the translation of the last sentence, see commentary.

Margin

1. Like your soul, which is full of Torah and commandments and talent, and like the soul of him who is subjugated to your service, who is writing
2. on the *Seder* of “You shall be holy” (Lev. 19.2), 23 for the counting (of the *ʿOmer*), in the year of “I will give the rain for [your land]” (Deut. 11.14; = 18 May 1489).

Below

1. [shall be given by the help of] God exalted to the hand of the master, the *ḥaver*, Saʿīd, may God save him, [who is known] as
2. Ibn Muhaḏḏab.

Commentary

Recto

Line 1:
For a similar motto, see letters P.3.a/1 and P.3.e/1.

Line 2:
“And its spring.” The exact meaning of the expression אלוף העדה ומעיניו is not clear. If the writer does indeed mean ‘spring’ (מעין), he should have written ומעינה in the feminine. Anyhow, the imagery of a leader as a spring is not frequent. We can, cautiously, suggest that the writer was influenced by the biblical verse והיה אם מעיני העדה נעשתה לשגגה ‘Then if it was done unwittingly without the knowledge of the congregation’ (Num. 15.24). The ex-

pression עיני העדה 'the eyes of the congregation' has been interpreted by rabbinic sources as an allusion to the sages (cf. C.7, 2v/3). If so, the correct form should have been אלוף העדה ועיניה, but the writer adhered to the idiom of the verse.

Line 3:
"Fears from the day that people pass (before God) like sheep." This is an allusion to the Day of Judgment in the next world. Originally, this was the description in the Mishnah (Rosh ha-Shanah 1.1) of the passing of all human beings before God "like sheep" on the first of Tishrei, but it is not plausible that the writer was actually referring here to Rosh ha-Shanah, especially in the light of the date of the letter (the eighth of Iyar).

It is possible to read in our letter כבנימרון as one word. The original version in the Mishnah, according to accurate manuscripts, was כבנומרון 'as *Numeron*', i.e., like a military unit, but already in the Babylonian Talmud (Rosh ha-Shanah 18a) the form כבני מרון occurs. One of the explanations for this expression given in the discussion there is 'sheep' in Aramaic (אמרנא), and this is the common interpretation in Jewish commentary. See also commentary on l. 28.

Line 4:
"Among the pupils of Aaron." The expression (following m. Avot 1.12) is probably a reference to the fact that the addressee is a *Kohen*.

Line 6:
"For remembrance." Moses is here writing associatively. The expression "among the pupils of Aaron" brought to his mind the

image of Aaron dressed in the priestly clothes, such as the *Ḥoshen*, which “remained always on his forehead” (Exod. 28.38). This verse reminded him of other verses in this chapter (Exod. 28.12, 29), from which he took the word לזכרון ‘for remembrance’.

Line 9:

Above the word נפשך ‘your soul’, the writer started to write a word that we cannot decipher ([(?)..]אפ).

Line 13:

חן וחסד ורחמים. The expression is frequent in some known liturgical passages: the first blessing of the grace after meals (*birkat ha-Mazon*); the last blessing of the ʿAmidah; the wayfarer’s prayer (*Tefilat ha-derekh*).

Line 22:

“Cubit.” The writer here uses a Hebrew term, *ammah*, which is a biblical and talmudic unit of length. He is probably referring to the local measurement of *ḏirāʿ*, which is more or less equivalent to the Roman cubit.

Line 26:

“Before the holiday.” It seems that the holiday mentioned here is the festival of Shavuʿot (Pentecost), whose date was 3 weeks later (15 May 1489).

“*Ḥalwa.*” A sweetmeat of sesame, oil, and nuts.

Line 27:

David the scribe is undoubtedly R. David ibn Shams.

Line 30:
“The book of Qanah.” A kabbalistic work by an anonymous author. It is mentioned also in letter P.7/23. On this book, see Introduction, §2.5.

Line 33:
“Copying their (tractate) of Avot of [R.] Israel.” The reading of the word “Avot” is not certain. If it is correct, the writer is probably referring here to the commentary of R. Israel of Toledo on tractate Avot, which was composed in Judaeo-Arabic in Spain in the fourteenth century. Nathan Sholal, the Nagid, also had this work in his library (see Introduction, §2.2.5). On this work, see, for example, Nahem Ilan (2006). Another option is that the writer means a scribe called Israel who copied this manuscript.

Verso

Line 1:
“He would not prevent it from me.” The translation is based on the reading ימנעֹו. If we read ימנעֻו, it should be translated ‘they would not prevent’.

Line 3:
[מ]קשיה. The reading of this word is difficult. Its form was deciphered by Aharon Maman, as quoted by Hacker (2000, 577 n. 19). מקשיה is a term used by Judaeo-Arabic speakers for biblical translations into Arabic (see, for example, Dayyan, *Divre Emet*; Avrahami 1994), but it seems that this term was not yet in use in the fifteenth century. Therefore, we preferred to leave this word without translation.

Line 4:
"*Kuḥl* (= kohl)." Due to a tear in the manuscript, the meaning here is not clear. In Hebrew and Arabic sources, כחל is usually a blue-black collyrium used by women (and also men) for colouring the eyes. In light of the context of the text, perhaps the writer meant here a blue colour for illuminating a manuscript? Another meaning of כחל (*keḥal* or *kaḥal*) in talmudic sources is 'cow's udder', which was eaten in some cases, but this understanding looks unlikely here, too.

Line 7:
"*Ketiv.*" The meaning here is not clear due to the condition of the text. Maybe the writer was discussing here a work on Masora, with a list of *Qeri* and *Ketiv* cases.

Lines 9–10:
"The translation of Rav Joseph." The writer refers here to an Aramaic translation of the *Ketuvim*. This name was given to it due to a wrong attribution to Rav Joseph, a Babylonian *Amora* who is known in the talmudic literature as an expert in Aramaic translation of the Prophets. In actual fact, this anonymous translation was written not in Babylonian Aramaic, but rather in Palestinian Aramaic.

Line 16:
"Abraham al-Shuwayḵ." He is mentioned also in letter P.3.g/12.

Line 18:
"Yeshuʿah Nushādirī." According to his name, he, or one of his ancestors, was a *nushādir* (ammoniac) seller.

Line 20:
"The Work." Jacob Mann (1926, 305) noted here: "By 'The Work'... no doubt Maimonides' *Mishne Torah* is meant."

Line 23:
"From the Work." See l. 20.

Line 24:
"The reminder." On the meaning of מזכרת, see the discussion in Hacker (2000, 577 n. 20).

Line 31:
"My brother R. Me'īr." This is an expression conveying friendly closeness, and it should not be understood literally. Me'īr's father, David the scribe, was not Moses' father.

"And also to... Ḥananya." The translation is based on the assumption that the words וגם כ"ר חנניה in fact mean וגם לכ"ר חנניה. If the absence of the *lamed* here is intentional, it should be translated as 'and also the honourable rabbi Ḥananya... and all those who accompany you for serving you (are greeting you)'.

Margin

Line 1:
"Who is subjugated." Literally: 'who is pierced'. The term refers to the law of the Hebrew slave in the book of Exodus: "If the slave declares: I love my master... I will not go out free... and his master shall bore his ear through with an awl; and he shall serve him for life" (Exod. 21.5–6).

Line 2:
"The *Seder* of 'You shall be holy'." The writer refers to the week which precedes the reading of the *parasha* of "You shall be holy" (Lev. 19.1–20.27) on Shabbat in the synagogues.

"In the year of 'I will give the rain for your land'." The Hebrew word מטר 'rain' is a hint for the Hebrew year רמ"ט ([5]249), which is equivalent to the Christian year 1488/9.

Below

The name "Saʿīd" is typical for the Mamlūk period. We have no more information on Saʿīd ibn Muhaḏḏab.

P.2: Letter to Moses b. Judah, Probably from Nathan Sholal

Bodl. MS Heb. c. 72/16

General Introduction

Concerning private issues between Sholal and Moses b. Judah. Hebrew.

The writer thanks Moses for the favours he bestowed upon Isaac, probably Isaac Sholal, Nathan's nephew and his successor in the Nagidate. The address line on the verso was written in the handwriting of Ṣedaqah Nis. This is a sign that Ṣedaqah was one of the Nagid's associates, and maybe responsible for the Nagid's correspondence for a period of time. The letter was delivered by a personal messenger (l. 12).

Physical Description

13.6 × 14.1; paper; 1 leaf; 13 lines (recto); 1 line (verso); torn, holes, red-brown stains.

Transcription

Recto

1. אמת
2. כבוד גדו' יק' מע' היקר הנכבד החשוב יקירנו אהובנו מה"ר
3. משה יצ"ו ב"ר יהודה ז"ל ישמרך השם ויהי בעזרך אחר שהשב[תי]
4. לך על כתבך שהגיעני לא ראיתי עוד מענה ממך והגיעני
5. מיצחק יצ"ו כתבים והוא מתפאר ומשתבח בך ומודה בכל
6. הטובות הרבות שעשית עמו עד שהוא מתבייש הרבה

 https://doi.org/10.11647/OBP.0352.12

7. מן הטובות שקבל ממך השם ישמרך לעד ויאריך ימיך
8. והוא ישלם לך שכר פעולתך אמנם אנחנו קצרי היד
9. לשלם לך גמול טוב והשם הוא שיגמלך כל טוב אבקשך
10. להודיעני כיצד הלך יצחק ואחותו אם הם בריאים ואם
11. הניחו אצלך שום כתב תשלחהו אלינו מהרה ועתה אי[ני]
12. יכול להאריך עליך לסבת היוצא נחוץ ושלום לך ולבי[תך]
13. ולכל הסרים אל משמעתך ואתה שלום

Verso

כבוד גדו' יק' מע' מה"ר משה יצ"ו ב"ר יהודה נ"ע באסכנדריה יע"א

Translation

Recto

1. Truth.
2. The honourable, great and respectful, the precious, the venerable, the noble, our dear beloved, our teacher Rabbi
3. Moses, may God save him, son of Rabbi Judah, rest in peace, may the Name save you and be your assistance. After I answered
4. you concerning your letter, which I received, I have not seen a reply from you yet. I got
5. letters from Isaac, God save him. He glorifies and praises you, and is grateful for all
6. the many favours you did him, to the degree that he is very ashamed
7. because of the favours he received from you. May the Name save you forever and extend your life,

8. and he will pay you your work's reward. Although we do not have the ability
9. to reward you well, it is the Name who will reward you all the best. Please
10. inform me what happens with Isaac and his sister. Are they healthy? If they
11. left any letter (for me) with you, send it to us soon. Now I [cannot]
12. draw out (this letter) to you, because the messenger is in a hurry. Peace be upon you and [your family]
13. and all those who are under your authority. And peace be upon you (1 Sam. 25.6).

Verso

The honourable, great, and respectful, the precious, our teacher Rabbi Moses, may God save him, son of Rabbi Judah, his soul rest in Eden, in Alexandria, may God protect her.

Commentary

Recto

Line 1:
"Truth (*emet*)." This is the *ʿalāma* of the Nagid. Beginning in the Fāṭimid period, Jewish leaders—Geonim, exilarchs, and Negidim—imitated the Muslim rulers' custom of using a permanent motto. This motto appears at the head of the letter or at its end and is usually based on a biblical phrase, a wish for redemption, etc. The *ʿalāma* of Nathan, 'truth', is unique, and to the best of

our knowledge, was not used by any other leader in Medieval Eastern Jewry.

Line 8:
"We do not have the ability to reward you well." This line may reflect the weakness of the Nagidate in the fifteenth century and its reliance on the Jewish elite of rich traders and clerks in the Mamlūk administration.

Line 10:
Isaac probably exited Cairo, where his uncle lived, and arrived in Alexandria. After a stay in the city, supported by Moses b. Judah, Isaac continued on to an unknown destination. The Nagid was asking Moses to give him information on Isaac's journey and to send him Isaac's letters, if there were any.

P.3.a: Letter from David ibn Shams to Moses b. Judah

Bodl. MS Heb. c. 72/19

General Description

Unknown content. Judaeo-Arabic.

Only the beginning of the letter is preserved. The address line, in Arabic script, mentions Moses' profession as the dragoman (of the Venetian consulate) in Alexandria.

Physical Description

7 × 13.6; paper; 1 leaf; 4 lines (recto); 2 lines (verso); torn, holes, red-brown stains.

Transcription

Recto

1. שיל"ת לק"י מעאמי"ל[1]
2. [...] אלדי יעלם [בה כ"ר] משה אבקאה [אללה תע' פי] כיר ועאפיה ונע[מת]
3. [אן שאפיה ... ... כ]תאב [...]

[1] = שויתי י"י לנגדי תמיד; לישועתך קויתי י"י; מגני על אלהים מושיע ישרי לב

 https://doi.org/10.11647/OBP.0352.13

Verso

1. يصل ان شا الله الى ثغر اسكندرية يسلم ليدالمعلم موسي بن يهودة الترجمان من عند المملوك داود شمس
2. יסלם ליד מוסי א' יהודה י"ל

Translation

Recto

1. I am ever mindful of the LORD's presence (Ps. 16.8). I wait for your deliverance, O LORD (Gen. 49.18). My shield is with God, who saves the upright in heart (Ps. 7.11).
2. [This letter] which informs [the honourable rabbi], may [God make his life] lasting [...] in well-being and good health and [pleasantness]
3. [...] a letter [...]

Verso

1. (The letter) should arrive, God willing, to the port of Alexandria, to be given to the *muʿallim* Mūsā b. Judah the dragoman from the servant Daʾūd Shams.
2. To be given to Mūsā b. Judah, may he live for ever.

P.3.b: Letter from David ibn Shams to Moses b. Judah

Bodl. MS Heb. c. 72/20

General Introduction

This is the beginning of a letter, with praises for Moses b. Judah, in Hebrew (the letter itself was probably written in Judaeo-Arabic).

The friendship between David and Moses is reflected especially well in this letter. The author chooses an intimate quotation from Song of Songs to describe the kinship between them. It is not a relationship between a master and his apprentice, as we find in some other letters in our corpus, but an equal relationship between two close friends. This closeness is illustrated well also in the address line, where David calls the addressee "the brother," and not 'the master' etc. (see also P.3.c).

This torn letter does not provide us with much historical information, and we know nothing of the subjects David wanted to discuss, but it has special importance in that it portrays Moses' status, his reputation, and his public image as a leader and associate of the authorities on the one hand, and as an intellectual and a local scholar on the other.

Physical Description

19.7 × 13.8; paper; 1 leaf; 18 lines (recto); 1 line (verso); torn, holes, rubbed, red-brown stains.

 https://doi.org/10.11647/OBP.0352.14

Transcription

Recto

1. בשמׄא רחמׄנא וחנׄנא לׄקׄיׄ
2. אני לדודי ודודי לי הרועה בשושנים
3. שלום רב לאוהבי תורתיך ואין למו
4. והתענג על י"י ויתן לך משאלות
5. ואמרתם כה לחי ואתה שלום וביתך
6. והאיש משה עניו מאד מכל האדם אשר
7. שמר תם וראה ישר כי אחרית לאיש
8. י"י עוז לעמו יתן י"י יברך את
9. אלעבד אלאצגֿר ואלמחב אלאכבר
10. דוד בר יעקב ידיע א' שמס
11. אל מבחר החבירים . גזע הישרים . מחמד החכמה הפנימית
12. הנאוה השולמית . שׂר צבא י"י . אביר צבאות י"י . אופן השכל
13. במהלכו נהלך . וחיות המדע לפניו תהלך . נהרי דינור מבינתו
14. נמשכת . להט החרב המתהפכת . הוא כג"ק מ"ו משה התרגמן
15. נטע נעמן . לכל מדה טובה מזומן . שולחנו מלא כל טוב דומה לירידת
16. המן . אהוב המלכים . ידיד הנסיכים . מדותיו לטובות נמשכים .
17. נוצר תעודות ואיש חמודות יתמכו בימינו אלהי עולם . וישמר יודע
18. כל [.................... עו]לם [...] יחיד(?) נעקד וחז סולם אנ"ס

Verso

יצל אלי תגר אסכנדרייה יסלם ליד אלאך מוסי א' יהודה מ[...]

Translation

Recto

1. In the name of the merciful and the gracious. I wait for your deliverance, O LORD (Gen. 49.18).
2. I am my beloved's, and my beloved is mine; he pastures his flock among the lilies (Song 6.3).
3. Great peace have those who love thy law; nothing can make (them) stumble (Ps. 119.165).
4. Take delight in the LORD, and he will give you the desires (of your heart) (Ps. 37.4).
5. And thus you shall salute him: Peace be to you, and (peace be to) your house, (and peace be to all that you have) (1 Sam. 25.6).
6. Now the man Moses was very meek, more than all men that (were on the face of the earth) (Num. 12.3).
7. Mark the blameless man, and behold the upright, for there is posterity for the man (of peace) (Ps. 37.37).
8. May the LORD give strength to his people; may the LORD bless (his people with peace) (Ps. 29.11).
9. The humblest slave and great friend
10. David b. Jacob, known as Ibn Shams.
11. For the choicest of friends, the descendant of the righteous, the delight of the inner wisdom,
12. the wonderful *Shulammite* (following Song 6.4; 7.1), the commander of the army of the LORD (Josh. 5.14), the mighty one of the hosts of the LORD (following Isa. 1.24); the wheel of mind

13. is going in his route; the animals of knowledge are walking in front of him; a fiery stream (following Dan. 7.10) is flowing
14. from his comprehension; the fiery ever-turning sword (Gen. 3.24), which is his honourable highness and sanctity, our master and rabbi, Moses the dragoman;
15. plant of pleasantness (following Isa. 17.10), ready to any good virtue; his table is full of all the best, which is similar to the falling
16. of the Manna; beloved by Kings; friend of princes; his good virtues are flowing;
17. the observer of the written law and the oral law (see Isa. 8.16; see also commentary), and the one who is greatly beloved (Dan. 10.11); may the LORD of the universe uphold him in his right hand (following Isa. 41.10), and the one who knows
18. [everything] will save [...............] the world (or: forever) [...] the only (son) (following Gen. 22.2) who was bound (= Isaac), and the one who saw the ladder (= Jacob). Amen, forever.

Verso

(This letter) should arrive to the port of Alexandria, to be given to the hand of the brother Mūsā b. Judah [...]

Commentary

Recto

Lines 2–8:
The biblical blessings allude to some of the good virtues of the addressee, such as love of knowledge (l. 3), humility (l. 6), moderation, and integrity (l. 7).

Line 6:
"Now the man Moses was very meek." An allusion to the name of the addressee.

Line 11:
"The delight of the inner wisdom." A reference to Moses' proficiency in mystical knowledge, probably Kabbalah. The phrase 'the inner wisdom' first appeared in Jewish literature, as far as we know, in 1080 CE, in the book *The Duties of the Heart* by R. Baḥyā ibn Paqudā. Ibn Paqudā used the Arabic term العلم الباطن, which probably came from the Sufi tradition (Ibn Paqudā, *The Duties of the Heart*, p. 468). The term *al-ʿilm al-bāṭin* in Sufism (and also Ismāʿīlīsm) is equivalent to the known term *maʿrifa*, which designates direct, unmediated, experiential knowledge granted by the divine, as opposed to *ʿilm*, which would be knowledge obtained by rational means.[1] R. Baḥyā's book was translated from Judaeo-Arabic into Hebrew in the twelfth century by Judah ibn Tibbon, who chose to render this term with the Hebrew phrase החכמה הפנימית. Apparently, David ibn Shams did not

[1] We want to thank Dr Nathan Hofer for his assistance in this matter.

adopt this term directly from the Sufi literature (interest in Sufism subsided among Rabbanite Jews in this period), but rather from the Kabbalistic vocabulary. In the thirteenth century, this phrase (in Hebrew) was used by Spanish Kabbalah sages, such as R. Moses de Leon and R. Joseph Jiqatilia, and the Italian kabbalist R. Menachem Recanati, as well as in the *Zohar* (חכמתא פנימאה).[2] In this period, the meaning of the term probably became 'the Kabbalah'. R. Simon b. Ṣemaḥ Duran (1361–1444) wrote explicitly: כי החכמה הפנימית, אשר אין בה תרמית, ומעלתה על שאר החכמות גדולה, היא חכמת האמת חכמת הקבלה 'The inner wisdom, which has no false… it is the wisdom of truth, the wisdom of Kabbala' (*Tashbeṣ*, Amsterdam 1738, II, §52). It is quite certain, therefore, that by this term David is here referring to the Kabbalah.

Lines 12–13:

The image of the wheel and animals is following Ezekiel's vision (Ezek. 1). *Nehelakh* in the *nifʿal* is very rare, and is not documented in the Historical Dictionary Project of the Academy of the Hebrew Language until the nineteenth century. The inconsistency in the Hebrew—*ḥayot* being plural while the verb *tihalakh* (for this form, see Exod. 9.23; Ps. 73.9) is in the singular—could be due to the influence of Arabic grammar (we want to thank Prof. Judith Henschke for this suggestion).

---

[2] It is possible that they adopted this term from the Hebrew translation of *The Duties of the Heart*, but there is no clear evidence for this supposition.

Line 16:
"Princes." Probably the Mamlūk emirs, with whom Moses was in close contact. Compare the phrase אדון הנסיכים 'the master of the princes', which is a description of the biblical Moses (C.7/f1/v8). See also the description of the addresses in C.7: הרואים פני המלך בנסיכות 'who princely see the king's face' (C.7/f1/16).

מידותיו לטובות נמשכים. The phrase is not correct grammatically. There is a gender disagreement here—*midotav* is feminine while *nimshakhim* is masculine. The selection of the masculine form was probably influenced by rhyme (*nesikhim–nimshakhim*). More problematic is the word *la-ṭovot*. We translated it according to the assumption that there is a scribal error here and it should be הטובות instead of לטובות. If the *lamed* here is intentional, maybe the writer wanted to write לטובים 'for the good ones', which is a nickname for the Jews (or for the righteous), but wrote incorrectly לטובות, maybe because of the gender switch in the next word. According to this suggestion, the phrase should be translated as 'his (good) virtues are flowing for the good ones'. However, this suggestion is quite speculative.

Line 17:
"The observer of the written law and the oral law." The writer follows Isa. 8.16: "Bind up the testimony, seal the instruction among my disciples" (צוֹר תְּעוּדָה חֲתוֹם תּוֹרָה בְּלִמֻּדָי). צור is from the root צר"ר, not from נצ"ר. The term תעודה was used by the early poets not to mean 'testimony' but rather as a synonym for the Torah. The plural form תעודות refers to the two kinds of Torah—the written one and the oral one. See, for example, Rav Saʿadiah's *viduy*: זנחנו שתי תעודות חיללנו שבתות ומועדות (Bodl. e.54 [2744], 3–

8). For the plural form תעודות with the same meaning, see also letter C.7/v17.

The phrase used here is based on a creative commentary on the biblical phrase, not as 'bind up the testimony', but rather as 'keep the Torah'. This commentary is reflected already in the early *piyyuṭim*; see, for example: תורה לשמר תעודה לנצור (anonymous *piyyuṭ*, Bodl. f.44 [2722], 17–25). The phrase נוצר תעודה/ תעודות appears in the writings of Sephardi sages. The earliest example we have found is from the twelfth century (see Abulafia 1871, 25) and it was also popular among Sephardi sages in the next centuries (see, for example, Al-ashqar, *Responsa* §9).

Line 18:

חז is a poetic form of the verb חזה 'he saw'. "Ladder" (סולם) here is a symbol of the divine presence (following Gen. 28.12). The phrase *ḥaz sulam* appears already in the early *piyyuṭim*, as in a *piyyuṭ* by an anonymous poet from the sixth century (Cambridge, University Library Or. 1080, 3.52) and another by Elʿazar ha-Qalir (Oxford, Bodl. e.37.71–72). Yanai used a similar phrase in one of his *piyyuṭim*: זרע חז עולים וירדים 'the descendants of the one who saw (the angels) who were ascending and descending' (T-S, NS 111.63). The nickname *ḥaz sulam* for Jacob was also in use among later poets, such as an anonymous poet of the eighth century (ENA 2932.1); Saʿadiah Gaon (Sassoon Collection, 216.4–8); Judah b. Benjamin (tenth century; ENA 2859.26–27); Joseph al-Bardānī (tenth century; Budapest, Library of the Hungarian Academy of Sciences, Geniza 50[8]); and more.

"Amen, forever." It seems that the writer here blessed the addressee that he would be blessed by the merit of the three Patriarchs, Abraham (in the unpreserved part of the line), Isaac, and Jacob.

P.3.c: Letter from David ibn Shams to Moses b. Judah

Bodl. MS Heb. c. 72/22

General Description

Concerns family and trade affairs. Hebrew and Judaeo-Arabic.

In this letter, David gives Moses information about his wife and also offers some tips about how to deal with her. The relationship between Moses and his wife was in crisis and Moses wanted to divorce her. It seems that David is trying to induce Moses to think again about this decision ("You should only think good about your wife, all her thinking is about you. You should not listen to any other word [of those hostile towards her] regarding her"). On David as an intermediary element between Moses and his wife, see also letter C.3.

Physical Description

24.5 × 14.2; paper; 1 leaf; 25 lines + marginalia (recto); 7 lines (verso); verso is written inversely in relation to recto; torn, holes, red-brown stains; distinctive wormholes.

 https://doi.org/10.11647/OBP.0352.15

Transcription

Recto

1. בשמ̇א רחמ̇נא וחנ̇נא
2. כי שמש מגן[1] י"י אלהים חן וכבוד וכו'
3. ומצא חן ושכל טוב בעיני אלהים וכו'
4. בורא ניב שפתים שלום וכו'
5. ואמרתם כה לחי ואתה שלום ובית[ך] וכו'
6. י"י עוז לעמו יתן י"י יברך את וכו'
7. <אלממ' דוד א̇ שמס> אלי חצ̇רה אלאך אלעזיז אלמחב אלצדיק אלחביב אללביב אלמולא
8. אלאג̇ל ה"ר משה א' יהודה אבקאה אללה תע' פי כיר ועאפיה
9. ונעמת אן שאפיה אללה תע' יג̇מענא נחן ואיאך̇ פי מסתקר
10. רחמתה א'נ'ס' וינהי אלי עלמה אלכרים באן וצלת משרפת אלמכדו'
11. ופהמת̇ מצ̇מונהא ושכרת אללה תע' עלי צחת מג̇אזכם ואבקאך̇
12. פי כ̇יר ועאפיה אמא מא דכרתה מן ג̇הת ביתך̇ פהי מא הי
13. כארהא פי אלמכדו' חתי אנהא תכ̇תאר קבצ̇ אלגט והי צברת מן
14. יום אן סאפר אלמכדו' מן ענדהא אלי יום תאריכה והי מסתרג̇ייה
15. חצ̇ורך פענד מא קרב וקת חצ̇ורך̇ תג̇פיהא באלכלאם פקד
16. אערף̇ אלמכדו' אנהא אמתתלת מר[צ]ומך̇ ותצבר אלי דלך̇ אלעאם
17. אלדי דכרתה ומהמא כאן ג'רצ̇ך̇ תפעלה בגיר כלאם מוו[ד]י וקד
18. סאלהא אלממ' ען אלזביב פדכרת אן וצל אליהא עלי יד אלולד אסחאק
19. ולד אלח' שמואל סכנדרי [..........] זביב ברימה ובאעת [מנה] פי
20. נביד̇ אלכ̇לף ואלמוג̇ב כמס קנאטיר וצפי להא אתנעשר קנטאר
21. מכ̇לצה ושהדנא עליהא בדלך̇ כמס תמנהם(?) והם מקסמין ענדה[א]
22. פיכון דלך̇ עלי עלמכם אלכרים ולא יכון כאטרך̇ אלי טייב מן גהת̇

---

[1] Should be: ומגן.

23. ביתך וכׄאטרהא כלה אליך ולא תסמע פיהא כלאם אלאעד[א ...]
24. חאמלה אלמצׄ בסבבך חתי לא יתג'ייר כׄאטרך עליהא [... ...]
25. ללמכדו' פי כל וקת בופא אלדין וחצׄארך אליהא סרעה [... ...]

Verso

1. אן יופי דינך ודיננא ודין כל ישראל ויקרב הגואל בחיינו ובחי[כם ובחיי]
2. כלל עמו בית ישראל בעד תגׄדיד תקביל אלארצׄ ואלסלאם עלי גׄמיע
3. אלאצחאב ואלמחבין כל ואחד באסמה ועלי כל מן יחיט בה עלמך אלכר[ים]
4. ושלום

In a different hand

5. חצׄר אלממ' דלך
6. אהרן בר חסדאל
7. הלוי שׂצׄ

Translation

Recto

1. In the name of the merciful and gracious
2. For the LORD God is sun and shield; (the LORD bestows) grace and glory etc. (Ps. 84.12).
3. You will find favour and approbation in the eyes of God etc. (Prov. 3.4).
4. I create the speech of the lips: Peace, Peace etc. (Isa. 57.19).
5. Say as follows: “To life.” Greetings to you and to your household etc. (1 Sam. 25.6).
6. May the LORD grant strength to his people, may the LORD bestow etc. (Ps. 29.11).

7. <The servant David ibn Shams> to the majesty of the great brother, the beloved, the just, the dear, the skilled, the accomplished
8. master Rabbi Moses b. Judah. May God exalted keep you in the best (of states) and health
9. and true well-being. May God exalted unite us, us and you, in a permanent resting place
10. of his mercy. Amen, forever. (The writer) would like to inform the honourable that the letter of the addressee arrived,
11. and I understood its content. I thanked God exalted for the good state of your passage. May he keep you
12. in a good state and wellbeing. Concerning what you mentioned of your wife: she is what she is,
13. spiteful about you until she will choose to receive the divorce document (*geṭ*). She has been patient since
14. the day you travelled away from her until now. She is hoping
15. for your presence, and when the time of your arrival is near, you may treat her harshly with words.
16. You already know that she is obedient to your command. You should have patience until that day
17. I mentioned: Whatever your intention is, do it without any insulting(?) word.
18. I have already asked her about the raisins, and she mentioned that they arrived to her by the hand of the boy Isḥāq,
19. son of the *ḥaver* Samuel Skandarī (the Alexandrian) [...............] mixed-colour raisins. She bought from him
20. red-brown wine. What was needed amounted to five *qinṭārs*, but he decanted 12 *qinṭārs* of pure quality for her.

21. We witnessed for her in this matter a price(?) of five. They are currently divided up at hers.
22. This should be to your honourable knowledge. You should only think good about
23. your wife, all her thinking is about you. You should not listen to any other word [of those hostile towards her] regarding her.
24. [She] is in agony for the reason that you do not change your mind about her [...]
25. to you at all times in dutiful fashion, you should come to her quickly [...]

Verso

1. that he may (let us) fulfil your and our religion and the religion of the whole people of Israel. May he bring close the redeemer in our lifetime and in your [lifetime and the life of]
2. his entire people, the house of Israel. After repeatedly kissing the earth (before the addressee, we are sending you) greetings to all
3. (our) co-religionists and beloved ones, everyone by his name, and to everyone you know.
4. Peace (will be).
5. The sender attended this (= witnesses the validity of this letter).
6. Aaron b. Ḥesedel
7. ha-Levi, may God preserve him.

Commentary

Recto

Line 13:
It seems that Moses had decided to divorce his wife, but she refused to receive the *geṭ*. Although, according to talmudic law, a man can divorce his wife if she is unwilling, from the tenth century (following the rule accepted by R. Gershom), it was a common practice in Ashkenazi Jewish courts to approve divorces only when both sides agreed on it. It is difficult to determine what the halakhic policy concerning this question was in Alexandria in this period.

Verso

Line 6:
Aaron b. Ḥesedʾel is known from a document written in Cairo in 1466 (British Library Or. 4856.2). He lived in Cairo and was one of the leaders in the community. The name Ḥesedʾel is not very common but appears in some documents. It was popular mainly among the Karaites; see, for example, MS St Petersburg, RNL Evr.-Arab. I 4531 (1401 CE?); II 1412 (1433 CE); II 1456 (1776 CE).

P.3.d: Address of a Letter to Moses b. Judah, Written by David ibn Shams

Bodl. MS Heb. c. 72/29

General Description

Only the address line is preserved from this letter. It was written in the handwriting of David ibn Shams and may be a part of one of the other chopped-up letters by David found in our corpus.

Physical Description

4.8 × 7.5; paper; 1 leaf; 6 lines (recto; verso is blank); torn, holes, rubbed, beige stains.

Transcription

יצל אלי תגר אסכנדרייה יסלם ליד אלמ"[1] מוסי א' יהודה י"ל

Translation

(This letter) should arrive to the port of Alexandria to be given into the hand of M. Mūsā b. Judah, may he live forever.

Commentary

"Mūsā b. Judah." The abbreviation אׄ for *ibn* 'son' is not a common one in the Genizah material and does not occur in any of the epistolary material investigated by Wagner (2011).

---

[1] אלמׄ = אלמעלם.

 https://doi.org/10.11647/OBP.0352.16

P.3.e: Letter to Moses b. Judah, Written by David ibn Shams

Bodl. MS Heb. c. 72/32

General Description

Mainly concerned with business affairs. Judaeo-Arabic.

Physical Description

28.2 × 6.5; paper; 1 leaf; 28 lines + marginalia (recto); 22 lines (verso); torn, holes, rubbed, red-brown stains; distinctive worm-hole the same as the one in P.4.b and P.4.c.

Transcription

Recto

1. שיל"ת לק"י מע[אמי"ל][1]
2. אלדי יעלם בה אלאך אלע[זיז כ"ר משה בן]
3. י[הוד]ה אבקאה אללה [תע' פי כיר ועאפיה]
4. אנ"ס וינהי אלי עלמה [אלכרים ...]
5. אלשׁ יוסף באלכרקה ואל[...]
6. לזבונךּ אלזהר ופא ו[...]
7. פוג̇דת רשע מא ק[אל ...]
8. אלנאקע פארסל עין [...]
9. תמאן אשרפייה אלקנט[אר ...]
10. 1/3 236 ועדתהם 39 ל[...]
11. סת אשרפייה פוגדנא [...]

---

[1] = שויתי י"י לנגדי תמיד; לישועתך קויתי י"י; מגני על אלהים מושיע ישרי לב.

 https://doi.org/10.11647/OBP.0352.17

12. כתיר פחצל ביני ובינ[...]
13. יוסף ~~ובחצ̇רה~~ ובחצ̇ר[ת̈ ...]
14. אלמג'רבי אלדי באע אל[...]
15. וקלת לה אעטיתה כל [...]
16. אשרפי טלע קלנג בא[...]
17. פטאיבוה אלדי כאנו ח[...]
18. אשרפי באלף עלאג̇ פק[...]
19. אנה וכיל וינזלו פי צ̇א[...]
20. בה פמא וג̇ד יוסף ביד[ה ...]
21. ידכ̇ל בנפסה פי האדה [...]
22. ירסל ליוסף וכאלה באלגוי[...]
23. אלש[ה]ו[ר ...] עפיף באל [...]
24. באלע[ש]רין אשרפי ותנ[...]
25. ולא תג̇עלה וכיל מטל[...]
26. עליה חתי יסתג'לק כל [...]
27. כאן תאיה פא[...]
28. אלאצל [ת]מאנין ומנזל [...]

Margin

1. ומתאכר פיהא 32 אשרפי תם צ̇הר אלמצטור בעד דלך̇ וגדנא פיה מתאכ̇'ר 45 אשרפי פקצדו ילג'ו אלדי הו ינזל לך̇
2. מנזל פי אלמסודה ונחן מא נעלם באטן אלאמר כיף הו פאלמכדו' ירסל וכאלה באסם יוסף או באסם מרדוך

Verso

1. אלעשרין פא[נה]ם אכדהם [...]
2. אלתנזיל ואלמכדו' לא תרסל [...]
3. פאנני מא אלתזק לה ולו פי [...]

4. מנّי נהאר מן אישם אלנהא[ר ...]
5. תכלץ הא[ד]ה אליהודי בכיר [...]
6. אברא[... ...] אלאמיר [...]
7. דלך̇ עלי עלם אלמכדו' ת[...]
8. אלכחל אלוטי פי אלקאהרה [...]
9. ואלטייב יסוא 750 ואלזביב [...]
10. ואחסאנך̇ תפעל גהד מקד[ור ...]
11. בעוץ̇ אלצמג' ועוץ̇ אלכרקה [...]
12. אלטריק פאן אלצ̇רורה דאעיה [...]
13. אכלאל עלי צדקאתך̇ ופצ̇לך [...]
14. מא תכצר ורצאנא שיי ויע[...]
15. מכאפאת אלמכדו' תם בעד [דאלך̇ ...]
16. אולאד אלאעזא ועלי כל מן [יחיט בה עלמך אלכרים]
17. ושלום
18. צטר יום אלתלאתה מ"ז [לעומר(?) ... תזכו]
19. לשנים רבות נעימות וטו[בות ...]
20. פנערף אלמכדו' באן יוסף חלף א[נה ...]
21. פאלמכדו' יוכל אחדא גירה מן [...]
22. ולעל פצ̇לך̇ תעלם אלמ̇ נגיב באנ[ה ...]
23. ענדה בתאע יעקוב א' אלנג[יד ...]

Translation

Recto

1. I am ever mindful of the LORD's presence (Ps. 16.8). I wait for your deliverance, O LORD (Gen. 49.18). My shield is with [God, who saves the upright in heart] (Ps. 7.11).
2. (This letter) which informs the [magnificent] brother [the honourable rabbi Moses ben]

3. J[uda]h, may God keep you [in the best (of states) and health].
4. Amen, forever. It should reach his [honourable] knowledge [...]
5. Sheikh Joseph with a cloth [...]
6. for your partner al-Zuhr's death [...]
7. I found wickedness. He did not [say ...]
8. tearing clothes. He sent [...]
9. eight *ashrafī* dinars per *qinṭār* [...]
10. 236 and 1/3. Their number is 39 [...]
11. six *ashrafī* dinars. We found [...]
12. many. Between me and [...] happened [...]
13. Joseph. In the presence of [...]
14. the Maghrebian who bought the [...]
15. I told him: "I gave him all [...]
16. *ashrafī* dinars. Qulnaj went up with [...]
17. They were pleasant with him, who had been [...]
18. *ashrafī* dinars, for a thousand doses of medication. [...]
19. he is the agent. They will settle in [...]
20. with him. Joseph did not find in his hand [...]
21. he will enter himself in this [...]
22. he should send to Joseph a power of attorney with a Muslim [...]
23. [months ...] ʿAfīf with the [...]
24. for twenty *ashrafī* dinars [and two(?)...]
25. You should not make him agent [...]
26. to him until he makes the whole sale final [...]
27. it was ... [...]
28. the real estate eighty, and an apartment [...]

Margin

1. delayed (payment) of it, 32 *ashrafī* dinars. Then the document emerged. After that we found in it a delayed payment of 45 *ashrafī* dinars. They wanted to talk about the one who lives for you
2. in the apartment (that appeared) in the register (or: record). We do not know the inner (meaning) of the matter, how it is. The master should send a power of attorney in the name of Joseph or in the name of Mardūḵ.

Verso

1. The twenty. He took them(?) [...]
2. send down. (O) master, do not send [...]
3. I am not stuck to him! If in [...]
4. from me a day of any day [...]
5. the release of this Jew in good (condition) [...]
6. [...] the emir [...]
7. this to the knowledge of the master [...]
8. low (quality) *kuḥl* (=kohl) in Cairo [...]
9. good quality comes to 750, and raisins [...]
10. by your generosity, do your utmost possible [...]
11. instead of the gum, and instead of the cloth [...]
12. (on) the way. If the necessity requires it, [...]
13. exhausting your generosity and grace [...]
14. You should not suffer harm. Our satisfaction (will be achieved by) anything [...]
15. the worries of the master. Then after [that ...]
16. the beloved children and to everyone [you know]

17. Peace (will be).
18. Written on Tuesday, 47 [of the counting of *ʿOmer*(?) … may you have]
19. many pleasant and [good] years […]
20. We inform the master that Joseph swore [that he …]
21. The master should appoint an agent other than him of […]
22. Perhaps by your grace could you inform M. Najīb that […]
23. with him belonging to Yaʿqūb son of the [Nagid …]

Commentary

Recto

Line 3:
אבקאה אללה [תע' פי כיר ועאפיה]. For this completion, compare letters P.3.c/8, 11; P.3.g/3.

Line 4:
וינהי אלי עלמה [אלכרים]. For this completion, compare letters P.3.c /10; P.3.f/v2.

Margin

Line 2:
"Mardūk̲." This is probably Mardūk̲ Qarqūsa, the presumed writer of letter P.8.

Verso

Lines 18–19:
The letter was written on Tuesday, but the precise date was not preserved, due to the condition of the fragment. The word מ"ז

(47) seemingly refers to 47 of the counting of *ʿOmer* (compare P.1, line 23), that is to say, three days before the festival of *Shavuʿot*. The blessing תזכו לשנים רבות וטו[בות] is typical of the days of the Tishrei festivals, around Rosh ha-Shanah, but it was in use also before other festivals such as *Shavuʿot*; see, for example, TS 13J14.1. (We thank Dr Liran Yadgar for this reference.)

Line 23:
"Yaʿqūb son of the Nagid." Concerning his identity, see commentary on letter C.5/m2. However, the reading of the word is not certain. We can read only אלנג clearly. The letter after the *gimel* seems like *yod*, and the completion אלנג[יד] is inferred. It could alternatively be completed as אלנג'[יב] 'the noble, the generous'. Maybe he is the one mentioned in the previous line. Al-najīb was a common honorific title in Judaeo-Arabic. Compare P.6/19, "to the honourable Joshua known as Najīb."

P.3.f: Letter from David ibn Shams to Moses b. Judah

Bodl. MS Heb. c. 72/39

General Description

Concerning trade matters and books which Moses wanted to purchase. Judaeo-Arabic.

Physical Description

20.5 × 14.3; paper; 1 leaf; 21 lines (recto); 23 lines + marginalia (verso); verso is written inversely in relation to recto; torn, holes, rubbed, red-brown stains; distinctive wormhole.

Transcription

Recto

1. [... ...] בה הו מש[... אבקאה] אללה תע' [פי כיר ועאפיה ונעמת]
2. אן שאפיה אנ"ס וינהי אלי עלמה אלכרים באן אכ̇ר [... ...]
3. ארסלתה לך צחבת אלקאצד אלדי מן ענד אלפרנג̇ ולם וצל לנ[א]
4. ג̇ואב מן ענד אלמכדו' לא מן ג̇הה̈ אלעדים אלדין יעיש ולא מן גהת
5. שריכה מנצור ואלחדר תם אלחדר אן תוצלו יעיש דרהם פלוס מן
6. ג̇הה̈ תספירה אלמאצ̇י פאנה אכ̇ד מני ארבע אשרפיה ועשרין
7. נצף̇ ורבע פיכון דלך̇ עלי עלמך̇ ותעלם אלמ' סלימאן כראת
8. בדלך̇ תם אערף̇ אלמכדו' עלי אן אלממ' למן חאסבת אלדכירה ואכ̇דו
9. מני אלמבלג' אלמתעלק במביע אלממ' ובמביע זין אלדין א' מג̇וד
10. פקבץ̇ אלצירפי מני [illegible Coptic number] אסקט מנהם 426 מן ג̇הה̈

 https://doi.org/10.11647/OBP.0352.18

11. סידי זין אלדין ומן גֹהֹה אלממ' [illegible Coptic number] אשרפי ושהדו שהוד
12. אלדכירה בדלך ואשהדו עלייה בחצׄור אלכואגֹה ובחצׄור סידי
13. צלאח אלדין אלדיבי באן אל 426 אשרפי מן מאל זין אלדין דון מאלי
14. ושהדת להם באלואקעה עלי אנהם יכׄצמו בדלך פי מצטור
15. זין אלדין תם אן אלממ' למא וצל אלי אלקאהרה חאסבת זין אלדין
16. וולדה עלי' האדה אלחסאב ואכׄצמת פי חסאבהם באלארבעמאיה
17. סתה ועשרין אשרפי באסם אלדכׄירה פלמא [וצלת] אלמצאטיר
18. בתאע אלדכירה פמא אכׄדו מן אלמצאטיר שי אלא בעד מות
19. זין אלדין פוגֹדת אלמצטור בתאע זין אלדין מכׄצוץ [...] 360
20. אשרפי ותאכד מן אלחסאב 65 אשרפי אלדי צׄהר ללמלוך
21. אן אל 65 אשרפי אכׄצמו בהא מן אלפרט כׄארגֹ ען אלדי פי
22. אלמצטור פעד פיצאל אלממ' מנהם בעד מות זין אלדין טאלבך
23. אלממ' [... ... ...]

Margin

1. פאקצד פצׄל אלמכדו' ואחסאנה אן תערף סידי צלאח אלדין בדלך ותאכׄד לי מנה כתאב ללצבי או לסידי צל[אח אלדין]
2. במא עליהם ללדכירה ובמא קבצׄוה מני ואן כאן תאכׄד עליהם שי בעד דלך ארסל אעלמני ותערף אלכוא[גה ...]

Verso

0. [... ... ...]
1. אללה עבדה וסידי אחמד א' אלצפי ותוקפהם עלי אלכואגֹה ועלי סידי
2. צלאח אלדין ואן אכׄתארו יכשפו מן חסאב אלדכירה מן קדאם
3. אלשהוד כׄאן אחסן פלעל פצׄלך ואחסאנך וצדקאתך לא תדע
4. האדה אלכתאב מן ידך חתי' תנהי לי האדה אלשגל ותאכד לי [כׄ]טהם
5. ותרסלו לי מן כלבד וסבב פאנני כנת ראיח אשתכי אלצבי ללמלך

6. ולא תסתג̇נא במקאבלת̇ אלעבד כ̇יר אללה וסידי אחמד אלא' כ̇ט יד סידי
7. צלאח אלדין או כ̇ט אלכ̇ואג̇ה לצלאח אלדין [עמי] ואנא אערף אן מא עמלו
8. דלך̇ אלא מן ג̇הה̈ אלפרט אלדי תאכ̇ר להם פי אלמביע בראני פקצדו
9. אן יעומו עלי אלפרט יאכ̇דוה אללה אללה פי אלג̇ואב סרעה צחבת מן
10. יחצ̇ר סרעה ואמא קצ̇ייה̈ אלאנכ̇אך̇ פאשתרית לך̇ 25 נך̇ ועקיב
11. דלך̇ יחצ̇רו לך̇ פי אול מרכב אן תדכ̇ל אלכ̇ליג̇ ואמא תג̇ריד אלחקאיק
12. פנערף אלמכדו' אנני אכ̇דת לך̇ אלג̇זא אלאול פי ורק דיואני כאן
13. אסתנסכני פיה שכ̇ץ מן זמאן ולם כ́מל בקא פיה בעץ̇ שי פאלממ'
14. ביטייבה פיאכ̇דו מנה ואכמלו לך̇ בכ̇טי יתאכ̇ר פיה יג̇י רבעה ואמא
15. אלג̇זא אלת̇אני ענדי בכ̇ט רבי עמרם אן אכ̇תרת ארסלתה לך̇ ואלמכדו'
16. כאן רא״ה ענדי פיכון ג̇מיע דלך̇ עלי עלם אלמכדו' ואלקצד מן פצ̇לך̇
17. סרעה̈ אלג̇ואב מן ג'יר תאכ̇יר ואקצד פצ̇לך̇ תנהי לי אמר אלכאפור
18. ואלזנג̇ביל אלמרבה כד לי פיהם איש מא אכ̇תרת ג̇וך̇ או ג'ירה ולא
19. תאכ̇רהם ואלמכדו' מא יעג̇ז ען האדה אלאמר אלפשרי ואן כאן אנטון
20. יאכדהם אעטיהם לה וכד לי בהם ורק או גוך מנה תם בעד סלאם ושלום

Translation

Recto

1. [… … … may] God exalted [keep them in comfort, wellbeing, and health]
2. healing […]. Amen, forever. (The writer) would like to bring to his honourable knowledge that on the last […]
3. I sent it to you with the messenger who belongs with the Europeans, but we did not receive
4. a reply from the master, neither (with information) concerning the pious pauper Yaʿīsh, nor concerning
5. his partner Manṣūr. Warning, warning! If you send Yaʿīsh a dirham of money on behalf of

6. his consignment, he (already) took from me four *ashrafī* dinars and twenty
7. half-dinars and a quarter. You should know this! You should inform M. Sulaymān Karāt
8. about this (too). I also inform the master that when the servant settled the accounts of the provisions,[1] they took
9. from me the corresponding sum of money from the sale of the servant and the sale of Zayn al-Dīn b. Majūd.
10. The banker received from me [illegible Coptic number]. Subtract from it 426 on behalf of
11. my lord Zayn al-Dīn and on behalf of the servant [illegible Coptic number] *ashrafī* dinars. The witnesses witnessed
12. the provisions regarding this. They witnessed about it in the presence of the Doctor and in the presence of my lord
13. Ṣalāḥ al-Dīn al-Ḏiʾbī that the 426 *ashrafī* dinars are from the property of Zayn al-Dīn without my property.
14. I witnessed to them concerning what had happened so that they would subtract according to that in the document
15. for Zayn al-Dīn. Then, after the servant arrived in Cairo, I settled the accounts with Zayn al-Dīn and
16. his son regarding that account, and I subtracted in their account 426
17. *ashrafī* dinars in the name of the provisions. When the documents
18. belonging to the provisions [arrived], they did not take any of the documents, until after the death

---

[1] See Wahrmund (1898, 704).

19. of Zayn al-Dīn, when I found the document concerning Zayn al-Dīn, (which was) particularly dealing with [...] 360
20. *ashrafī* dinars. You should take from the account 65 *ashrafī* dinars. It became evident for the servant
21. that the 65 *ashrafī* dinars which they subtracted regarding it from the interest exceeds those (mentioned) in
22. the document. ... ... the servant of them after the death of Zayn al-Dīn, the servant claimed from you
23. [... ... ...]

Margin

1. I present to the grace of the master and his good deeds that you should inform my master Ṣalāḥ al-Dīn of this. You should take for me from him a letter to the boy or to my master Ṣal[āḥ al-Dīn]
2. regarding the provisions and of what they received from me. If you take anything on their behalf after that, then send to inform me and you should (also) inform the Doctor [...]

Verso

0. [... ... ...]
1. may God [protect] his servant and my master, Aḥmad b. al-Ṣafī. You should acquaint them with the Doctor and my master
2. Ṣalāḥ al-Dīn. If they prefer to reveal the accounts of the provisions before
3. witnesses, that would be best. Perhaps, by your grace, your beneficence and your charity, do not put

4. this letter down from your hand until you have informed me about this business. You should take for me their signature
5. and send it to me in any case. The reason (for that) is that I was going to lodge a complaint against the boy about the property,
6. and you should only collect in the presence of the servant Ḵayrullah and my master Aḥmad the signature of my master
7. Ṣalāḥ ad-Dīn or the signature of the Doctor for Ṣalāḥ al-Dīn, my paternal uncle. I know that they only did
8. this for the interest, which defaulted for them in the sale. … They intended
9. to include all in the interest. They should receive it quickly in the reply letter, immediately, in a *ṣuḥba*-transaction of anyone
10. present, quickly! Concerning the matter of carpets, I bought for you 25 carpets, and following
11. this, they should come for you on the first ship that goes up the delta. Concerning the *Tajrīd al-Ḥaqā'iq* ('The Abstract of Speculative Truths'),
12. I inform the master that I obtained for you the first part on *dīwān*-quality paper, which
13. someone had copied for me a while ago. It was not completed; some things had remained (uncopied). The servant
14. is currently having it amended. They should take it from him and complete it for you on my order. If it is delayed, it will go out in its (present) state. As for
15. the second part, I own one (written) in the hand of Rabbi ʿAmram. If you prefer, I shall send it to you. The master's

16. opinion guides me. All this should be known to my master. If you please
17. (could send) a short reply quickly without delay. Please inform me about the matter of the camphor
18. and ginger jam. Take for me of those anything that you see fit, (also) cloth or anything else. And do not
19. delay them. The master is not idle on account of this … matter. If Anton is there,
20. he should take them, give them to him. Take for me from their (profit) paper or cloth from him. Greetings. Peace (will be).

Commentary

Recto

Line 1:
"The Europeans." This designates European Christian traders.

Line 7:
"M. Sulaymān Karāt." See commentary on letter C.5/16.

Verso

Line 7:
"Ṣalāḥ al-Dīn, my paternal uncle." Names that include the component *Dīn* were traditionally only given to Muslims. It is possible that Ṣalāḥ al-Dīn, the writer's relative, was a converted Jew.

Line 9:
"*Ṣuḥba*-transaction." On these kinds of transactions, see, for example, Cohen (2017, 70–104).

Line 11:

"Concerning the *Tajrīd al-Ḥaqāʾiq* ('The Abstract of Speculative Truths')." On this work, written by David ha-Nagid II, see the detailed discussion in the Introduction, §2.5.

Line 19:

"Anton." Probably a Christian trader.

P.3.g: Letter from David ibn Shams to Moses b. Judah

Bodl. MS Heb. c. 72/42

General Description

A letter concerned with business matters regarding foodstuffs. Judaeo-Arabic.

Physical Description

21.1 × 9.9; paper; 1 leaf; 21 lines + marginalia (recto); jottings (verso); torn, holes, red-brown stains; the fragment is vertically torn in the middle, with the wormholes mirroring each other, suggesting it was bound or kept in folded form.

Transcription

Recto

1. לק"י
2. אלי חצ̇רה̈ אל[אך אלא]ג̇ל אלסייד אלכאמל
3. הד' ר' משה [אבקא]ה אללה תע̇ פי כיר
4. ועאפיה ו[נעמת אן] שאפיה א'נ'ס' ואלדי
5. אערפך בה [לא אער]פך אללה מכרוה באן
6. נחן משתאק[ין פ]אלמכ' כתיר אללה לא
7. יכלי מנכם [...] מכאנכם אללה יפרחך
8. באלאולאד אל[...]תל מא תחב ותשתהי
9. ואן מן יום אן [ספ]ר אלמכ' לם וצל לנא
10. מן ענדכם [שי] ואני ג̇מעת אלאשתיואן
11. וחזמתה וק[ד ...] גא וזנה ת'כ' רטל

 https://doi.org/10.11647/OBP.0352.19

12. וארסלתה לל[מע'] אבראהים שויך עלי יד
13. ר' צדקה ניס י'ל' [...] בלגני אן וצל ענדכם
14. זביב פאלמכ' [יג]י לי מנה ותאכד מן
15. אבי חקה ואן מא מעה שי פאלמכ'
16. יאכד לי מן י[דה] ותרסל תעלמני אל
17. תמן נרסל ל[ך] תרסל אלזביב סרעה
18. ולא ארסל ל[אל] מכ' ג̇ואב מן ג̇הה אבי
19. ואן אלמכ' יעלם אן אלממ' מא הו כארה
20. [... ...] אל[א ... ...] אלואלדה לא תסאל פי אל
21. [... ... ...]א אבי וא[...]

Margin

1. ואני אעטית פצׄלהׄ אלגוד ללמ' מוסי אבו שערה ואן אלח' פרג̇ אללה אבאד[.] שר חבי א[...]
2. וקאל לי עלי אן אלמכ' קאל לו בט'ו' מאי' אלדראע פהו אלא אלאן לא ג̇אב אלכתאב אלדי קאל אל[...]
3. בעד אלסלאם אלתאם עלי אלמכ' ועלי אל[...] אלח' יוסף ועלי אלאולאד אלאעזא ועלי אהל אל[...]

Translation

Recto

1. I wait for your deliverance, O LORD (Gen. 49.18).
2. To the majesty, the splendid [brother], the accomplished master,
3. the majesty Rabbi Moses. May God exalted keep you in the best (of states)
4. and health and [true] well-being. Amen, forever. (This letter, in) which

5. I inform you, may God [protect] you from all that is hateful, that
6. we long for you very much. May God
7. not forsake you [...] (in) your place, and may God gladden you
8. with [...] children such as you want and desire.
9. Since the day when you [left], no[thing] has arrived to us
10. from you. I collected the Black Spleenwort
11. and put it into bundles. [...] Its weight exceeded 420 *raṭl.*
12. I sent it to [the *muʿallim*] Ibrahim Shuwayḵ by the hand of
13. R. Ṣedaqah Nis, may he live forever. [It] reached me that raisins arrived at yours,
14. the master [should send] me some of them—take a box from
15. my brother. If he does not have any, then you
16. should take (it) for me from his [own] (supply). You should send to inform me of the
17. price, we will send (it) to you. You should send the raisins quickly.
18. You have not sent [the] master an answer (yet) concerning my father,
19. although the master knows that the servant only hates
20. [... ... ...] the mother. Do not ask about
21. [... ... ...] my brother [...]

Margin

1. I gave the surplus of the cloth for M. Mūsā Abū Sha'ra. The *ḥaver* Faraj Allah … … […]
2. He said to me that you had told him that is at fifteen hundred *mu'ayyadī* per *ḏirā*'(?). He has not yet brought the book (or: the letter), which he said […]
3. After complete greetings to the master, to the […] the *ḥaver* Joseph, to the beloved children, and to the wife of […]

Commentary

Recto

Line 10:
אלאישתואן. The meaning of this term is unclear. The term appears also in letter P.1/13, 17. Here and there it is connected with Ibrahim Shuwayḵ, and it seems that the two letters deal with the same transaction.

Line 12:
"Ibrahim Shuwayḵ." He is mentioned also in letter P. 1/16–17.

Margin

Line 1:
"Mūsā Abū Sha'ra." He is mentioned in a letter written by Ṣedaqah Nis to the Nagid Nathan Sholal (TS 10J24.3 + CUL Or. 1080J174; published by David 1999, 303–7); in two payments lists from the fifteenth century (TS J 1.34; ENA 2148.3); and also in few *waqf* documents (CCA 51, 61, 62), from the years 893 H

(1488 CE), 899 H (1493/4 CE), and 914 H (1508/9 CE). These documents are not accessible today, but we have an Arabic register of them made by Israel b. Zeʾev in the 1930s. We can learn from the *waqf* documents that Abū Shaʿra was a wealthy and respected person in the Cairo community. He bequeathed to the community some pieces of land near the old synagogue in Cairo. In one of these documents (CCA 61), he is mentioned, if we rely on Bez-Ze'ev's transcription, as موسى بن ابراهيم بن سليمان الفرنجي الترجمان المعروف بابي شعرة (*Mūsā bin Ibrāhīm bin Sulaymān al-faranjī al-tarjumān, al-maʿrūf bi-Abī Shaʿra* 'Moses b. Abraham b. Solomon the *faranjī* [= West-European], the dragoman, who is known as Abī Shaʿra').[1] It therefore seems that, like Moses b. Judah, Moses Abū Shaʿra was a dragoman who offered his services to European traders in Egypt. His European background (probably Spanish or Italian) would have given him the ability to translate from Arabic to Romance languages. However, other sources state that Abū Shaʿra was a descendant of a Maghribian family, which had arrived in Egypt from Tunisia (see Berav, *Responsa*, §§56–57; see also Hacker 2000, 583 n. 55). It is possible, however, that it was a Sephardi family, who immigrated to the Maghreb after the riots of 1391 CE in Spain, and later settled in Egypt.

The family of Abū Shaʿra was known in Egypt in the sixteenth and seventeenth centuries. A deed of sale written in Adar 1519 documented a purchase of a property in Cairo 'known as the house of Abū Shaʿra' (הידוע בבית אבו שערא, EVR II A 1256). One of the synagogues in Cairo was called Kanīs Abū Shaʿra,

[1] His profession as dragoman is mentioned also in CCA 62.

which indicates that it was established by a member of this family (TS AS 146.230, a list written in 1672). One of the known scholars in Egypt in the seventeenth century was R. Jacob Abū Shaʿra (Conforti, *Qore ha-Dorot*, 50a; Ben-Simeon 1908, 19a; Shtober 1994, 419).[2] Other family members appear in documents from the fifteenth to seventeenth centuries. For example, a certain Judah Abū Shaʿra is mentioned in a record from 1588 in the accounts notebook of the Mustaʿrib community of Cairo (ENA NS 1.57); Aaron Abū Shaʿra is mentioned in a list of names from that period (BL Or. 10,599/27); a certain Abū Shaʿra signed a deed (TS NS 32.81) that was written between 1440 and 1540; and another appears in a payments list from this period (TS AS 145.45).

[2] Ben-Simeon (1908, 19a) attributed the synagogue of Abū Shaʿra to Rabbi Jacob: ועד היום יש במצרים בית הכנסת הנקראת על שם הרב כמוהר"ר יעקב אבושערה ז"ל 'and till nowadays there is a synagogue in Cairo, which is called after the rabbi Jacob Abū Shaʿra, of blessed memory', but this tradition is not certain and needs further research.

P.4.a: Letter from Ṣedaqah Nis to Moses b. Judah

Bodl. MS Heb. c. 72/11

General Description

Letter mainly concerned with business issues. Hebrew.

Physical Description

20.1 × 10.8; paper; 1 leaf; 31 lines (recto); 2 lines (verso); verso is written inversely in relation to recto; holes, red-brown stains.

Transcription

Recto

1. בס"ד
2. שלומות אלף על מעט קלף לשר האלף האדון הנעלה מה"ר משה יצ"ו
3. אחרי דרישת שלום תורת האדון באתי להודיעך אופן בריאותי שהוא
4. על נכון ~~בעש~~ הודאה לאל ית' ועוד הגיעני כתב גלילות אצבעותיך היקר
5. מפז והודעתני סבת מיעוט כתביך וכתבי והוא שקרות המגיד ומכל
6. ענין אין חדש להשיב למעלתך רק מזכרת אהבה וכבר הודעתיך שהשני
7. ספרים מצויים ואין הדבר מתעכב רק מצד המעתיקי' שאינם כראי
8. חזקי' ובאורך מעט יגיעך חפצך בע"ה והניירות הגיעו עם עמירא
9. וחפצך אשלים בקניית הבסבאסה עם שהיא נעדרת עתה שלא הגיע
10. ממנה דבר עדין וכשאקנה שלי אעשה חשבון בעבורך וכן תדרוש
11. שלומי למסי"ר לוי"ז ביזר"ו ויראה לי שלא יגיעהו דבר בכליג ועכ"פ
12. בזמן המוכרח שהוא הקטאיע יקבל שלו משלם כרצונו וכן דמינגו
13. ומענין הספרי' שנדר לך כבו' מעלת אדוננו יצ"ו הם ספרי מנחם יצ"ו
14. וכבר עשאני מורשה עליהם והם ברשותי בע"ה נתראה פנים ונכתוב
15. לפני כל שאתה צריך ויגיעך כשאלך כי כן המצוה איש את רעהו

 https://doi.org/10.11647/OBP.0352.20

16. יעזורו ואמנם הב' תרגומים אין בספרי מנחם והשם יזמנם ממקו'
17. אחר הבסמים בסכומם עומדים ורובם ביד גדולי הארץ וגם מאספי'
18. המועט שביד אחרי' והנייר הוזל במצרים מידי ומיד אחרי' אבל
19. ברוך הש' אין הפסד ומעניין העלייה מצד הדיר"א של מרדוך כבר רוצים
20. האנשי' שעמם לצאת וגם הוא לפעמי' אומר לצאת איך שיהיה אם ישאר
21. לא ישאר כי אם הוא לבדו כרצונכם ומענין המכירה השתדלתי בכל
22. עוז ולא מצאתי כי רבים כמו כן בקשו קונים ולא מצאו ואולי יזמן השם
23. כי חן נפשי ב'כל תאותי להשלים רצונכם בכל ענין ודבר כראוי לי מחק
24. האהבה וחק הגמול והצוף וה[..] עם נאמן ראשון שיגיע יגיעוך
25. והבראד שציוית לאבו אלכיר עליהם יגיעוך בע"ה כי אני הולך אליו
26. יום ב' ומה שאמצא מהנשאדר אביא אע"פ שנתייקר סכומו
27. במצרים הרבה ואיני יודע אם יזדמן לי בשוה(?) קודם ר"ה או אחר
28. המועדים והש' יזמן הטוב ואין כל חדש להאריך כי אם בשלום מעלתך
29. ובניך ונות ביתך מב"ת וכל הנלוים אליך וסרים אל משמעתך
30. יום ששי בהכנסת כלה
31. צדק[ה] ניס

Verso

0. [...]
1. ש[ח]שבון(?) זה מבן מהד[.] ושלחו פא[1]
2. מפי חסן יצ"ו דורש שלומך הרבה ושלום לך

[1] Maybe: פ"א (= פעם אחת)

Translation

Recto

1. With God's help.
2. Thousands of greetings on a little (piece of) vellum, to the leader of a thousand (people), the honourable lord, our teacher Rabbi Moses, may God save him.
3. After inquiring about the wellbeing of the master's *Torah*, I come to inform you of the state of my health, which is
4. well, thanks to God, shall he be blessed. Also, I got a letter from your fingers, which is more dear
5. than gold, and you informed me of the reason for the small number of your letters and my letters, which is the lying of the informer. There is nothing
6. new in all the matters to reply to your honour, just the mentioning (maybe: memento) of love. I have already informed you that the two
7. books are available. The matter is only delayed because of the copiers, who are not strong as a molten
8. mirror (following Job 38.17). You will get what you want in a short time with God's help. The papers arrived with ʿUmayra.
9. I will fulfil your wish by buying the mace, although it is missing now—nothing
10. of it has arrived yet. When I will buy mine, I will do the accounts for you. Also, deliver greetings
11. to Monsieur Louis Bizro. I think he would not get anything via the *Ḵalīj*, but nevertheless

12. in the obliged time, which is (the time of) the partnership dissolution, he will get his part completely, according to his will. The same is true for Domingo.
13. Concerning the books that our honourable lord (= the Nagid) vowed (to give) you, they are Menachem's books, may God save him.
14. He already appointed me as a proxy for them, and I have them. With God's help we will see each other (2 Kgs 14.8) and write
15. to me whatever you need, and you will get as you wish, since this is the commandment: "Each one would help
16. his fellow" (Isa. 41.6). Indeed, the books of Menachem are not including the two translations. The Name will provide them from another
17. source. The perfumes stay on their price, and the majority of them are in the hands of the rich men. They also collect
18. the little which others hold. The paper, of mine and of others, became cheaper in Cairo, but
19. thanks to God there is no loss. About the attic beside Mardūḵ's flat,
20. the people who are (living there) with them already want to leave, and he also sometimes thinks of leaving. Anyway, if he stays,
21. he will stay alone, as you wish. About the sale, I made an effort with all
22. my strength, but I did not find (a buyer), as many looked for buyers and did not find (any). Maybe the Name will provide (one),

23. I swear,[2] my desire is only to fulfil your wish in any matter and any issue, as is appropriate to me according to the decree
24. of love and the decree of reward (maybe: gratefulness). (About) the wool and the […]—It will arrive to you with the first trustee who will come.
25. The kettle you commanded Abū l-Ḵayr (to buy) for them will arrive to you with God's help, because I am going to him
26. on Monday. I shall bring any ammoniac I will find, even though its price has risen
27. very much in Cairo and I do not know if I will find an equal(?) (price) before Rosh ha-Shanah, or after
28. the holidays. The Name will provide the good. There is nothing new (to report) for extending (this letter), only with the peace of your honour
29. and your sons, and your wife, above all women in the tent shall she be blessed (Judg. 5.24), and all those who accompany you, and who are under your authority.
30. Friday, at the wedding of the bride (i.e., on Friday afternoon).
31. Ṣedaqah Nis

Verso

0. […]
1. that this account from the son(?) of […], and he sent it once(?).
2. (This information arrived) from Ḥassan, may God save him, who is inquiring a lot about your wellbeing. Peace be upon you.

---

[2] The translation here is based on the assumption that this is a scribal error, and it should be *ki ḥey nafshi.*

Commentary

Recto

Line 2:
"The leader of a thousand." A biblical term for a leader who is responsible for 1,000 people and serves as their judge (Exod. 18.21–26), or a military commander who commands 1,000 soldiers (for example, Num. 38.48; 1 Sam. 17.18; 18.13; 1 Chron. 13.1).

Line 9:
"Mace" (بسباسة, *myristica moschata*). See Kazimirski (1860, 124); Goitein (1967, 438 n. 20).

Line 10:
"When I will buy mine, I will do the accounts for you." In addition to carrying out Moses' business as an agent, Ṣedaqah had his own mercantile enterprise. He promises his patron here that he will do accounts of how much of the goods he bought belongs to him and how much to his patron.

Line 13:
"The books that our honourable lord vowed (to give) you." Given the "two translations" of these that are mentioned (l. 16), they were probably books from the Bible. The description here may refer to Nathan Sholal, the Nagid. Nathan felt grateful for Moses' generosity, as we see in one of his letters (P.2), in which Nathan mentions Moses' grace and adds: "We do not have the ability to reward you well, it is the Name who will reward you all the best." Maybe Nathan decided to give two books from his big library as a gift to Moses, in order to express his gratitude.

Line 19:
"About the attic beside Mardūḵ's flat." This is probably a house in Cairo belonging to Moses, which was rented to residents, under the supervision of Ṣedaqah.

Mardūḵ was one of Moses' associates and he is mentioned also in letters P.5.a and P.3.e. He can probably be identified as Mardūḵ Qarqūsa (see letters C.4 and P.8). The name Mardūḵ is not common but appears in some documents from the fifteenth to sixteenth centuries (such as BL Or. 5566 B22; TS J 1.34; TS NS 32.81; and more).

Line 21:
"About the sale." This probably refers to the attic mentioned before. Moses may have asked Ṣedaqah in a previous letter to try to sell his real estate, but Ṣedaqah did not succeed in finding any buyers.

Line 25:
"Abū l-Ḵayr." A very common name in Jewish Egypt in the Classical Genizah period (e.g., Gil 1997 IV:824) as well as in the late Mamlūk period.

Line 30:
"At the wedding of the bride." A literary expression for Shabbat eve (see also P.4.d/22). This image is based on the midrashic motif which compares the Shabbat to a bride (see Gen. Rabbah 10.9; 11.8; b. Shabbat 119a; b. Bava Qama 32b). The literal meaning of בהכנסת כלה is the time that the bride is entering her *ḥuppah*. The writer probably means that he wrote his words close to the beginning of Shabbat, a short time before the sunset.

Verso

Line 1:

"he sent it once(?)." the reading here is difficult due to the condition of the fragment. Our translation is based on the possible reading פ"א, i.e., פעם אחת 'once'.

P.4.b: Letter from Ṣedaqah Nis to Moses b. Judah

Bodl. MS Heb. c. 72/12

General Description

Concerns trade affairs. The writer alternates between Hebrew and Arabic throughout the entire letter.

Physical Description

28.4 × 6.7; paper; 1 leaf; 38 lines (recto); 27 lines (verso); verso is written inversely in relation to recto; torn, holes, red-brown stains; distinctive wormhole the same as the one in P.4.c and P.3.e.

Transcription

Recto

1. [שותה] ממי תבונה שתול כנחלי עדני[ם]יתר מרעהו צדיק שם
2. [...]ות מרוממות מחבילי חכמות בנ[פש]ו תשכונה ולמקור
3. [...] תשובנה עת אשר תשבע ימים ב[ט]וב זקנה תנחיל
4. [...]יה חכמה ובינה.   אחרי דרישת שלום אדוני
5. [כרא]וי למעלתך באתי להודיע למעלתך שהגיעני כתבך
6. [...]ה היום והקפתי בכל חלקיו ואני מצותך אשמרה בבל
7. [כח(?)]י להכיל בכל ענין והבנתי מכתבך שאקנה לך מ"ג
8. [... מ]שלם נשאדר עד ל"ו פלפל עד נ"ז בלדי עד נ"ט
9. [...] בזה הסכום אמתין עד שיקנו הסוחרים ואלכה
10. [לי בא]שר ילכו אמנם דע אדוני עם שעדיין לא נמכר
11. [...]ך נראה לי שלא ימכר פחות מכ' מפני שרובו

 https://doi.org/10.11647/OBP.0352.21

12. [כ]בר הגיע אצלכם בכליג ביד בעליו ר"ל[1] שלוחיהם
13. [...] נמכר בס' לעטארין טוב ונקי ולסוחרים
14. [... ולא] קבלו כמעט מהממון והרוב נשאר עד אחר הדוגיות
15. [...] קרנפל מ' והענין תלוי ועומד ובע"ה הבורא יתע'
16. [ישמור נפ]שך[2] והנני סומך על כתבך זה והש' יעזור וכבר
17. [...] על מה שכתבתי לכבודך מענין השולחנים
18. [שיש] להם כמו ו' חדשים שלא הרויחו כבר וכמעט
19. [...] אלא שסובלים וממתינים באולי וזה ידעתי
20. [... מפ]ני שחקרתי היטב וכבר נתתי ה' פרחים
21. [... מ(?)]אתים מן נשאדר בסכום ל"ה שהם עושים
22. [...]ם והתנינו שאם יעלה טוב יהא שלי ואם לאו
23. [... ק]פץ א' חדאיד מעשרה אלפים שלא מצינו עתה
24. [...] בו' פרחים וקפץ וחבל ובואבה ותעביה וחמאר
25. [...]א והספינה [.] מאידי ומשם תקבלהו ויגיעך
26. [...] והקפל שהיה ביד כ"ר יוסף והטלית בידי ליתנה
27. [...]ם ויגיעך האפסנתין והזופא והברוד חצרם
28. [...] האפסנתין וקרטאס רטל כתירא לחתני עבד
29. [...]ע כלם תוך כרקה זרקא מכויטין ומענין
30. [...]ן מצד השעל שיש לו הגדתי לרופאים ואמרו
31. [...]תו ואיכות [ב]יאתו(?) וכל [ע]ניניו ואם יש עמו
32. [...]א ובלאו הכי לא יוכ[ל] לדבר נכונה ואמרו
33. [... ב]ענין ר' סעדיה יצ"[ו[3] ישב] עמכם ושלום לכם
34. [... אל] נ[ג]יד(?) יצ"ו אמ' לי והזכירני שעשה עמי חשבון על
35. [...] לי נתן ע"ב לגאליה ועדיין יש לי בידו ב' פרחי'

---

[1] = רוצה לומר.

[2] Or: יעשה כנפ]שך].

[3] = ישמרהו צורו ויחייהו.

36. [... ... מ]עניך הכ'זאני[4] ואתקן בד' אבנת[5] ובעאדי א'

37. [... ... ... ב]לויים כי בלאו הכי הם נכתבים

38. [... ... ... ד]וגיות אבל עתה

Verso

1. ומה ש[יגיע]ך שלי הם כ"ד תכרה מהם [...]
2. וא' ג[וז]ה ועוד בקס מנינם ס' ומש[קלם ...]
3. ומשקלם תשס"ה ומשקל הבלדי ה' [...]
4. שמ"ד והג̇וזה שס"ו ובבלדי יש א[...]
5. בהגיעם קודם שיעלום מהספינה [...]
6. שייחיטנה עליה וכן הג̇וזא טאק א[...]
7. יש עוד א' ~~מנשור~~[6] את̇ניך ותלאת ס[...]
8. ועודין גלאט מדלוך מן כל ואחד תל[אתה(?)]
9. מכייטה כל דאלך̇ מן ג̇מלה̈ אלעדד [...]
10. הדארא יצ"ו שהוא עם חפציו וחפצי[ך ...]
11. י"ב פרחים מהם ז' זהב וה' פחות [... כסף]
12. לנאצ̇ר וללג̇מאלה אלדי ידכלו בהם [...]
13. ארסל להם צבי אכר אמא צהרי [...]
14. ימשי מע אלג̇מאל אללה אללה לא ת[...]
15. אלצבי אלמספר עליהם צחבה̈ [..]א[...]
16. ואיצ̇ה אנה מא יכפי חרצהם פ[...]
17. לצביאן אלגמאל חתא ידכלו בהם ס[...]
18. טלועהם מן אלמרכב ותתאמל [...]
19. וכדאלך̇ עדה̈ אלבקס ואלצנדל ו[...]

---

[4] Or: הבזאני.

[5] אבות(?).

[6] The word was probably deleted.

20. תצרף עליהם מן ידך באסם [...]
21. ואלקרנפל מתאעך מאיתון מן [...]
22. למן תעתאוהם כדהם בגרבלה [...]
23. אללה אללה פי דאלך גֹמיעה ויגיעך [...]
24. על המכזן שתשים בו החפ[צים(?) ...]
25. אלגרמאני ודבריו ידעתי כי ל[א ...]
26. ואין להאריך כי אם בשלו[מ]ך [...]

Translation

Recto

1. [... drinks] from wisdom's water, planted (like a tree on the banks of) Eden's rivers (Ps. 36.9; see also Ps. 1.3). A righteous man gives his friend direction (Prov. 12.26),[7] there
2. [...] exalted [...] of parcels of wisdom, shall dwell in his [soul], and to the origin of
3. [...] will return, at the time you shall prolong days, well and aging, and bequeath
4. [...] wisdom and understanding. After inquiring about the wellbeing of my master,
5. [as is appropriate] to your standing, I come to inform your honour that I received your letter
6. [...] today and I passed through all its parts. I am keeping your commandments with all
7. [my efforts(?)], to complete(?) every matter. I understood from your letter, that (you want) me to buy for you 43

---

[7] Here is the King James translation, but this difficult phrase has been explained in many ways by different commentators.

8. [...] whole [...], ammoniac—a maximum of 36; pepper—a maximum of 57; *baladī*—a maximum of 59;
9. [...] With this amount, I will wait until the merchants will buy, and I will go
10. [wherever] they go. But my master should know that although the [...] has not been sold yet,
11. it appears that it would not be sold for less than 20, because most of it
12. already arrived to you via the *Ḵalīj* with its owners, i.e., their messengers.
13. And the [...] was sold for 60 (each) to the perfume sellers, good and clean, and to the merchants
14. [...] (they) got hardly [any] of the money, and the majority left until the (time/season of the) boats
15. [...] cloves 40, and the matter is pending, and with God's help, the creator exalted
16. [will save] you.[8] I rely on this letter of yours, and the Name will help. Already
17. [...] on what I wrote to your honour about the bankers.
18. [It has been] for them about six months already that they did not earn, and almost
19. [...] but they are bearing and waiting, maybe (that it would change). I know this
20. [... because] I investigated it well, and I already gave five florins

---

[8] Alternatively, if the phrase is completed as הבורא יתע' [יעשה כנפ]שך, it should be translated 'the creator exalted [will do according to] your [wish].

21. [...] 200(?) of ammoniac for the amount of 35, that they are doing
22. [...] and we made conditions that if (the price) would go up well, it would be mine, and if not
23. [...] basket, one iron bar from ten thousand, because we cannot find now
24. [...] for six florins, and basket, rope, container, litter, and donkey.
25. [...] and the boat (costs) [illegible Coptic number] *muʾayyadī* and you will get it from there and it will reach you
26. [...] and the metal lock which the honourable R. Joseph holds, and the *tallit*—I can give it (or: and the *tallit* which I hold, to give it)
27. [...] it will reach you. The wormwood, and the ... and the ...
28. [...] the wormwood and many *raṭls* of paper to my son-in-law ʿAbd
29. [...] word concerning blue stitched *Ḵirqa*-cloth. Concerning
30. [...] because of the cough he has—I told the doctors and they said
31. [...] and the quality of [...] and all his matters, and if he has
32. [...] and in any case he cannot speak rightly, and they said
33. [...] Concerning R. Saʿadiah, may God save him, [he can sit] with you, and peace be upon you
34. [... the] Na[g]id(?), may God save him, told me and reminded me that he settled (his) accounts with me regarding
35. [...] to me, he gave 72 for the poll-tax, and he still owes me two florins

36. [… … …] about the *ḵazanī*. And I will fix(?) in (the amount of) four … and one …
37. [… … … worn] because in any case they are being copied
38. [… … … … … … … … … boats], but now

Verso

1. Concerning what [reaches] you of my (wares), they are 24, you should buy(?) from them […]
2. and one (consignment of) [nutmeg], and also brazil wood, their number is 60 and their [weight …]
3. their weight is 765. The *baladī*'s weight is five […]
4. 344, and the nutmeg is 366. There is […] of *baladī* […]
5. when it arrives, before it is discharged from the boat, […]
6. … on it, and also the nutmeg …
7. There is one aloe wood, two and three […]
8. thick and polished pieces of aloe wood, of each [three],
9. stitched, all of this, of the whole number […]
10. Hadara, may God save him, that he is with his wares and [your(?)] wares […]
11. 12 florins, seven of them gold, and five minus [… silver]
12. for Nāẓir, and for those who will go (into the ship) with them […]
13. Send them another boy! Concerning my brother-in-law […]
14. he should go together with the camel driver. Quickly, do not […]
15. the boy, who is travelling to them (within the framework of a) *ṣuḥba* (business relationship) […]
16. also, their solicitude is not sufficient […]

17. for the the camel driver's boy until they go (into the ship) with them [...]
18. They come down from the ship. You should monitor carefully [...]
19. also, some brazil wood and sandal wood and [...]
20. pay for it from your account in the name of [...]
21. and your cloves, 200 of [...]
22. to whom you should give them. Take them for examination [...]
23. quickly in this matter, all of it. It will reach you [...]
24. in the storeroom where you are putting the [wares(?) ...]
25. Al-Gharamānī(?), and about his words I know that he [would not...]
26. There is no need to extend, except for (sending) greetings to you [...]

Commentary

Recto

Line 14:
"The majority left until the (time/season of the) boats." Ṣedaqah probably means here the Venetian boats that were sailing at regular times to Alexandria.

Line 30:
"Because of the cough he has." It is difficult to know if השעל is an Arabic word (سُعَال), or a Hebrew word (שַׁעַל, for שיעול). If it is Hebrew, this is a unique form. We did not find it in any other medieval Hebrew texts.

Line 34:
"[The] Na[g]id(?), may God save him." The reading of the first word נ[ג]יד is uncertain, but it is clear that a person is mentioned here, due to the blessing יצ"ו 'may God save him'. If it is a personal name that terminates in *dalet*, it could be, for example, ע[ב]ד (ʿAbd).

Lines 34–35:
The writer refers here to the payment of the *jizya/jāliyya* poll-tax. It seems that the transaction documented here was intended to help poor people in the community with their payment of the tax.

P.4.c: Letter from Ṣedaqah Nis to Moses b. Judah

Bodl. MS Heb. c. 72/13

General Description

Concerns trade affairs and refers to transactions with Muslim merchants. Judaeo-Arabic.

Physical Description

22.4 × 9.5; paper; 1 leaf; 23 lines (recto); 1 line (verso); holes, slightly rubbed, red-brown stains; distinctive wormhole the same as the one in P.4.b and P.3.e.

Transcription

Recto

1. בס"ד
2. אלעלום אלכרימה מחיטה בכתרת אלשוק ועדם אלפצ̇א
3. ואלראחה מן טלב אלנאס ועס[ר אל]תחציל ולטף
4. אללה תע' אגלה ופצ̇לה אע[.....]א הו ען ג̇הת
5. אלע[ת]ל פהו פי שכא[תיר ... ...]ת אמיר
6. כביר וקד כלמת אלמו' אלמע' ווער באלמסעדה
7. ואמא ען אלגוך פאכברני סרעה תפצילה ואסעארה
8. ותפציל אלביעה אלמתחצלה ללג̇הה̈ אלמעלומה
9. ומקצוד אלמע' שמואל אן תסאעד בכל ג̇הדך מע
10. ס'[1] בדר אלדין אלמצרי פי ביע אלכיאר ואשתהד[2]

---

[1] = סייד.

[2] For אגתהד.

 https://doi.org/10.11647/OBP.0352.22

11. פי דאלך מא תכצר עליה שי וקד ארסל הו
12. כתאב ידכר פיה אן קרקשונה טלבהם לאגֹל
13. וגֹואב אלכתאב ואצל לס' בדר אלדין מפצל ען
14. כל שי אלמעתמד עליה פי דאלך ואלמו' אלמע'
15. שמואל קאל לי נכתב ללמכ' ומע כוני נערף
16. אנך מא תכלם קרקשונה מא ארדת נקול לה
17. דאלך בל קלת לה אני נכתב לך ואנך תסאעד
18. ותעמל פאלקצד אנך אן לם תקדר תעמל תתכפל
19. עלי אלמעלם מחמד יסאעד ויעמל אללה אללה
20. פי דאלך ומהמא כאן לסיידי מן חאגֹה ערפני
21. נפוז בקצאהא בעד אלסלאם אלמכתץ בסיידי
22. אליה יצ"ו ואלאולאד ואהל בית וכל מן יכוד
23. במנזלך אלכרים ושלום צדקה ניס כ"ד לעומ[ר]

Verso

לי[ד ... ...] כ"ר משה יצ"ו [ב"ר] יהודה זלה"ה צדקה ניס

Translation

Recto

1. With God's help.
2. (Your) honourable knowledge should comprise the magnitude of longing for you and (our) lack of money
3. and respite because of the demands of people, and their urge to obtain (it). May
4. God exalted make (matters) favourable. May his grace […] Regarding the
5. maintenance money, it is in the boa[ts … …] of a great

6. emir, and I already spoke with the master *al-muʿallim*, and he promised support.
7. Concerning the cloth, you should inform me quickly regarding its cut, its prices,
8. and details of the collected lot on behalf of a certain viewpoint known (to you).
9. It is the intention of the *muʿallim* Samuel that you assist in all your efforts
10. M. Badr al-Dīn al-Maṣrī (the Cairene) in the sale of the *cassia fistula*. Make an effort
11. in this, so that you don't suffer losses. He already sent
12. a letter in which he mentions that Qarqashūna claimed them for (himself).
13. The answer to that letter is arriving to M. Badr al-Dīn, detailing
14. for everything its respective agent. The master, the *muʿallim*
15. Samuel told me that I should write to you, although we should inform you
16. that you should not talk to Qarqashūna. I did not want to tell him
17. this but I told him that I would write to you and that you would help
18. and work (on it). The intention is that you, if you cannot work (on it), then you should pledge (it)
19. to the *muʿallim* Muhammad to assist and work (on it), (act) quickly
20. in this (matter). Anything my master needs, let me know,

21. we will gladly carry it out. (This letter ends) after sending special greeting to my master
22. Elijah, may God save him, and the children and the wife and everyone who belongs
23. to your honourable house. Peace (will be). Ṣedaqah Nis, 24th of [the counting of the] *ʿOmer*.

Verso

To [… …] the honourable rabbi Moses, may God save him, [son of R.] Judah, may his memory live in the world to come. Ṣedaqah Nis.

Commentary

Recto

Line 10:
"Badr al-Dīn al-Maṣrī." His name testifies that he is a Muslim, as the component *al-Dīn* 'the Religion' in personal names only occurs with Muslim individuals, whereas Christians and Jews did not use this element in their names.

"*Cassia fistula.*" Known as 'golden rain tree'. On its medical use in the Middle Ages, see Amar (1995). On the medieval trade in this fruit, see David (2011, 109–10) and the literature mentioned there (110 n. 68).

Line 12:
"He mentions that Qarqashūna claimed them." Qarqashūna could be identified with ʿAbd al-ʿAzīz al-Qarqashūnī, who is mentioned in letter P.4.f, which is also a letter from Ṣedaqah Nis. The name

could also be pronounced as Qarqasūna. This *nisba* attests to a provincial origin, from Carcassonne, in the South West of France.

Line 15:
“Although.” For *maʿa kon* as ‘although’, see Spiro (1895, 517).

P.4.d: Letter from Ṣedaqah Nis to Moses b. Judah

Bodl. MS Heb. c. 72/15

General Description

Concerns trade affairs. Hebrew.

Physical Description

18.5 × 11; paper; 1 leaf; 22 lines (recto); 1 line (verso); holes, red-brown stains.

Transcription

Recto

1. בס"ד
2. אחרי דרישת שלום מעלתך אלפים כפלים משעור הראוי למעלתך
3. באתי להודיע לכבודך שהיו' חדש לא הגיעני כתב מכבודך ונצטערתי
4. ושוב שמעתי כי פקדך אלהיך להיטיב לך באחריתיך(!) ומיד שלח מלאכו
5. וירפאך ונצטערתי ושמחתי וקושט אמרי אמת לא ידעתי בכתב
6. לכן אני מחלה פני כבודך בעבור שלא נשאר לי כל כך זמן שתמהר
7. להודיעני אופן בריאותך וסדר מצבך ותודיעני ענין אבו אלכיר
8. של נשאדר מה הביא ומה נתת לו ותודיעני ענין הסמים בפי'
9. כל דבר ומה נראה לך מסכומו . ומענין הצאבון והנחאס
10. ששלחת לומ' לסיידי א' אלגִיעאן התשובה אינם רוצים לתת רשות
11. למורשה שלהם לעשות שום דבר עד זמן המוסם של דוגיות
12. אמנם אמרו לי שהם חפצים מאד במעשיך ותאותם שתעמוד
13. תמיד באוצרם ובפרט בזמן הדוגיות ושתשרתם מלב ומנפש
14. ולא להתראות ושהם ייטיבו לכבודך בכל זמן ויהיו לך למסעד
15. היום ולמחר ואמנם מהבורית והנחשת שאמרת עשה

 https://doi.org/10.11647/OBP.0352.23

16. כל השתדלותך בסכומים ושלחו להודיעם [סוף המעשה] אם יישר בעיניהם
17. יקיימו ואם לאו לאו וכל אשר שאלת בע"ה יגיעך עמי ואם
18. תצטרך עוד דבר תודיעני מהר ומפני שאין זמן להאריך לכן
19. לא הארכתי ואין להאריך כי אם בשלום מעלתך ושלום בניך שי'
20. כנפשך ונפש המזומן למאמרך הדבק באהבתך צדקה ניס(?)
21. וחתוך כתב קטן זה ושלחהו לאחות מב"ת
22. בהכנסת כלה ואברכך[1] מברכיך

Margin

1. ותן האחד
2. למה"ר יוסף יצ"ו

Verso

ליד האדון מה"ר משה יצ"ו בכ"ר יהודה זלה"ה מעם צדקה ניס

Translation

Recto

1. With God's help.
2. After inquiring about the wellbeing of your honour, thousands and double of the appropriate amount to your honour,
3. I come to inform your honour, that today it has been a month that I have not received a letter from your honour, and I was worried.
4. Again, I heard that your God remembered you, to do you good at your latter end (Deut. 8.16), and immediately sent his angel

---

[1] In Gen. 12.3, it is ואברכה.

5. and healed you. I was worried and I was happy, but I did not get to know the exact truth from a letter.
6. Because of that, I am begging your honour, since I do not have much time, hurry
7. to inform me about your health and your condition. Inform me about the matter of Abū l-Ḵayr,
8. how much ammoniac he has brought and how much you paid him. Inform me about the matter of the drugs explicitly.
9. (Let me know) everything and what you think its appropriate price is. About the soap and copper,
10. of which you sent a mention to my master Ibn al-Jayʿān, the answer is: they do not want to give permission
11. to their proxy to do anything until the time of the caravan of the boats.
12. Indeed, they told me they are very satisfied with your activities, and their desire is that you would
13. always stand in their store, especially in the time of the boats, and that you would serve them from heart and soul,
14. not (just) to meet each other, and that they would benefit your honour at any time, and will be your assistance
15. today and tomorrow. Indeed, about the soap and the copper that you mentioned, make
16. all your efforts on the amounts and send to inform them (what happened) finally with the matter. If it looks well in their eyes,
17. they will make it, and if not—not. Everything you asked, with God's help, will arrive to you by me. If

18. you need anything else, inform me quickly. Since there is no time to extend,
19. I did not extend (this letter). I shall not draw out, only in (sending) greetings to Your Honour, and greetings to your sons, shall they live
20. like your soul and the soul of the one who awaits your commandment and is attached to your love. Ṣedaqah Nis.
21. Cut off this little letter and send it to the sister, above (all) women in the tent shall she be blessed (Judg. 5.24).
22. At the wedding of the bride, of "I will bless those who bless you" (Gen. 12.3).

Margin

1. And give the other one
2. to our teacher Rabbi Joseph, may God save him.

Verso

To the master our teacher Rabbi Moses, may God save him, son of the honourable rabbi Judah, may his memory live in the world to come. From Ṣedaqah Nis.

Commentary

Recto

Line 8:
"About the matter of Abū l-Ḵayr, how much ammoniac he has brought." See letter P.4.a/25.

Line 9:
“About the soap and the copper.” Here the writer uses the Arabic terms (הצאבון והנחאס) but later he mentions the same items again by their Hebrew names (הבורית והנחושת). This phenomenon reflects the effort of the writer to write in Hebrew. Even when he uses Arabic terms at first, he later corrects his language and adopts the Hebrew alternatives. For a discussion of this, see Arad (2009, 113–14).

Line 21:
“Cut off this little letter and send it to the sister.” The meaning is not clear, but evidence from other collections, such as the Arabic and Hebrew Prize Papers from The National Archives, London, dating to the middle of the eighteenth century, shows that letters often had other letters glued to them.[2]

Line 22:
“At the wedding of the bride.” A literary expression for Shabbat eve. See the other letter of Ṣedaqah, P.4.a/30.

“I will bless those who bless you.” This is a clue to the time when the letter was written. A common custom among writers was to mention a phrase from the weekly *parasha* that was being read in the synagogue. Here is a phrase from *Lekh lekha* (Gen. 12.1–17.27), which is usually read in the month of *Marḥeshvan*.

---

[2] For details on the collection, see Wagner and Ahmed (2017).

Margin

"Rabbi Joseph." Several people called Joseph are mentioned in the documents of our corpus (see index), and it is therefore impossible to identify this Joseph exactly.

P.4.e: Letter from Ṣedaqah Nis to Moses b. Judah

Bodl. MS Heb. c. 72/25

General Description

Concerned with business affairs. Hebrew.

Physical Description

20.3 × 5.9; paper; 1 leaf; 28 lines + marginalia (recto; verso is blank); torn, holes, beige stains.

Transcription

Recto

1. [... ... ...] בידי עד שלחי
2. [...]ות נמצא הוא ונשתדל בהעתקתו וסכום
3. [...] קרפה חסיני עד בלדי גוזה ניל
4. [...] 22 7(?) 8 16 32 22
5. [...] לא נודעו עדיין וגם אלו לא כל כך נמצאים
6. [...]ם והשמועה יש שיבואו סמים במצוע הרגיל
7. [...] ואמנם ע[ת]ה במדינה אין שום משא ומתן
8. [... בח]סדך אדוני מענין הדאר פלפל והתנכאר
9. [... כת]בתי למעלתך הסכומים של מעות והם
10. [... תנ]כאר צנדל וכל זה בשאני אפרע הדכירא
11. [...] 20 30 כמנהג אם עתה יש שמן
12. [... למעל]תך עשה והצלח ולך חסד בענין
13. [...] השמן שם אם הוא נמכר מפני שבמצרים
14. [...] למחלא וכבודך חכם ועשה מה שיראה לך
15. [...] ולא אני ומכל שאר ענייניך בעז' הש' אני

 https://doi.org/10.11647/OBP.0352.24

16. [... כל ש]אפשר ואחר אשלח להודיעך וכבודך כתב
17. [... ח]אצֿר נראה לי שאדרבה אם אכתוב יחשוב
18. [...] בדבר ובאמרך לו שהם שלי לא ימנע
19. [... ה]פסד וגם ששרתתי אותו בכאן וגם נתתי
20. [... חש]בון הדכירא יותר על מה שנתנו אחרים
21. [...] קונים במעות או בנחשת יותר טוב
22. [...] צביחה גליטה או שריט או שאר סחורות
23. [...] הם היותר טובים לי לכוונתי ואם יש
24. [... הדכי]רא תחסר מהסכום בשיעור הראוי לכך
25. [...]ק שיש שמועת מלחמה מדרך היבשה והנה
26. [...]ם[1] ללכת יהי רצון ש'מהר קץ משיחנו בימנו אנ"ס
27. וכתב אחיך   המזומן למצותך
28. צדקה ניס

Margin

1. [...]
2. [...]ושנאש

Translation

Recto

1. […] in my hands until I will send
2. […] it can be found, and we will make (or: he made) an effort to copy it. The amount
3. […] cinnamon, *ḥusaynī*, agarwood, *baladī* ('local'), nutmeg, indigo
4. […]   22,   7(?),   8,   16,   32,   23
5. […] It is not known yet, and even those can rarely be found

---

[1] Maybe: [נחפזי]ם.

6. [...] there is a rumour that drugs are going to be brought, with the regular brokerage fee(?)
7. [...] Indeed, there is now no business activity in the country (or: in the city).
8. [...by your grace] my lord. Concerning the long pepper and the borax,
9. [...] I have [written] to your honour the amounts of money. They
10. [...] borax, sandal wood. All that when I will repay the storage fee
11. [...] 20 30 as it is customary. If the oil can be found now
12. [...] (to) your [highness], do and prosper, and you have grace in the matter (or: you have grace. Concerning)
13. [...] the oil there, if it is sold, because in Cairo
14. [...] to Maḥalla. Your honour is smart, so do what seems best to you.
15. [...] and not me. About all your other matters, with the Name's help I will
16. [... make all that] possible, and after that I will send to inform you. Your honour wrote
17. [...] Ḥāḍir, I think that vice-versa, if I will write, he would think
18. [...] in the matter. If you will say to him that it is mine, he will not prevent
19. [...] loss, and also that I have served him in the *Khan*, and I also gave
20. [...] the [account] of the storage fees is more than others have given

21. […] buying with money or with copper is better
22. […] thick metal plate or wire or other merchandise
23. […] those are the best for my aim. If there is
24. [… the storage fees] will be less than the amount in appropriate extent
25. […] that there is rumour of war on the land route, and
26. [hurry] to go. May it be the will (of God) that he will bring soon the time of our Messiah in our days. Amen, forever.
27. Written by your brother who is ready for your order.
28. Ṣedaqah Nis

Margin

1. […]
2. […]

Commentary

Recto

Line 2:
Ṣedaqah mentions here a book which he tried to source for Moses' library.

Line 3:
"*Ḥusaynī.*" A nisba (i.e., adjective of provenience) for a product, probably a kind of textile.

Line 7:
"The country." *Medina* in Hebrew can be interpreted both as 'country' and as 'city' (as it can in Arabic, مَدِينَة).

Line 14:
"Maḥalla." Maḥalla (al-Maḥalla al-Kubrā) is a city in northern Egypt, on the Damietta branch of the Nile. The Jewish community of Maḥalla was in existence from at least as early as the tenth century until the twentieth century. There are many references pertaining to this community in the Genizah documents from the Classical Genizah period, and also some in the documents from the Mamlūk era, for example, a deed written in Maḥalla in 1374 CE (TS NS 264.7). The nickname מחלי (ENA 2763.20) or מחלאוי (TS AS 200.149; Mosseri II 111.1) appears in documents from the Mamlūk and Ottoman periods. In the early Ottoman period, the Jewish population in the city grew—as reflected in many documents in the Genizah, in the Cairo Community Archive, and in the responsa literature—following the waves of Jewish immigrants arriving in Egypt. On the life of the last generation of the community, see Fargeon (1938, 282–86).

Line 25:
"There is rumour of war on the land route." Ṣedaqah's letters are not dated and it is therefore difficult to determine exactly which event is mentioned here, but it seems that the information refers to the Ottoman-Mamlūk war, which occurred in Syria and Anatolia in 1485–1491.

Margin

The meaning of these words is not clear.

P.4.f: Letter from Ṣedaqah Nis to Moses b. Judah

Bodl. MS Heb. c. 72/26

General Description

Probably concerns business affairs. Hebrew.

Physical Description

7.7 × 8.8; paper; 1 leaf; 6 lines (recto); 1 line (verso); verso is written inversely in relation to recto; torn, red-brown stains.

Transcription

Recto

1. בס"ד
2. שלומות אלף במעט קלף לשר האלף האדון הנעלה לשם לתהלה כה"ר
3. משה יצ"ו באתי להודיע למעלתך שהגיעוני הכתבים האחרונים
4. לי ולסיידי עבד אלעזיז אלקרקשוני ונתתיו לו וקודם לכן כבר נת[ן]
5. השר ביד מי שנדר בקוטע ומחבור והנה הוא [...]

Verso

יצל ליד אלמו' אלאג'[1] אלפאצ̇ל כ"ר משה יצ"ו בר כ"ר יהוד[ה]

---

[1] = אלמולא אלאג̇ל.

 https://doi.org/10.11647/OBP.0352.25

Translation

Recto

1. With God's help.
2. A thousand greetings on a little (piece of) vellum, to the leader of a thousand (people), the exalted master, (who is known) for his name and glory, the honourable rabbi
3. Moses, may God save him. I come to inform you that I received the last letters
4. for me and for my master ʿAbd al-ʿAzīz al-Qarqashūnī (or: Qarqasonī). I gave it to him. Before that
5. the minister already gave to the hands of him who vowed … …, and he […]

Verso

(This letter) should arrive to the admirable master, the generous, the honourable rabbi Moses, may God save him, son of the honourable rabbi Judah.

Commentary

Recto

Line 2:
For the phrases in this line, compare P.4.a/2.

"The leader of a thousand." See commentary to P.4.a/2.

Line 4:
"ʿAbd al-ʿAzīz al-Qarqasūnī." See commentary to P.4.c/12. It is difficult to know whether he was Muslim or Jewish.

Line 5:
“The minister already gave to the hands of him who vowed.” Our translation is based on the reading ביד מי. Another option is to understand the phrase as בירמי, being the minister’s name. If so, the words should be translated as: “Minister Vermes already gave…” Although this reading seems perhaps to accord better with the handwriting in the manuscript, it is less plausible in terms of meaning. See also P.4.f/5.

P.4.g: Letter from Ṣedaqah Nis to Moses b. Judah

Bodl. MS Heb. c. 72/27 + 43

General Description

Concerned with business matters. Judaeo-Arabic.

Physical Description

Fragment 27: 5.9 × 10.3; paper; 1 leaf; 4 lines + marginalia (recto); 1 line (verso); torn, holes, red-brown stains.

Fragment 43: 16.3 × 10.1; paper; 1 leaf; 14 lines + marginalia (recto); 14 lines (verso); torn, holes, beige stains; fragment is cut in half in the middle vertically, and wormholes on both sides mirror one another, i.e., the fragment was probably bound folded in the middle.

Transcription

Recto

1. שלום שלום
2. אלדי יעלם בה סיידי אן ענד חצ̇ורי לביתי בעד אן כתבת
3. לך̇ מן פוה מא קד כתבת ועליה אלמעתמר ראית
4. פי [... ...]ב במצר אתם שב מע גנוי ויא[כד(?)] דמ[...]
5. [...][1]
6. כדה לי מן כל ובד[2] ס[וה(?) ...] באלכיאר ולך̇ בחצץ פלפל
7. ולא תצ̇ן מא [... ...] עאתב מולאי סיידי שי

---

[1] Fragment Bodl. MS Heb. C. 72/43 begins in this line.

[2] This seems to be a scribal error or unusual variant of כל בד.

 https://doi.org/10.11647/OBP.0352.26

8. פי קלם אלארסאל אלפצׄ[ה ...]א קלת לדׄ צדקא מן אולאדדׄ
9. לא מסאלם ל[...] וטריק[ה ...] דכלך וקד קלת לסיידי אן
10. תאכד כמסין אשרפי [... ו]קד וצל אלחסאב מן אלמכ' ועקיבה
11. יצלני חסאבי ונרסל [... ל]למכ' באקי מתאמן וגׄמיע
12. מא [ת]טלבהא איצׄה יצל[... ל]ך מע אול מן [יצל] ושלום לדׄ
13. לם תם וקת לל[צעוד(?)] ניל
14. צדקה ניס

Margin

1. מן אמר אל[...] כירה סאעד כל מא תקדר מן ברא ברא
2. ועלם ר' יע[קב ...]ן כיף עמל ושיר עליה ומא יכון בחסד

Margin Below

1. אלאכל כיר ואפחץ ואעלמני [... ...]ל [..]יא אחדא בתור [.]ואני
2. ואעמל בחילה אן ידכל כמאנה א[... מ]א יגלבני אלא באלמשפט
3. בחית אן יכתב כדא לוכילא [פי]קע פי ידי ומא יכון לי
4. גראמה כתיר ושלום

Verso

יצל ליד [...] ר' משה בכ"ר יהודה זלה"ה [מ]עם צדקה ניס

Translation

Recto

1. Peace, Peace (will be).
2. (This letter) which informs you, my master, that during my stay in my house, after I had written
3. to you from Fuwwa what I had already written, and (pondered) about it repeatedly, I saw

4. in [... ....] in Cairo, the best alum (is found) at Ġanawī's (hands), [and he will take(?) ...]
5. [...]
6. Take it for me in any case [...] with the *Cassia fistula* and for you in shared pepper.
7. You should not think that [... ...] my lord my master any blame.
8. Concerning the reed pens, the consignment [...] what I told you truthfully of your children
9. He is not sending [...] ... [...] by means of your revenue. I already told my master that
10. you should take 50 *ashrafī* dinars. [...] The account just arrived from the master, and immediately after that
11. my accounts should arrive to me. We (or: I)[3] will [...] send to the master the rest of the entrusted (goods) and everything
12. that you asked for should also arrive [... at yours] with the first one [who arrives]. Peace be upon you!
13. The time for [the rise of the] Nile has not come to pass (yet).
14. Ṣedaqah Nis

Margin

1. Concerning the matter of [...] better. Support everything you can (to be shipped) over land.
2. Inform R. Ja[cob ...] how did he do. [...] It should not be at the mercy

---

[3] See §III.2.7.4 under *1st Singular/Plural.*

Margin Below

1. of the family. Investigate and let me know [... ... ...] one ... ...
2. Work with guile if he comes in like this [...] He only defeated me because of the legal ruling.
3. Insofar as he writes thus to an agent, [it remains] in my hand, and I will not have
4. many debts. Peace (will be).

Verso

(This letter) should arrive to the hand of [...] R. Moses b. the honourable R. Judah, may his memory live in the world to come, from Ṣedaqah Nis.

Commentary

Recto

Line 3:
"From Fuwwa." Fuwwa is a small town, located on the Nile, east of Rosetta. The 'classical Genizah' documents contain information on the Jews there (see Ashtor 1967–69, 7; Golb 1974, 129). Meshullam of Voltera and Rabbi Obadiah of Bertinoro, however, who used to record the existence of a local Jewish community in every place they visited, did not mention any Jewish presence in Fuwwa.[4] It seems therefore that there was no Jewish community

[4] Obadiah remained in the town for two days and was impressed by its fertility: "We remained two days in Fooahm because the wind was not favorable; It is a large and beautiful place, and fish and vegetables can

present at the time when our corpus was composed (see David 1988, 22). There is some evidence for commercial activity of Jews in the town in the sixteenth century. R. David ibn Zimra discussed the case of someone who "went from his home to Fuwwa, where he had business, and left his wife in her period. After 15 days, people came and said to him that his wife was pregnant, and he shouted and said that she became pregnant in prostitution and that the fetus is *mamzer*" (Ibn Zimra 1882, I, §321). Another source mentioned a Jew who said "every week I was going to Fuwwa" to take part in the slave trade there (Bodl. MS Heb. b. 13/45; this letter was published and discussed by Assaf 1940, 272–73, 277–78). This is an important source for the involvement of Jews in the slave trade in Ottoman Egypt, but also an additional testimony to the presence of some Jews in the commercial centre of Fuwwa. Our letter gives us earlier evidence for this phenomenon.

---

be got almost for nothing" (Adler 1930, 223). It is implausible to suppose that he spent this time in the town without making any connection with the local Jewish community. In every place he passed, he looked for the Jews and described their customs, their demographical details, etc. We have to infer, therefore, that there was already no Jewish congregation in the town in his time.

P.5.a: Letter from Elijah b. Elyaqim to Moses b. Judah

Bodl. MS Heb. c. 72/10

General Description

The letter, written in Hebrew, was sent from Damietta to Alexandria, probably on 30 November 1486, and was written two and a half years after another letter from Elijah b. Elyaqim, sent from Candia, which is also preserved in our collection (P.5.b). Elijah responded after two letters from Moses had reached him. Moses had expressed his disappointment about the quality of the paper and the script in one of the books Elijah bought for him, and the latter sought to justify himself in that regard. Moses was also dissatisfied with the price he had to pay for the book and Elijah tried to explain the details of the expenditure. He updated the addressee about other purchases of books. In addition, he offered a suggestion as to with whom the addressee could send his money and his response letter, and pleaded with him to pay attention if letters addressed to the writer should arrive in the port of Alexandria from other people. The letter was first published by Benayahu (1984).

The letter reflects the central place that the Jewish holidays took in people's minds. The writer wrote his letter on the eve of Hanukah, and his mind was already on the next holiday, Purim. The year of 5247 (1486/7) was a leap year in the Hebrew calendar, so Purim fell on a date four months later (on 18 March 1487). Nevertheless, the writer was worried that he still did not

 https://doi.org/10.11647/OBP.0352.27

have an Esther scroll and asked the addressee: "If you have one old (scroll), send (it) to me for Purim, and I will send it back immediately [with those who come first]."

Another two letters probably written by Elijah (MS Budapest, Kaufman 36.11r and 371; published by David 2016, 391–97) were sent by him from Candia to Egypt, to the brothers Leon and Elijah, and dealt with his trade businesses.[1]

Physical Description

14.5 × 19.5; paper; 1 leaf; 27 lines (recto); 2 lines + 13 partial lines of mirrored script (verso); verso is written inversely in relation to recto; torn, holes, red-brown stains.

Transcription

Recto

1. לק"י[2]
2. [יברכך ה]אל[3] מציון וראה בטוב ירושלם כל ימי חייך וראה בנים לבניך אהובי היקר כ"ר משה י"א אחרי רוב שלו' מודיעך
3. [שקבל]תי מכבודך ב' כתבי' ע"י אבראימי טורצמן הא' שש[לח] לי מקנדיאה כ"ר שלמה והאחר ששלח לכבודך שתקבל
4. [...] ובאותו הכתב כתב לי כבודך איך קבלת הספרים וכתבת לי גם איך הכתיבה לספר תורת האדם אינה

---

[1] The signature of the author is missing but the handwriting looks similar to Elijah's handwriting in our corpus.

[2] = לישועתך קויתי י"י.

[3] In Ps. 128.5: יברכך ה'.

5. [משוב]ת בעני כבודך. ויש הפרש מהנייר ששלחתי לכבודך מקנדיאה . ועל זה האל יודע כמה השתדלות עשיתי
6. [ולא] יכולתי[4] לקיים גזרתך. ופעם ופעמים באתי בדברים עם הסופר. ובזמן שהייתי אני בקנדיאה הכתיבה היה טוב
7. [...] ויותר יפה מהנייר ששלחתי לכבודך. ומשם ואילך איני יודע מה נהיה בו . ועל זה הוקשה לי מאד בראותי כי
8. [אינ]ך מפויי[ס] בו. מ"מ אדוני האל יודע כמה שיכולתי ומה שהיה באפשרות ממני לא היה מניעה ממני. ואם אין
9. [נראה ב]עני[5] כבודך אהיה מנוצל מכבודך. מצורף לזה על אודות המעו' אדוני כבודך יודע כאשר כתבתי
10. [אליך][6] ותבקש כתביי וכן תמצא איך נתפשרתי עם הסופר כ'[7] מרצלוש בקונטרס ויתרון על כל הספר מרצלוש
11. [ואני] חושב שיעלה כל הספר קונטרסים ט"ו ובעת נסיעתי מקנדיאה חשבתי שיעלה יותר מי"ז קונטרסים.
12. [והנה] הספר הוא בידך ותמדוד אותם כמה חסרים. ותעשה החשבון כבודך כמה הם עולים בחשבון י"ב מרצלוש
13. [...(?) בד]וקט ונצייאן. ועל הספר יוסף בן גוריון נראה לי אם אני זוכר בטוב נתפשרתי בדוקטי ב' או ב' וח' כי בעונותיי
14. [איני זוכ]ר[8] כל כך ותתפוס כתביי ותראה כמה כתבתי לכבודך. עם כל זה אני בספק אם לא תמצא כתביי וכתבתי

---

[4] Benayahu reads: [כמה ש]יכולתי; Hacker (2000, 575 n. 9) offers: [עד ש]יכולתי.

[5] Benayahu: [זה נראה ב]עיני.

[6] Benayahu: [מקודם].

[7] Benayahu: ב'.

[8] Benayahu offered: [נחלש הזיכרון], but it does not fit the linguistic style of that period. Hacker: [איני זכו]ר.

15. [לקנדיא]ה שיודיעוני כמה עלו ואכתו' לכבודך עו' כמה שיתחדש. עו' בעד מגילת אסתר עלה ~~לי~~ לי חצי

16. [דוקט ונ]צייאן ואני צריך בו בגרותי ותשלחהו לי במצרים ביד מורדוך והוא ישלח אותו לי הנה ע"י הבאים. ואם

17. [הנך ח]פץ בו איני לזוז מגזרתך. אמנם אם יש לכבודך א' ישן תשלח לי בעבור הפורים ומיד אשלח אותו

18. [עם הקודם] ותשובתך יגיעני ע"י המוביל כתבי שהולך ל[ידי(?)] אלוייזא פיזן. והמעו' הנז' תשלחם לידי מורדוך והוא

19. [יביאם] הנה ע"י יודים(!) שהולכים ובאים בכל יום ~~ה~~[9] ממצרים הנה. ר' שלמה מקנדיאה כתב לי איך שלח לי

20. [ב' כת]בים אחרים על ידך ואני לא קבלתי כתבי' אחרים זולת אלה הנז' ובחייך יהיו עניך פקוחות אם יגיעו

21. [לך הכ]תבים שלי שתשלחם לי תכף. ומובטח אני בזה. על אודות הכמוכדש שכתב לי כבודך לא הביאו

22. [עדיין מא]ותו המין שכתב לי ~~כ~~ כבודך לכן לא ~~-~~ קניתי לכבודך. ותודיעני אם כבודך צריך בהם אולי יביאו עד

23. [בוא ה]גריפרייש שעתידים לבואו[10] הנה. ואם תצטרך דבר מפה תגזרני ואקיים גזרתך. והמעות שתשלח לי

24. [...]תם דוקטי ונצייאני. או מרצלוש אחר אין להאריך רק אתה שלו' וביתך שלו' וכל אשר לך שלו'

---

[9] Benayahu, wrongly: יום ה'. In our opinion, the scribe started to write הנה and changed his mind.

[10] Benayahu, wrongly: להביאו. However, this may be what the writer actually intended.

25. [ואחר] הקדות[11] רוב השתחויות ממני. בפרט לכ"ר צדקה י"ל ולכל ביתו רוב
שלו' מאדון השלו' ותודיעני
26. [מכל הע]ובד וברוך שובר אויבים ושמחתי מאד על זה
27. עבדך אליא הכותב יום ג' כ'ד' לכסליו בטמייאט

Verso

1. המתהלך בתומו צדיק הוא איהו הנכ"ר[12] משה י"ל
2. בהנ"ר[13] יודה תנצב"ה[14] ושוי"א[15] בסכדרייא ינתן לשלו'

Translation

Recto

1. I wait for your deliverance, O LORD (Gen. 49.18).
2. [The] LORD [bless you] from Zion; may you see the prosperity of Jerusalem all the days of your life. May you see your children's children (Ps. 128.5–6). My dear beloved, the honourable rabbi Moses, may God save him. After many greetings, I inform you

[11] Benayahu: הקדוש [מהאל]; Hacker: הקדוש [לקהל], but it is clear that the word has been corrected. It looks as if the author first wrote הקדוש and then changed it to הקדות. See the translation.

[12] = הנכבד כבוד רבי.

[13] = בן הנכבד רבי.

[14] = תהא נשמתו צרורה בצרור החיים.

[15] Benayahu offers: ושלום וישע יקרב אמן/ ששון ושמחה ישיגו אמן/ ושולחו ומגיעו יבורך אמן. The last option seems the best, and it is similar to other typical blessings in address lines.

3. [that I have got] from your honour two letters by Ibrāhīm the dragoman, the first which the honourable rabbi Shlomo sent me from Candia (= Heraklion, Crete), and the other which he sent to your honour, which you are going to receive
4. [...]. In that letter, your honour wrote to me that you got the books, and you wrote also that the (scribe's) handwriting of the book of *Torat ha'Adam* is not
5. [beautiful] in your honour's eyes, and that there is a difference between it and (the quality of) the paper I have sent to your honour from Candia. About this—God knows how many efforts I made
6. [but] I could [not] fulfil your commandment. I talked once or twice with the scribe. And at the time I was personally in Candia the handwriting was good
7. [...] and much nicer than the paper I have sent to your honour. From this point I do not know what happened to it. Because of that, it was very difficult for me when I saw that
8. [you are not] satisfied with it. Anyhow, my master, God knows my abilities, and that everything I was able to do, I did not avoid doing. If it does not
9. [seem well in] your honour's view, your honour will accept my apology. In addition, about the money, my master, your honour knows as I wrote
10. [to you], look in my letters and you will find that I reached a compromise with the scribe for 20 *marcellos* for each *quntres,* and one more(?) *marcello* for the whole book.

11. [I] think that the whole book would come to 15 *quntreses,* but when I travelled from Candia I thought it would come to more than 17 *quntreses.*
12. [After all,] the book is in your hands. Measure them (= the *quntreses*), how many they decreased, and do the accounts, your honour, how much they cost, at a rate of 12 *marcellos*
13. [in one(?)] Venetian ducat. Concerning the book of Joseph ben Gurion, I think, if I am remembering well, I reached a compromise at two ducats, or two (ducats) and eight [*marcellos*(?)],[16] because, due to my sins,
14. [I do not remember] so well. Take my letters and see how much I have written to your honour. Nevertheless, I still have a doubt. If you do not find my letters, I have written
15. [to Candia], (to ask them) to inform me how much they cost. I will write more to your honour, according to the news. Another (issue): for the Esther scroll, it cost me half a
16. Venetian [ducat], and I need it in my state as a foreigner. Send it to me to Cairo via Mordukh, and he will send it to me here by the people who come, but if
17. [you want] it (for yourself), I submit to your command. Indeed, if you have one old (scroll), send (it) to me for Purim, and I will send it back immediately
18. [with those who come first] (or: [after Purim]). I will get your answer with those who carry my letter, which is going [to(?)] Eloisa(?) Pizan. Send these monies by the hand of Mordukh, and he

---

[16] Another option is that ב̇ וח' means ב̇ וח[צי] ‘two and a half (ducats)’.

19. [will bring them] here via Jews who come and return every day from Cairo to here. R. Solomon from Candia wrote to me that he sent me
20. [two(?)] other letters through you, but I did not get other letters except those mentioned before. Please open your eyes (to ensure that) if [the] letters
21. of mine would arrive [to you], send them to me immediately. I trust you on this matter. On the ... which your honour wrote me (about it), it was not [already] brought
22. from the same kind your honour wrote me about, so I did not buy it for your honour. Inform me if your honour needs it, maybe it will be brought by the time
23. the ... [will arrive], because they are expected to bring it here. If you need anything from here, command me and I shall fulfil your commandment. The money you will send
24. [...] Venetian ducats, or *marcellos*. After (all of that), I shall not draw out (this letter). Just peace be upon you, and upon your house (i.e., 'your wife', or 'your family'), and upon all that you have (1 Sam. 25.6),
25. [and after] bowing down, many prostrations from me. Especially for the honourable rabbi Ṣedaqah, may he live forever, and to all his family, a lot of peace from the master of peace. Inform me
26. [on everything that] happened (with you), and praised be the one who defeats enemies. I was very happy about it.
27. Your slave Eliya (Elijah), who is writing on Tuesday, the 24th of Kislev, in Damietta.

Verso

1. He who walks in his integrity as a righteous man (see Prov. 20.7), he is the notable, the honourable rabbi Moses, may he live forever,
2. the son of the notable rabbi Judah, may his soul be bound in the bundle of life. May he who sends it and gives it be blessed, Amen. In Alexandria, will be given in peace.

Commentary

Recto

Line 4:
Torat ha'Adam 'The Laws of Man' is a known halakhic book of Nahmanides (Rabbi Moses b. Nahman, 1194–1270), which contains the laws of mourning and burial.

Line 9:
"Your honour will accept my apology." The meaning of the Hebrew phrase is not clear. Our translation relies on the supposition that the author here used the word התנצלות (apology) as a verb in the passive form (מנוצל). Another option is that מנוצל is a unique form of the verb להינצל in the *pu'al* form, and the meaning is אנצל מכבודך, i.e., "I will be saved from (the anger of) your honour."

Line 10:
A *marcello* is a Venetian silver coin, named after Nicolo Marcello, the Duke of Venice (died in 1474). The book should cost, therefore, about 300 *marcellos* (20 *marcellos* per *quntres*), i.e., 25 ducats.

quntres 'quire, gathering' is a basic term in Hebrew codicology. Every *quntres* was made from some bifolia. Every bifolium was folded in half and contained four pages (from both sides). The number of bifolia per *quntres* was different from one book to another, but was regularly no more than ten. The standard size of a *quntres* in Italy and in the East in the Middle Ages was five bifolia, as compared to four bifolia in France, Germany, and Persia, and six bifolia in Spain and Byzantium (these details are based on the unpublished book by Malachi Bet-Arié, *Hebrew Codicology*). It is reasonable to assume that the local scribe in Candia followed the Byzantine-Jewish custom. If so, Elijah estimated that the book should contain 360 pages (90 bifolia). If the book was made according the Eastern-Italian custom, it would contain 300 pages (75 bifolia).

Line 13:
Joseph ben Gurion is the common Hebrew name of the book of Josippon.

Line 18:
"[to(?)] Eloisa(?) Pizan." The meaning is unclear, but it seems that the writer mentions here a Christian person, probably Italian. The name seems feminine; however, it is not reasonable to assume that Elijah was in contact with a female trader, and it is better to assume that he refers here to a man. Possibly this name is a different form of Louis Biz[a]ro (P.4.a/11).

Line 27:
The dated letters in our corpus come from the years 1481 to 1488. In 1480s, the 24th of Kislev fell on Tuesday only in ה'רמ"ז, 30 November 1486 (the closest other possible years are 1476 [19

December] and 1490 [16 December]). The other letter by Elijah in the corpus (P.5.b) comes from the year 1484, so the dating of this letter to 1486 is very likely.

P.5.b: Letter from Elijah b. Elyaqim to Moses b. Judah

Bodl. MS Heb. c. 72/14

General Description

This is a letter from Elijah b. Elyaqim to Moses b. Judah, in Hebrew and Venetian.

The letter was probably written on 12 June 1484. The year is not mentioned in the Hebrew text, but on the verso there is a short text in Venetian, in a different hand, from 8 June 1484, which was the festival of Shavuʿot (Pentecost), according to the Hebrew calendar. The Hebrew letter itself is dated at the end by mentioning the weekly Torah portion read in the synagogue: "on Thursday, in (the time of the reading of) the *parasha* of 'The seven lamps shall give light'" (Num. 8.2). This verse is from the *parasha* of *Behaʿalotekha* (Num. 8.1–12.16). In that year, this portion was read on Saturday 14 June 1484, so the letter was written two days before, on 12 June.

The deciphering of the Venetian text is difficult, even for researchers used to reading medieval Italian manuscripts. We want to thank Prof. Benjamin Arbel, Prof. Charles Burnett, Dr Christopher Wright, Dr Mike Carr, and Dr Renard Gluzman for their help.

The Hebrew part of the letter was published by Benayahu (1984, 263).

The fragment also contains mirrored script on both sides, which was transferred from two missing letters, probably while

 https://doi.org/10.11647/OBP.0352.28

stored in an archive. The text on the verso comes from the beginning of a letter by the Nagid to the community of Alexandria and is discussed under C.1.d. The beginning of the Nagid's letter preserved here was written in Hebrew but the letter itself was probably composed in Judaeo-Arabic. The text on the recto is a smaller piece from another unpreserved letter, which was written in Hebrew. Three blurred lines were copied to our letter, but we can only read כי באמ[ת] 'which indeed' from the first line, and the words וליהודים ולישמעלים(!) 'and to the Jews and the Muslims' from the second line.

Physical Description

22.4 × 20.1; paper; 1 leaf; 17 lines + 3 partial lines of mirrored script (recto); 3 lines + 7 partial lines of mirrored script (verso); torn, holes, beige stains.

Transcription

Recto

1. [א]הוב[י] היקר ונעלה כ"ר משה ת"ל יחד עם כל הדורשים בשלומך ממני אהובך אליא המודיעך
2. [א]יך קבלתי כתבך ודבריך בטוב הבנתיו. ובא אצלי הערל בעד היין ובעד הגבינה ובקשנו
3. [מ]אד בעבור היין ואינם רוצים פחות מדוקטי ז' והוצאות א'[1] אשר יעלה עד[2] הביצית דוקטי

---

[1] = אחד.

[2] Benayahu: עוד.

4. [ח]משה[3] ונראה לי ביוקר גדול ועוד כי השעה היה נחוצה ואם כבודך חפץ תודיע לערל וישלח
5. [א]ותו לכבודך עם הדוגייאות של ונצייאן ואשתדל לו כמה שעולה ~~בידך לא~~ ~~ב[.]~~ בידי לאהבתך
6. [וע]ל אודות הגבינה אינו נמצא כעת כל כך טוב ועם הקודם אמר לי הערל להשתדל לשולחו
7. [עם(?)] היותר טוב. ואם תרצה היין תודיענו עם הקודם לשלוח אותו עם הדוגייאות עכ"פ
8. [ב]עבור הספר פרוש התורה לרבנו משה ב"ר נחמן הלכתי ומצאתי השר ויטור דוגעו ואומר
9. [כי] אינו יודע דבר. ואני בקשתי בקהל ומצאתי א' של ניירים יותר חדש מיישן [בכ]תיבה[4] יפה
10. [וש]ואלים[5] דוקטי ח' לכן תודיעני רצונך ואקיים גזרתך. עו' נודע אלי איך יש במקום אחד ספר
11. [של][6] קלפי' ושואלי' דוקטי ט"ו ומה שיתחדש אקשיבך[7] עם הקודם תן רוב שלו' לכ"ר שולאימן
12. [...]אש ו[ל]כל ביתו ותאמר לכבודו בעד השופר איך עשו לו[8] ג' ולא יצא אחד מהם טוב עכ"ז
13. [ע]לי הדאגה לקיים גזרתו אחר[9] אין לי להאריך רק אתה שלו' וכל אשר לך שלו'

---

[3] Benayahu reads wrongly: שמונה.

[4] Benayahu: והכתיבה.

[5] Benayahu: [שו]אלים.

[6] Maybe: [על], or: ['א].

[7] Benayahu: אשיבך, but the reading אקשיבך is clear. It looks like a scribal error.

[8] Benayahu: לי.

[9] Benayahu reads wrongly: יותר. Compare P.5.a/24.

14. [ול]כל[10] הקהל הקדוש רוב שלו' מאדון השלו' [ו]לכ"ר[11] צדקה יצ"ו רוב שלו' ולכמ"ר[12] אברהם
15. [ת]למיד י"א אלף שלומות ולר'[13] יוסף קשטרו ספרדי אלף שלומות
16. [א]הובך אליא ב"ר אליקים מקניאה הכותב
17. בחפזון[14] בקנדיאה ביום ה' בפרשת יאירו שבעת הנרות
18. [אלי]א [ב"ר] א[לי]קים(?)

Verso

Various readings have been suggested:

a) In Christi nomine 1484 7 d(ie) de Jugo in chandia graciosso domino on ....mo d(ie) delpasato per via de damiata fo. Chandi culva destine don in persona atrovar nostra magistra
b) Ite(m) no(m)i(n)e 1484 [5] d(ie) de Zug(n)o i(n) Chandia |2 [G..c]ra[ss]o deci(m)o o[m(ni)mo(do?)] [a] [Q(ui ?)...] Delpastito Io(hannes) de Via de Damiata fo cul[ta] mia (et)c(etera) Chandida |3 ch[..]bi cul[t]a discrete dov[er] vegnir i(n) p(er)sona (et) trovar vost(ra) Mag(nificentia)
c) In C[hristo] no[m]in[o] 1484/ A d[ie] d[e] Jugo i[n] Candia – graciosso d[o]m[in]o omnino ad.. drepa..to per

---

[10] Benayahu: [ל]כל.

[11] Benayahu: ולכה"ר.

[12] It seems the word cannot be read as ולכה"ר.

[13] Benayahu: ולהר'.

[14] This is Benayahu's reading, but it is doubtful. The reading seems rather to be: [ב]חיפזון.

via d[omi]n[a] damiata fo. Cul .. n[ost]r[a] Candia .. Culva disrm..r do.. .. in persona atrovar nostra magistra

d) In Christo nomine, 1484 a dì 8 Zugno, in Chandia. Generosso d(o)m(in)o oner(andissi)mo a dì 14 del pasato p(er) via de Damieta f'u l'ult(im)a mia rechoma(n)da Michelli cusin di(Si)me dover vegnir in p(er)sona a trovar vostra mag(nificenti)a

Translation

Recto

1. My beloved, dear and exalted, the honourable rabbi Moses, shall you live forever(?),[15] together with all who inquire about your wellbeing, from me, your beloved Elijah, who informs you
2. that I got your letter, and I understood your words well. The Christian came to me for the wine and for the cheese. We were looking for
3. the wine very much. They do not want less than seven ducats, and expenses of one who charges it on the little boat
4. five (ducats), so I thought it is too expensive. Also, the time was busy. If your honour wants, inform the Christian, and he will send
5. it to your honour with the Venetians' ships and I will make an effort for him as much as I can, because I love you.

---

[15] If we read ת"ל as תחיה לעד. Maybe: תהילתו לעד ('his glory is forever').

6. About the cheese—it does not exist now in good enough (quality). The last time the Christian asked me to make an effort to send
7. [with(?)] the better. If you want the wine, let us know with the first one to send it by the boats anyhow.
8. For the book of the Torah's commentary of Our Rabbi Nachmanides, I went and found the Minister Vitorio Dujaou, and he says
9. [that] he does not know anything. I looked for it among the community, and I have found one on paper, more new than old, with [nice handwriting,]
10. and they [demand] eight ducats (for it), so inform me of your wish and I shall fulfil your commandment. Another (issue)—I have been informed that in one place there is a book
11. [on] vellum, and they demand 15 ducats. I will reply to you concerning what is new with the first one (who will come). Inquire about the wellbeing of the honourable rabbi Sulaiman
12. [...] and all his family, and tell his honour about the *shofar* that they made three for him, but none of them was made in good quality. Nevertheless,
13. the responsibility to fulfil his commandment is [upon me]. After (all of that) I shall not draw out, except (to bless): peace be upon you, and peace be to all that you have (1 Sam. 25.6),
14. and a lot of peace from the master of peace upon the whole holy community. [And also], a lot of peace upon the honourable rabbi Ṣedaqah, may God save him, and a thousand peace for the honourable our teacher(?) Rabbi Abraham

15. Talmid, may God save him, and a thousand peace upon R. Joseph Castro, the Sephardi.
16. Your beloved, Elijah, son of Rabbi Elyaqim from Chania, who is writing
17. hastily(?) in Candia, on Thursday, in (the time of the reading of) the *parasha* of "The seven lamps shall give light" (Num. 8.2).
18. [Eliy]a (Elijah) [son of R.] E[lya]qim

Commentary

Recto

Line 1:
"My beloved." See the other letter from Elijah, P.5.a/2.

Line 2:
"The cheese." On the import of cheese from Crete to Egypt, see Introduction, §2.3.

Line 3:
"Little boat." The term *beṣit* (ביצית) for a small boat is talmudic (see b. Bava Batra 73a). The usage here probably follows Maimonides: "When a person sells a ship, included in the sale are the mast, the sail, its anchors… Not included in the sail is the *beṣit*—the small boat in which one sails to land" (*Mishne Torah, Mechirah* 27.1–2). See also note to line 5.

Line 5:
"The Venetians' ships." The author uses two different terms, דוגית and ביצית. In the Talmud, however, the terms are considered the same: ביצית היינו דוגית '*beṣit* is the same as *dugit*' (b. Bava Batra

73a). According to the talmudic passage, *beṣit* was in use in the language of Babylonian Jews, while *dugit* was in use among Palestinian Jews.

Line 13:
"I shall not draw out" (אין לי להאריך). See the other letter from Elijah: אחר אין להאריך (P.5.a/24).

Line 14:
"Rabbi Abraham Talmid." *Talmid* means 'pupil'. Abraham was a rich man of Spanish origin who was active in Egypt in the last quarter of the fifteenth century and in the first quarter of the sixteenth century. He was one of the advisors of Solomon b. Joseph the Nagid and later banned by the last Nagid, R. Isaac Sholal, after a confrontation between them. He is mentioned in several Genizah documents (see Assaf 1946, 197–99; David 1991).

Line 15:
"R. Joseph Castro, the Sephardi." Castro was a well-known Sephardic family, its members settling in Cairo, Alexandria, Jerusalem, and other places after the expulsion from the Iberian Peninsula. The most famous figures of this family were Abraham Castro, who was one of the leaders of Egyptian Jewry in the first half of the sixteenth century, and Abraham's son, R. Jacob Castro, one of the famous rabbis in Egypt in the second half of the sixteenth century, and the author of the responsa collection *Ohale Yaʿaqov*.

Line 16:
"Chania." A city in Crete (Canea in Venetian, Χανιά in Greek).

Verso

Information gleaned from the different interpretations of the letter on the verso shows that the letter was written in June 1484 in Chandia and sent via the route of Damietta.

P.6: Letter from Isaac Bayt ʿAṭṭān to Moses b. Judah

Bodl. MS Heb. c. 72/18

General Description

A letter to Moses b. Judah from Isaac Bayt ʿAṭṭān, written in Judaeo-Arabic. Isaac, probably of northwest African origin judging by the handwriting and the linguistic properties of the letter, writes from Syracuse and informs the addressee about the troubles and hardships he had on his journey, and asks him to help a Christian Catalan trader who is preparing to come from Sicily to Alexandria.

Linguistic Description

The letter exhibits a number of colloquial features, such as מתע for the possessive particle and באש as a consecutive connector, which linguistically pinpoints the origin of the writer to North Africa. This is also confirmed by the distinctly North-African handwriting.

Physical Description

22.6 × 20.4; paper; 1 leaf; 20 lines (recto); 4 lines (verso); holes, red-brown stains; address on verso is written transversely in relation to recto— it is written between two folds, which suggests the letter was folded over into a small strip, with only the address visible on the outside, similar to Genizah letters from the eleventh century.

 https://doi.org/10.11647/OBP.0352.29

Transcription

Recto

1. בעד אל סלאם אל גליל אל חביב אל כרים אל עאלם אל שאמל ה"ר ~~ייד~~ משה בן יודה
2. נעלמך באן בעד אלדי אפתרקנה מנכום קאציינה כתיר פי אל טריק מן גהה̈ אל
3. אל[1] מרכב אלדי כאנת תעמל מא אכתיר ואל כאלק תעאלה פריג עלינה וצלנה
4. פי רודוס וקעדנה פי רודוס דקס שהריין. ואפתרקנה מאע ואחד אל בארכה
5. באש נמורו פי סרקוסה ומורנה למדון ונקצנה שוי כובז ונביד וגיירה נזל ר' צוריאל
6. ור' מצליח באש יאשתריו אל כובז ואל נביד נאס אל בלד ומר אל קארב ואל נאס ואל
7. יהוד אלדי כאנו מן פוק ועמרו זוג מראכב באש יאכדו אל מרכב מתענה.
8. אוחניו ריינה דאלךּ אל שי קטענה אל חבל והרבנה ובקיו אל יהוד פי מדון
9. וכדאלךּ בקא ר' צוריאל פי מדון ואנא אל יום סרקוסה נעלמך באן יגי ענדך
10. ואחד אל נצראני קטלאני אסמו מיסר ברנארד לו אזינה נסראני גיד נרגבך באן תאקף
11. שוי מעה בפיידה מתעך ומתעה אלדי דאלך אל נצראני אסתקסה אש אנסאן פי
12. סכנדרייא אלדי הו יסוא יאקף פי מטגר וגיירה ואנא קולת לה פיהא ואחד אסמו
13. ר' משה והו אנסאן סמסאר ויסוא פי כל שי. איצׄה הו יגיב מעה כמס מית
14. קטעה גבון טהור באל חותם מתענה ויגיב מעה ואחד אל כותאב מן אל דיין מתענה

---

[1] The word was twice written wrongly.

15. כאן דאלךּ אל גבון הו כשר וטהור ודאלךּ אל גבון אשתראה בריאיי אנא.
16. נעלמך באן אל ספרים אלדי ועתך באש נבעתך מא כאן לי זמן נכתובהם לך לאכן
17. מן דאלךּ אלדי ועת[ך] מוסרע יגיאוךּ וסלם מן גהתי כתיר לשלום ה"ר אברהם
18. תלמיד. איצׄה לחסיד הנכבד ה"ר צדקה קונטייס(?) איצׄה לנכבד ר' יושוע המכונה
19. נגיב. וסלם מן גהתי לגמיע אל חבאב. ושלום
20. מהיי לאמרך יצחק בית עטאן

Signature jotting

Verso

1. ליד היקר הנעים הנכבד
2. הנ[ח]מד איש חמודות
3. כה"ר משה בן יודה
4. מן סרקוסה לסכנדריי[א]

Translation

Recto

1. After greetings to the dear, the beloved, the honourable, the one of comprehensive knowledge, the honourable rabbi Moses ben Judah,
2. I inform you that after we separated from you, we suffered[2] a great deal because a lot of water was leaking into

[2] See Friedman (2016b, 819).

3. the ship,[3] but the Creator, may he be exalted, saved us,[4] and we arrived
4. in Rhodes and stayed in Rhodes for about two months. We departed with a *barca*
5. in order to go to Syracuse and went to Modon. We were lacking bread and wine, and other (things). R. Ṣuriel
6. and R. Maṣliaḥ went down (from the ship) in order to buy bread and wine (from) the country people, and then the (small) boat went off (to the shore), with both the (non-Jewish) people and the
7. Jews on it. Then a pair of ships approached in order to seize our ship.
8. They revealed themselves, and (when) we saw this, we cut the hawser and fled, while the Jews remained in Modon.
9. So R. Ṣuriel remained in Modon and I am now in Syracuse. I inform you that
10. a Christian Catalan will come to you, his name is Messer Bernard Lo Azina. He is a nice Christian. I want you to support
11. him somewhat, for your and his benefit: this Christian inquired about someone in
12. Alexandria who is (his) equal, to support (him) in the marketplace, and in other (things). I told him: there is someone in (Alexandria), his name is
13. R. Moses. He is an agent and equal (to you) in every regard. Also, he will bring with him five hundred

[3] See Friedman (2016b, 654).

[4] See Friedman (2016b, 713).

14. pieces of kosher cheese with our seal, and he will bring with him a letter from our *dayyan* (Jewish judge),
15. (certifying) that this cheese is indeed kosher and pure. He bought this cheese under my advice.
16. I inform you that the books which I promised you to send to you—I did not have time to copy them for you but
17. those which I promised to you—I am making haste so that they will arrive at yours (soon). Relay from me many greetings to the honourable rabbi Abraham
18. Talmid, and also to the honourable *ḥasid* (pious) rabbi Ṣedaqah Contias(?), and also to the honourable R. Joshua known as
19. Najīb, and greet for me all the loved ones. Peace (will be).
20. Ready for your command, Isaac Bayt ʿAṭṭān.

Verso

1. For the beloved, the pleasant, the honourable,
2. the lovely, a man greatly beloved (Dan. 10.11),
3. the honourable rabbi Moses b. Judah,
4. from Syracuse to Alexandria.

Commentary

Recto

Line 4:
"Rhodes." Rhodes is the central city in the island of Rhodes and is located at its northern end. During the period of our corpus, it was under the rule of the Hospitaller order. In 1480 CE, the Ottomans besieged the island, but did not succeed in conquering it,

and Rhodes remained under the knights' rule until 1522 CE, when Sulaymān the Magnificent occupied it. A small Jewish community existed in the city in this period, and its members were apparently the hosts of the writer and his group. According to Obadiah of Bertinoro, who visited the city in December 1487 CE, only 22 Jewish families lived there, but it seems that the community diminished through the 1480s CE and had been bigger before the Ottoman campaign.

"About two months." In Maltese, *daqs* means 'about, near, approximate' (see Aquilina 2006, 204). We wish to thank Prof. Michael Cooperson for this information.

"*Barca.*" A kind of a small boat (in Spanish and Italian).

Line 5:

"Syracuse." One of the most central cities in Sicily, Syracuse experienced a period of Islamic control, but was controlled by Christian forces again from 1086 CE. The Muslim and Jewish populations, however, remained part of the Arabic world to some extent. The Jews in Syracuse, as well as other Sicilian cities, continued to speak and write in Judaeo-Arabic (at least as a second language) and had strong ties with their co-religionists in North Africa and Egypt. Sicily came under Spanish influence from the end of the thirteenth century CE, and moved, in a continuous process, into the ownership of the Crown of Aragon. In 1460 CE it became officially part of the kingdom, under the rule of Ferdinand the Second. At the time when this letter was written, the Jews of Syracuse were still a flourishing community, but a short time later, in 1492 CE, all Sicilian Jews were expelled from the island, as from all Spanish territories. A large number of them settled in the Mamlūk state and in the Ottoman Empire.[5] The nickname סרקוסטי/סרקוסי/סרגוסי 'Siraqūsī' is common in the Genizah and in other documents, but it is difficult to determine, in some cases, if this refers to someone's origin from Syracuse in Sicily, or Saragossa in Spain. However, sometimes Syracusian origin is mentioned explicitly, as in the case of Siman-Ṭov, son of David Barceloni "from the town Syracuse of Sicily" (מן עיר סרקוסת אצקלייא), who copied the *Mikhlol* of R. David Kimḥi in Jerusalem and Hebron in 1439 CE (MS Paris, Bibliothèque Nationale heb. 1237).

"Modon." Modon is the Venetian name of Methoni, a city in the western Peloponnese (Italian: Modone; Spanish: Modona). While most of the Peloponnese, which was called Morea in this period, was ruled by the Byzantines, this city and some other cities close by[6] were under Venetian rule. The Ottomans had captured most of the peninsula by 1461 CE, but Modone remained in the hands of the Venetians until the second Ottoman-Venetian war (1499–1503 CE), when the city was conquered by the army of *sulṭān* Bayezid the Second (1500 CE). Modone's port was a central station in the maritime route from Venice to Palestine and Egypt (on this maritime route see, for example, TS 10J16.32, a Hebrew letter of a Jewish merchant, who probably lived in Egypt, from the fifteenth or the sixteenth century: הגיעה הספינה ממודון 'the ship from Modone has arrived').

---

[5] Concerning these communities in the Ottoman Empire, see Schwarzfuchs (1995).

[6] Koron, Navarino, Argos, and Nauplion (see *EI*[2], s.v. 'Mora').

"R. Ṣuriel." Maybe this is Ṣuriel Dayyan, the writer of letter P.7.

באש. The word *baš* is used throughout this letter as the connective 'so that', which points to the northwest African origin of the writer; see the detailed analysis in §III.2.10.3.

Line 6:
"R. Maṣliaḥ." The name is not known from other documents in the corpus.

Line 7:
The writer did not identify the nationality of the hostile sailors. The Mediterranean Sea was at that time a zone of activity for many naval forces: Mamlūks, Ottomans, Spaniards, Venetians, and others, as well as pirates. It is therefore difficult to know who those boatmen besieging the writer's boat were.

Line 10:
On the Catalan traders that settled in Sicily, see Dauverd (2006).

Line 14:
"Kosher cheese with our seal." According to the *halakhah*, a cheese made by a gentile, even if the milk itself is kosher, is forbidden (see m. ʿAvodah Zarah 2.5; b. ʿAvodah Zarah 35a; *Mishne Torah*, *Maʾakhalot Asurot* 3.13). In the Talmud, the practice of stamping a product with a seal as a testimony that the product is kosher is mentioned regarding a barrel of wine, but later it became popular also with other products, such as cheese. The seal serves the purpose of proving that no one has opened the package and replaced the kosher cheese with unsupervised cheese.

Line 16:

"I did not have time to copy them." Most likely, Isaac did not intend to copy them himself, but to pay a scribe to write them.

Line 17:

"Abraham Talmid." See commentary on letter P.5.b.

Line 18:

"Ṣedaqah Contias(?) and also... R. Joshua known as Najīb." We have no information on these two. The second appears to be a local Jew, while the first may be a Spanish immigrant. Najīb is probably also mentioned in letter C.5, where Moses is asked to send him regards. Ṣedaqah's title, *ḥasid* (pious), is very interesting for the time and means that R. Ṣedaqah engaged in spiritual praxis, although we cannot determine what exactly this implied.

P.7: Letter from Ṣuriel Dayyan to Moses b. Judah

Bodl. MS Heb. c. 72/23

General Description

A letter to Moses b. Judah, written in Judaeo-Arabic. The identity of the writer is not entirely clear. The handwriting is similar to that of Isaac Bayt ʿAṭṭān in letter P.6 (and it also seems he wrote the address lines on the verso). The last three lines were written in a different quill pen and were signed by Ṣuriel Dayyan. We know from P.6 that Isaac and Ṣuriel were partners, who probably worked for Moses b. Judah. It seems that the greater part of the letter was written by Isaac, and then Ṣuriel appended an addition, but the handwriting in both parts is very similar, and part of the letter (which perhaps contained Isaac's signature) is missing, so it is difficult to know exactly what part each of them had in composing this letter. The carrier of the letter was someone called David (l. 19). The letter contains details on Moses' business and information about scrolls and books he had asked be bought for him.

Physical Description

28.3 × 18.9; paper; 1 leaf; 35 lines (recto); 4 lines (verso); verso is written transversely in relation to recto; torn, holes, badly rubbed and faded, red-brown stains.

 https://doi.org/10.11647/OBP.0352.30

Transcription

Recto

1. [בעד אל סלאם ... ...]ל אל עאלם אל[שאמל וכל] גמעתה ה"ר משה בן יודה מע וגה [...]
2. [... ... ...]יא נח[נא(?)] פי [... ... ...] אל נסק יסמענה ענכום כייר ועפייה [אנ"ס]
3. נעלמכו[ם באן... ... ...] נגי סכנדרייא וכדאלך ענדי ביעה [...]
4. בעקׄ מתגה פי אל גרב באל [נ]צרייא ברצם אלדי נ[ש]תרי צׄהב באיש נגיבו סכנ[דרייא(?)] כדאלך [...]
5. פי ~~סכנדרייא~~ טרבלס אל דוכלה מ[..]רה תסווה כמסה וארבעין ענדי מו' [...] וכדאלך חסבה [...]
6. ב[עקׄ] אלנצרייא אלדי ענד[כום ..]תם ביהום צׄהב נציב אלדי נתלף דקׄ עושרין אל מייא וכמתל
7. נצ[ר]ייא לייס יכרגו פי אל שרק חסבת אלדי נק[עד] פי טרבלס חתי' אלרדא מתע אל טרא[בלסיין]
8. [וכמ]תל ד'י אל זמן [... נש]תרי לופה ונרגע לסכנדרייא בסלאם ונתכל באל כאלק אלדי ב[...]
9. [...]לד ש[... ... ...] נעלמך באן יתצלךׄ מע אל גלייאסה מתע גל[ייא]ס מושט עניא[...]
10. [... ... ...] ממלוץ(?) בפווא(?) ב754 איצׄה שוכרה אוכ[.....]ה ולד תכׄלץ
11. [... ... ...] פצׄה עדוד סע ~~תי [..]~~ כ"ה[1] מאידי אלי אש[תריית(?) ... ...]ה
12. [... ... ...] דלפיהא אסמו מ' נקלו קורניר זווג חצור פווה ותשתחץ(?) ולד תכלץ [...]
13. [...]פייא [...] א[...] יתצלך מע אל שכרץ אל מד' בלא ש[.]וקי דאכלהא עשרי פי

---

[1] The author first wrote ת"ה (405), and then deleted it and wrote כ"ה (25).

14. [...] וגי[...] בלא זנגאר דאכלהא נד[...] וזנ[הא] קנט' אלא רטל סרקוסי בלצ[..]ש ג[.] איצ̇ה סנה

15. ודכלת אל ספר תורה אלדי אשתריית לך ודכל אל סנדוק אל מד' ספר העקרים וד' נביאים ראשוני[ם]

16. ופירושם כפל קאלב נעלמך לאן אל ספר אלדי אשתריית אלק[..]ה ואמליח כתיר כתיר ומדחייה כתיר

17. כתיר כאם אפשר אלדי יכון פי אל ~~דונייא~~ עולם וכביכול יגדר יוקללו ספר עזרא ונסאל [...]

18. נכון ענדכום נערפכום כל שי בפרט איצ̇ה יתצלך מע אל שכרוץ אל מד' נקולו קורניר

19. אלמקר מסנון איצ̇ה יתצלך מע ר' דוד חאמל כותבנה די' ג' קצב פרפ[...] מן אל מד[..]

20. אלדי [..]יתני וכמתל יתצלך [.]תו[..]ך קודס גבון ח מעצם כולהום מן גהתי ומן גיהת ר' ישר[אל]

21. [...] איצ̇ה נעלמך באן ר' אברהם הרירא פי תונס עטאני זווג דודלי משחרה ורב[..]

22. עותמאנייא וזווג בראני מעגון נעלמך לאן דלך אל זווג בראני מעגון יתצלו לך מ[ע ר']

23. דוד אל מד' וזווג [ד]ודלי ואדה אכצהום מע ר' יצחק שולל עלי [כתי]בת ספר הקנה ועש[..]

24. נגי נציר נגיבו מעי נעלמך באן כאן כון תביעו כל שי' [.]אכ[.]ו ענכום ומגאייה בס[..]

25. נערפכום כל שי ובפרט נעלמך באן אל מאיורקיני ~~יק~~ יקומו גאליין כתיר כתיר אן [...]

26. פיהום סעי' טייבין תמיד ואן לם סברו חתי' מגייה בסלם ואל לאון [ו]מנשי אל מאיורקיי[ני]

27. בדי' אל ט[... ...] ד' אזרק מגלוק ד' אכצ̇ר מגלוק [..]אל וזן אל כרוגה. איצ̇ה נעל[מד]

28. [... ...] כותאב יתצלך אל פודסי מתע אל שכרוץ אל ואחד ואל אכיר ופי אל מאי[..]
29. [...] וספר ואלמקץ אלייס(?) ענדי פ[...] ולא וחדי [... ...] וקביית פי אל ש[...]
30. [... ...] כאן נקלו קורניר ולא הום מעכיין פי אל גוך וכו[...] דאלך אל[...]יס [........]
31. [...] לאן תווצל גמיע דאלך אל כות[אב] לצחבהום [...]

In a different (?) hand:

32. [... ... ...] תנעטי מן גה[ת א]ל[...]
33. [... ..]ייא אוכרין גייר אלדי כתב ל[ך ...]
34. [... ...] יין ג[.]ל מתע טרטר(?) וגיירה
35. [אוכתיב יום X] כ"ד סיון צוריאל דיין

Verso

1. יצל ליד אל גליל [אל ...]יל אל
2. [......] אל מעלם אל נגיב(?)
3. מקדם [.]מ[...] ה"ר משה [ב"ר]
4. יודה [מן ס]רק[וסה] ל[סכנדרייא(?)]

Translation

Recto

1. [After greetings to ... ...] the one of [comprehensive] knowledge [and all] his group, the honourable rabbi Moses ben Judah together with the presence of [...]
2. [... ... We] are in [a state of(?)] good order. May (God) let us hear from you (only) good news and well-being. [Amen, forever.]

3. We inform you [that... ... ...] we will come to Alexandria. Also, I have with me merchandise [...]
4. some of it destined for the West with the Christians, with the intention that I will buy gold(?) for everything that I will bring to Alexandria. Also, [...]
5. in Tripolis, the [...] import tax comes to 45. I have 46(?) [...] Also, the account of [...]
6. [some of] the Christians who are with [you ... ...] gold for them, we should chance upon someone who we can ... 20 per hundred. Likewise,
7. the Christians will not depart to the East so that we shall [stay] in Tripolis until the return of the Tri[politans]
8. [and likewise] that to [... we (or: I) will] buy cotyledon-plant and return to Alexandria safely. We will rely on the Creator who [...]
9. [... ... ...] we (or: I) inform you that it will reach you with the galleass-ship belonging with the [galleass-ships] of ... [...]
10. [... ... ...] ... in Fuwwa(?) at 754. Also ... [... ...] For you it will arrive
11. [... ...] silver number ... 25 *mu'ayyadī* [I bought(?) ... ...]
12. [... ... ...] ... his name is Mr Nicolo Cornier, a pair of mats ... ... for you, it will finish
13. [... ... ...] will connect(?) you with the mentioned ..., without hangings(?) inside it ......
14. [... ...] without verdigris inside it [... Its] weight is a *qinṭār* minus one Syracusian *raṭl* .... Also, ...

15. The Torah scroll which I bought for you arrived. The mentioned chest arrived, The Book of Principles, (the) Four Former Prophets
16. and their commentary … … We let you know because the book I bought is … and most beautiful, very much so, and very praiseworthy,
17. as much as there could possibly be in the world. So to speak, it is appropriate to call it 'Ezra's scroll'. We ask […]
18. we should be with you to inform you of everything in particular. Also, it should arrive to you with the mentioned … Nicolo Cornier
19. traditional … Also, it should arrive to you with R. David, the carrier of our letter, these three … of the …
20. which … likewise, it should arrive to you … … eight (pieces) of … cheese, all of them from me and from R. Isr[ael].
21. […] Also, we inform you that R. Abraham Herrera is in Tunis. He gave me a pair of black … and
22. Ottoman (Turkish) … and a pair of earthenware pots (filled with) *maʿjūn*. We tell you because this pair of earthenware pots (filled with) *maʿjūn* should arrive to you [with the]
23. mentioned [R.] David and a pair of … When he took them with R. Isaac Sholal for the [copying] of the *Sefer ha-Qanah* […]
24. (when) I go to Naṣīr, I will bring it with me. We inform you that you….. buy everything, we will … approaching […]
25. We inform you of everything. In particular, we would like you to know that (for) the Mallorcan, they will impose a lot of poll-tax that […]

26. of them good, always, and that they did not examine until (their) safe arrival. Al-Leon and Menashe the Mallorcan
27. with these [... ...], four blue closed, four green closed, ... departure weight. Also, we inform [you]
28. [that ...] books will reach you with ... . the first and the last, in the ...
29. [...] and a book, and ... ... with me, [...] ... ... I collected in the [...]
30. [...]was Nicolo Cornier. and they are not filling(?) the cloth [...] this [... ... ...]
31. [...] because you should send all of these [books] via their owners [...]

In a different (?) hand:

32. [...] was given from the side of [...]
33. [... ...] ... without those he wrote [to you ... ...]
34. [...] ... ... and so on.
35. [I am writing on X(day)] 24th of Sivan, Ṣuriel Dayyan.

Verso

1. (This letter) should arrive to the illustrious, [the ...], the
2. [... ...] the *muʿallim*, the generous(?)
3. [the] *muqaddam* [... ...] the honourable rabbi Moses [son of rabbi]
4. Judah [from Syracuse to Alexandria(?)]

Commentary

Recto

Line 1:

For the completion here, compare P.6.

Line 4:

"For the West." I.e., the Maghreb.

Line 5:

"Tripolis." This is the Libyan Ṭarābulus al-Ġarb, rather than the Lebanese Ṭarābulus al-Shām.

Line 9:

"Galleass" (from Italian *galeazza*). Although later this term was attributed to a military ship, here it refers to a commercial ship, probably of Venetian sailors.

Line 12:

"Nicolo Cornier." An early fifteenth-century Nicolo Corner (Cornier) is mentioned in Chojnacki (1999).

Line 15:

"The Book of Principles." Written by R. Joseph Albo, this book is one of the central books in medieval Jewish philosophy. Albo (1380–1444 CE) was a rabbi in various communities in Aragon and Castile and took part in the Tortosa debate in 1413–14 CE. He discussed the list of principles by Maimonides (which contains 13 principles) and reduced them to only three (the existence of God, the revelation at Mt Sinai, and the divine Justice).

"(The) Four Former Prophets and their commentary." We do not know which commentary this was—perhaps that of R. David Qimḥi, a leaf of which (from his commentary on Kings) is contained in our corpus (W3).

Line 17:
The word "world" was first written in Arabic, then crossed out, and replaced with the Hebrew word. Evidently, the feeling was that the Arabic word did not quite convey the concept as fully as the Hebrew word.

"It is appropriate to call it 'Ezra's scroll'." The writer does not refer here to the biblical book with this name, but means 'Ezra's book', i.e., the Torah scroll written by Ezra the scribe. One of the explanations for the name of Ben-Ezra synagogue is that an old book was kept in it, which was held by the worshippers to be an ancient book written by Ezra the scribe himself. It seems that this legend is reflected in the words of the writer here. Ezra was a 'local cultural hero' in eastern synagogues, along with Elijah, and some synagogues were dedicated to him. One of the most famous among these was the old synagogue of Tedef (near Aleppo), where local inhabitants (both Jews and Muslims) identified the grave of Ezra/ʿUzair. Other 'Ezra synagogues' were located in Diyarbakir, Nusaybin, ʿAmadiya (Iraqi Kurdistan), and more. For a discussion of the 'Ezra synagogues', see Krauss (1928, 238–39); Ben-Yaakov (1974, 178–84). It seems that the writer wanted to praise the value of the Torah scroll he bought by comparing it to the famous 'Ezra scroll'. For wider discussion of the Ezra scrolls and the Ezra synagogues, see Arad (in press a).

Line 22:

"A pair of earthenware pots (filled with) *maʿjūn*." The term *maʿjūn* has various meanings in dictionaries. Here it is probably a hemp paste, a material which produces similar effects to hashish. The writer's intention is unclear. It is possible to interpret that he means the addressee will use this hemp for his pleasure, but maybe he only means to describe the pots as being made with this paste.

Line 23:

"R. Isaac Sholal." The absence of honorific adjectives here, and the mentioning of Sholal without the title 'Nagid', testifies that the letter was written before Sholal was appointed as Nagid in circa 1484.

"*Sefer ha-Qanah*." See commentary on P.1/32.

Line 26:

"Al-Leon." The prefix 'Al' (the prefix of definiteness in Arabic) here is strange and looks like a scribal error.

Verso

Line 4:

"[from Syracuse to Alexandria(?)]." For this possible completion, see P.6/v4.

P.8: Letter from Mardūḵ Qarqūsa to Israel ʿAṭāʾīn and Yeraḥmiel ʿAṭāʾīn

Bodl. MS Heb. c. 72/37
1488

General Description

Three fragments of letters concerning business affairs. Judaeo-Arabic.

The connection between these three fragments is not entirely clear. It seems that the first and the second were dictated and/or composed by Mardūḵ Qarqūsa. The first one was dictated by Mardūḵ but written out by a different scribe, who had more readable handwriting but little practice in writing Judaeo-Arabic, and did not finish his work. The second part was then written by Mardūḵ himself. Mardūḵ is also mentioned in the third fragment, written on the verso in a third hand. It is not clear who the writer is or what the connection is to the fragments on the recto.

In the right margin of the verso, there is a copy in mirror script of letter P.3.b/9–18.

Physical Description

28.4 × 20; paper; 1 leaf; 25 lines (recto); 7 lines + 4 lines written inversely + 8 lines mirrored script (verso); torn, rubbed, beige stains.

 https://doi.org/10.11647/OBP.0352.31

Transcription

Recto

0. [... ... ... ה"ר ישראל]
1. עטאין מני אנא מרדוך קרקוסה וליס עלימים כתיר [...]
2. י[רא]גבכום(?) בכול בא[ן] כלומירא ל[..]ן ~~עפ~~ עטלך טנ[...]
3. לרבי מושה יבעתלי קטר סכנדראני זביב לאין כ[...]
4. תקפייא מה בטע יצחק ורגבוה מין גהטי למוש[ה א']
5. יהודה לאין ידילוה דינאר ונופץ בכ[ול(?) ...] מין אל[...]
6. בטע יוסף מסרי והכדא נרגב ליוסף לאן אעוטיהו [...]
7. בגוארה מין גהת מרדוך והוא מספר ולא טכ[...]
8. מעוך יטעמלוה מזפא מה לא

In a different hand:

9. אני' מרדוך קרקוסה נעלמיך
10. יא ר' ירחמאל תיתוסי' בדי אלמסא[פר]
11. כיתיר כ[י]תיר יהדי' כייר מרגוב
12. אל[...] אנ[.] נרגאביך יא ר' ירחמאל
13. ב[פצל]ך תקול ליל מעלמי מוסה א'
14. [יהודה] בא[ן א]ני'(?) רוחת ענד אלכ[...]
15. [יב]עתלה עלי' אסמיט וקאל יתב[...]
16. [... מ]יידי' דהב v מתאקלה יבעת ק[...]
17. אל[...]ל אש סוי' יבעת פלוס אצית [...]
18. לילמעילים יוסף אלכאדים בילילייי'
19. [ב(?)]עד נרגאביך עלי' מחאבך אל[לה]
20. תעאלי' באניך תעתי לראאס ב[...]
21. ראאח סאת(?) ונופץ כליה ורוח[...]
22. עני' קביל לי' יעמיל דאהוי' ויבקי'
23. עון עליני יהדי' כייר מרגובי אליך

24. ושלום אוכאתיב יום ו ד' תמוז
25. שנת רח"ם ייי על ירא[יו]

Verso

In a third hand:

1. [......]ה ר' ירחמ[אל ..] כאן מרד[וך] קרקוסה [יסל]ם עליך
2. [ומן] פצ̇לך אנך תקול למוסי אבן יהודה אנה יעטי ליצחק
3. אשרפי ונוץ אמא מן ענדי אמא מן אלפלוס אלד̇י אילו ענד[ך]
4. אודה(?) [ד]אלך [..]יה צדק[ה] ואתוצו בו מן פצ̇לך כמתל מא
5. מועתדין בחלואסנא וקול לבנימין רומאן כאן עליה
6. בארבע [...] עיל[..] אן כאן יבעת לי קנטר גיבן.
7. מעך אבעת לו אלשטר ושלום רב

Verso Inverted

1. יסל אלגליל אל[..]דיל
2. ה"ר ישראל עטאין
3. ה"ר [ירחמ]אל עטאין
4. ש"צ[1] וש[לום(?)]

Translation

Recto

0. [Greet the honourable rabbi Israel]
1. ʿAṭāʾīn(?) from me, Mardūḵ Qarqūsa. There are not many learned ones(?) […]
2. [(God) would like(?) for you] everything (you want. I inform) that Kalomira […] your loss […]

---

[1] = שמרו צורו.

3. to Rabbi Moses that he should send to me an Alexandrian *qinṭār* of raisins because […]
4. … belonging to Isaac, they want it from me for Mos[es b.]
5. Judah because they will transfer you a dinar and a half, [of all …] from the […]
6. belonging to Joseph Maṣrī (or: Miṣrī) and thus we would like (it to go) to Joseph because I will give it […]
7. into his protection with regard to Mardūḵ. He is travelling and does not…
8. with you, they will work on it […] what has not…

In a different hand:

9. I, Mardūḵ Qarqūsa, inform you,
10. O R. Yeraḥmiel, that you should behave very generously with this [traveller(?)]
11. He brought the desired *Cassia fistula*
12. [… …] We would like you, O R. Yeraḥmiel, [to please]
13. talk to the *muʿallim* Mūsā b.
14. [Judah…] that I(?) went with the […]
15. he should send to him to Izmit. He said he will […]
16. […] *muʾayyadī* of gold, seven *miṯqals.* He should send […]
17. […] anything except sending money. […]
18. to the *muʿallim* Joseph the servant with the […]
19. [after that(?)], we would like your beloved, by God
20. exalted, that you will give to the leader […]
21. going, one and a half hours(?) everything. Went off […]
22. from me surety for me. He will do […] May (God) make
23. the protection over us lasting. He will bring good-quality *cassia fistula* to you.

24. Peace (will be). I am writing on Friday 4th Tammuz
25. of the year [5]248 (22 June 1488). "God has shown mercy to those who fear him" (Ps. 103.13).

Verso

In a third hand:

1. [… …] R. Yeraḥm[iel …] Mardūḵ Qarqūsa [sends] you [greetings]
2. by your grace that you tell Mūsā b. Judah that he should give to Isaac
3. an *ashrafī* dinar and a half. Now to my (own, i.e., the scribe's) matters, concerning the money which they sent [you],
4. […] this […] Ṣedaqah(?). Entrust it with him by your grace, just as that they do not
5. hesitate regarding our … Tell Benjamin Roman (or: Rūmān), if he has
6. four [… …] If he could send me a *qinṭār* of cheese
7. with you. Send the deed to him. Many greetings.

Verso Inverted

1. (This letter) should arrive to the sublime, the […]
2. the honourable rabbi Israel ʿAṭāʾīn,
3. the rabbi [Yeraḥm]iel ʿAṭāʾīn,
4. may God save them [and peace(?) (will be)].

Commentary

Recto

Line 2:
"Kalomira." A female Greek name. She is probably a Byzantine Jewish woman.

Line 6:
"Joseph Maṣrī (or: Miṣrī)." His name indicates he is of Cairene origin.

Line 15:
"Izmit" (Nicomedia). A city in northwestern Turkey.

Line 24:
"Friday 4th Tammuz." The fourth of Tammuz 5248 (22 June 1488) was indeed a Friday.

Verso

Line 5:
"Benjamin Roman." It seems this is a Sephardi Jew. Compare, for example, the name Ḥayyim Romano, which appears in a list of names in the Genizah (TS Misc. 11.208). It could also be read as Rūmān. Another option is to read the words as וקול לבנימין רומי̇ אן 'Tell Benjamin Rūmī (= the Greek) that…'.

P.9: Letter from an Anonymous Scholar to Moses b. Judah

Bodl. MS Heb. c. 72/24 + Bodl. MS Heb. c. 72/2

General Description

This letter, composed in Hebrew and Judaeo-Arabic, is unique within the material in this volume. It does not discuss trade, family, or communal affairs, as the other letters in our corpus do, but deliberates exegetical questions. The letter illustrates the central status of Maimonides in the circle of Moses b. Judah and his friends. The writer calls Maimonides simply 'Our Rabbi' (רבינו), without mentioning his name, and quotes from *The Guide of the Perplexed* in its original Judaeo-Arabic version. We are indebted to Dr Gregor Schwarb, Prof. Mordechai A. Friedman, Prof. Hannah Kasher, Dr Ariel Malachi, Dr Dan Grinberger, Tommer Shani, and Shmuel Polacheck for their invaluable comments on this letter.

Physical Description

Folio 24: 20.4 × 4.5; paper; 1 leaf; 23 lines (recto); 22 lines (verso); torn, holes, red-brown stains.

Folio 2: 20 × 15.5; paper; 1 leaf; 20 lines (recto); 24 lines (verso); torn, holes, red-brown stains.

 https://doi.org/10.11647/OBP.0352.32

Linguistic Description

The letter's linguistic style is very different to the documentary material that makes up most of the rest of the corpus under investigation. It is to a large degree influenced by literary norms and has thus been treated separately in the Linguistic Analysis section (§III.2.11).

Transcription

Folio 24 Recto

1. שלום שלום
2. אהובי וידידי ורעי ומיודעי כ'ר' משה אן לי לשון לספר ו[לא פה]
3. לדבר לפי כך שתקתי כי דוד אחר ששבח עד שאמרו ע[ליו]
4. כי הוא אדון המשוררים אמר לך דומיה תהלה [וביאר]
5. רבינו עליו השלום זה הדבר בעניין גדול והמשכ[יל יבין.]
6. אשאל מהשם ימלא משאלות לבך לטובה ומאמר [...]
7. כבודך יודע כי לב שם משותף ~~כאש~~[1] פיעלם ס[יידי]
8. באן קולי משאלות לבך אשׁיר בדלך אלי כמאל אלע[קל]
9. אלאנסאני אלבאקי בעד אלמות פאן קאל קאיל והל אל
10. עקל אלאנסאני יסמי לב קלנא ראינא נצוץ
11. תדלנא עלי דלך ואיש נבוב ילבב יעני יעקל וכ[דלך]
12. לב חכם לימינו וכדלך קול אלישע הנביא לגיחז[י]
13. לא לבי הלך קאל אלרב אלמעצֹם אליס כנת חאצֹ[ר]
14. בפכרי פקד צֹהר באן אלעקל יסמי לב פאן סאל
15. סאיל וקאל כיף יקול להו אולא מאין גחזי תם

[1] Maybe the writer started to write כאשר in Hebrew, and then changed his mind and continued the sentence in Judaeo-Arabic.

16. יקול להו לא לבי הלך אעלם אן קולהו מאין
17. גיחזי פתחון דבר והראייה הגמורה כאשר
18. כיחש ואמר לא הלך עבדך וכו' אז השיבו ואמ[ר]
19. לא לבי הלך בחמה וככה פירש רב' אבר' בן עז[רה]
20. כאשר אמר השם לאדם הראשון איכה וכן כאש[ר]
21. אמר לקין אי הבל אחיך וכאשר אמר לבלעם
22. מי האנשים כל זה פתחון דבר כי הוא יודע
23. [...]

Folio 2 Recto

1. התשובה שמ[...] כי קין כיחש ואמר השומ[ר]
2. אחי והשם השיב ואמר קול דמי אחיך ופירוש
3. קול דמי כאשר אמר המתרגם פאן קלת באן
4. לא יחצל כמאל אל עקל אלי בעד תוטיאת קד צ̇הר
5. ען אל מכ' ~~באנהו משתגל~~ באנהו משתגל פי מא
6. יאדי אלא דלך ובכאצה אשתגאלך פי אל מצוות
7. עלמן ועמל אלדי הם אל גאית אלקצוי ובהם
8. יחצל אלכמאל אל אכ̇יר כמא קאל אל תנא הפוך בה
9. והפך בה סיב ובלי בה פקד צ̇הר מן קולהו הפוך
10. בה והפך בה באנך תתאמל בה(?) מעאניהא אלדי להו
11. באטן מע אקראנה בל צ̇אהר פקד[2] וכדלך
12. קאלו אל חכמים למה היו דברי תורה דומין
13. קודם שבא שלמה[3] ~~למים~~ לבאר שהיו ממיה עמוקין
14. וצוניך[4] מה עשה פקח אחד ספק חבל בחבל ומשיחה

---

[2] The author here wrote פקד for פקט.

[3] In the opening of *The Guide of the Perplexed*: עד שלא עמד שלמה.

[4] Guide of the Perplexed: עמוקים וצוננים ולא היה אדם יכול לשתות מהן.

15. למשיחה ודלה ושתה וכו' כך היו דברי תורה
16. קאל רבינו פלא ארא אחדן מן סאלמי אלקראיה יעתקד
17. אן דברי תורה אל מקול הנא הוא שעור שופר וסוכה
18. ודין ארבעה שומרים בל ה[נא(?)] אל גואמץ̇ בלא שד[5]
19. פקד צ̇הר באן תם נצוץ להא צ̇אהר פקט ונצוץ להא
20. צ̇אהר ובאטן ונצוץ להא באטן אמא אל נצוץ אלדי ליס
21. לה[א] צ̇אהר מתל נעשה אדם בצלמינו ומתל ארדה
22. נא ואראה ומתל וינחם יוי וידלנא עלי דלך תרגמת
23. אנקלוס הגר ובעדה כל אסעאד ען דלך ואמא
24. אל נצוץ אלדי להא צ̇אהר פקט אלקצ̇ ואלמצוות

Folio 24 Verso

1. [...] אן תעתבר מן קולהם ע"ה פי אלציצית תכלת דומה ליס
2. [וים] דומה לרקיע וכו' ואמא אלדי להם צ̇אהר ובאטן
3. [מ]תל קול אל נץ ומשה עלה אל האלהים אל ההר בגופו
4. [ואל] השמים בשכלו פאן קאל קאיל אן מקרא יוצא
5. [מ]ידי פשוטו ~~ואן קולכם~~ אן תם נצוץ ליס להא צ̇אהר
6. [ל̇]ם נסלם דלך קלנא נחן באן למא אן וגדנא נצוץ̇
7. [ת]דלנא עלי דלך ודלך באן ראינא שמואל הרמתי
8. [י]קול בנפסה ניחמתי כי המלכתי ויקול הוא בנפסה
9. [ו(?)]גם נצח ישראל וכו' ופי אל תורה קאל וי׳חם יוי וקאל לא
10. [א]יש אל ויכזב ובן אדם כאנהו יקול ולא בן אדם מתל
11. [נ]ער הייתי ומתל יומם השמש לא יככה כאנה יקול
12. [ו]לא ירח ואיצ̇א קאלו מרגליה בפומיה דרב [...]

---

5 In Joel's edition of the *Guide* (Maimonides, *Dalālat al-Ḥāʾirīn*, p. 7): ומא ארי אן אחדא מן אלסלאמי אלקראיה יתכ'יל אן דברי תורה אלמשאר אליהא הנא אלתי תחיל פי פהמא כפהם מעאני אלאמת'אל הי אחכאם עמל אלסוכה ואללולב ודין ארבעה שומרים בל אלקצד הנא פהם אלגואמץ' בלא שד.

13. העולם הבא אן בו לא אכילה ולא שתייה ולא קנאה
14. ולא תחרות וכו' ואל ~~תאנא~~ חכם אל אכר יקול
15. עתיד הב"ה לעשות סעודה לצדיקים מבשרו
16. שללויתן פאן אכדנא גמיע דלך עלי צ̇אהרה
17. חצל תנאק̇ץ ואן אכד אל גמיע בגיר צ̇אהר חצל
18. תנאק̇ץ פלם יבק ענד כל די עקל סאלם מן
19. הוי אלא אן יגעלה ובן אדם ויתנחם הוא אל מטלוב
20. וכדלך וגם נצח ישראל וכדלך העולם הבא
21. אן בו לא אכילה וכו' ותלך אלנצוץ להא תאויל
22. [... ... ... ד]לאיל ובנצוץ עלי אן

Folio 2 Verso

0. [...]
1. דלך ענדהו יקין וחד אליקין חית לם יג̇ד אל[א]
2. מא תקרר מכאלף פאן לם ינה̇ץ לתלך אלדרג̇ה
3. נקול להו קאלו אל חכמים קולה כאפיה חאלא
4. לגמיע משכלאת אלשריעה באסרהא והו קולהם
5. דברה תורה כלשון בני אדם וקאל רבינו אברה[ם]
6. אבן עזרה ע"ה כי לא יוכל אדם לדבר דברים בגב[וה]
7. עליו [א]ו בשפל ממנו רק על דרך דמות האדם
8. כי השומע אדם גם המדבר על כן אמר פי
9. הארץ יד הירדן וראש עפרות תבל ולשון ים מצר[ים]
10. וחלילה חלילה להיות דמות לשם וכאשר ראה
11. הנבי דמות [כבוד] השם כמראה אדם והשם
12. הוא אחד והוא יוצר הכל והוא הכל
13. ולא אוכל לפרש הדא נצה ע"ה פארי
14. כיף עלל לנא ע"ה באן נחן מא נפהם
15. הדה אלנצוץ אלא בהדה אלעבארה והוא

16. קולה פי תעליל דלך כי המדבר אדם
17. גם השמומע(!)[6] אדם וכדלך קאל [ע"]ה
18. למא אראד יקרר לנא באן תם נצוץ
19. להא צ̇אהר ובאטן קולה פי שרח(?) [ש]מות(?)

Translation

Folio 24 Recto

1. Peace, peace (Isa. 57.19).
2. My beloved, friend, comrade, fellow, the honourable rabbi Moses. Neither do I have a tongue for expression [nor a mouth]
3. for speech, so I keep silent because David, after he praised (God so well) such that they said [about him]
4. that he is the Master of the poets,[7] said, "For you, silence is praise" (Ps. 65.2).
5. Our Rabbi, peace be upon him, [interpreted] this matter (giving it) a great importance, and the wise [man shall understand] (following Dan. 12.10).
6. I ask God to fulfil your heart's wishes (following Ps. 20.6; 37.4) and the saying [...]
7. Your honour knows that *lev* (heart) is a homonym ... and [my master(?)] should know[8]

---

[6] Should be: השומע.

[7] A common epithet given to poets writing in Arabic.

[8] Another option is to read: פי עלם ס[...]. In this case, the sentence should be translated 'is a homonym, with (the meaning) of "wisdom"'. We want to thank Dr Dan Grinberger for this comment.

8. that when I say "your heart's wishes," I mean by this that the perfection of the human
9. [intellect], which is remaining after death. If someone will ask (literally: 'say'): Is the
10. human intellect called *lev* (heart)? We will answer (literally: 'say') that there are phrasings
11. indicate this to us: "A stupid man will get understanding (*yilabev*)" (Job 11.12). It means 'he will understand', [similarly]
12. "A wise man's heart inclines him toward the right hand" (Eccl. 10.2). Similarly, what Elisha the prophet said to Geḥazi:
13. "Did I not go with you in spirit?" (2 Kgs 5.26). The sublime master said: "Wasn't I present
14. in my mind?" It has become apparent that *al-ʿaql* (the intellect) is called *lev*. If someone
15. asks: How did he (= Elisha) say to him, first: "Where have you been, Geḥazi?" (2 Kgs 5.25), and then
16. he said to him: "Did I not go with you in spirit?", you should know that his saying "Where
17. have you been, Geḥazi?" was a rhetorical question. And the absolute proof (for that is) when
18. he denied and said: "Your servant went nowhere" etc. (2 Kgs 5.25), then (Elisha) replied to him and said:
19. "Did I not go with you in spirit?", in anger. This is the interpretation of Rabbi Abraham ben Ez[ra].
20. When the Name said to the first man (Adam): "Where are you?" (Gen. 3.9), and also when

21. (God) said to Cain: "Where is Abel your brother?" (Gen. 4.9), and also when (He) said to Balaam:
22. "Who are these men?" (Num. 22.9), these are all rhetorical questions, because He knows
23. [...]

Folio 2 Recto

1. the answer [...], because Cain denied and said: "Am (I) my brother's keeper?" (Gen. 4.9),
2. And the Name replied and said: "The voice of your brother's blood" (Gen. 4.10). The meaning of
3. "the voice of (your brother's) blood" is as the translator said. If you say that
4. it does not result in a perfection of the intellect until after the preparations. It has become apparent
5. from the master that he is busy with what
6. is conducive to this—in particular your occupation with the religious commandments
7. with regards to knowledge and practice which are of the extreme limits, and in them
8. he will achieve the final perfection, just like the Tanna said: "turn it
9. and turn it again; grow old and worn in it" (m. Avot 5.22) It has become apparent from his statement "turn
10. it and turn it" that you study their meaning, which has
11. a hidden (level), with our confirmation of the obvious (meaning).

12. The sages also said: "To what were the words of the Torah compared
13. before the time of Solomon? To a well the waters of which are at a great depth
14. and cool. What did a clever man do? He joined cord with cord and rope
15. with rope, and drew up and drank, etc. In that way were the words of the Torah" (Song Rabbah 1.1).[9]
16. Our Rabbi said: "I do not believe that any intelligent man thinks
17. that 'the words of the Torah' mentioned here are the (required) dimensions of Shofar and Sukkah
18. and the laws of the four trustees, but [these are] the profound subjects, without doubt" (Maimonides, *The Guide of the Perplexed*, opening).
19. It has become apparent that (some) passages have only obvious meaning. (Other) passages
20. have obvious and hidden (meaning). (Other) passages have (only) hidden meaning. Concerning the passages which have
21. only obvious meaning, such as "Let us make man in our image" (Gen. 1.26), and like "I will go down
22. to see" (Gen. 18.21), and like "and the LORD repented" (Gen. 6.6; Exod. 32.14), the translation of Onkelos the proselyte guides us concerning this,
23. and after him, every guidance concerning this. Regarding
24. the passages which have only obvious meaning, (these are) the stories and religious commandments

[9] For a similar sermon, see b. Yevamot 21a.

Folio 24 Verso

1. [...] that you should observe what (the sages), peace be upon them, said regarding *tsitsit*: "Azure is similar to the sea,
2. [and the sea] is similar to the sky" (b. Sotah 17a) etc. It has obvious and hidden meaning,
3. such as the meaning of the phrase: "Moses went up to God," (which means:) to the mountain with his body,
4. [and to] the sky in his mind. If someone says: "A verse does not depart
5. from its literal meaning" (b. Shabbat 63a), there are (however) verses that do not have obvious (i.e., literal) meaning.
6. We [do not] accept it. We said that when we found passages
7. that guided us to this. That is, according to our opinion, Samuel ha-Ramati
8. says himself: "I regret that I made (Saul) king" (1 Sam. 15.11) and he himself says:
9. "Also, the glory of Israel (will not lie)" (1 Sam. 15.29) etc., and in the Torah he says: "And the Lord repented" (Gen. 6.6), and he also says: "God is not
10. man that he should lie, or a son of man" (Num. 23.19), it is as if he was saying "and not a son of man" like
11. "I have been young" (Ps. 37.25) and like "By day the sun will not strike you," as if he says
12. "Nor the moon" (Ps. 121.6). Also (the sages) said: (the Amora) Rav was regularly saying:
13. "In the next world, there is no eating or drinking, nor any jealousy

14. or competition" (b. Berakhot 17a) etc. ~~The *Tanna*~~ The other sage says:
15. "God, blessed be he, will make a feast for the righteous from the meat
16. of the whale" (b. Bava Batra 75a). If we take all of this in its literal meaning,
17. it results in mutual contradictions. If everything is taken in a non-literal meaning, it results
18. in a mutual contradiction. Accordingly, nothing remains for anyone whose mind is not
19. biased but to consider(?) that "and a son of man that repents" is the intended(?) issue.
20. And thus, "also the glory of Israel," thus "In the next world
21. there is no eating," etc. These passages have an interpretation
22. [... ... ...] evidence, and in passages on

Folio 2 Verso

1. This, it has certainty, a single certainty. When he finds only
2. what you stated, he will have a different opinion. If he is not encouraged to this step,
3. we tell him that the sages said that conditions suffice
4. for all the problems of the (religious) law, in their entirety. That is what they said
5. "the Torah spoke in human language" (b. Makkot 12a). Our Rabbi Abraham
6. ibn Ezra, peace be upon him, said that "A man cannot talk on what is [above]
7. him, [or] below him, only by allegory to human characters,

8. because the listener is a man, and also the speaker. That is why (the Torah) says 'the earth's mouth' (following Num. 16.32),
9. 'on the hand of the Jordan' (Num. 23.29), 'the head of the dust in the world' (Prov. 8.26), 'the tongue of the Egyptian sea' (Isa. 11.15).
10. God forbid that the Name has a figure ... When
11. the prophet saw the image of the Name's honour 'as the appearance of a man' (Ezek. 1.26). The Name
12. is one, and he who creates everything, and he is everything.
13. And I cannot interpret" (Ibn Ezra's commentary to Gen. 1.26). This is his wording, peace be upon him, and I see
14. how he explains (it) to us, peace be upon him, so that we only understand
15. these passages in this interpretation. This is
16. what he says in interpreting it: "because the speaker is a man.
17. Also, the listener is a man." So (Rabbi Abraham), peace be upon him, said
18. when he wanted to state for us that passages
19. have obvious and hidden meaning, he said in [the commentary on Exodus(?)]

Commentary

Folio 24 Recto

Line 4:
"The master of the poets." This expression appears in medieval texts, such as *ʿAqedat Yiṣḥaq* by R. Isaac ʿAramah (d. 1494). A similar expression appears already in the early *piyyuṭim.* In an

anonymous *piyyuṭ*, probably from the sixth–seventh century, it is said: למען ראש משוררים תאב שתות מים (Goldschmidt and Frenkel 1981, 200; we would like to thank Dr Yehoshua Granat for this reference). On the term 'poet' (*meshorer*) for David in *piyyuṭim*, see Granat (2001, 72–74).

Line 5:
"Our Rabbi, peace be upon him." There is no certainty as to who the scholar mentioned here is, but it seems the writer refers to Maimonides, who dedicated a long discussion to this verse and similar sources in *The Guide of the Perplexed* (part I, chapter 59). The expression "Our Rabbi, peace be upon him" shows us the centrality of Maimonides in the intellectual world of Moses b. Judah and his anonymous friend. On 'Our Rabbi' as a nickname of Maimonides, see also Friedman (2023, 94–95).

והמשכ[יל יבין]. For this completion, compare ENA 3366.7.

Line 7:
"A homonym." The term שם משותף comes from the vocabulary of medieval Arabic (اسم مشترك) and Judaeo-Arabic philosophy. Maimonides wrote (in the opening chapter of *The Guide of the Perplexed*) that one of his main goals in the book was to explain those words in the Bible which were understood wrongly by most people. The writer did not use the translation of Samuel ibn Tibbon (who translated the term *ʾism mushtarak* as שם משתתף and not שם משותף), or al-Ḥarīzī's translation, but used the Judaeo-Arabic original, as becomes clear from f2/16–18.

Line 17:
"A rhetorical question." Literally: 'a way of opening a matter', i.e., Elisha asked Geḥazi this question, although he was a prophet

and knew the answer anyway, as a way of opening a conversation with him, to give him the opportunity to confess. The expression *pitḥon davar* is taken from Ibn Ezra's commentary on Gen. 3.9 (טעם אַיֶּכָּה—פתחון הדברים), and on Num. 22.9 (פתחון ותחילת דבור). This interpretive direction had appeared already in Rav Saʿadiah Gaon's writings (in his response to Ḥiwi ha-Balḵi, in his Bible translation, and in his Bible commentary), and in Rashi's commentary.

Folio 2 Recto

Lines 1–2:
כי קין כיחש ואמר השומ[ר] אחי והשם השיב ואמר קול דמי אחיך. A paraphrase of Ibn Ezra's commentary on Gen. 3.9 (והנה כחש קין, והשיב לו השם: קול דמי אחיך צועקים); compare also his commentary on Num. 22.9.

Line 3:
"As the translator said." The writer probably refers here to Onqelos (המתרגם 'the translator' is the term by which Onqelos is consistently referred to in Ibn Ezra's commentary).

Line 5:
The writer unintentionally wrote the words באנהו משתגל twice, then deleted one of the occurrences.

Line 14:
וצונין. This is the original form of the word in accurate manuscripts of the talmudic literature. Later, the word צונין was understood wrongly as a single form, and the plural form צוננין was created.

Line 16:
"Our Rabbi." Maimonides.

Line 18:
"The laws of the four trustees." These laws are mentioned in Exod. 22.6–14, and discussed in the Mishnah and Talmud, mainly in Bava Meṣiʿa, chapters 1, 3, 7.

Folio 2 Verso

Line 19:
"[The commentary on Exodus(?)]." See Ibn Ezra's commentary on Exod. 19.20.

P.10: Letter from an Anonymous Writer to Moses b. Judah

JTS MS 2331, 217b–218a
Before 1484

General Description

This letter was sent to Moses by one of his associates and deals with Moses' request of the writer to copy for him a book of Kabbalah. It was first published by Hacker (2000, 592–93), who suggested that the writer is Meʾīr, son of David the scribe, who is mentioned in Moses' letter (P.1/29). We assume that Rabbi David Shemesh, who is mentioned in this letter, can be identified as David ibn Shams, who wrote many of the letters to Moses in our corpus; and that David ibn Shams is the "David the scribe" mentioned by Moses in his letter. The identification of the writer with Meʾīr, son of David the scribe, is therefore impossible: the writer mentions David as his friend and not as his father.

The letter was written at the end of a copy of the Kabbalistic work *Shaʿar ha-Shoʾel* 'The Section/Gate of the Questioner', R. ʿAzriel of Gerona's commentary on the Ten *Sefirot* (JTS 2331, 207a–213b; 214a–215b). It was a very popular work in the Middle Ages (more than 150 manuscripts of it have survived). The manuscript also contains samples of letters (214a–215a), which are also mentioned in our letter (l. 15).

The manuscript was held in Moses' library and later by Samuel Ḥalafta, a Maghribian Jew who lived in Jerusalem in the early sixteenth century (his ownership signature appears in

 https://doi.org/10.11647/OBP.0352.33

207a). Below the letter, a censorship signature by the famous converted censor Dominico Irosolimitano, dated to 1598, can be found (217b), which indicates that the manuscript later arrived in Italy. Irosolimitano's signature also appears on other copies of this work, such as MS Paris, Bibliothèque Nationale heb. 810 (a collection of Kabbalistic works in Italian-Ashkenazic script, including R. ʿAzriel's work).

The writer included an addition to the letter, with a request that Moses check whether he, or Nathan Sholal, had received any letters from the Maghreb. This could be evidence that the writer was of Maghribian origin, like Sholal. He wrote this addition on the previous page, in a free space left at the end of the book he had copied (217b), and added to it a special title (l. 1). However, both letters are unsigned, and it is therefore possible that they did not originally belong to the same letter.[1]

Physical Description

Codex; paper; folio 217b: 7 lines; folio 218a: 19 lines.

Transcription

Folio 218a

1. בשם יי"י אל עולם
2. יעלה ויגיע ביד האדון הנעלה לשם ולתהלה כג"ק
3. מה"ר משה ברכ"ה ר' יהודה זלה"ה. הכתב והמכתב

---

[1] Hacker understood the letter in 217b and the letter in 218a as two different letters, written by different persons, and attributed the first to an anonymous Maghribian Jew.

4. מאת אחיך הדל והצעיר אשר בים גלותו מצטער
5. ומתאנח עד אשר יניח אזי עלינו לשבח ליוצר הכל
6. אשר הוא הכל ישתב'.[2] ועתה אדוני אל תאשימני
7. ואל תבא במשפט את עבדך שאחרו פעמי דברותי
8. עד עתה כי זמננו זה זר ואכזר. ואינו מסכים לאשר
9. יחשוב החושב וגזר. והרי כבודך צוה לי אחי שאעתיק
10. לו פי' הספי'[3] ר"ל השאלות שבאו מנא אמון ליד אהובנו
11. הנאמן והותיק כג"ק מה"ר דוד שמש יצ"ו ואחר זה
12. פשפשתי ומצאתי נוסחא אחרת ביד המשכיל החכם
13. ה"ר עובדיה גזע ר' דוד הנגיד זלה"ה[4] והערכנום וראינו
14. לזאת שהעתקתי תועלת על האחרת ומה שהיא כעין
15. תוספת באחרת הרי הוא כתוב אחר המליצות וההזכרה
16. שכתבת לי בשביל המליצות לא ידעתי אנה אבדה ממני
17. והרי כתבתי מה שנזדמן עד אם תראה שצוית ביותר
18. או באופן אחר או תרצה השאלות הנזכרים כסדרן הנם
19. כתובים אצלי הודיעני ואני אשלחם לך ואתה שלום

Folio 217b

1. רודף צדקה וחסד כו'
2. והחסד אשר תעשה עמדי שתשתדל ותשגיח בכל מי שיבא
3. מן המערב לחקרו ולדרשו אולי יביא לי או לאהוב ה"ר נתן
4. שלאל איזה כתבים ותשלחם עליד[5] אחד מהנכבדים ותצווהו
5. שיש~~לחם~~ג׳עם ל~~מערב~~ידי ובזה ברכ'ת ינוחו על ראשך ויש שכר

---

[2] = ישתבח.

[3] = הספירות.

[4] = זכרונו לחיי העולם הבא.

[5] First the writer wrote ליד, then he added ע to make it על יד.

6. לפעולתך בזה ובבא והשם יזכנו יחד לחיי העולם הבא
7. אמן ואמן. ודי

Translation

Folio 218a

1. In the name of the LORD, the Everlasting God (Gen. 21.33).
2. (This letter) will reach the exalted master, who is renowned and praised (Zeph. 3.20), his honourable highness and sanctity,
3. our teacher Rabbi Moses, son of the honourable rabbi Judah, may his memory live in the world to come. The writing and the letter (following m. Avot 5.5)
4. is from your poor and young brother, who in the sea of his exile suffers
5. and moans, until (the LORD) gives rest (Deut. 3.20), then we shall praise the creator of all
6. that he will be praised for everything. Now, my master, do not blame me
7. and do not bring your servant into judgement (Ps. 143.2), that the hoofbeats of my words tarried (following Judg. 5.28)
8. until now, because our time is strange and cruel, and does not agree to what
9. a man thinks and plans. Your honour commanded me, my brother, that I will copy
10. for him the commentary on the *Sefirot*, i.e, the questions, which arrived from Alexandria to our beloved,
11. the loyal and pious, his honourable highness and sanctity, our teacher Rabbi David Shemesh, may God save him. After that

12. I looked for and found another version in the hands of the educated scholar
13. the rabbi Obadiah, descendant of R. David ha-Nagid, may his memory live in the world to come. We compared them and we saw
14. that the one I have copied has an advantage over the other one, and what is like
15. an addition in the other one is written after the samples of letters. Concerning the reminder(?)
16. that you wrote me for the samples of letters, I do not know where I lost it.
17. I have written according to what came upon (me) by chance till (now?). If you would see that you command (to copy) more
18. or in another way, or if you want the questions aforementioned in their order,
19. I have them written (already). Inform me and I will send them to you. And peace be upon you (1 Sam. 25.6).

Folio 217b

1. He who pursues righteousness and kindness etc. (Prov. 21.21).
2. And the favour you could do for me is making an effort and giving attention to anyone that comes
3. from the Maghreb, to investigate and ask him, maybe he brought to me, or to the beloved rabbi Nathan
4. Sholal, any letters. (If so,) send them by one of the notables, and command him

5. ~~to send them to the Maghreb~~ to bring it to me. By that, may blessings rest upon your head, and your work shall be rewarded (Jer. 31.15),
6. in this (world) and in the next (world), and the Name will grant us together to the life of the world to come.
7. Amen, Amen. And that's all.

Commentary

Folio 218a

Line 5:
"We shall praise the creator of all." An ancient prayer originally composed for the liturgy of Rosh ha-Shanah, which later became part of the daily liturgy and is recited at the end of each prayer.

Line 6:
"That he will be praised for everything." The syntax of this sentence (אשר הוא הכל ישתב'[ח]) is unclear. There is perhaps a scribal error here, and it should be, for example: אשר הוא על הכל ישתבח.

Line 7:
"That the hoofbeats of my words tarried." Following Judg. 5.28: "Out of the window she peered, the mother of Sisera gazed through the lattice: 'Why is his chariot so long in coming? Why tarry the hoofbeats of his chariots?'"

Line 10:
"*Sefirot.*" The ten emanations of God according to the Kabbalah.

"The questions." The author refers here to *Sha'ar ha-Sho'el* 'The Section/Gate of the Questioner'. See Introduction, §2.5.

Line 13:

"The rabbi Obadiah, descendant of R. David ha-Nagid." David the Nagid who is mentioned here is probably David the second of the Maimonidean dynasty. The year of his death is not known, and we only know that in 1409 he was still alive. Obadiah was not his direct son, but a descendant, as the Hebrew word *gezaʿ* indicates. We have no other information about this late figure of the Maimonidean family. Another option is to understand the word *gezaʿ* here as literally 'son'. Israel Ben-Zeʾev (1957, 14) claimed, on the basis of an Arabic court document from the eighth of Shaʿabān 887 H (1482/3), that between Solomon b. Joseph and Nathan Sholal there was a short tenure of a Nagid called David b. Abraham. This possibility is supported by a Hebrew letter of Nathan Sholal which mentions "ʿAbd Allah son of David ha-Nagid, may he rest in peace" (TS NS 167.17). As is well known, ʿAbd Allah is the Arabic equivalent of Obadiah. However, the Arabic document of 887 H is not accessible today, and it is impossible to check Ben-Zeʾev's reading. In addition, Ashtor (1970, 154) doubted the authenticity of the information adduced by Ben-Zeʾev. Therefore, the identity of the "rabbi Obadiah, descendant of R. David ha-Nagid" who is mentioned here remains unclear.

Lines 14–15:

"What is like an addition in the other one." The writer refers here to an additional part of 'The Section/Gate of the Questioner', which was copied in the manuscript previously, in 215b–217b.

Folio 217b

Line 2:

"You would make an effort and give attention to anyone that comes from the Maghreb." The writer probably lived in Cairo, as did Nathan Sholal who is also mentioned. Letters from the Maghreb arrived at the port city, Alexandria. The writer asked Moses, as a local Jew who had good connections among the traders in the port, and as a local leader, to look for letters that were sent to the writer (and to Sholal) and arrived in Alexandria, and to send them to Cairo.

Lines 3–4:

"The beloved R. Nathan Sholal." The mentioning of Sholal without the title 'Nagid' indicates that the letter was written before his appointment in 1484.

Line 5:

"May blessings rest upon your head." This expression follows a known talmudic phrase; see, for example, b. Shabbat 31a (ינוחו לך ברכות על ראשך); Berakhot 33a; Megillah 225b; ʿAvodah Zarah 60b; and more.

P.11: Letter from an Anonymous Writer to a Certain Yedidiah

Bodl. MS Heb. c. 72/50

General Description

Beginning of a letter of unknown content. Hebrew.

Only praises are preserved in this fragment, and we cannot learn much historical data from it. The addressee of the letter is not known from other documents in our corpus or any other source. The name Yedidiah was not common in the medieval Jewish diaspora in the Islamic world, although it appears from time to time in Genizah letters.[1] The rarity of this name calls us to take into account the possibility that it may only be a nick-name. Yedidiah 'the friend of God' was the name given by God to Solomon after his birth (2 Sam. 12.25). Is it perhaps a nick-name for Solomon b. Joseph, the Nagid?

One of the phrases in the letter, "the light of our eyes" (אור עינינו) is a typical epithet for a Nagid at that time. The expression is very common in letters addressed to leaders and rabbis in the Classical Genizah documents (e.g., Budapest, Hungarian Academy of Sciences, 278; TS 12.68; TS 8J13.14; TS Misc. 36.203), but in the Mamlūk period it is used only (to the best of our knowledge) in letters addressed to Negidim, such as David ha-

[1] For example, a certain Yedidiah who was living in Ṣanʿa (Yemen) in the time of R. Sherira Gaon (TS 16.95; Paris, AIU VII.E.23).

 https://doi.org/10.11647/OBP.0352.34

Nagid (the first; TS 16.63),[2] and his son Abraham (ENA 2592.17). In the fifteenth century, this expression appears in connection with Joseph the Nagid (TS 12.815; TS 13J4.16) and his son Solomon the Nagid (TS 13J4.16),[3] and Nathan Sholal (TS 16.216; TS Misc. 28.71). In light of this, we cannot reject the possibility that the addressee here was Solomon the Nagid. If so, it could be that this fragment is a draft of a letter from Moses b. Judah, which was sent to the Nagid, maybe as a response to his letters addressed to the Alexandrian community.

Nevertheless, this hypothesis is doubtful. The addressee of this letter is not characterised as a leader, and the word 'Nagid' (or any similar title) does not appear in it. He is characterised mainly as a prominent sage and is praised for his wisdom and for his good virtues. The writer also emphasises the origin of the addressee from a pious family (l. 9). It seems that his ancestors, and maybe he himself too, took part in the Judaeo-Sufi Ḥasidic movement, which was an important element in the spiritual life of Egyptian Jewry in the Mamlūk period.

---

[2] See also Bodl. MS Heb. d. 66/211, which was sent to the Nagid David I or David II. This epithet was given also to the head of the Maimonidean dynasty himself, Maimonides, as is well illustrated in his responsa (TS NS J 43; Maimonides, *Responsa*, §§275, 285, 373).

[3] TS 13J4.16 is a levirate agreement for Solomon's widow Faraj, 1482 CE. He is mentioned as כג"ק מ' ור' אור עינינו שלמה הנגיד ז"ל. His father is mentioned as כג"ק מר' ור' אור [עינינו] יוסף הנגיד ז"ל. The word עינינו was erroneously omitted by the scribe.

Physical Description

14.2 × 13.6; paper; 1 leaf; 15 lines + marginalia (recto; verso is blank); torn, red-brown stains.

Transcription

Recto

1. לכרוב ממשח אזרח צדיק כתמר יפרח חפץ כבוד יי"י עליו [יזרח] חפץ
2. יי"י בידו יצלח בתורתו כל לב ישמח שכלו דבק ביוצרו
3. תמיד ~~לא נח~~ כי מצא חפצו ונח במתק לשונו הצח כל יגון נשכח יעו כי הוא
4. ללומדי תורתו ושומעיה נזם וחח יושיב השם
5. לאהלו בהשקט ובטח כי הוא איש אלהים שפל
6. בעניו ויקר בעיני אדוניו ונודע בשם חכמה
7. וחשיבות בעיני אנשים יועץ וחכם חרשים ונבון
8. לחשים תחכמוני ראש השלישים[4] הוא עדינו
9. העצנו[5] נין החסידים הפרושים נכד הקדושים
10. אשר הם אל יי"י ניגשים הוא מוא"ע[6] ידידיה
11. אשר תורת אלהיו בלבו תמיד מצויה ומצוותיו בפיו
12. דרושים נודע בשערים ביופי מדותיו ההגונות
13. בשבתו עם זקנים וישישים לבו אמיץ בתורתו
14. כאריות וכלישים האל יעלה מעלתו בין המלאכים
15. הקדושים ואז יגלו לו שערים חמשים בה[...]

---

[4] ʿAdino the ʿEṣnite is called רֹאשׁ הַשָּׁלִשִׁי (1 Sam. 23.8, according to the Masoretic Text), but in the parallel in 1 Chron. 11.11 this hero of David appears (with a different version of his name) as רֹאשׁ הַשָּׁלִישִׁים (in the *Ketiv*: השלושים).

[5] This is the form of the word in the *Qere*, but the *Ketiv* is העצני.

[6] Probably: מורנו אור עינינו.

Margin

1. ואדוני חכם כחמת[7] מלאך ה'אלהים לדעת כל[8]
2. [אשר בארץ]

Translation

Recto

1. For the anointed cherub (Ezek. 28.14), Ezraḥ, a righteous man, who will flourish like the palm tree (Ps. 92.13), the glory of the LORD [has risen] upon him (following Isa. 60.1), and the good pleasure
2. of the LORD will prosper in his hand (Isa. 53.10), in his Torah every heart will be happy, his mind always cleaved unto his creator,
3. because he found his desire and rest, in his sweet and clear words every sorrow has been forgotten, because he is
4. like an earring and a nose ring for those who learn his Torah and hear it. May the Name establish
5. his tent in serenity and peace, because he is a man of God, humble
6. in his own eyes (following 2 Sam. 6.22), and respected in his master's eyes (following Ps. 116.15), and he is known for his wisdom
7. and respect in people's eyes. (He is) a counsellor, skilled craftsman and clever

---

[7] Read: כחכמת.

[8] In the Masoretic text: את כל.

8. enchanter (Isa. 3.3), the Taḥkemonite, the chief of the captains, he is ʿAdino
9. the ʿEṣnite (2 Sam. 23.8), the descendant of the *Ḥasidim* and the pious, the grandson of the holy people
10. who approaches the LORD (following Exod. 19.22), that is our master, the light of our eyes(?), Yedidiah,
11. the one who has the Torah of his God always in his heart (Ps. 37.31), and his commandments are learned
12. in his mouth. He is known in the gates (Prov. 31.23) by the beauty of his good virtues
13. when he sits with elders and old people (see Prov. 31.23). His heart is strong in his Torah,
14. just as lions.[9] God will raise his status among the holy
15. angels, and then the fifty gates (of wisdom) will be displayed for him. [...]

Margin

1. And my lord has wisdom like the wisdom of the angel of God to know all things
2. [that are on the earth] (2 Sam. 14.20).

Commentary

Recto

Line 1:
"Ezraḥ." Meaning 'home-born' (in Modern Hebrew 'citizen'), this is a synonym for Abraham, following 1 Kgs 5.11: "For he was

[9] ליש has usually been interpreted as 'old lion'.

wiser than all men, than Ethan the Ezrahite." Ethan the Ezrahite (Ps. 89.1; 1 Kgs 5.11) is identified in rabbinic literature with Abraham (see b. Bava Batra 15a).

Line 3:
First of all, the author wrote שכלו דבק ביוצרו, תמיד לא נח, 'he cleaved unto his creator, and did not stop (his intellectual activity) even for a moment', but following the correction the meaning is different (see translation).

Line 7:
"Skilled craftsman and clever enchanter." This expression could be interpreted as a reference to the skills of the addressee as a magical practitioner who writes amulets, etc. However, it is more plausible to suppose that the author refers here to a talmudic sermon on these words (b. Ḥagigah 14a):

> "The cunning"—this is a student who makes his rabbis wise. "Charmer [*ḥarashim*]"—this is one that when he begins speaking matters of Torah, all (those listening) are as though deaf [*ḥershin*]. "The skilful"—this is one who understands something (new) from something else. "Enchanter [*laḥash*]"—this is referring to one who is worthy of having words of the Torah that were given in whispers [*laḥash*].

Line 8:
"The Taḥkemonite." The word refers to one of King David's heroes (2 Sam. 23.8), but the sages attribute this adjective to King David himself (see b. Moʿed Qatan 16b).

"ʿAdino the ʿEṣnite." Again, even though the simple understanding of this phrase is that ʿAdino ha-ʿEṣni is a name (or a nickname) of one of David's heroes, the sages attributed it to David himself. The Talmud says: "He is ʿAdino the ʿEṣnite, (that is) when he was sitting engaged in the (study of) Torah he rendered himself pliant as a worm, but when he went marching out to (wage) war he hardened himself like a tree (or: a lance)" (b. Moʿed Qatan 16b). The *derasha* is explaining the name ʿAdino after מעדן את עצמו 'rendered himself pliant', and the name ʿEṣnite after מקשה עצמו כעץ 'hardened himself like a tree'. This phrase is intended to describe the dual faces of a sage who is also a political leader. He is gentle as a teacher of the Torah, but he is tough and decisive as a public leader.

Line 15:
"The fifty gates (of wisdom)." The notion of the fifty gates of wisdom is a talmudic concept, which was developed at length in the Kabbalah. In Tractate Nedarim it says: "Rav and Samuel both said: Fifty gates of understanding (בינה) were created in the world, and all but one were given to Moses" (b. Nedarim 38a). In *Sefer Yeṣirah*, an old mystical work (the date of its composition is under continual debate among scholars), it is said that God created the world with 32 paths of wisdom (חכמה). In biblical Hebrew חכמה and בינה are almost synonyms, but the early Kabbalists differentiated between the two and attributed to God two different virtues: *Ḥokhmah* (which contains 32 paths) and *Binah* (which contains 50 gates), which were considered the second and third *Sefirot* (after the first one, *Keter*). In light of the heavy influence of the Kabbalah on the Jewish elite in Egypt in the fifteenth century, it seems that by these words the writer does not mean the revealed Torah (as Talmud and *halakhah*), but intended to bless the addressee that he might discover the hidden Torah and understand the secrets of the Kabbalah.

P.12: Letter from an Anonymous Writer

Bodl. MS Heb. c. 72/54

General Description

This fragment has two different sets of imprints in mirrored script, both written in Hebrew; the one in the bigger script on the bottom of the recto is a letter. The original letter is not contained in the Bodleian collections, but an impression of it in mirror script has been preserved in this fragment. Both writer and addressee are unknown, but it is possible that it was sent to Moses b. Judah. The content is unclear, but it seems it was concerned with commercial affairs. The Hebrew of the writer is simple, and his spelling non-standard. He switches between ע and א (see ll. 3, 4, 7), and in at least one example he writes שלו instead of שלא (l. 8). The confusion between ע and א suggests that the writer is not of local origin and that Arabic is not his mother tongue, as this distinction would have been fairly evident for a native speaker of Arabic.

In the top part of the page there are few lines in different handwriting, also in Hebrew. These lines are very blurry, and it is extremely difficult to decipher them, but we can read the name אברה[ם] (Abraham) among the words.

Physical Description

28 × 19.8; paper; 1 leaf; 10 and 18 lines of mirrored script (recto; verso is blank); holes, red-brown stains; unusual blue-grey paper.

 https://doi.org/10.11647/OBP.0352.35

Transcription

1. [... ... ...] של
2. בו לקחת לידי לכן מכרו ה[...][1] [...] בש[..]
3. וה[...]מ[...] על כן עם[2] תו[כל(?)] לחזור יות[ר]
4. [טוב ... ...]ם ולהם ועים[3] לא תעשה מ[ה]
5. שתוכל כי אני לא ידעתי [מ]זה הענין [ו]לו היה
6. כבוד[ך] כותב לי שום כתב לא היה לך רע
7. על כן תדע מה תעשה וזה אד[4] ש[...]
8. [...] שלו[5] יעשה לך שום [רע ולא יבוא]
9. [ה]פסד ממנו תבקש ה' [...] עי[ם ...]
10. [...] מ[..]תי עמ[... ... ...]לי ולא [...]
11. יה[י]ה [... ... ...]יב ל[...]
12. [... ... ...] שיהי[ה ...]
13. ואני מודיע לכבודך כמ[...]
14. בהם יעשו [...]
15. [...]דה על כן [...]
16. [...] ש[...]
17. [...]
18. [...]
19. [...]

---

[1] Perhaps הנביד.

[2] Standard Hebrew אם.

[3] Standard Hebrew ואם.

[4] Standard Hebrew עד.

[5] Standard Hebrew שלא.

Translation

1. […] of
2. […] for taking to myself. Therefore, they bought the [wine(?) …]
3. […] therefore, if you [could] cancel (or: if you could come back), it is
4. [better … … …] and to them, and if not, do [what]
5. you can, because I did not know about this matter. If
6. [your] honour was writing me any letter, no bad (thing) did happen to you.
7. Therefore, know what to do, and this is till (you) […]
8. […] for that he will not do any [bad] to you, and any
9. loss [will not be caused] by him, demand five [… if …]
10. [… … … … …] to me, and [he will] not
11. have to […]
12. […] that will be […]
13. I inform your honour […]
14. With them, they will do […]
15. […] therefore […]
16. […]
17. […]
18. […]
19. […]

Commentary

Line 2:

“They bought the [wine(?)].” The reading here is not clear. On the trade of נביד, a kind of wine, see also P.3.c/19–20 and P.6/5–6.

Line 3:

“If you [could] cancel.” The subject here is apparently a deal, which the writer thinks will not be successful and he recommends that the addressee cancel it, if possible.

Line 9:

“Demand five […].” The missing word was probably a kind of a coin.

BODL. MS HEB. C. 72

PART II: LITERARY WORKS

W: LITERARY WORKS

Contents

8. Unidentified Work
   Bodl. MS Heb. c. 72/1

W.1: Qohelet Rabbah

Bodl. MS Heb. c. 72/3

General Description

This fourteenth-century fragment, in Sephardi script, contains a sermon on Eccl. 3.16 from Midrash Qohelet Rabbah, discussing the famous rabbinic legend about the murder of the prophet Zechariah in the temple (2 Chron. 24.17–22) and other sermons on Eccl. 3.16.[1] The reader can find a commentary on the text in Hirshman's critical edition to Qohelet Rabbah (Hirshman 2017, 217–21).

Due to the fact that there are not many manuscripts of Qohelet Rabbah, we thought it would be useful to compare our manuscript, which has not yet been discussed by scholars of rabbinic literature,[2] to the other extant manuscripts.[3] Preparing a

---

[1] For parallel accounts of the legend about the murder of Zechariah in rabbinic literature, see y. Taʿanit 4.5, 25a; b. Gittin 57b; Lam. Rabbah 4. On this legend in the monotheistic traditions, see Kalmin (2014). On Qohelet Rabbah, see Kiperwasser (2005; 2007); Sandberg (1999); Hirshman (2017).

[2] For a full description of the manuscripts and Genizah fragments of Qohelet Rabbah, see Hirshman (2017, introduction section, 126–40). Our manuscript is not mentioned there.

[3] These are the shelf-marks of the manuscripts mentioned hereinafter in the footnotes: Vatican, Biblioteca Apostolica ebr. 291/1; Oxford, Bodl. MS Ox.Uri. 154; New York, JTS Rab. 1914; St Petersburg, RNL Firkovich Evr. II A 272/1; Moscow, Russian State Library Günzburg 936; Paris, Bibliothèque Nationale Oratorie 073.

 https://doi.org/10.11647/OBP.0352.36

complete critical edition of this Midrashic passage is, however, beyond the goals of this book. We therefore limit ourselves to presenting the main differences between our manuscript and other manuscripts. We compared it also to the first printed edition of this Midrash (Constantinople 1512, hereinafter: C). In this comparison we were helped by Hirshman's (2017, 216–220) edition.

Physical Description

20.9 × 13.8; paper; 1 leaf; 21 lines (recto); 21 lines (verso); holes, beige stains.

Transcription

Recto

0. [ר' יודן[4] בעא קומי[5] ר' אחא באיזה מקום]
1. ה[ר]גו את זכריה [ה]נביא בעזרת ישראל או בעזרת הנשים אמ'
2. לו לא בעזרת ישראל ונשים אלא בעזרת כהנים וכוליה ענינא
3. במסכת גיטין.[6] ולא נהגו בדמו כדם הצבי וכדם האיל[7] בדם

---

[4] This is the version in all the manuscripts of Qohelet Rabbah. In C: ר' יונתן.

[5] According to most of the manuscripts. In C: קמיה.

[6] The same in MS New York (וכו' עניינא במסכ' גיטין). This is a reference to b. Gittin 57b. In MS Vatican the reference is to Lam. Rabbah (וכו' במגלת איכה). In C there is no reference at all.

[7] In MS Vatican: לא כדם צבי ולא כדם איל, and the same in MS Moscow and in C.

4. צבי[8] דכתי' ושפך את דמו וכסהו בעפר.[9] אבל בזכריה הנביא
5. שהיה צדיק גמור שפכו דמו על העצים ועל האבנים[10] דכתי'
6. כי דמה בתוכה היה על צחיח סלע שמתהו[11] כל כך למה
7. להעלות חמה ולנקום נקם. גרפו עליות לעפר[12] ובנו עליו
8. בנין ולא נח ועשו כל בערמה.[13] את מוצא בשעה שעלה נבוזר
9. אדן האכזרי להחריב את ירושלים רמז הב"ה[14] לאותו הדם
10. והיה תוסס ומרתיח אמ' לו הב"ה לדם הא ענתא דתיגבי
11. דיקי[15] דידך כיון שעלה נבוזארדן חמא יתיה מרתיח. אמ'
12. ליה[16] מה טיבו של דם זה תוסס כדין[17] אמרו ליה[18] דם פרים
13. וכבשים ואילים[19] ושחט עליו ולא שקט[20] ולא נח ולא עמד

---

[8] In the manuscripts: בצבי ואיל. In C: בדם איל וצבי.

[9] Lev. 17.13.

[10] MS Vatican: לא נהגו כן אלא שפכוהו על האבנים. C: לא נהגו בדמו לא כדם איל וצבי אלא שפכוהו על האבנים.

[11] Ezek. 24.7.

[12] Should be: עליו כל עפר.

[13] In MSS New York and St Petersburg, and in C: ועשו כל ערמה. In MSS Vatican, Oxford, and Paris, these words are missing.

[14] = הקדוש ברוך הוא.

[15] The same in MSS Vatican, Moscow, and New York. In C: דייתיקי.

[16] In MSS Moscow and New York, and in C: לון. In MS Vatican: לן.

[17] In most manuscripts, this word is missing. In MS New York: בכה. In C: כך.

[18] In all the manuscripts and in C: לו.

[19] Should be here: דם פרים וכבשים ואילים שהיינו שוחטין ומקריבין. הביא פרים וכבשים ואילים (the version in MS New York). This is a homeoteleuton of ואילים-ואילים.

[20] In MSS Vatican and New York, and in C: שתק.

14. [מי]ד הביאן תלאן בגרדון אמ' לו[21] אמרו לי מה טיבו של דם
15. ואי לא[22] אנא מסרקנא לכון בסרקי[23] דפרזלא. אמרו לו הואיל
16. והב"ה רוצה לתבוע דמו מידינו נגלה לך אמרו לו כהן ונביא
17. ושופט היה והיה מתנבא עלינו את כל הדברים[24] אשר אתה[25]
18. ע[ושה] לנו ולא היינו מאמינים לו והרגנוהו[26] על שהיה
19. מוכיחנו מיד הביא שמנים אלף פרחי כהונה ושחט עליו
20. ולא נח והיה הדם מבצבץ[27] ובוקע[28] עד שהגיע לקברו של
21. זכריה ועוד הביא סנהדרי גדולה וסנהדרי קטנה ושחט עליו[29]

---

[21] Should be: לון.

[22] In all the manuscripts and in C: ואם לאו.

[23] MS Vatican: במסרקא; MS New York: במסרקי; MS Moscow: במסריקא; C: במשרקא.

[24] In all the manuscripts, and in C: הדברים האלה.

[25] In all the manuscripts, and in C: שאתה.

[26] In all the manuscripts, and in C: מאמינים/ן בו ועמדנו עליו והרגנוהו.

[27] MS Vatican: מכסכס (in the others: מבצבץ).

[28] The same in MS Vatican. In MSS New York and St Petersburg: ובוקע והולך; Moscow: והולך ובוקע; C: בוקע ועולה.

[29] The same in all the manuscripts. In C: עליהם.

Verso

1. ולא נח באותה שעה נזף ב[יה] אותו רשע ו[א]מ'[30] מה טב את
2. ומה טימי[31] דידך יתירא יתירא(!) מדמין דאלהין[32] דקטלית בעי
3. את דנוביד[33] כל אומתך בגינך.[34] באותה שעה נתמלא הב"ה
4. רחמים אמ' ומה זה שהוא רשע[35] בן רשע ואכזרי ועלה
5. להחריב את ביתי נתמלא עליהם רחמים אנכי[36] שכתו' בי כי
6. אל רחום יי"י אלהיך.[37] וכתי' יי"י יי"י אל רחום וחנון ארך אפים.[38]
7. וכתי' טוב יי"י לכל ורחמיו על כל מעשיו.[39] על אחת כמה וכמה.
8. באותה שעה רמז הב"ה לדם[40] ונבלע במקומו. אמ' ר' יודן

[30] This is the version in most manuscripts. In C: באותה שעה בא אותו רשע וזעק על דמא ואמר.

[31] The same in MSS Vatican and New York (and probably also St Petersburg). In MS Moscow: טיבי; in C: דמא.

[32] In most manuscripts and in C: מדמי אילין. In MS Vatican: מדמי אלין; in MS St Petersburg: מדמי דכל [...]ן.

[33] In most manuscripts, and in C: דנובד. In MS Moscow: דמיביד. In MS New York it was fixed to: דאובד.

[34] C: בגינה.

[35] MS Vatican: ומה זה רשע; MS New York: ומה אם רשע; MS Moscow and C: ומה אם זה רשע.

[36] MSS Vatican and Moscow: אני.

[37] Deut. 4.31.

[38] Exod. 34.6. The words ארך אפים are missing in other manuscripts and in C.

[39] Ps. 145.9.

[40] In MSS New York and St Petersburg: לאותו הדם; in MSS Moscow and C: לאותו דם. In MS Vatican these two words are missing.

9. שבע עברות עברו ישראל[41] הרגו כהן ונביא ודיין ושפכו דם
10. נקי וטמאו את העזרה ויום שבת ויום הכפורים היה. ר'
11. יהושע פתר קרייה במעשה העגל מקום המשפט שמה
12. הרשע[42] מקום שעשה משה מדת הדין שנ' עברו ושובו
13. משער לשער.[43] שמה הרשע. שנ'[44] ויגוף יי"י את העם.[45] ורוח
14. הקדש צווחת ואומרת[46] מקום שצדקתים מקללותיו של
15. בלעם[47] וקראתים אלוהות שנ' אני אמרתי אלהים אתם[48] שמה
16. הרשיעו ועשו העגל.[49] ר' יודה[50] פתר קרייה בשטים[51] שנא'
17. קח את כל ראשי העם והוקע אותם[52] שמה הרשע[53] ויהיו

[41] MSS Vatican, Oxford, New York, and Moscow add here: באותו היום. MS St Petersburg: באו[תו] הדם; C: באותה שעה.

[42] Eccl. 3.16.

[43] Exod. 32.27.

[44] In most manuscripts: שמה הרשע שמה כתו'/כתי'.

[45] Exod. 32.35.

[46] C adds here: ומקום הצדק שמה הרשע.

[47] The words מקללותיו של בלעם were copied wrongly, due to the homeoteleuton מקום שצדקתים-מקום שצדקתים in the continuation.

[48] Ps. 82.6. Most manuscripts (and C) add here: שמה הרשע.

[49] All the manuscripts (and C) add here a reference to Exod. 32.8.

[50] MSS Vatican, New York, and Paris: יודן; MSS Oxford and Moscow: יהודה. C: יודה.

[51] Other manuscripts and C add here: מקום המשפט שמה הרשע מקום שעשה מדת הדין בשטים שנא' (with tiny changes).

[52] Num. 25.4.

[53] שמה הרשע only in MS Moscow and in C. In other manuscripts these words are missing. In MS Vatican wrongly: והוקע אותם שם.

18. המתים במגפה[54] ורוח הקדש צווחת ואומרת מקום
19. שצדקתי[55] מקללותיו של בלעם הרשע והפכתים לברכות
20. שנא' ויהפוך יי"י אלהיך לך את הקללה לברכה.[56] שמה הרשע
21. שזנו[57] שנ' וישב ישראל בשטים.[58] ר' לוי ור' יצחק ר' לוי אמ'
22. שני[59]

---

[54] Num. 25.9. MS New York also omits the numbers of the dead, but in MS Vatican and in C: כ"ד אלף. In MS Oxford: ד' ועשרים אלף, following the biblical version.

[55] Should be: שצדקתים.

[56] Deut. 23.6.

[57] In MSS Vatican, Oxford, St Petersburg, and New York: שמה הרשיעו וזנו; in MSS Paris and Moscow and in C: שמה הרשע שמה הרשיעו וזנו.

[58] Num. 25.1.

[59] A catchword for the first word on the (unpreserved) next page: שנים דברים ביד ושנים דברים בימין (in all the manuscripts: שנים; in C: שני).

W.2.a: *Mishne Torah*, Sheḥitah Laws (Maimonides)

Bodl. MS Heb. c. 72/4

General Description

Leaves from *Mishne Torah*, Sheḥitah laws, 3.10–18. Ashkenazi script. Fourteenth century. A later hand, probably from the fifteenth century, in Italian script, added some sentences in the margin, which were skipped by the original scribe.

Due to the fact we have today semi-critical editions of *Mishne Torah*, based on accurate manuscripts, mainly Yemenite, we did not think there was a need to recover the blurred text on the deleted sides of the folios. Therefore, hereinafter we attach only transcription of the well-preserved sides.

Physical Description

22.6 × 16.2; vellum; 1 leaf; 28 lines in two columns (recto + verso), on verso also marginalia in a different hand and ink; badly rubbed and faded on recto.

Transcription

Right Column

1. תחת המטלית הואיל ואין הסכין
2. גלוי הרי זו ספק נבלה וכן אם שחט
3. מיעוט הסימנין בחלדה וגמר
4. השחיטה שלא בחלדה הרי זו
5. ספק נבלה.   דרסה
6. כיצד כגון שהכה

 https://doi.org/10.11647/OBP.0352.37

7. בסכין על הצוואר כדרך שמכין
8. ~~בסכין~~ בסייף וחתך הסימנין בבת
9. אחת בלא הולכה והבאה או שהניח
10. את הסכין על הצואר ודחק וחתך
11. למטה כחותך צנון או קשות עד
12. שחתך הסימנין הרי זו פסולה.
13. הגרמה כיצד זה השוחט
14. בקנה למעלה
15. ממקום שאינו ראוי לשחיטה
16. וכמו שני חטין יש בסוף הקנה
17. למעלה <מטבעת הגדולה שחט בתוך החטין אם שייר מהן כל שהוא למעלה> הרי זו כשירה שהרי שחט
18. משפוע׳ כובע ולמטה והוא מן
19. המקום הראוי לשחיטה ואם לא
20. שייר מהן כלום אלא שחט למעלה
21. מהן הרי זו מוגרמת ופסולה.
22. שחט רוב האחד או רוב שנים
23. והשלים בדריסה או בהגרמה
24. הרי זו כשירה שהרי נשחט
25. ~~ב~~השיעור כראוי. הגרים בתחלה
26. שליש ושחט שני שלישים הרי
27. זו ~~שני~~ כשרה. שחט שליש
28. והגרים שליש [וחזר] ושחט שליש

Left Column

1. האחרון כשר. הגרים שליש ושחט
2. שליש וחזר והגרים שליש האחרון
3. הרי זו פסולה. ואם דרס או החליד

4. בין בשליש הראשון בין בשליש
5. האמצעי הרי זו פסולה.
6. עיקור   כיצד כגון שנעקרה
7. הגרגרת והיא קנה
8. או וושט ונשמט אחד מהן או
9. שניהם קודם גמר שחיטה פסולה אבל
10. אם שחט אחד בעוף או רובו ואחר
11. כך נשמט הסימן השני שחיטתו
12. כשירה.   נשמט אחד מהןם[1]
13. ואחר כך ~~נשחט~~ שחט את הסימן
14. השני שחיטתו פסולה.
15. שחט אחד מהן ונמצא השני
16. שמוט ואין ידוע אם קודם שחיטתו
17. נשמט אם לאחר שחיטה נשמט
18. הרי זו ספק נבלה. נמצא הסימן
19. השחוט שמוט הרי זו כשירה
20. שודאי אחר שחיטה נעקר שאלו
21. נעקר קודם שחיטה היה מתדלדל
22. ולא ישחט.   בד"א[2] בשלא תפס
23. סימנין בידו כששחט אבל אם תפסם ושחט
24. איפשר שתשחט אחר העיקור
25. ולפיכך אם נמצאת שמוטה
26. ושחוטה הרי זו ספק נבלה.
27. כל מקום שאמרנו בשחיטה
28. פסולה הרי זו נבלה ואם אכל ממנה

---

[1] It seems that the scribe first wrote מהן and then corrected to מהם (compare l. 23), but it is also possible that מהם was corrected to מהן.

[2] = במה דברים אמורים. It seems that the word was deleted.

W.2.b: *Mishne Torah*, Sheḥitah Laws (Maimonides)

Bodl. MS Heb. c. 72/5

General Description

Leaves from *Mishne Torah*, Sheḥitah laws, 10.8–9. Ashkenazi script. For more details, see W.2.a.

Physical Description

22.5 × 16.1; vellum; 1 leaf; 28 lines in two columns (recto + verso); rubbed and faded on verso.

Transcription

Right Column

1. בו [מות]רת **א** משום טרפה
2. ואסורה משום סכנת נפשות.
3. נמצאו כל הטריפות המנויות <כשיפרטו
4. ואיפשר שימצאו בבהמה וחיה
5. שבעים. ואלו הן על הסדר
6. שנתבארו בחבור זה. א' דרוסה
7. ב' נקב תרבץ הושט. ג' נקב
8. קרום המות. ד' נתמסמס המוח
9. עצמו. ה' נקב הלב לבית חללו.
10. ו' נקב קנה הלב. ז' נקבה המרה.
11. ח' נקב קנה הכבד. ט' נקבה הקיבה.
12. י' נקב הכרס. י"א ניקב המסס.
13. י"ב נקב בית הכוסות. י"ג נקבו
14. מעיה. י"ד יצאו המעים לחוץ

 https://doi.org/10.11647/OBP.0352.38

15. ונהפכו. ט"ו נקב הטחול בעביו.
16. י"ו חסרה המרה. י"ז נמצאו
17. שתי מררות. י"ח חסרה הקיבה.
18. י"ט נמצאו שתי קיבות. כ' חסר
19. הכרס. כ"א נמצאו שני כרסים.
20. כ"ב חסר המסס. כ"ג נמצאו
21. שני מססים. כ"ד חסר בית
22. הכוסות. כ"ה נמצאו שני בתי
23. כוסות. כ"ו חסר אחד מן המעים.
24. כ"ז נמצאו שני מעים. כ"ח
25. נקבה הריאה. כ"ט נקב הקנה
26. למטה במקום שאינו ראוי
27. לשחיטה. ל' נקב סימפון
28. מפמפוני(!) הריאה ואפלו לחברו.

Left Column

1. ל"א נאטם מקום מן הריאה. ל"ב
2. נמוק סמפון מסמפוני הריאה.
3. ל"ג נ[מצ]את לחה סרוחה בריאה.
4. ל"ד נמצאו [בה מ]ים סרוחים. ל"ה
5. נמצאו בה [מים] עכורים ~~אע"פ שלא~~
6. ~~[הס(?)]ריחו~~. ל"ו נתמסמסה הריאה.
7. ל"ז נשתנו מראיה. ל"ח נהפך
8. הושט במראיו. ל"ט חסרה הריאה
9. ממניין האונות. מ' נתחלפו
10. האונות. מ"א הותירו האונות
11. מ[גב]ה. מ"ב נסמכה אונא לאונא
12. שלא כסדרן. מ"ג נמצאת הריאה

13. בלא חיתוך [אזנים]. מ"ד ח[ס]רה
14. מקצת הריאה. [מ]"ה [יבש]
15. מקצת גופה. מ"ו נמ[צ]את הריאה
16. נפוחה ועומדת. מ"ז צמקה
17. הריאה מפחד אדם. מ"ח חסר
18. הרגל בין מתחלתו בריתו בין שנחתך.
19. מ"ט או שהיתה רגל יתירה. נ'
20. נטל צומת הגידין. נ"א נטלה הכבד
21. נ"ב ניטל לחי העליון. נ"ג כוליא
22. שהקטינה ביותר. נ"ד כוליא
23. שלקתה. נ"ה כוליא שנמצאת
24. בה לחה ואע"פ שאינה סרוחה.
25. נ"ו כוליא שנמצאו בה מים עכורים
26. ואע"פ שאינם סרוחים. נ"ז
27. כוליא שנמצאו [ב]ה מים סרוחים.
28. נ"ח נפסק חוט השדרה. נ"ט

W.3: Commentary on Kings (R. David Qimḥi)

Bodl. MS Heb. c. 72/45

General Description

Fragments from the famous Provençal commentator, R. David Qimḥi (1160–1235). The commentary of Qimḥi was first printed in 1486 (Soncino). We compared our manuscript to the 1547 edition published in Venice (hereinafter: V).

For easier reading, we put in red those words and phrases commented upon.

Physical Description

20.1 × 15.5; paper; 1 leaf; 18 lines (recto); 5 lines (verso); torn, holes, red-brown stains.

Transcription

Recto

0. [אשר במסלת שדה כובס.[1] המסלה היא]
1. [הדרך שמתקנים אותה באבנים כדי שיוכלו לל]כת בה בימות הגש[מים]
2. [ועיקר הלשון הוא לשון הרמה מע]נין ס[לו לר]וכב בערבות[2] רוממו[3] ~~והמק~~
3. [והמקום הזה היה בזה השדה והו]א מתוקן[4] באבנים ועל המקום הזה
4. [היו עומדים מכבסי הבגדים במי ה]תעלה ובשדה היו שוטחים הבגדים

---

[1] 2 Kgs 18.17.

[2] Ps. 68.5.

[3] V: שענינו רוממו.

[4] V: מורם ומתוקן.

 https://doi.org/10.11647/OBP.0352.39

5. [לשמש. וכת"י[5] שדה כ]ובס. חקל משטח קצריא. ויקראו אל
6. [המלך.[6] קראו לא]שר על החומה או לאשר מצאו בש[דה כובס] [... ...][7]
7. [שיאמרו למ]לך שיצא לדבר עמם ויצאו אליהם במצות המלך אליקים
8. [ושבנא] ויו[אח.] אליקים בן חלקיהו אשר על הבית. וכן אמ' בישעיה בז[את]
9. [הפרש]ה[8] אבל בפרשה שנאמ' על שבנא נאמ' לך[9] אל הסוכן הזה על ~~שב~~
10. [שבנא א]שר על הבית[10] ונב' [...][11] שיהדפנו מהשררה שהיה בה על[12] הבית
11. [ויתננה ל]אליקים בן חלקיהו ולא נוכל לומ' כי קודם המעשה הזה מרד ~~שב~~
12. [שבנא] ונתנה[13] שררותו לאליקים ומפני זה אמ' אליקים אשר על הבית כי אלו
13. [היו המל]אכים הראשונים אשר באו ממלך אשור לירושלם ושבנא יצא
14. [אליהם] עם אליקים ואמ' לרב שקה דבר נא אל עבדיך ארמית כי שומעים
15. [אנחנו][14] ונאמ' ויבא אליקים ושבנה[15] הספר ויואח קרועי בגדים[16] נראה כי עדין

---

[5] = וכתרגום יונתן, 'like the translation (attributed to) Jonathan (b. 'Uzziel)'.

[6] 2 Kgs 18.18.

[7] In V there is no word after בשדה כובס.

[8] See Isa. 36.3.

[9] Should be לך בא, as in V.

[10] Isa. 22.15.

[11] Maybe: ונב'[א] ישעיה(?). In V: ונבא עליו.

[12] V: שהיה בה על.

[13] V: ונתנו.

[14] 2 Kgs 18.26; Isa. 36.11.

[15] In 2 Kgs 18.18 and 18.26 it is indeed ושבנה, but here (18.37) it is ושבנא. In Isaiah, the spelling is in all cases ושבנא.

[16] The full version in 2 Kgs 18.37 is: וַיָּבֹא אֶלְיָקִים בֶּן חִלְקִיָּה אֲשֶׁר עַל הַבַּיִת וְשֶׁבְנָא הַסֹּפֵר וְיוֹאָח בֶּן אָסָף הַמַּזְכִּיר אֶל חִזְקִיָּהוּ קְרוּעֵי בְגָדִים (the same in Isa. 36.22, except חִלְקִיָּהוּ instead of חִלְקִיָּה).

Verso

1. [...]
2. [...]
3. קרוע [בגדים ...]
4. [...]
5. אמרת אך דבר [שפתים ...][17]
6. [... ... ...] וי"ת[18] א[מרת] במלל א[... ... ...][19]
7. כי מרדת בי.[20] שלא נתן את(?)[21] שהטיל עליו [שנה בשנה. הרצוץ.][22]
8. הרצוץ בראשו ואותם קסמים[23] נכנסים בכף [האדם בהשען עליו. הלא]
9. הוא אשר הסיר.[24] כלומ' כשהסיר חזקיהו ונתץ המ[זבחות לא עשה כ"א[25]]
10. לכבודו ולהנאתו כדי שיבאו כלם לירושלם כי המזבחו[ת בכל מקום לשם]
11. י"י היו וחזקיהו הסירם ונתצם איך תחשבו כי י"י יעזור אותו [ואיך תבטחו]
12. על[יו]. ליהודה ולירושלם. כתרגו'[26] לאנש יהודה וליתבי ירושלם [התערב]
13. נא.[27] הכנס עמי בערבון בזה הדבר אם תוכל לעשותם.[28] רכבים עלי[הם].

---

[17] 2 Kgs 18.20 (and Isa. 36.5).

[18] = ויונתן תרגם.

[19] V: וי"ת ברם במלל סיפוון במילך וגבורא אעביד קרבא.

[20] 2 Kgs 18.20 (and Isa. 36.5).

[21] V: מה.

[22] 2 Kgs 18.21.

[23] Plural of קיסם.

[24] 2 Kgs 18.22.

[25] = כי אם.

[26] = כתרגומו.

[27] 2 Kgs 18.23.

[28] V: לעשותו.

14. רכבים שיהיו פרשים. המבלעדי י״י.[29] להפחידם אמ' כן או פי' אח[ר שכל]

15. הארצות נתן בידי[30] וגם כל ארץ ישראל הוא אמר אלי עלה ע[ל[31] הארץ]

16. והשחיתה ואם רב שקה היה ישראל משומד[32] אמ' זה לפי שישעיה [נבא]

17. ואמ' הנני[33] מעלה את מי הנה(!)[34] העצומים והרבים את מלך אשור[35] [וגו'. כי]

18. שומעים אנחנו.[36] מבינים ומכירים בלשון ארמית. העל אדוניך.[37] [כמו האל]

19. וכן הוא בישעיה[38] ולאליקים אמר שהוא הגדול וכן הוא אומ' ויאמר [אליקים[39] וגו']

---

[29] 2 Kgs 18.25.

[30] V: נתן י״י בידי.

[31] V: אל.

[32] The same in V. In later editions it was changed by censorship to מומר. For the rabbinic tradition on Ravshaqe, see b. Sanhedrin 60a.

[33] The same in V, but in Isaiah it is: הִנֵּה אֲדֹנָי.

[34] Should be הנהר.

[35] Isa. 8.7.

[36] 2 Kgs 18.26.

[37] 2 Kgs 18.27.

[38] See Isa. 36.12. V adds here: וכן על האנשים כמו אל.

[39] 2 Kgs 18.26; Isa. 36.11.

W.4: *Mikhlol* (R. David Qimḥi)

Bodl. MS Heb. c. 72/47

General Description

A damaged and faded fragment from the *Mikhlol,* a grammatical work by R. David Qimḥi, from the section on verbal grammar (roots: *qbb, rkk, šmm*). Sephardi script, fourteenth to fifteenth centuries. There is on the manuscript a glued sheet containing a halakhic text in Aramaic and Hebrew, in mirror script.

Our version of the manuscript was compared to the printed edition published in Venice (1545, 47a–47c), one of the first editions of this work (hereinafter: V). We also checked the common edition of Ełk (1862, 133a–134a; hereinafter: E).

The biblical words were written in the manuscript with partial Tiberian vocalisation.

Physical Description

20.5 × 14.1; paper; 1 leaf; 20 lines + various mirrored script lines from another text physically stuck to the fragment (recto); 18 lines (verso); torn, holes, rubbed, beige stains; the very top layer of another fragment is stuck to much of the recto surface.

 https://doi.org/10.11647/OBP.0352.40

Transcription

Recto

0. [קבב. באה מלה זרה בשורש הזה וְקָבְנוֹ לִי מִשָּׁם.[1]
ורבי יהודה[2] כתב ששרשו קָבָן ואין זה נכון][3]
1. אחר שלא מצאנו זה [השר]ש ונכון
2. יותר[4] שתהיה ה[נו"]ן [נו]ספת כמו שכתב[נו]
3. בשלמים ב[טור הר]אשון[5] גם י[תכן לומ']
4. שהנו"ן והו"ו כנוי ה[פעול כמו שהוא באית"ן]
5. ישמרנו יזכרנו כן יהיה[6] [בצווי[7] והיה]
6. משפטו בדגש וְקָבֶנוּ[8] והוקלה ה[מל]ה [ונפ]ל
7. [הד]גש מן הכפל ומן הנו"ן ובא [בחולם כמו]
8. עונותיו ילכדונו את הרשע.[9] רכך
9. כתב ר' יהודה אך והבא[תי]
10. מֹרֶךְ[10] לא יבא מענין זה[11] והנכ[ון]
11. וה[ישר] להיותו מעיקר זה בפלס בְּמֹ[עַל]

---

[1] Num. 23.13.

[2] Judah b. David ibn Ḥayyūj, a Hebrew grammarian of the tenth century.

[3] Completion based on V.

[4] V: ויותר נכון.

[5] V adds here: או שתהיה הנון במקום אות הכפל כמו לַשְׁמִד מָעֻזְנֶיהָ, כִּי לֹא תָמְנוּ.

[6] V: וכן הוא.

[7] According to V. In E: בהצווי.

[8] V: בהדגש קָבֶנּוּ.

[9] Prov. 5.22. In MT: עֲוֺנֹתָיו יִלְכְּדֻנוֹ.

[10] Lev. 26.36. V: וְהֵבֵאתִי מוֹרֶךְ בִּלְבָבָם (MT: מֹרֶךְ).

[11] V: אינו מעקר זה.

12. [ידיה]ם[12] ששרשו עלל ומשפ[טו בתשלומו[13] מָרְכַּד][14]
13. בפלס וזובח מָשְׁחָת[15] כי מָשְׁחָתָם בם.[16]
14. [שמ]ם. למה תשומם.[17] כתב ר'
15. [יה]ודה שיה[יה][18] מבנין
16. [ה]תפעל והדגש[19] [השי"ן לחסרון תי"ו ה]תפעל ונכון[20]
17. אע"פ שתי"ו ה[תפ]על לא תבא על אותיות
18. זשס"ץ[21] לפניהם[22] אעפ"כ הדגש[23] מורה עליה
19. כי כן[24] היה מקומה לולי קריאת האותיות
20. [ש]לא יתכן[25] כמו שכתבנו בשלמים. גם

---

[12] Neh. 8.6.

[13] V: משפטם בתשלומם.

[14] V adds here: מָעְלַל.

[15] Mal. 1.14. In MT: וְזֹבֵחַ מָשְׁחָת. V: וְזוֹבֵחַ מָשְׁחָת לַייָ.

[16] Lev. 22.25. In V and E, in accordance with MT: בָּהֶם.

[17] Eccl. 7.16.

[18] V: שהוא.

[19] V: ודגש.

[20] V: ונכון הוא.

[21] V: ז"ס ש"ץ.

[22] V adds: כי אם לאחריהם.

[23] V adds: שיש בשין.

[24] V: כאן.

[25] V: שלא יתכן כן.

Verso

יתכן לומר שיהיה מבנין נפעל ואל תתמ' לפי שבא בחלם[26] ולא אמר תִּשָּׁמֵם בפלס תִּשָּׁמֵר תִּזָּכֵר כי הכל אחד כי בחסרונם באו כן. יִשּׁוֹם וְיִשְׁרוֹק[27] וַיִּדּוֹם[28] אהרן וַתִּתּוֹם השנה ההיא.[29] ואם תשלומם[30] יהיו יְשׁוֹמֵם יְדוֹמֵם[31] תִּתוֹמֵם וכן העוברים מן הנפעל יש[32] מהם בחלם ויש מהם בצרי ויש מהם בפתח[33] כמו שכתבנו[34] כי הכל אחד ואין לחוש על זה.[35] כל ימי

---

[26] The scribe writes the word *ḥolam* without *vav*; see l. 7.

[27] Jer. 50.13. In V and E, in accordance with MT: יִשֹּׁם וְיִשְׁרֹק.

[28] Lev. 10.3. In MT: וַיִּדֹּם.

[29] Gen. 47.18. In V and E, in accordance with MT: וַתִּתֹּם (without השנה ההיא).

[30] V: בתשלומם.

[31] In V with *ḥiriq*: יִשׁוֹמֵם יִדוֹמֵם, and the same in E.

[32] V: מנפעל באלה הפעלים יש.

[33] V: ויש מהם בחולם ויש מהם בפתח ויש מהם בצרי.

[34] V: שזכרנו.

[35] V adds here: ואם יאמר אומר כי יִשּׁוֹם ויִדּוֹם משפטם בתשלומם יִשָּׁמוֹם, יִדָּמוֹם כי בבנין הקל שהוא יסוד הפעלים גזר(ה)[ת] פָּעוֹל מצאנו ולא גזרת פּוֹעֵל, נאמר לו אף על פי כן אחר שמצאנו גזרת פועל בבנין פועל הכבד נאמר כי לקחו בכפולים גזרתו כמו שעשו בהתפעל בכפולים כן נהגו זה המנהג בנפעל במקצת מקומות, והנה ר' יונה כתב כִּי עַתָּה אֵרוֹמֵם מבנין נפעל משורש רָמַם, וכן כתב בהֵרֹמּוּ מִתּוֹךְ הָעֵדָה, ורבי אברהם אבן עזרא ז"ל כתב גם כן למה תִשׁוֹמֵם מבנין נפעל, בָּהְשַּׁמָּה מֵהֶם, בלא בית השמוש היה אומר הָשַּׁמָּה, וכשנכנסה עליו בית השמוש נהפך הקמץ חטף בבית השמוש להקל על ההא ומשפטו בְּהָשַּׁמָּה כמו שבא גם כן לְהַפְרְכֶם אֶת־בְּרִיתִי שהיה ראוי לַהֲפִירְכֶם כמו שכתבנו בשמוש האותיות.

10. הָשַּׁמָּה[36] הוא מקור וטרם הסמכו עם[37]
11. עם(!) הכנוי יאמר הושם[38] כמו המקור
12. מהופעל[39] בחסר[40] הפ"א הוּגֵד הוּגַד לי[41]
13. ובהסמכו עם הכנויין שב הדגש במ"ם
14. לחסרון אות הכפל כמשפט ונשאר הדגש
15. בשי"ן כמו שהיה טרם הסמכו.[42]
16. **כלו פעלי הכפל.[43] ויש פעלים**
17. **בני ארבע אותיות.** מְכַרְכֵּר
18. בבכל עז
19. תאמר ממנו כל הבנין כִּרְכַּרתָּ כִּרְכּ[ר]ת[44]
20. וכן[45]

---

[36] Lev. 26.34.

[37] V: אל.

[38] V: הֻשַּׁם.

[39] V: מֻהְפעל.

[40] V: בחסרון, and maybe our manuscript also should be read 'בחסר, i.e., בחסר'[ון].

[41] Ruth 2.11. In MT and in V: הֻגֵּד הֻגַּד.

[42] V adds here: פְּנוּ אֵלַי וְהָשַּׁמּוּ, נמצא במקצת הספרים בדגש השין, וההא אם כן תקרא בקמץ חטף ואם הוא כן נצטרך לומר כי הוא פעל עבר מוסב לעתיד מפני הוו כי אין צווי בבנין שלא נזכר פועלו כאשר כתבנו, ויש ספרים מדוייקים שאין השין דגושה וההא אם כן תקרא בקמץ רחב והיא הקריאה הנכונה, ויהיה צווי מבנין הפעיל כמו הָשֵׁמּוּ השין בצרי כמו שבא הָשַׁב אֶל תַּעְרָהּ בפתח והוא כמו הָשֵׁב בצרי.

[43] V adds: בני שלש אותיות.

[44] The reading here is difficult, and the dotting unclear. Probably כִּרְכַּרְתְּ. V: ויש פעלים בני ארבע אותיות. יש בלא כפל אות כמו כִּרְבֵּל, כִּרְבַּלְתָּ, כִּרְבַּלְתִּי וכולי. The root *krkr* appears in the continuation in V (47c).

[45] A catchword for the first word on the next page.

W.5: *Sefer ha-Yir'ah* (R. Jonah Girondi)

Bodl. MS Heb. c. 72/51–52

General Description

Sefer ha-Yir'ah is an ethical composition (*Musar*) of R. Jonah Girondi, one of the famous Jewish sages in Catalonia in the thirteenth century. This copy is in Byzantine script.

The book was first printed in Lisbon in 1490 (this edition is very rare), and, since then, has been reprinted many times. The comparison to a printed version given below is to the 1565 Istanbul version (hereinafter: I). We marked only significant changes between our manuscript and the printed one.

Physical Description

14 × 21 (11 one leaf); paper; 2 leaves (bifolium); 19 lines + marginalia (recto); jottings (verso); slightly torn, holes, beige stains; three distinct pricks in shape of a triangle in both side margins.

Transcription

[ספר היראה

טוב לגבר כי-ישא על בנעוריו.[1] כי טוב לאדם לשאת ולסבול עולו של הקדוש ברוך הוא ולתת מוסרות ומוטות על צווארו להיכנס לעבודת בורא העולם. ויזכור את בוראו בימי בחורותיו, ובכל יום ויום יוסיף אומץ ויתחזק במצות בורא עולם, ויכניס אהבתו בלבו, ויחשוב הבורא תמיד לנגד עיניו, ועל ידי כן ייתן יראת הצור על פניו, ויכניע לבו, וישפיל קומתו ואת רום עיניו, וילך שחוח, ויתהה על עוונות נעוריו, ויבכה עליהם תמיד, וישמור בכל כוחו מחטוא עוד במסתרים, ולא יעשה במחשך מעשיו, ואז יהיה אהוב ונחמד בעיני הבורא, וכל רואיו יאשרוהו.

אלה הדברים אשר יעשה אותם האדם וחי בהם חיי עולם. בכל בוקר בהקיצו משנתו ,יזדעזע ויהיה נרתע ונחפז מאימת הבורא בזכרו חסדו אשר עשה לו ואמונתו אשר שמר לו, כי החזיר לו נשמתו

[1] Lam. 3.27.

 https://doi.org/10.11647/OBP.0352.41

אשר הפקיד אצלו, ואז יברך בלבו את הבורא אשר הגדיל לעשות עמו, כי חידש והחליף כוחו. ובשומו הדברים האלה אל לבו, תבער אהבת הבורא בלבו, ואז אל ייסוב על מיטתו דרך עצל, אך במהירות וזריזות]

Folio 51 Recto

1. יקום מיד. ואם יפ[ג]ע בו מנוול זה[2] ויוליכנו [דרך] עצלות
2. ישיב אמריו לו וישים אל לבו, כי אם יקרא לו[3] [בעל]
3. חוב או אדם אחר אליו יקום מיד או מפ[ני כבו]ד
4. אדם או מפני ריוח שיבא לו חיי[4] שעה או מיראת
5. הפסד ממון כמו נפלה[5] דליקה בעיר יק[ום] מיד
6. במהרה ואל[6] יתרשל או אם יצטרך ללכת לעבודת
7. המלך יקום ואל יתרשל פן יעלילו עליו או למ[צוא]
8. חן בעיני המלך על אחת כמה וכמה לעבודת מלך
9. מלכי המלכים הקב"ה שיש לו להיזהר לקום במ[הירות]
10. ובזריזות ויירא פן יאחר לבו[7] וכל מע[שיו יח]שיב[8]
11. לעשות לשם שמים ולפי כחו ילך בדרכי החכמ[ים]
12. ויהיה נכנע[9] ושפל רוח[10] אל יעמוד אדם ערום

---

[2] זה is missing in I.

[3] אם יקרא לו. In I: אם יקרא אליו גוי. The word גוי was omitted also in later editions.

[4] I: שהוא חיי.

[5] I: כגון שנפלה.

[6] I: ולא. This change is widespread, and we do not mark it hereinafter.

[7] Should be: לבוא.

[8] I: יחשוב.

[9] I: צנוע. But in later editions: נכנע.

[10] ושפל רוח is missing in I.

13. ממטתו[11] אך מיושב[12] כמו שהיה מתפאר ר' יוסי
14. ז"ל מימי לא ראו קורות ביתי אמרי חלוקי[13] כמ' כן
15. יקח[14] חלוקו ויכניס בו ראשו וזרועו[15] ואז בקומו
16. יהיה מכוסה ואל יאמ' הרי אני[16] בחדרי חדרים
17. בבית אפל מי רואני מי יודיעני[17] כי מלא כל הארץ
18. כבודו[18] לפניו כחשכה כאורה[19] וילבש בגדיו ויהיה
19. לו טלת[20] קטן וילבשנו מתחת למדיו כי עקר מצ[ו]ת

Folio 51 Verso

1. ציצת לזיכרון[21] ללבשו תמיד כי לזכ[ר]ון מצוה[22] נתנה
2. ולמען לא יסור האדם אחרי שמירות[23] לבו ואחרי מראה
3. עיניו המחטיאים את הגוף והדרך הזה לא ימצא כי
4. [אם] בלכתו בדרך[24] אשר דברי ערוה מצויים שם על

---

[11] I: ממטתו ערום (the order of the words is reversed).

[12] I: אך ילבש מיושָב. In later editions it was corrupted to אף מיושב.

[13] b. Shabbat 118b.

[14] כמ' כן יקח. In I: אך יקח.

[15] I: וזרועותיו.

[16] הרי אני. In I: הנני.

[17] I: יודעני. In later editions: מעידני.

[18] Isa. 6.3.

[19] Following Ps. 119.12.

[20] The pronunciation *talet* or *tales* is known among some Jewish communities. In I it is pointed as טָלֵית. Cf. verso, l. 7.

[21] ללבשו is missing in I.

[22] I: המצות.

[23] Should be: שרירות.

[24] וזה מועיל מאד לאדם ההולך בדרך :I. והדרך הזה לא ימצא כי אם בלכתו בדרך.

5. כן ילבש [אותו מ]יד ולא יעשה בו ברכה[25] אם לא רחץ
6. ידיו וטוב להיות זריז ליטול ידיו קודם ויברך עובר
7. ל[ע]שייתו וצריך להתעטף מעומד ואותו טלת[26] קטן
8. [טו]ב שיהיה כעין סרבל כי בזה אין פקפוק וינעול
9. [מ]נעליו של ימין תחלה ואחר כך של שמאל ויקשור
10. [ש]ל ש[מאל] ואחר כך של ימין כמו שארז"ל[27] ירא השם[28]
11. [יצא את] כולם לקיים דברי המשנה[29] ודברי רבי יוחנן[30]
12. כתפילתו[31] כך מנעליו מה תפילין[32] בשמאל אף מנעליו
13. בשמאל. ומעת שיתחיל[33] להתהלך על הארץ
14. יכוף קומתו וישוח ראשו כי השכינה למעלה מראשו
15. ולכן הגון[34] לו לכסות ראשו ואל יהיה בגילוי ראש
16. וילך ויבדוק עצמו בבית הכסא ושם יהיה צנוע ואל
17. יגלה עצמו כי אם לפניו טפח מאחריו טפחיים
18. והאשה מלאחריה טפח ומלפניה ולא כלום ואל[35]
19. ישתיק[36] מעומד פן יהיו נצוצות נתזות על רגליו

[25] ולא יעשה בו ברכה. I: בלא ברכה.

[26] See above, n. 20 in this section.

[27] b. Shabbat 61a.

[28] I: השם also, but in some later editions: שמים.

[29] I: הברייתא.

[30] I adds here: שאמר.

[31] I: כתפליו.

[32] I: תפליו.

[33] ומעת שיתחיל. I: ומעת קומו.

[34] I: נכון, and לו is missing.

[35] I: ולא.

[36] In I wrongly: ישטין.

Folio 52 Recto

0. [ואם אתה אצל בני אדם שאתה חייב בכבודם כגון אביך ואמם כבדם]
1. ותירא מהם ואל[37] תשב במקומם ולא תסתור דבריהם
2. ואם אמרו לך דבר אפי' ידעת כי אינו כן[38] אל תאמר
3. ל[א] היה כן[39] ואם יש להם דבר עם שום אדם אל תכריע
4. ביניהם ואל תכנס לתוך דבריהם[40] כי אף דברי חבירו
5. אם יכנס בהם[41] נקרא גולם כללו של דבר כל מה שיוכל
6. לתלות הכבוד שבהם אם הוא מדבר בשמם או
7. בשליחותם יתלה הכבוד בהם ולא בו ומאד יש להזהר
8. בכבודם כי הוקש כבודם לכבוד הבור'[42] ית' והמכבדם
9. כאילו מכבד המקום ב"ה[43] והמצערם כאילו מצער
10. עצמו[44] וחייב להאכילם ולהשקותם ולהלבישם[45] ולהכניסם ולהוציאם
11. ואם אין לו יסבב על הפתחים ויתן להם[46] ומה שיעשה

---

[37] I: ולא.

[38] I: ולא תסתור דבריהם אפילו אם יאמרו דבר שאינו כן.

[39] I: אינו כן, and then adds: היה אביו עובר על דת אל יאמ' לו אבי עברת על דת אלא יאמ' לו אבי מקרא כתוב בתור' כך הוא ויבין מעצמו ולא יתבייש. See hereinafter ll. 14–16.

[40] I: אל יכריע ביניהם ואל יכנס בדבריהם.

[41] I: כי אף הנכנס בדברי חברו.

[42] = הבורא.

[43] והמכבדם כאילו כיבד המקום ב"ה is missing in I.

[44] Euphemism for God himself. I adds: כביכול.

[45] I adds: ולהנעילם.

[46] ואם אין לו יסבב על הפתחים ויתן להם is missing in I.

12. להם יהיה[47] דרך כבוד כי יש מאכילו לאביו[48] פסיוני
13. וטורדו מן[49] העולם ויש מטחינו ברחיים ומביאו לחיי
14. העולם הבא[50] היה אביו עובר על דברי תורה אל יאמ'
15. לו אבא עברת על דברי תורה אלא אומ' לו מקרא כתו'
16. בתורה כך הוא והוא יבין מעצמו ואל יתבייש[51] ולא
17. ידבר על מעשיהם[52] בשום עניין אפי' זרק ארניקו(!)[53] לים
18. או לאויר העולם[54] בפניו לא יכלימם ואם שמע אדם
19. מדבר עליהם שלא כהוגן יקהה את שיניו ויאמר לו

Folio 52 Verso

1. שקר אתה מדבר אין[55] לו לאדם להכות את חבירו על
2. כף[56] ואף שתיקה יפה במקום שאין כבודם כמו שהוא
3. יודע שאם ימחה או יוסיף האחר לומ' עליהם דבר[י]
4. [גנאי] לאחרים ורצונם הוא כבודם. והם שמחלו על
5. כבודם כבודו מחול[57] ויהיה אדם ירא[58] מן החכמים כמ'

---

[47] I: אך כל מה שיעשה להם יעשה.

[48] I: את אביו.

[49] The copyist first wrote ל and then corrected it to מ.

[50] b. Kiddushin 31a. I: ומכניסו לגן עדן.

[51] היה אביו עובר... ואל יתבייש is missing in I. See above, n. 39.

[52] I: אל ידבר על דבריהם.

[53] I: אירנקי.

[54] I: לאור או לים.

[55] I: אך אין.

[56] Should be: כך.

[57] I: במקום שהוא יודע שאם ימחה בו יוסיף עליו דבר גנאי יותר. ויעבור על רצונם ורצונם הוא כבודם שאם מחלו על כבודם כבודם מחול.

[58] I: והוי ירא.

6. שדרש רבי עקיבה[59] את יו"י אלוהיך תירא[60] לרבות[61] תלמ' חכמ'
7. וידבק בהם ובדרכיהם[62] הטובים ויעמוד[63] מפניהם ואף
8. מפני הזקנים אע"פ שאינם חכמ' ובטל רצונך מפני
9. רצונם וכבד אחיך הגדול ואחי אביך ואחי אמך ואיש[64]
10. אמך ואשת אביך כי כולם דרשו חכמ'[65] ז"ל מן המקרא[66]
11. [דכת'(?)] כבד אביך[67] ואמך[68] אל תרדוף אחר ישיבת עמי הארץ
12. ולצים כי מהם לא תלמד תורה[69] כי אם דברים רקים
13. ולצון אך רדוף אחר החכמ' כי מהם תלמד חכמה ואל
14. תהא בז לדבור אחיך[70] ואל תלעג לשום אדם ואל
15. תמנע טוב מבעליו אם שתלך[71] אדם על טובה
16. שבעולם[72] או דבר מצוה אל תמנענו מעשותה אך
17. אם לא[73] דעתך על הדבר אמור עשה כחכמתך והוה

---

59 b. Pesaḥim 22a.

60 Deut. 6.13.

61 I: את לרבות.

62 I: והדבק בהם ובדבריהם ובדרכיהם.

63 I: ועמוד.

64 I: ובעל.

65 b. Ketubot 103a.

66 I: דרשו חכמים מפסוק.

67 Should be: את אביך.

68 Exod. 20.12.

69 I: חכמה וטובה.

70 I: בז לדבריהם.

71 Should be: ישאלך or שאלך. I: ישאלך.

72 I: על דבר תורה.

73 I: אין.

18. רגיל בצדקה כפי כחך ולכל[74] שתשעבד עצמך לבור'[75]

19. ית'[76] לתת כופר נפשך חוק קבוע בכל שבוע פרוטה[77]

---

[74] Should be: ולכל הפחות.

[75] = לבורא.

[76] [ברך]'לבור'[א] ית is missing in I.

[77] I: מחצה או פרוטה.

W.6.a: Commentary on *Hilkhot ha-Rif*, Pesaḥim (R. Judah al-Madārī) [I]

Bodl. MS Heb. c. 72/6–7

General Description

This is an excerpt from R. Judah al-Madārī's commentary on the compendium of the Babylonian Talmud by R. Isaac al-Fasī (Rif) known as *Hilkhot ha-Rif*, Tractate Pesaḥim. The folio before us discusses b. Pesaḥim 40a–42a. Al-Madārī's commentaries on *Hilkhot ha-Rif* are discussed extensively by Ta-Shema (2010, 35–63). Ta-Shema's volume was printed posthumously, and Prof. Simcha Emanuel added supplements and updates to it. In his supplement to the chapter dealing with al-Madārī, Emanuel identified the folio before us, and W.6.b, as parts of al-Madārī's work (Ta-Shema 2010, 63). We thank Adiel Breuer for this reference.

Al-Madārī lived in Aleppo in the thirteenth century and composed commentaries on several tractates of *Hilkhot ha-Rif*. However, his work is not a systematic commentary on the *Hilkhot*. Rather, it is a commentary on the Babylonian Talmud, the framework of whose discussion is determined by the scope of the Rif's citations from the Talmud. Al-Madārī does not extensively engage with al-Fasī's own annotations on the Talmud. He frequently quotes from Rashi's commentaries on the Talmud and compares the Rif's halakhic rulings to other halakhic approaches. We have compared the Talmudic passages and quotations from Rashi cited here to the common printed edition (Vilna) and have noted only significant changes.

 https://doi.org/10.11647/OBP.0352.42

Physical Description

29.7 × 21.5; paper; 2 leaves (bifolium); 26–27 lines; slightly torn, holes, beige stains, mainly on 2v; particular pattern of pricking: three similar holes in a line, on lower margins and side margins.

Transcription

Folio 6 Recto

1. וכי ההיא כדאמרינן[1] לחם עוני מה דרכו של עני הוא
2. מסיק ~~חושתו~~ ואשתו אופה לו אף כאן הוא מסיק ואשתו
3. אופה. אמ' מר שר שלום[2] וליקח קמח מן השוק בשעת
4. הדוחק מותר דלא מחזקינן איסורא. ויוצא בו ידי חובתו
5. אבל לכתחילה לא משום שנאמ' ושמרתם את המצות.[3]
6. מצה המשתמרת לשם מצה בעינן שימור מתחלה ועד
7. סוף. ארבה.[4] ספינה. בחישתא.[5] שם הנהר טבעה קודם
8. הפסח והיו בה חטים שאבד בו כלאים שנארג בו חוט של
9. כלאים ואינו ניכר. הרי זה לא ימכרנו לשוק[6] דהואיל ואין
10. כלאים שבו ניכר אתי לזביני האי גוי לישר' ולבשי ליה
11. ולאו אדעתיה. ולא יעשנו מרדעת לחמור. דילמ' הדר

---

[1] b. Pesaḥim 115b–116a.

[2] Rav Sar Shalom Gaon was the head of the Sura yeshivah around 848–53. This Geonic tradition (ll. 2–7) is probably cited from R. Isaac ibn Ghayyat's *Hilkhot Pesaḥim*, which was one of the sources the author used in his commentary.

[3] Exod. 12.17.

[4] b. Pesaḥim 40b.

[5] From here to l. 18, there are short quotations from Rashi's commentary.

[6] In the Vilna edition: לנכרי. In the MSS of the tractate: לגוי/לגוים.

12. שקיל ליה מהתם ותופרו באחד מבגדיו. אבל עושה אותו
13. תכריכין למת דהתם[7] תו לא שקיל ליה דבגדי המת
14. אסורין בהנאה ומת אין מצוות נוהגות בו דכתי' במתים
15. חפשי[8] כיון שמת נעשה חפשי מן המצוות. והני חיטים
16. נמי כיון דלא מינכר חימוץ דידייהו אתי גוי ומזבין להו
17. לישר' קבא קבא לישר' קב לזה וקב לזה. ולא הרבה באיש
18. אחד.[9] אין מוללין את הקדירות נתינת קמח לתבשיל
19. קרי ליה מלילה. ור"ח[10] פי' מלילת הקמח בקדירה וכן כתב
20. ר"מ ז"ל[11] וכן ~~כשמואל~~ כשמולל הקדירות החדשות אין
21. מבשלין בהן אלא מצה אפויה שחזרו וטחנו אותה אבל
22. קמח קלי אסור. שמא לא קלהו יפה ויבוא לידי חימוץ. ואחר
23. כך נותן את החומץ ואין החומץ מניחו להחמיץ מפני
24. שהוא מבשלו. ויש אומ' אף נותן חומץ תחלה דאע"ג
25. דחומץ כבר מעורב בתבשיל הוא מבשל את הניתן
26. בתוכו אחד זה ואחד זה אסור. בין חומץ תחלה בין לבסוף
27. אסור.

Folio 6 Verso

1. מתני' אין נותנין את הקמח לתוך החרוסת.[12] חרוסת
2. יש בו חימוץ[13] ועשוי לטבל בו בשר. ורגילין לתת

---

[7] In the Vilna edition (in Rashi's commentary): דמהתם.

[8] Ps. 88.6.

[9] In the Vilna edition (in Rashi's commentary): לאיש.

[10] R. Ḥananel b. Ḥushiel.

[11] *Mishne Torah*, Ḥameṣ u-Maṣa 5.5.

[12] m. Pesaḥim 2.8.

[13] In the Vilna edition (in Rashi's commentary): חומץ.

3. בו קמח וכל דבר שמקהה את טעמו. וקמח לאחר זמן
4. מחמץ ומקהה את הטעם יאכל מיד קודם שיחמיץ. ור'
5. מאיר אוסר דשמא החמיץ. אין מבשלין את הפסח דכתי'
6. אל תאכלו ממנו נא ובשל. ואע"ג דכתי' במים מפרש בגמ'
7. דאפי' שאר משקין אסירי. אבל סכין בשעת צלייתו.
8. ומטבילין בשעת אכילתו. מי תשמישו של נחתום ישפכו
9. שמצנן בו ידיו ~~וטעה~~ בשעה שהוא עורך ומקטף את
10. המצה ישפכו. רמז"ל מים שרוחצין בו את הידיים
11. והעריבה אחר שלשין שמשתמשין[14] בו בשעת לישא(!) הרי
12. זה ישפך במקום מדרון כדי שלא יתקבץ במקום אחד
13. ויחמיץ.[15] גמ'[16] מקום מדרון מקום משופע שאין המים
14. נקוים בו. אשבורן מקום המים תרגום מוגרין
15. במורד[17] מתקבצים במדרון[18] שם ואין נבלעין ומחמיצין
16. ואשבורן לשון שבירה שמשתבר הקרקע ויש בו ~~ש~~יקעים[19]
17. אלא במים שלנו. שנשאבו בלילה ולנו שבימי ניסן
18. המעיינות רותחין[20] שעדיין הגשמים[21] הם ובימות הגשמים
19. חמה מהלכת בשיפולי הרקיע לפיכך כל העולם צונן
20. ומעיינות חמים הילכך מלינן בלילה ומצטננין. לא בחמה
21. לא תשב בחמה ותלוש מפני מפני שחום השמש מחמם לעיסה

---

[14] In accurate editions: וכן מים שמשתמשין.

[15] *Mishne Torah*, Ḥameṣ u-Maṣa 5.16.

[16] b. Pesaḥim 42a.

[17] כְּמַיִם מֻגָּרִים בְּמוֹרָד (Mic. 1.4).

[18] Targum Jonathan: דאשידין במורדון.

[19] In the Vilna edition (in Rashi's commentary): בקעים.

[20] In the Vilna edition (in Rashi's commentary): חמין.

[21] Should be: ימות הגשמים.

22. ויש מפרשים מין הניטלין מן החמה כגון חמי טבריה
23. וכיוצא בהן ואיתא להא ואיתא להא בהלכות בן גיאת ז"ל
24. ולא במים הגרופים מן הנהרות ומן המעיינות אלא במים
25. שלנו דהיינו מייא דביתא. וכיון שמים גרופין ממהרין
26. להחמיץ בין בלילה הראשון בין כל שבעה. אשה לא תלוש

Folio 7 Recto

1. אלא במים שלנו. אחר שמקטפת בו. טחה פני החרר'
2. במים. ואחר שמצננת בו ידיה דאותו שמקטפת בו
3. מתחמם מחמת חום ידיה.[22] עברה ולשה בחמ[י]ן או בחמי
4. חמין או במים גרופין רב אשי אסר וכן הלכה. רמז"ל[23] ואם
5. עברה ולשה תחת השמש או שלא ציננה ידה או שעשת
6. עיסתה יתר משיעור חלה הפת מותרת. וכמה שיעור חלה
7. כמ' מ"ג ביצים וחומש ביצה כגוף הביצה הבנונית לא
8. כמשקלה. והיכא דעֿבֿרא ולשא כהני דאמרינן אסור למיכל
9. מן ההיא נהמא ולא נפיק ביה חובת(!). דאיבעייא להו וכו'
10. והילכת' כרב אשי. וריב"ג[24] ז"ל סובר דמאי אסור באכילת
11. דמצוה בלבד משום שאינה משתמרת כהלכתה
12. אבל באכילה בעלמ' לא ובהנאה מותר.
13. **הדרן עלך כל שעה**
14. אלו עוברין בפסח. פר"ש[25] ור"מ ז"ל
15. עוברין עליהן בלאו דלא יראה ולא ימצא. ור"ת פי' עוברין

---

[22] In Rashi's commentary: דאותן שמקטפת בהן מתחממות מחום ידיה והעיסה.

[23] *Mishne Torah*, Ḥameṣ u-Maṣa 5.12.

[24] = ור' יצחק בן גיאת.

[25] = פירש רבנו שלמה (i.e., Rashi).

16. בפסח שמעבירין אותן מן השולחן אבל אינו[26] עליהן בבל
17. יראה ובל ימצא משום דקיימ' לן דחמץ של ישר' שעבר עליו
18. הפסח אסור בהנאה מטעם קנסא ואליבא דר' שמעון
19. הואיל ועבר עליה בבל יראה ובל ימצא אסר ליה בהנאה
20. ואמרינן בגמ' ה"מ בעייניה(!) אבל על ידי תערובת לא קניס
21. כלומ' לא קניס ר' שמעון לאחר הפסח אלא על חמץ של ישר'
22. בעינן[27] הואיל ועבר עליה בבל יראה ובל ימצא. אבל חמץ
23. ישר' על ידי תערובת שלא עבר עליו בבל יראה ובל ימצא
24. לא קניס ר' שמעון אלמא הנך דמתני' על ידי תערובתהן לא
25. עבר עלייהו בבל יראה ובל ימצא. כותח הבבלי וכו'. כולהו
26. מפרש בגמ'. אף טיפולי נשים מפרש בגמ'.[28] בנות עשירים
27. טופלין אותן [בסו]לת. רמז"ל וטיפולי נשים. הו איצא דקיק

Folio 7 Verso

1. יתכדה אלנסא[29] ואין הלכה כר' אליעזר. מין דגן [ה' מינ]ים[30]
2. חטים ושעורין וכוסמין שבולת שועל ושיפון הרי א[לו]
3. באזהרה [א]ם אכלן ודוקא אם אכל כזית חמץ בתוך
4. התערובת בכדי אכילת פרס והוא שלש בצים הוא שלוקה
5. מן התורה. אבל אם אין בתערובת כזית בכדי אכילת
6. ~~פרס~~ שלש בצים אע"פ שאסור הוא לאכול אבל אם אינו
7. לוקה אלא מכת מרדות מדרבנן והכי מפרש בגמ' ואין

---

[26] Should be: אינו עובר.

[27] Should be: בעינו.

[28] b. Pesaḥim 43a.

[29] A quotation from Maimonides' commentary to m. Pesaḥim 3.1.

[30] The completion follows Rashi's commentary on the Mishnah, b. Pesaḥim 42a.

בהם כרת אם אכלן. אלא לאו כמו שפירשתי. **גמ'**[31] קומנייתא דאומא עיפושא של פת שמתעפש לאחר זמן בתוך הכותח. רב שרירא גאון ז"ל[32] קומנייתא הוא העפוש וזומא[33] קמח שעורים מגבילין אותו ומייבשין אותו בחמה[34] עד שמתעפש ועושין ממנו כותח. ורמו ביה שערי. שמטילין בתוכו שעורין כדי שיחמיץ בשביל השעורין הוא אסור. קורט מיימיא דחיזרי. מי סובין. ר"מ ז"ל. עמילן של טבחים. רמז"ל הפת שעושין לשאוב הזוהמא של בשר שנקראת עמילן של טבחים. קולן של סופרים. רמז"ל שעושין מאבק הרחיים ומדביקין בהן מה שירצו. רחז"ל[35] שמדביקין בו הסופרים ניירותיהם כל מחמצת וכו' מלשון כל קא מרבה. ובגמ' מפרש לה שפיר אבל איסורא מהא איכא ולקי מכת מרדות מדרבנן חייב מלקות מן התורה. **מתני'**. בצק שבסדיקי עריבה וכו' בגמ' מפרש לה. וכן לעניין הטומאה קס"ד דהכי קאמ' אם נטמאת העריבה ויש בין סדקיה בצק והוא רוצה להטבילה אם הקפיד עליו חוצץ וכו' ודוקא ערבה של עץ הוא דאית ליה טהרה במקוה. אבל עריבה של חרס אין לה טהרה במקוה אלא שבירה. ומקשינן בגמ' מי דמי

---

[31] b. Pesaḥim 42a.

[32] The author knew the commentary of Rav Sherira, probably via R. Isaac ibn Ghayyat's *Hilkhot Pesaḥim*.

[33] In R. Isaac ibn Ghayyat's *Hilkhot Pesaḥim*: וזימא.

[34] In R. Isaac ibn Ghayyat's *Hilkhot Pesaḥim*: ברמץ.

[35] = רבנו חננאל ז"ל.

W.6.b: Commentary on *Hilkhot ha-Rif*, Pesaḥim (R. Judah al-Madārī) [II]

Bodl. MS Heb. c. 72/9

General Description

See General Description for W.6a. Al-Madārī interprets the Mishnah (Pesaḥim 1.1) according to the Babylonian Talmud's discussion (b. Pesaḥim 8b) and then continues to interpret the Babylonian Talmud in Pesaḥim 2a–3a. This part of the work quotes a lot from Rashi's commentary. We have therefore not noted these quotations, but we have marked some changes from the common printed version (Vilna).

Physical Description

21.7 × 15; paper; 1 leaf; 28 lines (recto and verso); slightly torn, holes, rubbed, faded, beige stains; belongs to the same manuscript as Bodl. MS Heb. c. 72/6–7, all of whose fragments show peculiar three-hole pricks in the lower and side margins.

 https://doi.org/10.11647/OBP.0352.43

Transcription

Recto

1. [הש]ניה ששתיהן עליונות ורואות את [שמ]י קורה[1] אפי' של'[2]
2. [של]פנים משתהן[3] לא אצטריך ל[...... ו]דאי שטתיה נמ'[4]
3. חיצונות. ראשונה ושתי(?) תחתונ[ות ......] הפתוחות
4. ושנייה לה חיצונה נקראת שלפנים [...] והיא נמי פנימית
5. נקראת לחיצונה והשלישית פנימית לה. נמצאת השלישית
6. פנימית לפנימית והיינו דקאמ' למעוטי גייאתא דגייאתא[5]
7. ואע"ג דקאמ[רי]נן הילכת' כרב באיסורי כיון דכולהו תנאי
8. מסייע ליה לשמואל הילכת' כשמואל.[6] ורב שרירא ורב האי

---

[1] b. Pesaḥim 8b.

[2] The writer wrote here the beginning of the next word as a filling for the end of the line, as he did several times (for example, l. 22: 'אור = אורחיה). We did not copy these fillings in the continuation.

[3] = משתיהן.

[4] = נמי.

[5] This form is not documented in other copies. MSS New York, JTS Rab. 1623: גואיאתא דגואיאתא; Munich, Beyerische Staatbibliothek Cod. Heb. 95: גוייתא דגוייתא; Vatican, Biblioteca Apostolica ebr. 134: גוויתא דגוויתא; ebr. 125: גווייתא גווייתא; ebr. 109 and London, Valmadonna Trust 9 (formerly Sassoon 594, current location unknown): גויאתא גויאתא; Vilna edition: גווייאתא דגווייאתא.

[6] The conclusion והלכתא כוותיה דשמואל, which appears in the Vilna edition, is missing in some manuscripts, though it appears in MSS Vatican, Biblioteca Apostolica ebr. 134; Nuremberg, State Archives Fr. 51–68; and CUL Oo. 6.70.2 (these last two were taken from books' bindings). It seems that these words were missing also in the copy of the Babylonian Talmud held by the commentator.

9. גאון הכין סבירא להו נמצא לדברי שמואל הלכה כ[...]ן
10. וצריך לבדוק ראשונות העליונות [ושור]ה שלפנים
11. ממנה ודלא כפי' ר"ח[7] ז"ל. ור"מ ז"ל כתב וכ[שבוד]ק המרתף
12. בודק ממני שתי שורות החיצונות שהן העליונות ושל
13. מטה ממנו[8] ודבריו תימה שפסק כרב וכל תנאי תנו כשמואל.
14. גמ' קרו נגהי.[9] קרו ללילה נגהי. ותנא דידן כלומ' תנא
15. דמתניתין מ"ט לא תני לילי לישנא דלית ליה ספיקא
16. ומשני לישנא מעלייא נקט. כלומ' לשון הגון ונקי. שדרך
17. נקיי הדעת לדבר בלשון נקייה. לעולם אל יוציא אדם דבר
18. מגונה מפיו לאו משום דלילי דבר מגונה הוא קמייתי
19. להא דר' יהושע בן לוי בעלמא יתיב(?) ומאי שמעינ' מינה דדרך
20. חכמ' לחזר אחר לשון מכובד 'נקי אשר איננה טהורה[10] ולא
21. כתי' מן הבהמה הטמאה. חמש אותיות. אשר איננה טהורה
22. י"ג אותיות יש(?). ואע"ג דבאוריית' כתי' טובא טמא. שני
23. אורחיה בחד דוכתא ללמדך לחזר על לשון נקייה. שהרי
24. בזב קראו מרכב. ובאשה קראו מושב.[11] דכתי' בזב וכל
25. המרכב אשר ירכב עליו הזב יטמא.[12] ובאשה קראו מושב

---

[7] R. Ḥananel b. Ḥushiel.

[8] *Mishne Torah*, Ḥameṣ u-Maṣah, 2.6. In accurate editions: שהן העליונה ושלמטה ממנה.

[9] b. Pesaḥim 3a.

[10] Gen. 7.8.

[11] b. Pesaḥim 3a.

[12] Lev. 15.9.

26. דכתי' וכל הנוגע בכל כלי אשר תשב עליו ~~הזבה~~[13] יכבס בגדיו
27. ורחץ במים וטמא עד הערב.[14] לפי שאין לשון[15] הגון להזכיר

Verso

1. רכיבה ופיסוק רגליים באשה ואע"פ שהמרכב והמו[שב]
2. בש[ניה]ן[16] לא הזכיר מרכב בפי' כאשר הזכיר בזב וכל
3. המרכב אשר ירכב עליו הזב יטמא[17] אלא הזכירו ברמז דכתי'
4. וכל הנוגע בכל ה[כלי(?)] אשר היא יושבת עליו[18] ודרשינן בכל[י]
5. ~~לה~~ לרבות את המרכב והכי מסיק בתורת כהנים[19] ואמ'
6. ותבחר לשון ערומים.[20] ודעת שפתי ברור מללו[21] [......]
7. גרסינן ה[כי] מאי קאמ' וכי תימ' הני מילי בלישנא דאורית'
8. אבל בלישנא דרבנן לית לן בה. ת"ש[22] ותבחר לשון ערומים פי'
9. וכי' תימ' ה"מ[23] בדאוריית' תורה הקפידה ע[ל לשונ]ה שיציאתה[24]
10. מפי הגבורה. אבל חכמי' במשנה ובבריי[תא] אין להקפיד

[13] The writer was probably influenced wrongly by Lev. 15.6: עַל־הַכְּלִי אֲשֶׁר־יֵשֵׁב עָלָיו הַזָּב.

[14] Lev. 15.22.

[15] In the Vilna edition (in Rashi's commentary), לשון is missing.

[16] In the Vilna edition (ibid.): שוין בשניהן.

[17] Lev. 15.9.

[18] The writer here mixed Lev. 15.22 (וְכָל-הַנֹּגֵעַ בְּכָל כְּלִי [אֲשֶׁר תֵּשֵׁב עָלָיו]) with 15.23 (אוֹ עַל הַכְּלִי אֲשֶׁר הִוא יֹשֶׁבֶת עָלָיו בְּנָגְעוֹ בוֹ).

[19] *Sifra*, Meṣorʿa, tractate Zavim, 2.3.

[20] Job 15.5.

[21] Job 33.3.

[22] = תא שמע.

[23] = הני מילי.

[24] In the Vilna edition (ibid.): שיצאתה.

11. על לשו[ונ]ם ת"ש ותבחר לשון ערומים שמענו [...] ערומים
12. בוחר' לשון [...] והדר פריך מאי ואומ' וכי [תימא ה"מ] בדרבנן
13. אבל במילי דעלמ' לא ת"ש ודעת שפתי ברור מללו. והני דוכתי
14. עיקם הכתו' ללמדנו שצריכין אנן [להאריך(?)] כדי לספר בלשון
15. נקייה ובדוכתי אחריני היכא דכי הדדי [מס]פר בלשון
16. כבוד. ואי לאו כהדדי מדבר בדרך קצרה ללמדך שישנה
17. אדם לתלמידו דרך קצרה לפי שמתוך [...] ירבה(?) מלה(?)
18. יות[ר] מן הארוכה. מפני מה בוצרין בטהרה.[25] בכלים טהורים
19. ואין מוסקין בטהרה. בזתים קרי מסיקה. ואין צריך
20. למוסקן בכלים טהורים[26] כדקאמרינן במסכת שבת ביציאות
21. שבת שתים שהן ארבע[27] דלא חשיב מוהל היוצא מהן
22. להכשיר[28] שאינו שמן גמור אלא היוצא על ידי הבד. אבל יין
23. היוצא מן הענבים אפי' בלא גת חשוב משקה [ומכשיר]
24. ואע"ג דלא ניחא ליה שהרי הולך לאיבוד אפי' הכי מכשיר
25. כדמפרש בפ"ק[29] דשבת שמא יבצרנו בקופות מזופפות
26. ואז ניחא ליה דלא אזיל לאיבוד. ודכולי עלמ' חמץ לא
27. איתסר אלא משש שעות בין לר' מאיר בין לר' יהודה
28. דאיפליגו במתניתין[30] בהרחקה דעבוד רבנן לדאוריית'

---

[25] b. Pesaḥim 3b.

[26] In the Vilna edition (in Rashi's commentary): למוסקן בטהרה.

[27] b. Shabbat 17a.

[28] See Tossafot, b. Shabbat 17a, incipit *gozrani.*

[29] = בפרק קמא.

[30] m. Pesaḥim 1.4.

W.6.c: Anonymous Commentary on b. Eruvin

Bodl. MS Heb. c. 72/8

General Description

An unknown commentary on b. Eruvin. Hebrew. Byzantine script, fourteenth to fifteenth centuries.

Physical Description

21.5 × 14.6; paper; 1 leaf; 23 lines (recto); 22 lines (verso); slightly torn, holes, rubbed, faded, beige stains; similar three-hole prick to Bodl. MS Heb. c. 72/6–7 on lower margin and side margin (recto right); drawings on both sides.

Transcription

Recto

1. ומחר(?) זיל כלומ' הלך. מפני הטעין[1] כלומ' כשהיו מונים
2. התחום היו מונים עם עם חבל[י]ם והיו טועים בטובה(?)[2] אמות
3. ולאחר מיכן נפרש היאך היו מונים. רגליך[3] קרינן למה אמ'
4. אומרו שתי פעמ' אחד חסר כתיב. שתים לא יכנסו אבל
5. אחד יכנס.
6. סליק פירק'.

---

[1] m. Eruvin 4.11; b. Eruvin 52b. Should be: הטועין.

[2] Should be: בטובא (= 'a lot' [Aram.]). For alternations between ה and א by this scribe, see, for example, W.6.a, 1v, l. 11.

[3] Isa. 58.13.

 https://doi.org/10.11647/OBP.0352.44

7. בית יוצא[4] כלומ' כך היא העיר ואז מונים כנגדה והוא חשוב
8. כל זה הוא בתים. ונפשות על הבניין של הקבר. רחבה מצד
9. אחד קצרה מצד אחר[5] כלומ' כמו מגן היתי(!) אומ' שהוא כמו
10. מרובעת קמ"ל שאינו כך. נעביד כאורכה כלומ' הייתי
11. אומ' שהיא מרובעת קמ"ל שאינו כך.

15. פחות מארבעת אלפים אמה כלומ' מורידין מן ההיתר[6] ואז
16. הוא חשוב כל זה בתים. ואם הוא ארבעת אלפים אמה
17. כו' מורידין מן הקשת אינו רוצה לומ' קשת ממש אלא
18. מלמטה. והא דכי אתא במקום ששוכבין הבהמות. אלא
19. מפתח בתיהן[7] כלומ' היו עשרים שיושבין בשדות ושומרין
20. זה אחר זה מפני חיות אומ' שזה נמדוד אותו מכאן וזה
21. מכאן קמ"ל שאינו כך אלא מודדין כל אחד מפתח ביתו.
22. נותנין קרפיף לעיר[8] כלומ' שם[9] יש בכאן עיר אז משימים
23. [ה(?)]שבעים אמה ומודדין משם התחום [..]שתי עירות

---

[4] m. Eruvin 5.1; b. Eruvin 52b.

[5] b. Eruvin 55a.

[6] Should be: היתר.

[7] b. Eruvin 55b.

[8] m. Eruvin 5.2; b. Eruvin 55b.

[9] Should be: שאם(?).

Verso

1. בלבד ואם יש בין שתיהן ~~ב~~' שתי פעמ' שבעים אמה
2. הוא הכל חשוב כאחת. וכן שלשה כפרים המשולשין[10]
3. כלומ' ~~א~~ שאם יש בכאן כך 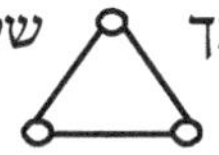 שלושה כפרים בכאן אחד
4. ובכאן אחד ולמטה אחד אז אנו מחשבים שזה
5. לשם ואז אם יש בין זה לזה שבעים אמה ובין אותו
6. שבעים אמה הכל חשוב כאחד. רב הונא אמ' אין נו[ת]נין
7. קרפיף פי' מה שאומ' למעלה חכמי' אין נותנין קרפיף אלא
8. לשתי עיירות בלבד זה רוצה לומ' קרפיף אחד. ליכנס
9. בתחומה כלומ' בתוך אלפים אמה. ואסור ליכנס בעיבורה
10. פי' בשבעים אמה. ולא ימוד פי' למעלה אלא כנגד לבו.[11]
11. והגיע לגיא כלומ' שאם היה מודד הגיא יש לו הרבה למדוד
12. כי הוא עמוק אימתי ימדוד למטה ולמעלה אלא לוקח
13. אותו בשוה. מפני שמרבה[12] כלומ' כשהוא מושך החבל שאם
14. הוא קצור(!) אז מושך אותו [......]. ולא יתיר מפני
15. שממעיט כלום כשהוא מושך [חבל] ארוך אז ממעיט והוא
16. טועה. ~~של נצרים לסוטה כלומ' כשהוא מושך החבל [...]~~
17. ~~ארוך או ממעס~~ט ~~והוא טועה~~. של נצרים לסוטה כלומ' היו
18. קושרים אותה והיו משקים אותה. כמו שאומ' הפסוק איש
19. כי ישטה אותו(!).[13] תנינא להא דתנו רבנן כלומ' מכיון שהברית'
20. מביאה ראיה מן המשנה טובה היא. של חמשים אמה
21. מבליעו עלומ' כשהוא מודד אם היה מודד הגיא למעלה
22. ולמטה יש לו הרבה לעשות אלא לוקח ~~ה[.]~~ הרחב שלמעלה

---

[10] m. Eruvin 5.3; b. Eruvin 57a.

[11] m. Eruvin 5.4; b. Eruvin 57b.

[12] b. Eruvin 58a.

[13] Should be: תשטה אשתו (Num. 5.12).

23. והולך. ואם לאו הולך למקום כלומ' למעלה הוא יתר רחב
24. מחמשים אמה הולך למטה שהוא פחות והוא מרויח כל אותן
25. של מעלה. ואם היה הגיא מעוקם כלומ' שאינו יכול למצוא
26. פחות מחמשים כי אם חוץ לתחום ואז אם ילך חוץ לתחום
27. או ימדוד יסברו העולם שהתחום הולך עד לשם אז מקדר.

W.7: List of Biblical Quotations for Use in Letters

Bodl. MS Heb.c.72/46

General Description

A list of biblical verses, arranged by subject. Oriental script. The verses are quoted by their initial words. The titles of the divisions are in Hebrew and Judaeo-Arabic. The aim of this list is to help letter writers to interweave biblical quotations in their correspondence. Line 1 contained the title for the first division. However, the line is torn and it is hard to decipher the remains of the letters.

Physical Description

28.5 × 15.1; paper; 1 leaf; 30 lines + intralinear additions (recto); jottings (verso); torn, holes, red-brown stains; jottings on verso may have served as index.

Transcription

Recto

1. [...]
2. ישושום מדבר וצייה[1] גו' רנו שמים כי עשה יי"י[2] גו' חסדי יי"י אזכ[יר][3]

[1] Isa. 35.1.

[2] Isa. 44.23.

[3] Isa. 63.7.

 https://doi.org/10.11647/OBP.0352.45

3. ויחן יי"י אותם[4] גו' עברו עברו בשערים[5] וגו' ובאו ורננו בשערים[6]
4. פצחו ורננו[7] יחדיו וגו' קול צופיך נשאו[8] וגו' ויראו ממערב
5. את[9] וגו' וראיתם ושש לבכם[10] וגו' מה נאוו על ההרים[11] וגו'
6. ואר(?) ושפכתי על בית דוד[12] וגו' תכבדני חיית השדה[13] וגו' אלי הנא
7. נחמות וגירה מלכים אני קראתיך בצדק[14] וגו' לא יתיצב איש[15] וגו' והוכן בחסד כסא[16] וגו' בימיו תושע יהודה[17] וג[ו]'
8. נהר פלגיו ישמחו מלך[18] וגו' ימים על ימי מלך[19] וגו' באור פני מלך חיים[20] וגו' מלך במשפ[ט]

---

[4] 2 Kgs 13.23.

[5] Isa. 62.10.

[6] Jer. 31.11.

[7] In the Masoretic text: פִּצְחוּ רַנְּנוּ.

[8] Isa. 52.8.

[9] Isa. 59.19.

[10] Isa. 66.14.

[11] Isa. 52.7.

[12] Zech. 12.10.

[13] Isa. 43.20.

[14] Isa. 42.6. In the Masoretic text: אֲנִי יי"י קְרָאתִיךָ בְצֶדֶק.

[15] Deut. 7.24; 11.25; Josh. 1.5.

[16] Isa. 1.5.

[17] Jer. 23.6.

[18] See commentary.

[19] Ps. 61.7.

[20] Prov. 16.15.

9. יעמיד[21] וגו' מלך ביפיו תחזינה עיניך[22] וגו' חסד ואמת יצרו מלך[23]
10. וגו' מלך שופט באמת[24] וגו' ויראו מפני המלך[25] וגו' חן שפתיו
11. רעיהו[26] מלך[27] וגו' ויאמר יי"י אלהיך לך[28] וגו' כל איש אשר ימרה[29] וגו'
12. [..]עד לאמ[..] וגו' לא יתיצב איש בפניך[30] וגו' אשריך ואשרי אנשיך[31] וגו' ופינחס בן אלעזר
היה נגיד[32] וגו'[33] חזק ואמץ אל תע[רץ][34]
13. וגו' ולמי כל חמדת ישראל[35] וגו' ואדוני חכם כחכמת מלאך[36] וגו' וראו
14. כל עמי הארץ[37] וגו' יפקוד יי"י אלהי הרוחות וגו'[38] יהי יי"י אלהיך

---

[21] Prov. 29.4.

[22] Isa. 33.17.

[23] Prov. 20.28.

[24] Prov. 29.14.

[25] 1 Kgs 3.28.

[26] In the Masoretic text: רעהו.

[27] Prov. 22.11.

[28] 1 Chron. 11.2.

[29] Josh. 1.18.

[30] See n. 15 in this section.

[31] See commentary.

[32] 1 Chron. 9.20. In the Masoretic text: וּפִינְחָס בֶּן אֶלְעָזָר נָגִיד הָיָה עֲלֵיהֶם.

[33] An addition below the line.

[34] Josh. 1.9.

[35] 1 Sam. 9.20.

[36] 2 Sam. 14.20.

[37] Deut. 28.10.

[38] Num. 16.27.

15. ברוך[39] וגו' יפיפית מבני אדם[40] וגו' חגר חרבך על ירך[41] וגו' והדרך צלח רכב[42] וגו'
16. אהבת צדק ותשנה(!)[43] וגו' מור ואהלות קציעות[44] וגו' ומצה(!)[45] חן ושכל טוב[46] וגו'
בי מלכים
17. ימלוכו[47] וגו' בי שרים ישרו[48] וגו' אני אהבי אהב[49] וגו' באורח
18. צדקה אהלך[50] וגו' עיר גבורים [עלה חכם][51] וגו' ויאמר אל תירא
19. איש חמודות[52] וגו' עקב ענוה יראת יי"י[53] וגו' והיה סחרה ואתננה
20. קודש[54] וגו' אשרי העם שככה לו[55] וגו' העם ההולכים בחשך ראו[56] וגו' מים קרים על
נפש עייפ[ה][57]

---

[39] 2 Chron. 9.8.

[40] Ps. 45.3.

[41] Ps. 45.4.

[42] Ps. 45.5.

[43] Ps. 45.8. Should be ותשנא.

[44] Ps. 45.9.

[45] Should be ומצא.

[46] Prov. 3.4.

[47] Prov. 8.15.

[48] Prov. 8.16.

[49] Prov. 8.17.

[50] Prov. 8.20.

[51] Prov. 21.22.

[52] Dan. 10.19.

[53] Prov. 22.4.

[54] Isa. 23.18.

[55] Ps. 144.15.

[56] Isa. 9.1.

[57] Prov. 25.25.

21. וגו' ואורח צדיקים כאור[58] וגו' כצנת שלג ביום קציר[59] וגו' אורח לצדיק מישרים[60] וגו'
22. יפרח בימיו צדיק[61] הולך צדקות ודובר[62] וגו' ושפט בין
23. בין(!) הגוים[63] וגו' ודבר שלום לגויים ומשלו[64] וגו' מלכי תרשיש ואיים[65]
24. וגו' מתוך ומחמס[66] וגו' יחוס על דל ואביון[67] וגו' ישפוט עניי עם[68] וגו' כי יעמוד לימין
25. אביון[69] וגו' יהי שמו לעולם[70] וגו' מ[...] כהנים וכרתי להם ברית[71] וגו'
26. בריתי היתה אתו[72] וגו' לכן אמור הנני[73] וגו' בשלום ובמישור
27. הלך[74] וגו' כי שפתי כהן ישמרו[75] וגו' כהניך ילבשו צדק[76] וגו'

---

[58] Prov. 4.18.

[59] Prov. 25.13.

[60] Isa. 26.7.

[61] Ps. 72.7.

[62] Isa. 33.15.

[63] Isa. 2.4.

[64] Zech. 9.10.

[65] Ps. 72.10.

[66] Ps. 72.14.

[67] Ps. 72.13.

[68] Ps. 72.4.

[69] Ps. 109.31.

[70] Ps. 72.17.

[71] See commentary.

[72] Mal. 2.5.

[73] Num. 25.12.

[74] Mal. 2.6.

[75] Mal. 2.7.

[76] Ps. 132.9.

28. וכהניה אלביש ישע[77] וגו' צדק לבשתי וילבשני[78] וגו' והקמתי
29. עליהם רועה[79] וגו' אני קראתיך בצדק[80] וגו' ונתתי להם [בביתי][81] וגו'
30. [...]

Verso

מליצות

Partial Translation

Recto

Lines 6–7

אלי הנא נחמות וגירה מלכים ...

Until here condolences and similar (quotations). (Verses related to) Kings: ...

Line 25

מ[...] כהנים

[...] (verses related to) Priests: ...

Verso

Verses for Letters

---

[77] Ps. 132.16.

[78] Job 29.14.

[79] Ezek. 34.23.

[80] Isa. 42.6. In the Masoretic text: אֲנִי י"י קְרָאתִיךָ בְצֶדֶק.

[81] Isa. 56.5.

Commentary

Line 3:

ויחן יי"י אותם. There is an unclear correction in the text. Maybe the writer wrongly wrote יי"י צבאות, and then deleted the beginning of the word and completed it as אותם.

Line 4:

In the Masoretic text פִּצְחוּ רַנְּנוּ, but the writer was probably influenced by Ps. 98.4 (פִּצְחוּ וְרַנְּנוּ וְזַמֵּרוּ).

Line 8:

נהר פלגיו ישמחו מלך. There is no such verse. The writer mixed—intentionally—Ps. 46.5 (נָהָר פְּלָגָיו יְשַׂמְּחוּ עִיר אֱלֹהִים) with Hos. 7.3 (בְּרָעָתָם יְשַׂמְּחוּ מֶלֶךְ).

Line 12:

אשריך ואשרי אנשיך. There is no such verse. The writer misquotes the words of the Queen of Sheba to King Solomon: אַשְׁרֵי אֲנָשֶׁיךָ וְאַשְׁרֵי עֲבָדֶיךָ אֵלֶּה (2 Chron. 9.7).

Line 25:

וכרתי להם ברית. This expression appears a few times in the Bible (Jer. 32.40; Hos. 2.20; etc.). It seems the writer refers here to Ezek. 37.26 (וְכָרַתִּי לָהֶם בְּרִית שָׁלוֹם, בְּרִית עוֹלָם יִהְיֶה אוֹתָם). This verse does not speak exclusively about the priests, but it was understood as such, following the similar verses in Num. 25.12–13 (הִנְנִי נֹתֵן לוֹ אֶת בְּרִיתִי שָׁלוֹם וְהָיְתָה לּוֹ וּלְזַרְעוֹ אַחֲרָיו בְּרִית כְּהֻנַּת עוֹלָם).

Line 28:

צדק לבשתי וילבשני. It is possible that the writer wrote wrongly ילבשנו. This verse was considered to be speaking about priests, not only because of the expression ‘I wear justice’ (as in the previous verse) but also because of the mentioning of *meʿil* and *ṣanif*, which are parts of the priest’s clothing (see Exod. 28.31–34; Zech. 3.5).

W.8: Unidentified Work

Bodl. MS Heb. c. 72/1

General Description

The page is in very bad condition. The vellum is dark, rubbed and stained, and the handwriting is almost impossible to read, not helped by the fact that it is all mirrored script, left behind by other texts. The verso side is even more difficult to decipher. Due to these limitations, we could not identify the work, but we assume it is a part of an exegetical work, perhaps on Exodus. The clue for this is the sentence in the last line of the recto (l. 19): ויורהו. הורה לו לקחת עץ '*vayorehu*: he commanded him to take a log'. There is no doubt that the subject discussed here is the story of the bitter water in Exodus. The writer refers here to the verse: "and the LORD showed him a log, and he threw it into the water, and the water became sweet" (Exod. 15.25). He explains the word ויורהו not as 'he showed him', as some commentators understood, but rather as 'he commanded him'. The existence of the dot after the word *vayorehu* reinforces the impression that this is indeed a remainder of an exegetical work. In such works, the author usually differentiates the word he is about to interpret and its commentary by a dot (whose syntactic role is equivalent to that of a colon in modern texts). The words in l. 18, which speak about a "complaint and cry," refer perhaps to the complaint of the children of Israel and to the prayer of Moses: "And the people murmured against Moses, saying, 'What shall we drink?' And he cried to the LORD" (Exod. 15.24–25). Here are some of the

 https://doi.org/10.11647/OBP.0352.46

significant sentences in the text that we succeeded in deciphering from the recto side:

3. למלך [על] כל הארץ לעול[ם] ועוד

5. ואתה הוא ושנותיך לא יתמו

13. בינינו וביניכ[ם]

18. מפרש(?) תלונתו [ו]יצעק התפלה אל השם מכ[ל לבו]

19. ויורהו. הורה לו לקחת עץ

Physical Description

12.4 × 19; vellum; 1 leaf; 19 lines of mirrored script (recto); 30 lines of mirrored script (verso); verso is written transversely in relation to recto; badly rubbed and stained.

PART III: LINGUISTIC ANALYSIS OF THE JUDAEO-ARABIC IN THE CORPUS

The Judaeo-Arabic letters of our corpus provide a significant contribution to the study of Late Judaeo-Arabic in general and of utilitarian prose in Judaeo-Arabic in particular. While the various literary and documentary registers of 'classical' Judaeo-Arabic, i.e., Judaeo-Arabic of the tenth to the fourteenth century, have been studied in greater detail and depth (see, e.g., Blau 1980b; 1981; 1988; Polliack 1997; Friedman 2016b, 933–41; Wagner 2010), Late Judaeo-Arabic from the fifteenth century onwards has yet to win the same measure of scholarly attention. This is partly due to the dearth of sources. For the period from the fifteenth to the seventeenth century, scholars lack a basic corpus of utilitarian prose that would enable systematic study of the language, although we have a few studies of literary sources.[1] More material is available from the late eighteenth and early nineteenth centuries, and studies on epistolary material have been carried out (Khan 1991; 1992; 2006; 2013).

For this reason, the publication of our fifteenth-century corpus makes a unique contribution to the number of sources available to scholars interested in Judaeo-Arabic linguistics, and we offer a linguistic analysis of notable phenomena and a summary

[1] See Hary (1992; 1994) for sixteenth-century Bible translations; Schorreel (2011) for a version of Qissat Hannah.

 https://doi.org/10.11647/OBP.0352.47

of the epistolary formulae and style of the Judaeo-Arabic letters in this volume.

1.0. Introduction

The letters vary greatly in the degree to which they emulate Classical Arabic and Classical Judaeo-Arabic standards. Some letters, such as P.4.b, are written in a comparatively classicising style and show a lot less variation than, for example, P.6. All letters written by David ibn Shams show a register of Judaeo-Arabic that is very close to Classical Judaeo-Arabic norms. Other letters, such as C.4 and P.8, are extremely colloquial, to the degree that it is doubtful whether they were composed by competent speakers of Arabic, or perhaps better, competent writers of Judaeo-Arabic. For this reason, they are treated in a special section at the end of this chapter, although they will be mentioned for purposes of comparison throughout the following analysis. The pages belonging to the same manuscript found under P.9 are a letter only in form; the text is a discussion concerning biblical exegesis that has little in common with the documentary material investigated in the rest of the corpus, and is therefore also analysed separately.

2.0. Lexicon and Style

2.1. Abbreviations

Most commonly, we can find abbreviations for the addressee and the writer himself: the addressee (*al-maḵdūm* ‘the served’) is normally abbreviated as 'מכ, whereas the writer (*al-mamlūk* ‘the servant’) appears as 'ממ. Similarly, we find a range of abbreviated titles, such as *sayyid* or *sayyidī* (*sīdī*) 'lord' or 'my lord' as ס', and *muʿallim* (originally 'teacher' but also an honorific title for a merchant, and commonly used as an address) as אלמע'. The title *al-mawlā* 'the master' is found as אלמו'. Other titles include כה"ר 'the honourable rabbi'. A variety of Hebrew blessings are also abbreviated, such as יצ"ו, 'may God save him and keep him alive'.

2.2. Introductory Formulae

The most typical contemporary Judaeo-Arabic letter introduction of the fifteenth century contains some form of the verb *ḥwṭ/ḥyṭ* 'comprise', for example: יחיט אלי עלם אלמכאדים '(this letter) brings to the knowledge of the addressees' (C.1.a/18, and very similar P.3.c/v3); אלעלום אלכרימה מחיטה בכתרת אלשוק '(your) honourable knowledge should comprise the magnitude of longing for you' (P.4.c/2).

Other letters are introduced by more traditional formulae, for example: אלדי יעלם בה '(this letter,) which informs' (P.3.e/2); אלדי יעלם בה סיידי '(my letter,) which informs my master' (P.4.g/2); בעד אל סלאם אל גליל אל חביב אל כרים אל עאלם אל שאמל ה"ר יוד משה בן יודה 'after greetings to the dear, the beloved, the honourable, the one of comprehensive knowledge, the rabbi Moses b. Judah' (P.6/1); ואלדי אערפך בה '(the letter in) which I inform you' (P.3.g/4–5).

2.3. Dating

Not all the letters are dated, but in those that are, the dating follows the Era of Creation, for example: אוכתיב יום בֹ הֹ ניסאן שנת הֹרֹמֹהֹ 'I am writing on Monday 5th Nissan 5245 (of the Era of Creation

= 30 May 1485)' (C.4/v16); אוכאתיב יום ו ד' תמוז רח"ם 'I am writing on Friday 4th Tammuz (5)248 (of the Era of Creation = 22 June 1488)' (P.8/24–25). We also find a Latin date (1484 7 d[ie] de Jugo) on the verso of letter P.5.b.

2.4. Loanwords

A number of Hebrew loanwords occur in the letters, such as: אל חותם 'seal' (P.6/14); אל ספרים 'the books' (P.6/16); אלעונש 'the penalty' (C.1.a/20, 24, 25, 26); שבעה טובי העיר 'seven town elders' (C.1.a/21, 27); ויסתחלו גזל רבים 'they should judge this as "stealing from many"' (C.1.a/23); אלגט 'the divorce document' (P.3.c/13). Code-switching may occur mid-sentence, for example: והתרתי העונש ללק[הל ...] 'I release the fine for the [community]' (C.1.a /30).

2.5. Vocabulary

A very striking colloquial feature of the letters is the occurrence of *mataʿ* and *bitaʿ* to circumscribe genitival or possessive relations: אל מרכב מתענה 'our ship' (P.6/7); ואלקרנפל מתאעך 'your cloves' (P.4.b/v21); בפיידה מתעך ומתעה 'for your and his benefit' (P.6/11); באל חותם מתענה ויגיב מעה ואחד אל כותאב מן אל דיין מתענה 'with our seal, and he will bring with him a letter from our *dayyan*' (P.6/14); פוג̇דת אלמצטור בתאע זין אלדין 'I found the document concerning Zayn al-Dīn' (P.3.f/19); מה בטע יצחק 'that belongs to Isaac' (P.8/4). The forms are not necessary a Late Judaeo-Arabic phenomenon. For example, *mataʿ* can already be found in eleventh-century material, as in L-G (formerly Westminster) Misc.

100/29, a letter written by the merchant prince Nahray b. Nissim, which dates to ca 1053.

The colloquial verbs *rāḥa* and *marra* for 'to go, walk' occur in various places: רוחת 'I went' (P.8/14); ומר 'he went' (P.6/5, 6).

The colloquial verb *jāba* 'to bring' occurs, for example, in הו יגיב מעה 'he will bring with him' (P.6/13, and similarly 14); נגיבו 'I will bring it' (P.7/4); and in the Spanish letters, for which see below.

The form אש for 'anything' and 'what' occurs in many examples in the Spanish letters, and in דאלך אל נצראני אסתקצה אש אנסאן פי סכנדרייא 'this Christian inquired about someone in Alexandria' (P.6/11–12).

In the Spanish letters, the verb *qāla* 'speak' is often combined with the preposition *li-* 'to' to form, for example: קאלי 'he told me' (C.4/30, v3); קולתלו 'I told him' (C.4/31); etc. In the rest of the corpus, it is rarer, but does occur, for example in יוקללו 'it is called' (P.7/17).

The short form *ḥad* occurs in עלי' חדא פי אלמדינה 'via someone in Palermo' (C.5/12); חד תקא 'a trustworthy person' (C.5/11–12).

2.6. Orthography and Phonology

2.6.1. Punctuation

The different writers of the letters vary greatly in the way they mark those Hebrew letters that represent more than one Arabic phoneme, such as *kāf*, *ḵā*ʾ, *jīm*, and *ġayn*. To disambiguate between *jīm* and *ġayn*, often the *gimel* receives a dot above to indicate *jīm*. But some writers also mark *ġayn* in a similar way. For example, David ibn Shams, the scribe who composed a number of letters in the corpus, uses a dot above the *gimel* to mark it as *jīm*, e.g., P.3.c/9 and P.3.c/12, and a stroke above the *gimel* to mark *ġayn*, such as P.3.c/17 and P.3.c/24. Occasionally, however, he also marks *ġayn* with a dot, such as in P.3.b/9. The writers of letters P.4.b, P.4.g, and P.3.g indicate *jīm* with a dot below the *gimel*, e.g., גּ in P.4.b/v12. In P.4.b, even Hebrew words may receive a dot, such as in P.4.b/v4.

Similar variety can be observed with regard to the abbreviation signs. For example, P.3.c was written by David ibn Shams, who uses a stroke above to indicate abbreviations, such as for *mamlūk* and for *maḵdūm*, but the person for whom he writes the letter, the undersigning Aaron b. Ḥesedel, uses a dot above the abbreviation for *mamlūk*.

Final *kāf* is marked in most letters, such as in P.4.b/v20 and P.6/8. Some letters appear to mark some of the final *kāfs*, such as the one in *ḏālika*, but not others; this could reflect pronunciation patterns, such as palatalisation of the pronominal suffixes, but may also simply accentuate the literary nature of the demonstrative pronoun used.

The *tāʾ marbūṭa* is indicated in a number of letters, such as P.4.b/v9 and P.3.g/2.

2.6.2. Short Vowels

From the later part of the Classical Judaeo-Arabic period onwards, short vowels are more frequently spelled *plene* in documentary writing, and the letters under investigation are no exception. The short vowel /u/ is most likely to be spelled, but we also find a number of examples in which short /a/ and /i/ are spelled *plene*, although these examples mostly occur in only three different letters that show a greater colloquial repertoire than others, and thus are less standardised compared to other material within our corpus. Two of those three are the letters analysed separately, C.4 and P.8, so of the correspondence used as a basis for this section, it is really only P.6 in which *plene* short /a/ and short /i/ are found. Compared to earlier material from the thirteenth century and to other fifteenth-century sources analysed in Wagner (2010), the lack of *plene* spelling is conspicuous. The picture may be slightly distorted, however, by the fact that a great number of the letters under investigation were written by David ibn Shams, who writes in a very 'classical' way.

Short /a/: מאע 'with' (P.6/4), יאקף 'he supports' (P.6/12), תאקף 'you support' (P.6/10), יאשתריו 'they buy' (P.6/6). More examples from C.4 and P.8 can be found below.

Short /i/: אכתיר 'more' (P.6/3). More examples from C.4 and P.8 can be found below.

Short /u/: מנכום 'from you' (P.6/2), נמורו 'we go' (P.6/5), ומורנה 'we went' (P.6/5), כובז 'bread' (P.6/5), ענכום 'from you' (P.7/2), פזולנא 'we stopped' (C.3/6), יועצא 'he opposes' (C.1.a/22).

2.6.3. Long Vowels

Perpendicular *ʾAlif*

Classical Arabic perpendicular *ʾalif* is often spelled, such as in דאלך 'this/that' (in *ka-ḏālika*; P.4.b/v9; P.4.b/11; P.6/9; P.7/3), in לאכן 'but' (P.6/16), or in האדה 'this' (P.3.f/4). In those authors writing a more classicised Judaeo-Arabic, such as David ibn

Shams, we find the defective writing דלך (e.g., C.1.a/22; P.3.c/21; P.3.e/m1; C.1.a/53). The latter source, however, shows perpendicular *ʾalif* in the form בהאדה 'in this' (C.1.a/46).

Final *ʾAlif* for CA *ʾAlif Maqṣūra* Spelled with *Yāʾ*

Final *ʾalif* for CA *ʾalif maqṣūra* spelled with *yāʾ* occurs in יתשכא 'he complains' (C.1.a/48); בקא 'he remained' (P.6/9); יסוא 'he is similar' (P.6/11–12); אלא (*ʾilā*) 'until' (P.3.g/m2).

Final *Yod* for CA *ʾAlif Maqṣūra* Spelled with *ʾAlif*

In the Spanish letters, final long ā is mostly spelled with *yod*, for example in להי 'for her' (C.4/19); וקולהי 'her speech' (C.4/21); עליני 'over us' (P.8/23).

Tāʾ Marbūṭa for CA *ʾAlif Maqṣūra* Spelled with *ʾAlif*

Tāʾ marbūṭa for CA *ʾalif maqṣūra* spelled with *ʾalif* occasionally occurs, for example in עלינה 'to us' (P.6/3); וצלנה 'we arrived' (P.6/3); אפתרקנה 'we separated' (P.6/2); קאציינה 'we spent' (P.6/2); מה 'what' (P.8/8; P.4.g/1).

It also occurs for the CA adverbial ending *-an* spelled with *ʾalif*: איצה 'also' (P.4.b/v16; P.6/13, 18).

Tāʾ Marbūṭa for CA *ʾAlif Maqṣūra* Spelled with *Yāʾ*

Tāʾ marbūṭa for CA *ʾalif maqṣūra* spelled with *yāʾ* occurs in תעאלה 'exalted' (P.6/3); אסתקצה (*istaqṣā*) 'he inquired' (P.6/11–12); מוסה 'Mūsā' (C.4/2); and in *zurqā* in אלזרקה אלכרקה 'the green cloth' (C.5/m2). In most cases, this may reflect length of pronunciation.

ʾAlif for CA *Tāʾ Marbūṭa*

ʾAlif for CA *tāʾ marbūṭa* occurs in אלפצ̇א 'money' (P.4.b/2); הי כארהא 'she hates' (P.3.c/13); חד תקא 'a trustworthy person' (C.5/11–12).

Long *ī*

Long *ī* may be spelled defectively, which probably reflects the length of the pronunciation, e.g., פלמכדום (*fī l-maḵdūm*) 'for the master' (C.5/6).

Tāʾ Marbūṭa

Tāʾ marbūṭa is often spelled with *tāʾ* within the genitive construction, for example in בכתרת אלשוק 'with much longing' (P.4.b/2); ונובת יעקוב 'the rotation (of public address) of Jacob' (C.1.a/40); מן גֹהת ביתך 'on behalf of your wife' (P.3.c/12). The letter from which the last example comes, however, shows also a clear marking of the *tāʾ marbūṭa* a few lines later: גהה̇ ביתך 'on behalf of your wife' (P.3.c/22–23). We also find spelling of *tāʾ marbūṭa* with *tāʾ* in those constructions whose form has been impacted by *Tanwīn*, for example: ונעמת אן שאפיה 'true wellbeing' (P.3.c/9).

Double Spelling

Double spelling of *yod* is very common, both in places where the *yāʾ* is geminated in pronunciation and where it is not: אשתריית 'I bought' (P.7/15); לסיידי 'to my master' (P.4.b/20); וגיירה 'and other things' (P.6/5); מכייטה 'stitched' (P.4.b/v9); שהריין 'two months’ (P.6/4); עלייה ‘on him’ (C.1/26; P.3.f/12); ואיי מן ‘who-ever’ (C.1/27); טייב ‘good’ (P.3.c/23); כייר ‘good news’ (P.7/2); לסייד ‘my master’ (P.4.g/2); אשרפייה ‘*ashrafī* dinars’ (P.3.e/9).

However, occasionally we find only single spelling even in places of geminated *yāʾ*: גיד ‘good’ (P.6/10).

Similarly, *vav* maybe be doubled in spelling: תסווה ‘it equals’ (P.7/5).

Hamza

Often, *hamza* is spelled with *yod*, following the *rasm* of the Arabic spelling: מהיי (*muhayyaʾ*) ‘prepared’ (P.6/20), or מית ‘hundred’ (P.6/13), omitting the *ʾalif* of the Classical prescribed spelling. Occasionally, however, it is spelled with *ʾalef*, as in ענדי ראאה כאן ‘his opinion guides me’ (P.3.f/v16), and it also appears in hyper-correct form in the Spanish letters, in לראאס ‘to the leader’ (P.8 /20) and ראאח ‘going’ (P.8/21).

2.6.4. Consonants

/š/ for /j/ occurs in ואשתהד ‘I am busy’ (P.4.c/10).

Tafḵīm of /t/ can be found in מטגר ‘place of business’ (P.6 /12). In particular in the Spanish letters, one of the writers displays repeated *tafḵīm* of /t/, for example in בטע ‘belonging to’ (P.8/4, 6); גהטי ‘my side’ (P.8/4); and יטעמלוה ‘they will work on it’ (P.8/8). *Tafḵīm* of /s/ occurs in ברצם ‘with intention’ (P.7/4) and in תכצר ‘you suffer loss’ (P.4.c/11). Possible *tafḵīm* of /ḏ/ may be in צ̇הב ‘gold’ (P.7/4). Possible *tafḵīm* of /k/ occurs in one of the Spanish letters and may point to the Spanish origin of the writer: יסקונו ‘they inhabit’ (C.4/v1).

Tarqīq of /ṭ/ occurs in תעתאוהם 'you should give them' (P.4.b/v22). *Tarqīq* of /ṣ/ is found in נסראני 'Christian' (P.6/10), as opposed to נצראני in same line. The Spanish letters show *tarqīq* of /ṭ/, for example: תיתליבני 'it will be demanded from me' (or: 'you should ask me'; C.4/v7); תיתוסי 'you should behave generously' (or: 'you will be solicited for help'; P.8/10); and תעתי 'you should give' (P.8/20). *Tarqīq* of /ṣ/ is found in בטע יוסף מסרי 'belonging to Joseph Maṣrī' (or: 'Miṣrī'; P.8/6).

2.6.5. Article

The article may be spelled defectively, such as in פלמכדום (*fī l-maḵdūm*) 'for the master' (C.5/6).

2.6.6. Assimilation

In two examples, we find that in forms of the verb *waʿada*, the *d* has assimilated with the *-t* of the verbal suffix, forming *waʿatt*: ועתך 'I promised' (P.6/16, 17). A similar process can be found in the Spanish letters where Classical Arabic /ḏ/ assimilates to following /t/: Classical Arabic *ʾaḵaḏtu* to *ʾaḵatt*, in אכאת מינו 6 מיידי' 'I took from him six *muʾayyadī*' (C.4/22); and אכאת מינהי' 'I took from her' (C.4/24).

2.6.7. Vocalisation

Interesting vocalisation patterns can be found in עושרין אל מייא 'twenty per hundred' (P.7/5) and גבון 'cheese' (P.6/13, 15).

2.7. Morphology

2.7.1. Nouns

The nominative, visible in plural and dual forms, has never been a real part of written documentary Judaeo-Arabic, and naturally plays no role in our corpus. There is, however, the hypercorrect form מאיתון '200' (P.4.b/v21).

Accusative endings can be found in a few examples, but only in adverbial endings and fixed expressions involving the pronoun *aḥad/ḥad* 'one, someone': ויציר כל אחדא מסתמר פי נובתה 'everyone should remain in their rotation (of public address)' (C.1.a/42–43); וכצוצא אדא כאן לבסה חזאיני 'in particular as his clothes are (that of) mourning' (C.1.a/50); תחילונא עלי' חדא פי אלמדינה 'you should give us a bill of exchange via someone in Palermo' (C.5/12); וכל אחדא ביתעפף ען אלתפלה 'everyone is withdrawing from prayer' (C.1.a/33–34); אחדא (P.4.g/margin below 1). In the case of other adverbs, however, the original accusative adverbial ending has been re-interpreted and is spelled with *he*, such as in ואיצ̇ה 'also' (P.4.b/v16).

An interesting *Mischform* of Arabic and Hebrew plurals occurs in אנביאים in בזכות גמיע אנביאים וצדיקים כולהי' 'for the merit of all the prophets and righteous men, all of them' (C.4/20).

2.7.2. Pronouns

The independent 1st plural pronouns occur, for example, as ונחנא 'we' (C.5/v9). The form appears to be a mix between Classical Arabic *naḥnu* and colloquial *iḥna*. Two different 2nd masculine singular forms occur in the letters that were probably written by

Spanish non-native speakers of Arabic: ואנתו 'you' (C.4/6) and ואנתי 'you' (C.4/8), both deviating from the expected masculine vowel pattern of *anta*.

The 3rd person masculine singular pronominal suffix is usually spelled with ה, as in Classical Arabic and Classical Judaeo-Arabic, but may occasionally be spelled with ו, for example in אסמו 'his name' (P.7/12; P.6/10, 12). Particularly in the aforementioned non-native letters, the suffix is exclusively spelled this way, such as in ומראתו 'and his wife' (C.4/v11); מינו 'from him' (C.4/22). In these letters, the singular feminine suffix is always spelled with *yod*, such as in נכריהי' 'I hire it out' (C.4/29) and להי' 'to them' (C.4/10), whereas all 2nd masculine singular pronominal suffix endings are spelled with *yod*, i.e., as יך, for example in נעלמיך 'we inform you' (C.4/4).

Demonstratives have become gender indifferent. Only *ḏālika* and no *tilka* appears, whereas, because of the spelling of final short and long /a/ with *he*, no difference can be found between *hāḏihi and hāḏā*—both are spelled האדה: עלי האדה אלצפה 'on that bench' (C.1.a/51); ען האדה אלאמר 'on account of this matter' (P.3.f/v19); פי האדה אלאיאם 'in these days' (C.1.a/35); האדה אלכתאב 'this letter' (P.3.f/v4). A plural demonstrative occurs in the Spanish letters analysed separately: הוולאי 'those' (C.4/17).

2.7.3. Lative

The lative (indicating motion to a location) may be expressed by verb government alone without a preposition, for example in נגי סכנדרייה 'I am coming to Alexandria' (P.7/3); נגיבו סכנדרייא 'I will bring it to Alexandria’ (P.7/4); and 'אני' נגי אסכנדריי' ‘I come to Alexandria’ (C.4/v9). This is similar to the Classical Arabic accusative that may function as a locative, but this accusative cannot function as a lative. The government of the lative may be restricted to the verb *jā* (Classical Arabic *jāʾa*) alone, as the same letter from which two of the examples above come also has the following example: ונרגע לסכנדרייא ‘we will return to Alexandria’ (P.7/8).

2.7.4. Verbal Forms

Weak Verbs

Final wāw and yāʾ: Traces of Maghrebian morphology may be found in the letters. For example, תעתאוהם ‘you should give them’ (P.4.b/v22) follows the modern Maghrebian forms for the final weak verbs, in which both final *yāʾ* and *wāw* of the forms *faʿala* and *faʿila* have merged in the perfect, and the forms of the 3rd singular feminine and 3rd plural masculine perfect are, for example, *mšāt* and *mšāw*. See M. Cohen (1912, 192) and D. Cohen (1964, 15).

Another Maghrebian feature can be found when the *yāʾ* is retained in the imperfect of plural forms, thus treating it like an ordinary consonant, for example in יאשתריו ‘they buy’ (P.6/6). This phenomenon does not occur in Modern Egyptian Arabic but can be found in the Maghrebian vernacular; see M. Cohen (1912, 192). The *yāʾ* may also be retained in the perfect, for example in ובקיו ‘they remained’ (P.6/8) and אוחניו ‘they turned’ (P.6/8). All examples come from the same letter. This letter also shows double spelling of *yod* in another perfect form of a final *yāʾ* verb, in

קאציינה 'we stayed' (P.6/2); and the spelling of final /a/ with *he* in a final *yāʾ* verb in אסתקצה 'he inquired' (P.6/11). Double spelling of *yod* in final *yāʾ* verbs, however, is a common phenomenon, for example in אשתריית 'I bought' (P.7/15), and less reflects morphological change than orthographical conventions.

Verbs with hamza in the root: The spelling of *hamza* in the root shows a lot of variation. In some letters, we encounter Classical spelling, such as in ראית 'I saw' (P.4.g/3); יאכדו 'they seize' (P.6/7); יג׳אוך 'they will reach you' (P.6/17); תאכד 'you should take' (C.5/v6); whereas in others, we find spellings such as ריינה 'we saw' (P.6/8); ויכד 'he takes' (C.5/v4).

Passive

The internal passive occurs, and is often indicated either by a *plene* written vowel or Arabic vocalisation signs: ולם ערפת תפציל מא עומל 'I did not know the detail of what was done' (C.5/m2–3); ולם כֻּמל בקא פיה בעץ שי 'it was not completed; some things had remained (uncopied)' (P.3.f/v13).

The internal passive occurs in one of the Spanish letters: מא אנבעאת 'it has not been sold' (C.4/v5).

Moods

As in Classical Judaeo-Arabic, the subjunctive has completely replaced the indicative, and no indicative forms are attested. The *bi*-imperfect occurs in וכל אחדא ביתעפף ען אלתפלה 'everyone is withdrawing from prayer' (C.1.a/33–34), and in פאלממ׳ ביטייבה 'the servant is currently having it amended' (P.3.f/v13–14).

Traces of the *bi*-imperfect may possibly be found in unusual noun phrases in the two letters that were most likely written by non-native speakers of Arabic: אנתו בעמלי כתאב 'you are busy with (drawing up) a document' (C.4/30), and ואנתו בעאריפ[...] 'you should know' (C.4/6).

Stems

The pattern *itfaʿala* for the fifth stem can be found in the more colloquial Spanish letters in ואתבקי כרייתהי' 'it remained on its hire' (C.4/23), and in ואתוצו בו מן פצ̇לך 'entrust it with him by your grace' (P.8/v.4), but cannot otherwise be found in the corpus.

1st Singular/Plural

In many examples, the conjugation of the 1st singular and plural shows an opposition of sg. *nafʿal* vs pl. *nafʿalū*, although sg. *afʿal* vs pl. *nafʿalū* also occurs. 1st sg.: מא ארדת נקול לה 'I did not want to tell him' (P.4.c/16); אני נכתב לך 'that I will write to you' (P.4.b /17); 1st pl.: נמורו 'we go' (P.6/5).

This is also found in the Spanish letters.

2.8. Syntax

2.8.1. Demonstratives

In our corpus, the demonstratives seem to have given up the Classical Arabic near–far deixis system, as already observed in the case of Classical Judaeo-Arabic (Wagner 2010, 117–32). Instead, *ḏālika* mainly serves as a pronominal demonstrative, whereas *hāḏā* is predominantly used attributively. We do, however, also find attributive *ḏālika*, in particular in letter P.6, as well as cases of pronominal *hāḏā*, and examples of the colloquial pronouns *di* and *da* used attributively.

Pronominal *ḏālika*: מא עמלו דלך̇ אלא מן ג̇הה אלפרט 'I know they only did this for the interest' (P.3.f/v7–8); תעלם דלך̇ 'you should know this' (C.3/13); עלי' האדה אלחסאב 'regarding that account' (P.3.f/16).

Attributive *hāḏā*: עלי האדה אלצפה 'on that bench' (C.1.a/15); ען האדה אלאמר 'on account of this matter' (P.3.f/v19); פי האדה אלאיאם 'in these days' (C.1.a/35); והאדה אלאמר יבקא 'this matter remains' (C.1.a/32); האדה אלכתאב 'this letter' (P.3.f/v4); האדה אלשגל 'this business' (P.3.f/v4).

In פי הדא אלאמר 'regarding this matter' (C.5/v10) and וג̇אליה הדא אל סנה 'the poll tax of this year' (C.5/v2–3), the author first wrote the colloquial pronoun *da* and then changed it—probably in an attempt to elevate the language—with a superscribed *he* to form the more literary demonstrative *hāḏā*.

Attributive *ḏālika*: The author of letter P.6 in particular likes to use attributive *ḏālika*, but it also occurs in another letter: דאלך אל נצראני אסתקצה אש אנסאן פי סכנדרייא 'this Christian inquired about someone in Alexandria' (P.6/11–12); דאלך̇ אל גבון הו כשר 'this cheese is kosher' (P.6/15); ודאלך̇ אל גבון אשתראה בריאיי 'he bought this cheese under my advice' (P.6/15); אלי דלך̇ אלעאם 'until that day' (P.3.c/16).

Pronominal *hāḏā*: והדא כלה בסבב 'this is all because' (C.5 /14); פיפעלו מא יכ̇תארוה בהאדה 'they should do what they choose in this (matter)' (C.1.a/46).

The colloquial pronouns *di* and *da* occur on a number of occasions. In addition to the above-mentioned corrections of *da* to *hāḏā* in C.5, the same letter also features פי דל אמר 'in this matter' (C.5/v11). In the following example, ד'י אל זמן 'this time' (P.7 /8), the *dalet* receives a stroke above, marking it as an interdental fricative. Similarly, *di* can be found in one of the Spanish letters, in בדי אלמסא[פר] 'with this [traveller]' (P.8/10). In all cases, *da* and *di* act as attributive demonstratives, probably because *ḏālika* is firmly established as *the* pronominal demonstrative.

2.8.2. Negation

The Particle *Lam*

The particle *lam* is arguably the most interesting of the Judaeo-Arabic negation particles. Originally a Classical Arabic particle that can prescriptively only negate the past and governs a particular mood (the apocopate), and that is very strongly marked as 'literary', it flourished in Judaeo-Arabic with broader functions: first negating present and future actions, before becoming the major, if not only, negation particle in Late Judaeo-Arabic documentary writing, serving as verbal and nominal negator alike.

In the material at hand, a few examples of *lam* are still following Classical Arabic usage, i.e., it requires the imperfect (although not the apocopate) and negates past action. It is not surprising that the Classical construction occurs in an 'official' context, i.e., inter-communal correspondence, which has a more literary air than private letters: [...] ולם יעלמו בית דין ולם יוצל 'they did not inform the *Bet Din* and it was not brought to [...]' (C.1.a/24–25); והאדה אלאמר יבקא מתעלק בדמתהם מא לם יכברונא במן יעציהם 'this matter remains their responsibility as long as they do not inform us who rebels against them' (C.1.a/32). In the following example, the present in the protasis of the conditional sentence is a matter of the English translation—in Arabic the past is required, expressed by *lam* + imperfect: אן לם תקדר תעמל תתכפל עלי אלמעלם מחמד 'if you cannot work (on it), then you should pledge it to the *muʿallim* Muhammad' (P.4.c/18–19).

However, *lam* occurs most commonly with the perfect: ואן [שי] מן יום אן [ספ]ר אלמכֿ לם וצל לנא 'since the day you (lit. the master) [left], no[thing] has arrived to us' (P.3.g/9); ולם ערפת תפציל מא עומל 'I did not know the detail of what was done' (C.5/m2–3); ולם וצל לנא גואב מן ענד אלמכדו' לא אלעדים אלדין יעיש ולא מן גהת מן גהה שריכה מנצור 'no answer reached us from the master, neither concerning the pious pauper Yaʿīsh, nor concerning his partner Manṣūr' (P.3.f/3–5); ולם כֿמל בקא פיה בעץׄ שי 'it was not completed; some things had remained (uncopied)' (P.3.f/v13); לם תם וקת (*lam tamma waqt*) 'the time has not come to pass' (P.4.g/13).

In the same context, we can also find *lam* as a nominal negation particle, anticipating its frequent use in this function in Late Judaeo-Arabic, for example in תם אן בלג'נא אן אלחזנים וחידין ולם ענדהם מן יסאעדהם 'then it reached us that the cantors are on their own, with no one to support them' (C.1.a/33).

To sum up, *lam* mainly negates the past, a function inherited from Classical Arabic usage, but it most commonly occurs with the perfect and only occasionally with the imperfect. There is also a case of *lam* acting as a nominal negation particle.

The Particle *Laysa*

The negation particle *laysa* is less common, and we find it as a nominal particle: ליס לה קלב אן יחצׄר פי בית הכנסת 'he does not have the heart to present himself in the synagogue’ (C.1.a/49); also in one of the letters analysed separately below: וליס עלימים כתיר ‘there are not many learned ones(?)’ (P.8/1). It also occurs as a verbal negator to negate the future in לייס יכרגו פי אל שרק ‘they will not depart to the East’ (P.7/7).

The Particle *Mā*

The particle *mā* is a versatile particle in Classical Judaeo-Arabic, and functions as a nominal and verbal negator in the corpus. Nominal *mā* occurs, for example, in יכונו ראשי החזנים ומא דונהם אלדי דכרנאהם אעלאה ‘they should be the heads of cantors, no one else except for those we mentioned above’ (C.1.a/44); ואן כאן מא יזן ללמכדום אלמבלג אלמדכור ואלא עוק עליה אלבאב ‘if he does not pay the mentioned sum to the master, block him from the door’ (C.5/v8–9); ואלמכדום יעלם אן אלממ' מא פי חאלה שיי ‘the master should know that the servant currently has nothing at all’ (C.5/v7); ואן מא מעה שי פאלמכׄ יאכד לי מן ידה ‘if he does not have any, you (lit. the master) should take it for me from his own (supply)’ (P.3.g/15).

Verbal *mā* occurs commonly with the perfect to negate the past, and slightly less often with the imperfect to negate the present and future: מא אלזמנאכם בה ‘we did not compel you concerning it’ (C.1.a/46); פמא וגׄד יוסף ‘Joseph did not find’ (P.3.e/20); ומא ארסל שי ‘he has not sent anything’ (C.5/10); מא ארדת נקול לה ‘I did not want to tell him’ (P.4.c/16); ונחן מא נעלם באטן אלאמר ‘we do not know the inner [meaning] of this matter’ (P.3.e/m2); ואן כאן מא יזן ללמכדום אלמבלג אלמדכור ואלא עוק עליה אלבאב ‘if he does not pay the mentioned sum to the master, block him from the door' (C.5/v8–9); ומא יכון לי גראמה כתיר 'I will not have many debts' (P.4.g/margin below 3–4).

In the following example, *mā* occurs with the perfect in jussive function, but this is due to the verbal syntax of the apodosis in the conditional sentence, as can also be seen in the case of the verb *rasamta* just before the negative phrase: ולו דרית אנה יסאפר רסמת עליה ומא כליתה יסאפר חתי' יזן אל מבלג אלמדכור 'if you learn that he is travelling, write about him and do not let him leave to travel unless he pays the mentioned sum' (C.5/v7–8). There is, however, another example in which *mā* negates the jussive: ומע כוני נערף אנך מא תכלם קרקשונה 'although we should inform you that you should not talk to Qarqashūna' (P.4.c/15–16).

The construction with *mā… illā* occurs: ואלחכאם מא להם ג'רץ̇ אלא[...] 'the arbiters only had the intention to…' (C.1.b/16). The phrase *mā… siwā* is found in אנה מא יסאפר סוי' לאסכנדריאה 'that he only ever travels via Alexandria' (C.5/v4).

The main functions of *mā* are nominal negation and negation of the past (with the perfect), but it also occurs for present and future negation (with the imperfect), and in the jussive.

The Particle *Lā*

In our corpus, the particle *lā* functions as a prohibitive with the imperfect: אללה לא יכלי מנכם 'may God not forsake you' (P.3.g/6–7); לא תדע האדה אלכתאב מן ידך חתי' תנהי לי האדה אלשגל 'do not put this letter down from your hand until you have informed me about this business' (P.3.f/v3–4); פלא תכלוה יחצ̇ר 'do not let him attend' (C.3/13); לא תמכנה לספר אלגרב אלי' אן תאכד מנה אל תסעה וכמסין נצף פצ̇ה 'do not let him travel to the West except after taking from him those 59 half-dinars of silver' (C.5/v5–6); ולא תסאל מא אל ממ' פיה מן אלצ̇יקה 'do not ask about (the trouble) the servant is in because of poverty' (C.5/13); ולא תג̇עלה וכיל 'you should not make him an agent' (P.3.e/25).

With the perfect, it negates the past: לא ג̇אב אלכתאב 'he has not brought the book' (P.3.g/m2); ולא ארסל ל[אל] מכ̇ ג̇ואב 'he has not sent an answer to the master' (P.3.g/18); with the imperfect it negates the present or the future: ומן לא יקבל דלך יחצ̇ר אלינא ילחן בחג̇תה 'anyone who does not accept this should present himself to us to explain his need' (C.1.a/47); חאמלה אלמצ̇ץ̇ בסבבך חתי לא יתג'ייר כ̇אטרך עליהא 'she is in agony for the reason that you will not change your mind about her' (P.3.c/24).

The phrase *lā... lā* 'neither... nor' occurs, for example, in ולם וצל לנא ג̇ואב מן ענד אלמכדו' לא אלעדים אלדין יעיש ולא מן גהת מן ג̇הה שריכה מנצור 'we did not receive a reply reply from the master, neither (with information) concerning the pious pauper Yaʿīsh, nor concerning his partner Manṣūr' (P.3.f/3–5).

2.9. Numerals

2.9.1. 1 and 2

The numeral 'one' occurs in a number of examples that are part of a common Judaeo-Arabic phenomenon, described by Blau (1980b, §237), in which *wāḥid* replaces *aḥad* 'one of the...', preceding the noun: ויג̇יב מעה ואחד אל כותאב 'he will bring with him a letter' (P.6/14); מאע ואחד אל בארכה 'with a *barca*' (P.6/4); ואחד אל נצראני 'one of the Christians' (P.6/10); ודכר אן כל ואחד מ[ן] האדה [...] 'he mentioned that every single one of this [...]' (C.1.b/22).

The numeral 'two' occurs in אתֹנין ותלאת 'two and three' (P.4.b/v7).

2.9.2. 3–10

In those numerals that are written out, in most cases it is the masculine (short form) numeral used to quantify both feminine and masculine nouns: כמס מית קטעה גבון '500 pieces of cheese' (the numeral 'five' and the counted noun '100'; P.6/13–14); באלארבעמאיה '400' (P.3.f/16); אכֹד מני ארבע אשרפיה 'he took from me four *ashrafī* dinars' (P.3.f/6); כמס קנאטיר 'five *qinṭars*' (P.3.c /20); תמאן אשרפייה 'eight *ashrafī* dinars' (P.3.e/9); סת אשרפייה 'six *ashrafī* dinars' (P.3.e/11); סת אנצאף 'six half-dinars' (C.5/20). A similar result was found in Wagner (2010) for fifteenth/sixteenth century material. There is only one example that shows the feminine (long form) numeral quantifying a masculine noun: תסעת שהור 'nine months' (C.5/10). The counted noun stands in the plural, with the exception of the 'hundreds' in a compound of multiple hundreds.

When the numeral stands by itself, it also appears to take the masculine form (short form): אתֹנין ותלאת 'two and three' (P.4.b/v7).

2.9.3. 11–19

Only one example of a written-out numeral between 11 and 19 can be found in the corpus, which shows the counted noun in the singular, as in Classical Arabic, where it takes the accusative in addition: אתנעשר קנטאר '12 *qinṭars*' (P.3.c/20).

2.9.4. 20–99

Numerals 20–99 take the counted noun in the singular, for example ועשרין נצף 'twenty half-dinars' (P.3.f/6–7); נֹך 25 '25 carpets' (P.3.f/v10); באלע[ש]רין אשרפי 'for 20 *ashrafī* dinars' (P.3.e/24); כמסין אשרפי '50 *ashrafī* dinars' (C.1.b/19; P.4.g/10).

Only one example from a letter, probably written by a non-native speaker of Arabic, shows a plural after a numeral 20–99: אשהר 144 '144 months' (C.4/28).

A number of written-out numerals between 20 and 99 with single digits occur, such as תסווה כמסה וארבעין 'it comes to 45' (P.7/5); ואתאכר ענ"ה סתה ותלתין נצ[ף] 'I am still owed 36 half-dinars by him' (C.5/20); ואכֹצמת פי חסאבהם באלארבעמאיה סתה ועשרין אשרפי 'I subtracted in their account 426 *ashrafī* dinars' (P.3.f/16–17); אתנין וארבעין נצף '42 half-dinars' (C.5/v3); תסעה וכמסין נצף '59 half-dinars' (C.5/v3). In all examples, the single digit is the feminine (long form) numeral, and when there is a counted noun, it is masculine, which may reflect gender polarity. This is interesting as gender polarity seems to have been abandoned in the numerals 3–10.

2.9.5. Even Hundreds

In Classical Arabic, the counted noun after even hundreds and thousands stands in the genitive singular. Although the cases have been lost, the counted noun in Classical Judaeo-Arabic follows suit and is counted in the singular. In our corpus, only one example of an even hundred with a counted noun can be found, and the counted noun stands in the singular: כמס מית קטעה גבון '500 pieces of cheese' (P.6/13–14). Another example shows the numeral by itself, with the hypercorrect nominative ending *-ūn*: מאיתון 'two hundred' (P.4.b/v21).

2.9.6. Definite Numbers

Due to the character of numerals as a type of word somewhere between nouns and adjectives, and the rare occurrence of definite numeral constructions, definite numeral constructions were not strictly standardised in Classical Arabic. There are four different competing constructions: (a) by analogy with the indefinite construction: *ṯalāṯatu r-rijāli*; (b) by the numeral standing in apposition to the noun and both receiving the article: *ar-rijālu ṯ-ṯalāṯatu*; (c) *aṯ-ṯalāṯatu r-rijāli/u*;[2] and (d) *aṯ-ṯalāṯatu rijālin*. Construction (d) is the most usual form in all dialects (see the examples in Mörth 1997, 171–74), and it also occurs in Modern Written Arabic (see Haywood and Nahmad 1962, 307f; Buckley 2004, 926). Unsurprisingly, this is the form we encounter most in Classical Judaeo-Arabic, and it is also the construction used in our corpus: אל 65 אשרפי 'the sixty-five *ashrafī* dinars' (P.3.f/21); אל 426 אשרפי 'that the 426 *ashrafī* dinars' (P.3.f/13); ואל ארבע באלאת אלורק 'the four bales of paper' (C.5/m2); אנה יזן אל סתה ותלת[ין] נצף 'that he pays the 36 half-dinars' (C.5/21–22); לא תמכנה לספר אלגרב אלי' אן תאכד מנה אל תסעה וכמסין נצף פצה 'do not let him travel to the West except after taking from him those 59 half-dinars of silver' (C.5/v5–6). In the last three examples, the numeral is written out and we can see gender polarity between the single digits and the

[2] The prescriptively correct case ending is not clear, according to Arab grammarians.

counted noun—something that could not be observed in the numerals 3–10 but that we could observe in numerals 20–99. Admittedly, all three examples come from the same letter. As in Classical Judaeo-Arabic, the counted objects behave syntactically as they would with indefinite numbers, i.e., they stand in the plural following numerals 3–10 and in the singular in all higher numbers.

2.9.7. Ordinal Numbers

The attributive ordinal numbers 'first' and 'second' can be found in אנני אכׄדת לך אלג̇זא אלאול פי ורק דיואני '(I inform you) that I got for you the first part on *dīwān*-quality paper' (P.3.f/v12); ואמא אלג̇זא אלת̇אני 'as for the second part' (P.3.f/v14–15). In יחצ̇רו לך פי אול מרכב אן תדכל אלכׄליג̇ 'they should come for you on the first ship that goes up the delta' (P.3.f/v10–11), the ordinal forms the first noun in a genitive construction, but the second noun in that construction does not have the article, although the phrase is definite.

2.10. Subordination

2.10.1. Adverbial Clauses in Judaeo-Arabic

When investigating adverbial connectives in Judaeo-Arabic (and in Middle Arabic in general), one of the most striking phenomena is the great variation of adverbial connectives. Compared to the Classical Arabic repertoire, we find a number of introductory particles that have changed semantics and/or which consist of compounds of 'older' connectives combined with relativisers or complementisers (for a more detailed discussion, see Wagner 2014).

2.10.2. Temporal Clauses

In temporal clauses, a variety of compounds of relativisers or complementisers plus prepositions occur. The relative pronoun *allaḏī* (although in the reading tradition of the time probably pronounced *əldi*) serves as temporal conjunction in combination with prepositions such as *baʿd* 'after': נעלמך באן בעד אלדי אפתרקנה מנכום קאציינה כתיר 'we inform you that after we separated from you, we suffered a great deal' (P.6/2).

The complementiser/relativiser *mā* on its own may serve as a temporal connective, a function it can also hold in Classical Arabic (see Fischer 2002, 234): והאדה אלאמר יבקא מתעלק בדמתהם מא לם יכברונא במן יעציהם 'this matter remains their responsibility as long as they have not informed us who rebels against them' (C.1.a/32). It also occurs, for example, in a compound with *ʿinda*: פענד מא קרב וקת חצֿורך תגפיהא באלכלאם 'when the time of your arrival has come near, you may treat her harshly with words' (P.3.c /15); but *ʿinda* also appears by itself: ענד חצֿורי לביתי בעד אן כתבת לך מן פוה מא קד כתבת 'during my stay in my house, after I had written to you from Fuwwa what I had already written' (P.4.g/2–3). In the latter example, the complementiser *ʾan* is also combined with *baʿd* to form the temporal connective בעד אן. This *ʾan* may also be combined with *ilā* to form the temporal connective in לא תמכנה לספר אלגרב אלי' אן תאכד מנה אל תסעה וכמסין נצף פצֿה 'do not let him travel to the West except after taking from him those 59 half-dinars of silver' (C.5/v5–6).

A Classical Arabic adverbial connective that appears to have survived the transition into written Judaeo-Arabic utilitarian prose is *ḥattā*, possibly due to its double function as preposition and connective: ולו דרית אנה יסאפר רסמת עליה ומא כליתה יסאפר חתי' יזן אל מבלג אלמדכור 'if you learn that he is travelling, write about him and do not let him travel until he pays the mentioned sum' (C.5/v7–8); לא תמכנה לספר חתי' אנה יזן אל סתה ותלת[ין] נצף 'do not let him travel until he pays those 36 half-dinars' (C.5/21–22); כארהא פי אלמכדו' חתי אנהא תכ̇תאר קבץ̇ אלגט 'she will be spiteful about you (lit. the master) until she will choose to receive the divorce document' (P.3.c/13); לייס יכרגו פי אל שרק חסבת אלדי נק[עד] פי טרבלס חתי' אלרדא מתע אל טרא[בלסיין] 'they will not depart to the East so that I will [stay] in Tripolis until the return of the Tri[politans]' (P.7/7); לא תדע האדה אלכתאב מן ידך חתי' תנהי לי האדה אלשגל 'do not put this letter down from your hand until you have informed me about this business' (P.3.f/3–4).

The preposition/connective *ḥattā* also occurs in the following sentence with a slightly changed function, possibly as a sort of complementiser within a causal connotation, forming a compound with *bi-sabab* 'for the reason that': חאמלה אלמץ̇ץ̇ בסבבך חתי' לא תג'ייר כ̇אטרך עליהא 'she is in agony for the reason that you do not change your mind about her' (P.3.c/24).

Lammā is a frequent temporal connective, as in תם אן אלממ' למא וצל אלי אלקאהרה חאסבת זין אלדין 'then, after the servant arrived in Cairo, I settled the account with Zayn al-Dīn' (P.3.f/15); פלמא [וצלת] אלמצאטיר בתאע אלדכירה פמא אכ̇דו מן אלמצאטיר שי אלא בעד מות זין אלדין 'when the documents belonging to the provisions [arrived], they did not take any of the documents, until after the death of Zayn al-Dīn' (P.3.f/17–19); פלמא בלגנא דלך קצדנא אן נזידכם מחאסן 'after we received this, we wanted to give you good advice'

(C.1.a/37). *Lammā* also occurs in the merged form *laman*, from *lammā ʾan*: תם אערף אלמכדו' עלי אן אלממ' למן חאסבת אלדכירה ואכֿדו מני אלמבלג' אלמתעלק 'then I inform the master that, when the servant settled the accounts of the provisions, they took from me the corresponding sum' (P.3.f/8–9).

The connective *ʾiḏā* carrying causal-temporal connotation occurs in וכצוצא אדא כאן לבסה חזאיני 'in particular as his clothes are (that of) mourning' (C.1.a/50).

Asyndesis may occur in [...] ועליה אלמעתמר ראית '(pondering) about it repeatedly, I saw [...]' (P.4.g/3), although parts of the sentence have been torn.

The question particle *kayfa* can also be found as a temporal connective in letter C.4, treated below in an extra section: כיף אני' נגֿי אסכנדריי' נגֿיבו פי ידי 'when I am coming to Alexandria, I will bring it with my own hands' (C.4/v9).

2.10.3. Final and Consecutive Clauses

In documentary texts such as the ones under investigation, it is often difficult to differentiate between final and consecutive meaning, so these two types of adverbial clauses are grouped together here.

In one of the letters, P.6, we find the particle *baš or bēš* used as a final connective: ואפתרקנה מאע ואחד אלבארכה באש נמורו פי סרקוסה 'We departed with a *barca* in order to go to Syracuse' (P.6/4–5); נזל רֹ צוריאל ורֹ מצליח באש יאשתריו אל כובז ואל נביד 'R. Ṣuriel and R. Maṣliaḥ went down in order to buy bread and wine' (P.6/5–6); ועמרו זוג מראכב באש יאכדו אל מרכב 'a pair of ships approached in order to seize the ship' (P.6/7). This *baš* may represent a colloquial form of *bi-mā*, in which Classical Arabic *mā* is replaced by colloquial *ayš*, which is then either monophthongised to *ēš* or shortened to *aš*.[3] For example, Wahrmund (1898, 258) has *bi-mā* for "so dass" (so that) in a consecutive/final sense. The phrase *bi-mā ʾan* also carries the meaning 'for the reason that', which is semantically close to final 'in order to'. This *baš* also occurs as a complement connective in נעלמך̇ באן אל ספרים אלדי ועתך באש נבעתך מא כאן לי זמן נכתובהם לך 'I inform you that the books that I promised to send to you—I did not have time to copy them' (P.6/16).

The relative pronoun *allaḏī/əldi* may serve as a consecutive conjunction in combination with the preposition *ḥasaba* 'according': לייס יכרגו פי אל שרק חסבת אלדי נק[עד] פי טרבלס חתי אלרדא מתע אל טרא[בלסיין] 'they will not depart to the East so that we shall [stay] in Tripolis until the return of the Tri[politans]' (P.7/7).

In other clauses, asyndesis serves to express consecutive/final meaning: ומן לא יקבל דלך יחצ̇ר אלינא ילחן בחג̇תה 'anyone who does not accept this should present himself to us to explain his need' (C.1.a/47); מן דאלך̇ אלדי ועת[ך] מוסרע יג̇יאוך 'those which I promised to you—I am making haste so that they will arrive at yours' (P.6/17); ואן כאן תאכ̇ד עליהם שי בעד דלך̇ ארסל אעלמני 'if you take anything on their behalf after that, then send to inform me' (P.3.f/m2).

---

[3] The orthography allows for both possiblities; see Wagner 2010, 63. The form *aš* is a typical Maghrebian form; see Blau (1981, 62).

2.10.4. Causal Clauses

Causal connection is sometimes expressed by *min jihha*: בעד אלדי אפתרקנה מנכום קאציינה כתיר פי אל טריק מן גהה אל מרכב אלדי כאנת תעמל מא אכתיר 'after we separated from you, we suffered a great deal because a lot of water was leaking into the ship' (P.6/2–3).

As mentioned above, *ʾiḏā* may carry causal-temporal connotation: וכצוצא אדא כאן לבסה חזאיני 'in particular as his clothes are (that of) mourning' (C.1.a/50).

The Classical Arabic connective *li-ʾanna/ li-ʾan* also occurs: לא תמכנה לספר אלגרב אלי' אן תאכד מנה אל תסעה וכמסין נצף פצׂה פצׂה לאן אלממ' וזנהא ענה 'do not let him travel to the West except after taking from him those 59 half-dinars of silver, because the servant paid them on his behalf' (C.5/v5–7).

A more unusual causal connective can be found in *kawn/ kon*: אלמׄ שמואל י"ל ארסל יתשכא לנא מן גהה נפסה כון אנה מכסור אלכאטר 'M. Samuel, may he live forever, sent to complain to us on his own behalf, because he is exhausted of mind' (C.1.a/48–49). A related connective occurs in Spitta's nineteenth-century colloquial Egyptian dictionary as *likon* 'for, because'. A similar form, probably read as *maʿa koni*, occurs in a concessive clause: ומע כוני נערף אנךְ מא תכלם קרקשונה 'although we should inform you that you should not talk to Qarqashūna' (P.4.c/15–16).

2.10.5. Conditional Clauses

In synthetic conditional clauses, Classical Arabic constructions can be found with the perfect in the protasis and apodosis: אן אכׄתרת ארסלתה לךְ 'if you prefer, I shall send it to you' (P.3.f/v15); ואן אכׄתארו יכשפו מן חסאב אלדכירה מן קדאם אלשהוד כאן אחסן 'if they prefer to reveal the accounts of the provisions before witnesses, that would be best' (P.3.f/v2–3). There are examples of the perfect or *lam* + apocopate in the protasis and jussive in the apodosis, such as אן לם תקדר תעמל תתכפל עלי אלמעלם מחמד 'if you cannot work (on it), then you should pledge it to the *muʿallim* Muhammad' (P.4.c/18–19). The jussive in the apodosis can also be found with a nominal clause in the protasis: ואן מא מעה שי פאלמכֿ יאכד לי מן ידה 'if he does not have any, then you (lit. the master) should take (it) for me from his own (supply)' (P.3.g/15). The same writers, however, may also use clauses where the protasis contains the verb in the imperfect: אן תוצלו יעיש דרהם פלוס מן גֿהה תספירה אלמאצֿי פאנה אכֿד מני ארבע אשרפיה ועשרין 'if you send Yaʿīsh a dirham of money on behalf of his consignment, he (already) took from me four *ashrafī* dinars and twenty half-dinars and a quarter' (P.3.f/5–7). The same letter may also contain the more analytical connective *ʾinkān*, which makes the use of a perfect verb in the protasis redundant: ואן כאן תאכֿד עליהם שי בעד דלך ארסל אעלמני 'if you take anything on their behalf after that, then send to inform me' (P.3.f/m2); ואן כאן מא יזן ללמכדום אלמבלג אלמדכור ואלא עוק עליה אלבאב 'if he does not pay the mentioned sum to the master, block him from the door' (C.5/v8–9). In the latter example, *wa-ʾllā* is used to introduce the apodosis, which lends extra emphasis to the command expressed.

More colloquial writers use *ʾinkān* as an introductory particle, although they may still analyse the individual parts. For example, the (probably) Spanish writer of letters C.4 and P.8 differentiates between singular and plural *ʾinkān*/*ʾinkānū*, which means he does not use *ʾinkān* as a lexicalised conditional connective. Whereas *ʾinkān* occurs in ואנכאן הוי' לא ירידהי' אני' אמי' נסכון אוולי חתי נכריהי' 'if he does not want it, my intention is surely to live (there) at first until I hire it out' (C.4/28–29), the plural form *ʾinkānū* can be found in אנכאנו פי אלקעה ואנא גיד 'if they are in the apartment, I am fine (with it)' (C.4/32).

Law, which serves as an irrealis connective in Classical Arabic, can also be found for the construction 'in case'. In the apodosis, we find a chain of perfect forms functioning as jussives (*rasamta wa-mā ḵallaytahu*): ולו דרית אנה יסאפר רסמת עליה ומא כליתה יסאפר חתי' יזן אל מבלג אלמדכור 'if you learn that he is travelling, write about him and do not let him travel until he pays the mentioned sum' (C.5/v7–8).

2.10.6. Relative Clauses

Relative clauses in the investigated material seem to largely follow the rules that have been observed for medieval documentary Judaeo-Arabic (see Wagner 2010, 211–25). Only the masculine singular form אלדי occurs, and introduces relative clauses following definite singular (masculine and feminine) and plural antecedents: ודכל אל ספר תורה אלדי אשתריית לך 'the Torah scroll which I bought for you arrived' (P.7/15); בסבב אלעונש אלדי אטלקנאה 'concerning the penalty that we imposed' (C.1.a/20); יכונו ראשי החזנים ומא דונהם אלדי דכרנאהם אעלאה 'they should be the heads of cantors, no one else except for those we mentioned above' (C.1.a/44); [סת אלא]מל שקרה א' אלש' יוסף אלבריקי נ"ע אלדי בעלה או זוגה [אלמע'] יעקוב סהלאן נ"ע '[Sitt al-A]mal Shaqara, the daughter of *Shaykh*

Joseph al-Brīkī, may his soul rest in Eden, who was the wife of [*Shaykh*] Jacob Sahlān, may his soul rest in Eden' (C.6/11–12).

In the case of indefinite antecedent nouns, the relative clauses are normally constructed asyndetically: וקד ארסל הו כתאב ידכר פיה אן קרקשונה טלבהם 'he already sent a letter in which he mentions that Qarqashūna claimed them' (P.4.c/11–12).

While in Classical Arabic, indefinite antecedents are normally followed by asyndesis, they may occasionally stand before אלדי (*allaḏī/əldi*) in the fifteenth-/sixteenth-century material. In the following example, it is probably the gap between the antecedent and the relative pronoun that makes asyndesis impossible and requires the use of a relative pronoun: דאלך אל נצראני אסתקצה אש אנסאן פי סכנדרייא אלדי הו יסוא יאקף פי מטגר וגיירה 'this Christian inquired about someone in Alexandria who is (his) equal, to support (him) in the marketplace, and in other (things)' (P.6/11–12).

Judaeo-Arabic also employs another innovative method to construct relative clauses after an indefinite antecedent. The form *ʾan*, homophonous with the complementiser, occurs as relativiser in various examples: ונעמת אן שאפיה 'true well-being' (P.3.c/9, and probably P.3.f/2).

Most of the examples of independent relative *ʾan*, however, occur between a noun and relative clause: ועקיב דלך יחצׄרו לך פי אול מרכב אן תדכל אלכׄליגׄ 'following this, they should come for you on the first ship that goes up the delta' (P.3.f/v10–11); יגׄלס פי מוצׄע אן יכתאר 'he will sit in a place he chooses' (C.1.a/53); ואן מן יום אן [ספ]ר אלמכׄ לם וצל לנא מן ענדכם [שי] 'since the day when you (lit. the master) [left], no[thing] has arrived to us from you' (P.3.g/9–10); והי צברת מן יום אן סאפר אלמכדו' מן ענדהא אלי יום תאריכה 'she has been patient since the day you travelled away from her until now' (P.3.c/13–14). In general, *ʾan* appears to be used as a regular relative particle used for particular relative constructions in the investigated material.

Headless relative clauses use *man* for an animate indefinite referent: וכל מן יכוד במנזלך אלכרים 'everyone who belongs to your honourable house' (P.4.c/22–23); ואיי מן כאלפהם יפעלו פיה אלמשפט 'anyone who does not obey them, they should take him to court' (C.1.a/27); ואן אל ממ' ירסל לך אלוצול צחבת מן תרסל מעה אלפלוס 'the servant will send the receipt to you with whoever you send the money by' (C.5/15). They use *allaḏī* for an animate definite referent: פקצדו ילג'ו אלדי הו ינזל לך מנזל 'they wanted to talk about the one who lives for you in the apartment' (P.3.e/m1–2).

2.10.7. Complement Clauses

The complement clauses in the material under investigation are relatively inconspicuous. They are introduced by *ʾan* or *biʾ-an*; in particular, the verb *ʿarrafa* 'to inform' is typically combined with *bi-ʾan*: בל קלת לה אני נכתב לך ואנך תסאעד ותעמל 'but I told him that I would write to you and that you would help and work (on it)' (P.4.c/17–18); נעלמך באן יג׳י ענדך ואחד אל נצראני קטלאני 'I inform you that a Catalan Christian will come to you' (P.6/9–10); פדכרת אן וצל אליהא עלי יד אלולד 'she mentioned that they arrived to her by the hand of the boy' (P.3.c/18); אערף אלמכאדים באן אלמ̇ שמואל י"ל ארסל יתשכא לנא מן גהה נפסה 'then I inform the masters that M. Samuel, may he live forever, sent to complain to us on his own behalf' (C.1.a/47–48).

In a few examples, *allaḏī* is used as an introductory particle. The use of *allaḏī* as a complementiser is not entirely alien to written Standard Arabic, as particular complement clauses may be introduced by *allaḏī* in post-Classical Arabic in the fixed syntagma *al-ḥamdu lillāhi allaḏī* ‘thank God that’ (see Spitaler 1962): ברצם אלדי נ[ש]תרי צ̇הב באיש נגיבו סכנדרייא ‘with the intention that I will buy gold(?) for everything that I will bring to Alexandria’ (P.7/4).

We also find examples of asyndetic subordination, although they are not as common as in, for example, letters from the Classical Genizah period: שמואל קאל לי נכתב ללמכ ‘Samuel told me that I should write to you’ (P.4.c/15); מא ארדת נקול לה ‘I did not want to tell him’ (P.4.c/16).

2.11. A Literary Letter: P.9

A text in letter form concerned with biblical exegesis, which consists of the folios Bodl. MS Heb. c. 72/24 and Bodl. MS Heb. c. 72/2, deserves separate linguistic analysis. Unlike the other letters in our corpus, it is not a true document, but to a large degree is influenced by literary norms. This manifests in a number of linguistic features, such as a more consistent Hebraised orthography and constant code-switching between Hebrew and Judaeo-Arabic, which mark the text as very different from the utilitarian prose analysed in the previous section.

The writer uses few extralinear signs, but occasionally indicates *jīm* by pointing below the letter: אלדרג̣ה ‘the step’ (P.9/f2 /v2). Abbreviations are indicated by a stroke or pointing above the words, whereas *ẓāʾ* and *ḍāl* are in all cases indicated by a dot above the צ. On occasion, he also uses שׂ for *šīn*, כּ for *k̲ā*ʾ, and a *dagesh* in final *kāf*, but these features appear in no consistent manner.

On an orthographic level, the spelling of the singular masculine pronominal suffix as הו is the most obvious feature. This form also occurs occasionally in some of the other letters, but in P.9 it is almost always spelled as such, by analogy with Medieval Hebrew orthography, e.g., להו 'for him' (P.9/f2/v3 and P.9/f24/15); באנהו 'that he' (P.9/f2/v5); קולהו 'his statement' (P.9/f2/9). Exceptions can be found, such as כאנה 'as if he' (P.9/f24/v11); and עלי צׄאהרה 'in its obvious meaning' (P.9/f24/v16). In the case of the latter, the prescribed Classical Arabic reading *ʿalā ẓāhirihī* with the genitive may have influenced the spelling.

Other Hebrew spelling conventions emulated in the Judaeo-Arabic of the text include the spelling of *tāʾ marbūṭa* with ת, such as in גאית 'extremity' (P.9/f2/7); and תרגמת 'translation' (P.9/f2/22). This spelling with ת occurs both in the construct form, as in the previous examples (where the *tāʾ marbūṭa* would have been pronounced as /t/), but also in the pausal form, where the pronunciation would have been a short /a/ vowel, e.g., in אלקראית 'the reading' (P.9/f2/16). These examples can only be judged as hypercorrections. The final vowel of the plural pronominal suffix ending, colloquially /a/ and Classical Arabic /ā/, may be spelled with ה, e.g., אקרארנה 'our confirmation' (P.9/f2/11), apparently in a slip into Hebrew orthography. In most examples, however, it is spelled according to Classical Arabic norms, such as וידלנא 'guides us' (P.9/f2/22).

The accusative is spelled as well, which is rare in the documentary sources of the corpus. The spelling does not, however, follow Classical Arabic conventions of marking with an *ʾalif*, but is spelled with *nun*: פלא ארא אחדן ‘I do not see anyone’ (P.9/f2/16). In the case of the adverb איצׄא ‘also’ we find the regular Classical Arabic spelling, for example in P.9/f24/v12.

The feminine demonstrative pronouns *tilka* and *hāḏihi* also occur, which is rare in the corpus, for example in ותלך אלנצוץ ‘those passages’ (P.9/f24/v21); לתלך אלדרגֿה ‘for this step’ (P.9/f2/v2); בהדה אלעבארה ‘in this interpretation’ (P.9/f2/v15); and in הדה אלנצוץ ‘these passages’ (P.9/f2/v15). The writer appears to have made careful separation between feminine and masculine pronouns. The masculine appears, for example, in the presentative הדא נצה ‘this is his wording’ (P.9/f2/13).

A rare apocopate form features in the text in the form *yabqi* in פלם יבק ענד כל די עקל סאלם ‘in all of this no sound mind remains’ (P.9/f24/v18; an alternative translation is provided there), demonstrating the literary nature of the letter. Interestingly, this is combined with the demonstrative די, which probably reflects colloquial *di*, instead of the more literary-marked *hāḏā* or *ḏālika*. Despite its Classical Arabic morphology, *lam* + apocopate is used for the present tense, which it cannot convey in Classical Arabic, although it could be argued that the expression may be understood as a general fact, which is expressed by the perfect in Classical Arabic and can be extended to *lam* + apocopate in the negative. A similar construction can be found in לם יגֿד ‘he does not find’ (P.9/f2/v1), which could also be taken as a general fact.

To sum up, the writer appears to have a greater appreciation of Classical Arabic conventions than most of the other writers in our corpus, with the exception of David ibn Shams, and he is careful to follow certain Classical conventions, for example in his use of the apocopate and of feminine demonstratives. At the same time, we find a more Hebraised orthography, which is probably due to the genre of the text.

2.12. Letters C.4 and P.8: Elijah Qarqūsa

Letter C.4 and part of letter P.8 are written in the same hand. They were most likely composed by Elijah, who introduces himself in C.4. P.8 was composed by three different scribes. The first lines of the document are written in one hand, by someone introducing himself as Mardūk Qarqūsa. The handwriting stops in the middle of a sentence, and the writer of letter C.4, Elijah Qarqūsa, takes over. Probably a close relative, as he bears the same name, he continues writing in the name of Mardūk Qarqūsa, before a third scribe—the most skilled and accomplished of the three with regard to writing Judaeo-Arabic—takes over on the verso.

Because these two letters exhibit a number of phenomena that are unusual for this corpus, they are analysed separately.

2.12.1. Supralinear Signs

Elijah Qarqūsa marks Classical Arabic *jīm* with a dot above the *gimel*, and also puts a *dagesh* in all final *kafs* to mark the differences between Arabic *kāf and ḵā*ʾ. He marks *ḍāḍ* with a dot, as most writers do. The most conspicuous feature of his hand, however, is the way he carefully marks all of his *ʾalif maqṣūra* spelled with *yā*ʾ with an extra stroke—a convention that normally betrays familiarity with Arabic-script spelling conventions, such as in עלי' 'over' (C.4/7). In his case, however, he occasionally writes any final long /a/ sound with *yod* and apostrophe, such as in all 3rd feminine singular pronominal suffix endings, e.g., ופיהי' 'and in it' (C.4/5) and להי' 'to them' (C.4/10), i.e., he analyses the final /ā/ as *ʾalif maqṣūra* spelled with *yā*ʾ. This is even extended to the independent feminine singular pronoun היי' 'it' (C.4/12) and הוי' 'he' (C.4/27, 28), where *yod* appears to designate short /a/. In some of the examples, a possible explanation is that the *yod* indicates an *imāla* of the final vowel, but Elijah also adds a stroke to the *yod* in examples such as אני' 'I' (C.4/2, 9); יר'שלימי' 'Yerushalmī' (C.4/13); and ותאעתי' 'you should give' (C.4/16), where the *yod* can only be read as an /i/-sound, making the marking redundant. Although the writer carefully marks all of his *ʾalif maqṣūra* spelled with *yā*ʾ with an extra stroke, he writes מוסה with ה and not י, as in Classical Arabic spelling. He thereby creates a *Mischform* between the Hebrew spelling for Moses/Moshe and the Arabic Mūsā. In C.4/4, מוסי' appears to be spelled according to Classical Arabic orthography.

All this evidence taken together creates the impression that the writer did not really know what he was doing. He may have picked up the habit of marking final *yod* with an apostrophe from someone who was perhaps a native speaker and familiar with Arabic spelling conventions and who only used it to mark original Classical Arabic *ʾalif maqṣūra* spelled with *yā*ʾ. But Elijah appears to extend it to almost any final *yod*, no matter what its pronunciation.

2.12.2. Vowels

The writer spells many short vowels in *plene*, which may indicate that he was familiar with European writing and spelling of vowels, although *plene* spelling of vowels also appears abundantly in the documentary writing of fifteenth-century native speakers of Judaeo-Arabic. All vowel qualities are spelled *plene*, such as:

/a/, in ראטליין 'two *raṭls*' (C.4/11); יארוח 'may it be sold' (C.4/13); נרגאביך 'I want you to' (C.4/15, v10); מא אנבעאת 'has not been sold' (C.4/v5); אכאת 'took' (C.4/22).

/i/, in מיני 'from me' (C.4/2); ומסלים 'given' (C.4/3); ואחיד 'one' (C.4/6); מא עריפת 'I did not know' (C.4/12); מין 'from' (C.4/13); אוכתיב 'I write' (C.4/v16); אוכאתיב 'I am writing' P.8/24).

/u/, in וקולתו 'I said' (C.4/10); תנפוד 'you should send' (C.4/10); אוכתי 'my sister' (C.4/18); אוכתיב 'I write' (C.4/v16; P.8/24).

In addition to the cases mentioned above (§2.12.1) and below (§2.12.4), possible cases of *imāla* appear in עליני 'over us' (P.8/23); וליד 'son' (C.4/19); and לילמעילים יוסף 'to the *muʿallim* Joseph' (P.8/18).

Some of the vocalisations are unusual, such as ואנתו 'you' (C.4/6) and מחאבך 'your beloved' (P.8/19). In מיאה 'hundred' (C.4/9), we encounter a colloquial spelling, as opposed to Classical מאיה. Anaptyctic vowels occur in יביקי הו להי' 'may he remain (a support) for her' (C.4/19), and possibly in ובזכות סיידיני' 'for the merit of our master' (C.4/21), although the latter example may reflect the reading of a Classical Arabic genitive.

Hebrew words may also contain *plene* vowels, such as שלומה 'Solomon' (C.4/v2), and הנאבי 'the prophet' (C.4/v15), although the latter appears to be a *Mischform* of Hebrew and Arabic.

2.12.3. Consonants

Hamza is spelled with *ʾalef*, as in לראאס ‘to the leader’ (P.8/20) and ראאח ‘going’ (P.8/21). Such forms occur, for example, in Saʿadiah’s Bible translation, whereas in many Classical Judaeo-Arabic letters, in these specific cases the writers would tend to write according to Classical Arabic, ראיס and ראיח, or in colloquial fashion, רייס. In הוולאי ‘those’ (C.4/17), we may have an example of *vav* for *hamza*, but this could also be a plain double spelling of *vav*. In סאת ונופץ ‘one and a half hours’ (P.8/21), the *hamza* may be dropped or the long /a/ shortened or spelled defectively, while the *tāʾ marbūṭa* is spelled with *tav*.

No cases of *tafk̠īm* of /t/ occur (as opposed to the second writer in P.8), but we find an example of *tafk̠īm* of /k/, which points to the Spanish origin of the writer: יסקונו ‘they will live’ (C.4/v1).

There are a number of examples displaying *tarqīq*: ואני' עת[ית] לעזיז מיאה ‘I gave to ʿAzīz 100’ (C.4/9); ותאעתי' ‘you should give’ (C.4/16); תעתי ‘you will give’ (P.8/20)—all from the root *ʿaṭā* ‘give’—and תיתליבני ‘it will be demanded from me’ (C.4/v7), from the root *ṭalaba* ‘demand’.

Assimilation of Classical Arabic /d̠/ to following /t/, by which Classical Arabic *ʾak̠ad̠tu* becomes *ʾak̠att*, appears to occur in אכאת מינו 6 מיידי' ‘I took from him six *muʾayyadī*’ (C.4/22), and אכאת מינהי' ‘I took from her’ (C.4/24).

2.12.4. Pronouns

Various independent pronouns can be found. Two different 2nd masculine singular forms occur, ואנתו ‘you’ (C.4/6) and ואנתי ‘you’

(C.4/8), both deviating from the expected masculine vowel pattern of *anta*. A parallel variation between /i/ and /u/ vocalisation for the 2nd masculine singular, although not in the pronoun but in the conjugation of the verb, can be found in a Late Judaeo-Arabic letter from the nineteenth century, in וערפתינא 'you informed us' (TS 10J19.24/4), and עמלתו טייב 'you did well' in the same line. In 'היי 'it' (C.4/12) and 'הוי 'he' (C.4/27, 28), short final /a/ appears to be spelled by *yod* with an apostrophe (see above §12.2.1).

The writer spells all 2nd masculine singular pronominal suffix endings with *yod*, i.e., as יךְ, for example: נעלמיךְ 'I inform you' (C.4/4); נקוליךְ 'I tell you' (C.4/v2); נרגאביךְ 'I would like you' (C.4/15, v10); and ידיליךְ 'he should suggest to you' (C.4/28). The addressee is a man, but it seems unlikely that the writer mistakenly used the feminine form for the ending. Perhaps the /i/ sounds reflects an *imāla* of the short vowel in the suffix. In חצ̇ארתך אלשריף 'your honourable majesty' (C.4/3), we may be dealing with a mixed-up Arabic-Hebrew form in חצ̇רתיך, as, prescriptively, a plural is required.

The singular feminine suffix is always spelled with *yod*, such as 'נכריהי 'I hire it out' (C.4/29) and 'להי 'to them' (C.4/10).

Demonstrative pronouns occur in בדי אלמסא[פר] 'with this [traveller]' (P.8/10), featuring the colloquial demonstrative pronoun *di*, and הוולאי 'those' (C.4/17).

2.12.5. Cases

Traces of cases appear in Elijah's writing, which could be an indication that he was somewhat familiar with Classical Arabic grammar. The accusative appears to occur in שיין 'anything' (C.4/v5). Possible genitive forms may be found in ליל מעלמי מוסה 'to the *muʿallim* Mūsā' (P.8/13) and in ובזכות סיידיני' 'for the merit of our master' (C.4/21).

2.12.6. Verb

The pattern *itfaʿala* for the fifth stem occurs in ואתבקי כרייתהי' 'it remained on its hire' (C.4/23).

Conjugation of the 1st singular and plural shows an opposition of singular *nafʿal* vs plural *nafʿalū*, for example: כיף אני' נגי אסכנדריי' נג׳יבו פי ידי 'when I am going to Alexandria I will bring it in my hands' (C.4/v9); נרגאביך 'I would like you' (C.4/15, v10); and נקוליך 'I tell you' (C.4/v2), vs נסאכנו 'we will rent out' (C.4/v1). The Classical Arabic 1st singular, however, also appears, in the very formulaic dating formulae at the end of the letters: אוכתיב 'I write' (C.4/v16); אוכאתיב 'I am writing' (P.8/24).

The vowel pattern *kānit* for the 3rd feminine singular is reflected in מתל לו כאנית אוכתי 'as if she was my sister' (C.4/18), but we also encounter מא אנבעאת 'has not been sold' (C.4/v5).

Vocalisation of verbs shows colloquial patterns, such as תיבעת 'you should send' (C.4/v7) and תיתוסי' 'you should behave very generously' (P.8/10), but also a preference for /i/ or perhaps vowel harmony where we would expect a /u/ vowel in the stem, such as in תיתליבני 'it will be demanded from me' (C.4/v7) and נבריגהום 'I will let them go' (C.4/v8). In other examples, the vocalisation agrees with Classical Arabic and colloquial patterns: תסלימלי 'greet from me' (C.4/15, v10); סלימלי 'greet from me' (C.4/v13); אוכתיב 'I write' (C.4/v16).

2.12.7. Lexicon

The colloquial verb *jāba* 'to bring' occurs, for example, in וג̇בני רבאייעי 'he brought me a box(?)' (C.4/5) and in כיף אני׳ נג̇י אסכנדריי׳ נג̇יבו פי ידי 'when I am going to Alexandria I will bring it in my hands' (C.4/v9). In the first example, in וג̇בני 'he brought me' (C.4/5), the defective spelling of /ā/ probably reflects a short pronunciation of /a/.

The spelling *nufṣ* for *nuṣf* 'half' occurs in שהר ונופץ 'a month and a half' (C.4/24) and in סאת ונופץ 'one and a half hours' (P.8/21). The second author of P.8 also uses *nufṣ*, whereas the third author chooses the form *nuṣṣ*.

The form אש for 'anything' and 'what' occurs in אש 'anything' (P.8/17); מא עריפת נ״ית אש היי' 'I did not know what it is' (C.4/12); and עליש 'everything' (C.4/25).

The verb *qāla* 'speak' is often combined with the preposition *li-* 'to', to form קאלי 'he told me' (C.4/30, v3); קולתלו 'I told him' (C.4/31); and נקוליך 'I tell you' (C.4/v2). In a similar fashion, *sallama* 'greet' forms a compound with *li-* in וסלמלי 'greet from me' (C.4/v11); ואסלמלי 'greet from me' (C.4/v12); סלימלי 'greet from me' (C.4/v13); and תסלימלי 'greet from me' (C.4/15, v10).

Both the forms ליסעי' (C.4/v5) and ואסעי' (C.4/v10) for 'now' can be found.

2.12.8. Verbal Syntax

Plural verbs governed by inanimate subjects—normally expressed by the verb in the feminine singular, both in Classical Arabic and in Classical Judaeo-Arabic—appear, for example, in ראחו אלמושתיין 'the *mštyyn* sold' (C.4/7), and probably also in לא

ירוחו 'they are not selling' (C.4/9). On the other hand, when the object is animate and a plural pronoun is required, the writer uses the feminine singular pronoun, as if following the convention for inanimate objects, for example in בזכות גמיע אנביאים וצדיקים כולהי' 'for the merit of all, prophets and righteous men, all of them' (C.4/20). This may, again, betray a speaker of an Indo-European language.

2.12.9. Syntax

In מא עריפת נ״ת אש היי' 'I did not know what it is' (C.4/12), the colloquial form אש can be found introducing the complement clause.

The writer seems to use quite unusual connectives to introduce adverbial clauses. In מתל לו כאנית אוכתי 'as if she was my sister' (C.4/18), *miṯla law* appears as a comparative connective, while in כיף אני' נג'י אסכנדריי' נג'יבו פי ידי 'when I am going to Alexandria I will bring it in my hands' (C.4/v9), *kayfa* functions as a temporal connective.

The writer differentiates between singular *ʾinkān* and plural *ʾinkānū*, which means he does not use *ʾinkān* as a lexicalised conditional connective. Whereas *ʾinkān* occurs in C.4/27, 28, *ʾinkānū* can be found in l. 32.

Unusual noun phrases appear to replace finite verbs in אנתו בעמלי כתאב 'you are busy with (drawing up) a document' (C.4/30) and [...]ואנתו בעאריפ 'you should know' (C.4/6). Because of the limited number of examples, however, and in particular as the second example is corrupt, this phenomenon cannot be investigated until the appearance of further examples.

Taking together his crude hand, family name, and the general linguistic properties of his letters, it seems quite likely that the author was a Spanish Jew, who was able to write in Judaeo-Arabic to a degree. The writing is not entirely crude, certain polite letter-writing conventions are adhered to, and the language of the letter is relatively homogeneous in itself, so it is likely that the man himself was educated, but simply not a skilled writer of the Arabic language, nor of the Hebrew alphabet.

2.12.10. The Other Two Hands of P.8

Even though the handwriting is neater, the author of ll. 1–8 in letter P.8 appears to be an even more unskilled writer of Judaeo-Arabic than Elijah Qarqūsa, and very often, it is difficult to understand the basic meaning of his words. It is probably the handwriting of Mardūk Qarqūsa himself, before Elijah Qarqūsa starts acting as scribe for him from l. 9. The writer's inexperience or lack of practice may explain why he stops mid-sentence, and why Elijah Qarqūsa takes over.

One of the most obvious features of this writer's prose is the repeated *tafkīm* of /t/, for example in בטע 'belonging to' (P.8/4, 6); גהטי 'from me (lit. my side)' (P.8/4; although compare מין גהת in P.8/7); and יטעמלוה 'they will work on it' (P.8/8), which may point to a non-Arabic, Spanish origin of the writer. In the same way as Elijah, the author metathesises דינאר ונופץ 'dinar and a half' (P.8/5).

The writer writes a number of vowels *plene*, such as מין 'from' (P.8/4, 7), and strays from Classical Judaeo-Arabic orthography by writing והוא 'he' (P.8/7), which either reflects the vowel pattern or imitates Hebrew orthography. The same phenomenon can be found in מה ‘what’ (P.8/8), where the spelling with *he* instead of *ʾalef* may indicate a short /a/ vowel in the pronunciation or follow Hebrew spelling. In a few words, interesting vocalisations occur, such as אעוטיהו ‘I will give it’ (P.8/6), and מעוך ‘with you’ (P.8/8). In the first example, the /u/ may reflect an epenthesis of a *Murmelvokal* between Arabic *ʿayn* and *ṭāʾ* as perceived by the writer in the emphatic environment, or it may reflect a usual vowel pattern in an intensive stem (II form).

The third hand, in which the verso is written, is superficially closer to the hand of ll. 1–8, but shows some deviations, and linguistically adheres more closely to Classical Judaeo-Arabic conventions. There are still some colloquial features, such as the pattern *itfaʿala* for the fifth stem, e.g., ואתוצו ‘entrust it’ (P.8 /v4), and the 3rd masculine pronoun in בו ‘with him’ (P.8/v4). The writer also uses the vernacular form *nuṣṣ* in אשרפי ונוץ ‘an *ashrafī* dinar and a half’ (P.8/v3), whereas the other two authors write *nufṣ*.

3.0. Summary

As perhaps would be expected in letters written during a time that marks the big divide between Classical Judaeo-Arabic and Late Judaeo-Arabic, the letters of the corpus display features both of a more Classical Arabic nature and of a more progressive, Late Judaeo-Arabic linguistic register. There is great variation between the authors, with some retaining conservative forms throughout their writing, while others embrace spelling and forms influenced by colloquial norms. This shows that, by the time they were written, the education system had already undergone substantial changes, and that only the very elite of Jewish society was still familiar with the old prescriptive Arabic norms that had still been prevalent in eleventh- and twelfth-century middle-class utilitarian prose from the Genizah. Yet, a difference between documentary and literary Judaeo-Arabic can still be observed, as is obvious in letter P.9, with literary works still showing a stronger leaning towards Classically-influenced prescriptive norms. This is a strong indication that the abandonment of Classical Arabic style was not only a result of the decline of the education system but also a choice, at least in correspondence. In a society where Classical Arabic forms were marked as specifically literary and had less social prestige than in previous Genizah periods, colloquial forms would have been preferred in letters as a way to express immediacy between writers, in particular between those educated in an environment of pragmatic literacy (see Parkes 1973; Wagner 2017).

ABBREVIATIONS

Manuscript Collections

AIU Alliance Israélite Universelle, Paris
Bodl. Bodleian Library, Oxford
BL British Library, London
CUL Cambridge University Library
ENA Elkan Nathan Adler collection, Jewish Theological Seminary, New York
IMHM Institute of Microfilmed Hebrew Manuscripts, the National Library, Jerusalem
JTS Jewish Theological Seminary, New York
RNL Russian National Library, St Petersburg
TS Taylor-Schechter Collections, Cambridge University Library

Other Abbreviations

b. year of birth
b. son of (ben/bar/ibn)
C Communal documents
ca circa
d. year of death
f folio
H Hijri year
l. line
m margin
n. footnote

P	Private letters
pl.	plural
sg.	singular
W	Literary works
v	verso

REFERENCES

Primary Sources

Abravanel, Isaac. 1828. *Yeshu'ot Meshiḥo.*

ישועות משיחו. קרלסרוה [סדילקוב?]:[1] חסר שם מדפיס. תקפ"ח.

Abulafia, Meir ha-Levi. 1871. *Kitāb al-Rasā'il*, edited by Jehiel Bril.

כתאב אלרסאייל: ספר אגרות לרב רבינו מאיר הלוי ז"ל, מהד' יחיאל ברי"ל. פריז: חסר שם מדפיס. תרל"א.

al-Ashqar, Moses. 1554. *Responsa.*

שאלות ותשובות. סביונטה: דפוס טוביה פואה. שי"ד.

de Avila, Samuel. 1725. *Keter Torah.*

כתר תורה. אמסטרדם: דפוס שלמה פרופס. תפ"ה.

Berav, Jacob. 1663. *Responsa.*

שאלות ותשובות. ונציה: דפוס אנדריאה מורישיני. תכ"ג.

Conforti, David. 1846. *Qore ha-Dorot.*

ספר קורא הדורות. ברלין: דפוס דניאל פרידלאנדר, תר"ו.

Dayyan, Mordecai Ḥay. 1937. *Divre Emet.*

ספר דברי אמת: תעריב אלמקשייה באללוגה אליהודייה-ערבייה. תוניס: דפוס וזאן. תרצ"ז.

---

[1] The place of printing given on the title page is Karlsruhe, but it is well known that this record is false, and its intention was to avoid Russian censorship. Many cities have been put forward by scholars as the real place of printing (Lwów, Żółkiew, Tarnopol, and Ostroh) but it seems that it was in fact printed in Sudilkov (Sudylkiv, Ukraine). See Lieberman (1984, 536–40).

Duran, Shimon. 1738. *ha-Tashbeṣ.*

ספר התשב"ץ. אמסטרדם: דפוס נפתלי הירץ לוי. תצ"ח.

al-Ḥarīzī, Yehudah. 2009. *Kitāb al-Durar.*

כתאב אלדרר: והוא ספר פניני המוסרים ושבחי הקהלים, מהד' יהושע בלאו, יוסף יהלום ויוסף ינון־פנטון. ירושלים: מכון בן־צבי. תשס"ט.

Ibn Zimra, David. 1882. *Responsa.*

שו"ת הרדב"ז, א-ז. וורשה: דפוס נתן שריפטגיססער. תרמ"ב.

Ibn Paqudā, Baḥyā. 1973. *The Duties of the Heart,* edited by Yosef Qafiḥ.

תורת חובות הלבבות, מהד' יוסף קאפח. ירושלים: דפוס עקיבא יוסף. תשל"ג.

ha-Levi, Eliyahu. 1734. *Zeqan Aharon (Responsa).*

זקן אהרן. קושטנדינה: דפוס יונה בן אהרן אשכנזי. תצ"ד.

Maḥzor Aram Ṣoba. 1527.

מחזור: כפי מנהג ק"ק של ארם צובה. ונציה: דפוס דניאל בומבירגי. רפ"ז.

Maḥzor Ashkenza (Sukkut). 1981. Edited by Daniel Goldschmidt and Jonah Fraenkel.

מחזור סוכות: שמיני עצרת ושמחת תורה, לפי מנהגי בני אשכנז לכל ענפיהם. ירושלים: קורן. תשמ"א.

Maimonides, Abraham. 1937. *Responsa.*

תשובות רבנו אברהם בן הרמב"ם, מהד' אברהם חיים פריימן ושלמה דב גויטיין. ירושלים: מקיצי נרדמים. תרצ"ז.

Maimonides, Moses. 1931. *Dalālat al-Ḥā'irīn,* edited by Issachar Joel.

דלאלה אלחאירין לרבנו משה בן מימון; מהד' יששכר יואל, המקור הערבי לפי הוצאת שלמה בן אליעזר מונק. ירושלים: דפוס עזריאל. תרצ"א.

Maimonides, Moses. 1958–1986. *Responsa,* edited by Joshua Blau.

תשובות הרמב"ם, מהד' יהושע בלאו, א-ד. ירושלים: מקיצי נרדמים. תשי"ח–תשמ"ו.

Mujīr al-Dīn al-ʿUlamymi. 1968. *al-Uns al-Jalīl.*

كتاب الانس الجليل بتاريخ القدس والخليل. النجف : المطبعة الحيدرية. ١٣٨٨هج. ١٩٦٨.

Ṣahalon, Yom Tov. 1694. *Responsa.*

ספר שאלות ותשובות. ונציה: דפוס ונדראמין. תנ"ד.

Secondary Sources

Abrams, Daniel. 2013. 'A Commentary to the Ten Sefirot from early Thirteenth-Century Catalonia: Synoptic Edition, Translation and Detailed Commentary'. *Kabbalah* 30: 7–63.

Abulafia, David. 1988. 'The Levant Trade of the Minor Cities in the Thirteenth and Fourteenth Centuries: Strengths and Weaknesses'. *Asian and African Studies* 22 (1–3): 183–202.

———. 1994. 'The Role of Trade in Muslim–Christian Contact during the Middle Ages'. In *The Arab Influence in Medieval Europe*, edited by Dionisius A. Agius and Richard Hitchcock, 1–24. Reading: Ithaca Press.

Ackermann-Liebermann, Philip. 2024. *The Business of Identity: Jews, Muslims, and Economic Life in Medieval Egypt*. Stanford: Stanford University Press.

Adler, Elkan Nathan (ed.). 1930. *Jewish Travellers in the Middle Ages: 19 Firsthand Accounts.* London: Routledge.

Adler, Mordechai. 1907. ספר מסעות של ר' בנימין ז"ל, מהד' מרדכי אדלר. London: H. Frowde.

Allony, Nehemia. 1984.

'הספר ומלאכת הספר בארץ ישראל בימי הביניים'. שלם ד (תשמ״ד): 1–25.

Allouche, Adel. 1994. *Mamluk Economics: A Study and Translation of al-Maqrīzī's Ighāthah*. Salt Lake City: University of Utah Press.

Almagor, Ella. 1995.

כתבי היד של מדרשי ר' דוד הנגיד: מחקר ביבליוגרפי. ירושלים: מכון בן־צבי. תשנ"ה.

Amar, Zohar. 1995.

'השימוש בכסית האבוב בארץ־ישראל ובסוריה בימי הביניים'. קורות יא (תשנ"ה): 56–64.

ʿAodeh, Ṣabīḥ. 1992.

'המכתבים הערביים של הסוחרים היהודים בגניזת קהיר במאה האחת־עשרה'. עבודת דוקטור, אוניברסיטת תל אביב. תשמ"ב.

Aquilina, Joseph. 2006. *Concise Maltese–English English–Maltese Dictionary*. Sta Venera, Malta: Midsea.

Arad, Dotan. 2008.

'לדמותו של בעל הלכה מוסתערבי במאה השש–עשרה: ר' יוסף ן' ציאח'. שלם ח (תשס"ט): 134–248.

———. 2009.

'ערבית-יהודית ועברית בקרב יהודי סוריה, ארץ־ישראל ומצרים במאה החמש-עשרה והשש-עשרה'. פעמים 121 (תש"ע): 101–129.

———. 2011.

'הקהל כגוף כלכלי, הקדש המוסתערבים בקהיר לאור תעודות הגניזה'. גנזי קדם ז (תשע"א): 25–69.

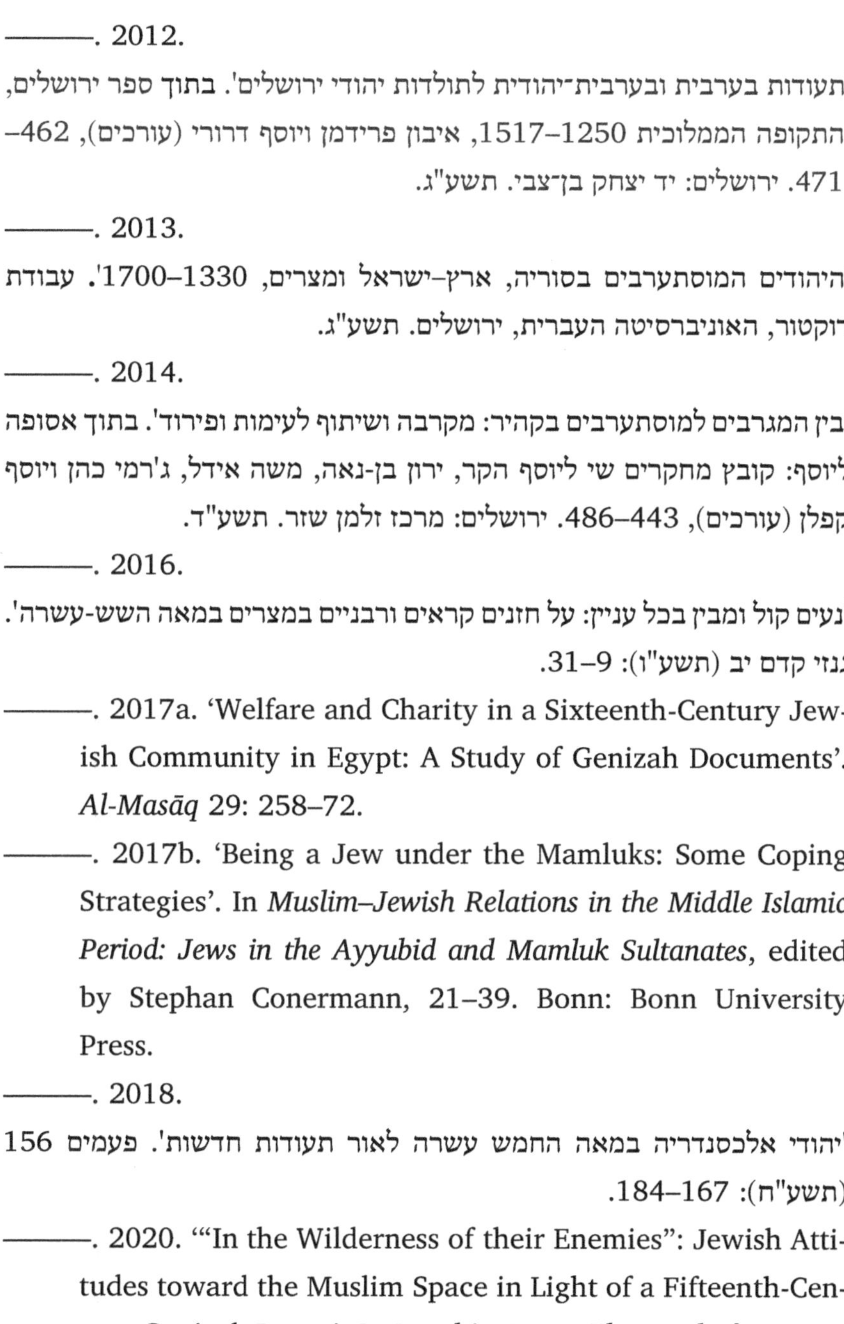

———. 2012.
'תעודות בערבית ובערבית־יהודית לתולדות יהודי ירושלים'. בתוך ספר ירושלים, התקופה הממלוכית 1250–1517, איבון פרידמן ויוסף דרורי (עורכים), 462–471. ירושלים: יד יצחק בן־צבי. תשע"ג.

———. 2013.
'היהודים המוסתערבים בסוריה, ארץ־ישראל ומצרים, 1330–1700'. עבודת דוקטור, האוניברסיטה העברית, ירושלים. תשע"ג.

———. 2014.
'בין המגרבים למוסתערבים בקהיר: מקרבה ושיתוף לעימות ופירוד'. בתוך אסופה ליוסף: קובץ מחקרים שי ליוסף הקר, ירון בן-נאה, משה אידל, ג'רמי כהן ויוסף קפלן (עורכים), 443–486. ירושלים: מרכז זלמן שזר. תשע"ד.

———. 2016.
'נעים קול ומבין בכל עניין: על חזנים קראים ורבניים במצרים במאה השש-עשרה'. גנזי קדם יב (תשע"ו): 9–31.

———. 2017a. 'Welfare and Charity in a Sixteenth-Century Jewish Community in Egypt: A Study of Genizah Documents'. *Al-Masāq* 29: 258–72.

———. 2017b. 'Being a Jew under the Mamluks: Some Coping Strategies'. In *Muslim–Jewish Relations in the Middle Islamic Period: Jews in the Ayyubid and Mamluk Sultanates*, edited by Stephan Conermann, 21–39. Bonn: Bonn University Press.

———. 2018.
'יהודי אלכסנדריה במאה החמש עשרה לאור תעודות חדשות'. פעמים 156 (תשע"ח): 167–184.

———. 2020. '"In the Wilderness of their Enemies": Jewish Attitudes toward the Muslim Space in Light of a Fifteenth-Century Genizah Letter'. In *Israel in Egypt: The Land of Egypt as*

Concept and Reality for Jews in Antiquity and the Early Medieval Period, edited by Alison Salvesen, Sarah Pearce, and Miriam Frenkel, 640–47. Leiden: Brill.

———. 2021.
'מיעוט בתוך מיעוט: קראים באימפריה העות'מאנית בצילם של יהודים רבניים'. היסטוריה 46–47 (תשפ"א): 63–102.

———. 2023.
'הרועה העושק והמשורר שקם להושיע: לתולדות הקראים באלכסנדריה בתקופה הממלוכית'. בתוך שמעו כי נגידים אדבר: ספר היובל לפרופ' מנחם בן־ששון, נחם אילן, חגי בן־שמאי ומרים פרנקל (עורכים), 47–68. ירושלים: מכון בן־צבי ומאגנס. תשפ"ד.

———. In press a. 'Elijah, Ezra and Samuel: The Cult of Biblical Figures among Jews in the Mamlūk and Early Ottoman Periods'. In *The Sacred in Mamlūk Society*, edited by Tetsuya Ohtoshi. Tokyo.

———. In press b. 'From the Synagogue to the Sharīʿa Court and Back: What Led to the Conflict within the Jewish Community in Cairo in 1466?'. *Medieval Encounters*.

Arad, Dotan, and Esther-Miriam Wagner. 2013. 'The Preacher who Speaks Like a Parrot: Two Versions of a Letter by R. Joshua ha-Nagid'. Cambridge University Library, Taylor-Schechter Genizah Research Unit, Fragment of the Month: January 2013. https://api.repository.cam.ac.uk/server/api/core/bitstreams/277d245a-1033-418e-86e3-4f6f3260a8b6/content (accessed 25 April 2025).

Arbel, Benjamin. 1988. 'Venetian Trade in Fifteenth-Century Acre: The Letters of Francesco Bevilaqua (1471–1472)'. *Asian and African Studies* 22: 227–88.

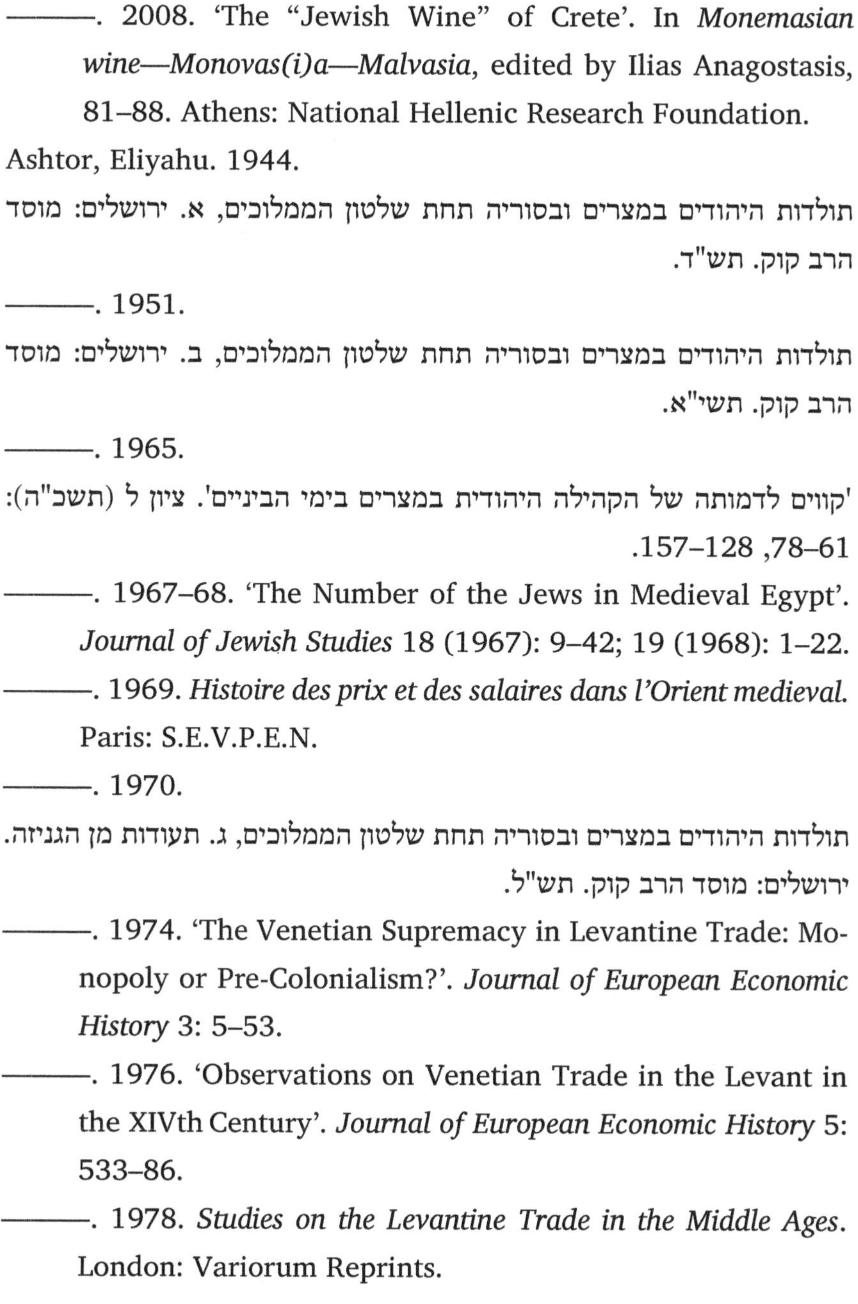

———. 2008. 'The "Jewish Wine" of Crete'. In *Monemasian wine—Monovas(i)a—Malvasia,* edited by Ilias Anagostasis, 81–88. Athens: National Hellenic Research Foundation.

Ashtor, Eliyahu. 1944.

תולדות היהודים במצרים ובסוריה תחת שלטון הממלוכים, א. ירושלים: מוסד הרב קוק. תש"ד.

———. 1951.

תולדות היהודים במצרים ובסוריה תחת שלטון הממלוכים, ב. ירושלים: מוסד הרב קוק. תשי"א.

———. 1965.

'קווים לדמותה של הקהילה היהודית במצרים בימי הביניים'. ציון ל (תשכ"ה): 61–78, 128–157.

———. 1967–68. 'The Number of the Jews in Medieval Egypt'. *Journal of Jewish Studies* 18 (1967): 9–42; 19 (1968): 1–22.

———. 1969. *Histoire des prix et des salaires dans l'Orient medieval.* Paris: S.E.V.P.E.N.

———. 1970.

תולדות היהודים במצרים ובסוריה תחת שלטון הממלוכים, ג. תעודות מן הגניזה. ירושלים: מוסד הרב קוק. תש"ל.

———. 1974. 'The Venetian Supremacy in Levantine Trade: Monopoly or Pre-Colonialism?'. *Journal of European Economic History* 3: 5–53.

———. 1976. 'Observations on Venetian Trade in the Levant in the XIVth Century'. *Journal of European Economic History* 5: 533–86.

———. 1978. *Studies on the Levantine Trade in the Middle Ages.* London: Variorum Reprints.

———. 1983. *The Jews and the Mediterranean Economy, 10–15th Centuries*. London: Variorum Reprints.

———. 1986. *East–West Trade in the Medieval Mediterranean*. London: Variorum Reprints.

———. 1992. *Technology, Industry, and Trade: The Levant versus Europe, 1250–1500*. London: Variorum Reprints.

Assaf, Simha. 1943.

באהלי יעקב, פרקים מחיי התרבות של היהודים בימי הביניים. ירושלים: מוסד הרב קוק. תש"ג.

———. 1946.

מקורות ומחקרים בתולדות ישראל. ירושלים: מוסד הרב קוק. תש"ו.

Avrahami, Isaac. 1994.

'תרגום המקרא לערבית יהודית של תוניס מאת ר' מרדכי חי דיין'. בתוך יצירה ותולדות בקהילות ישראל בספרד והמזרח, תמר אלכסנדר, אפרים חזן, גלית חזן־רוקם ואברהם חייג (עורכים), 73–88. ירושלים: משגב ירושלים. תשנ"ד.

Ayalon, David. 1939.

'ענייני נגידות במצרים בימי הביניים'. ציון ד (תרצ"ט): 126–149.

———. 1993. 'Some Remarks on the Economic Decline of the Mamlūk Sultanate'. *Jerusalem Studies in Arabic and Islam* 16: 108–24.

Baer, Fritz [Yitzhak]. 1929. *Die Juden im Christlichen Spanien*. Vol. 1. Berlin: Akademie-Verlag.

Bareket, Elinoar. 1999. *Fustat on the Nile: The Jewish Elite in Medieval Egypt.* Leiden: Brill.

———. 'Karaite Communities in the Middle East during the Tenth to Fifteenth Centuries'. In *Karaite Judaism: A Guide to its History and Literary Sources*, edited by Meira Polliack, 237–52. Leiden: Brill.

———. 2003. 'The Head of the Jews ("Ra'is al-Yahud") in Fatimid Egypt: A Re-evaluation'. *Bulletin of the School of Oriental and African Studies* 67 (2): 185–97.

Beeri, Tova. 1999.

'עולמו של יוסף בן אברהם הלוי; חזן מדמשק באמצע המאה השש עשרה'. ספונות כב (תשנ"ט): 241–273.

Behrens-Abouseif, Doris. 2019. *The Book in Mamluk Egypt and Syria (1250–1517)*. Leiden: Brill.

Beit-Arié Malachi, Colette Sirat, and Michael Glatzer. 1986. *Manuscrits médiévaux en caractères hébraïques*. Paris: Centre national de la recherche scientifique.

Ben-Sasson, Menahem. 1987.

'בני המגרב וקשריהם לארץ־ישראל במאות ט'–י"א'. שלם ה (תשמ"ז): 31–82.

———. 1991. 'Maimonides in Egypt: The First Stage'. *Maimonidean Studies* 2: 3–30.

Ben-Sasson, Menahem et al. 1991.

יהודי סיציליה, 825–1062. עזרו במחקר: נדיה זלדס ומרים פרנקל. ירושלים: מכון בן־צבי. תשנ"א.

Ben-Simeon, Aaron Raphael. 1908.

ספר טוב מצרים – רבני מצרים וגאוניה. ירושלים: שמואל צוקרמן. תרס"ח.

Ben-Yaakov, Abraham. 1974.

קברים קדושים בבבל: תיאורם של קברי אישים מתקופת התנ"ך, התלמוד והגאונים. ירושלים: מוסד הרב קוק. תשל"ד.

Ben-Ze'ev, Israel. 1957.

'בית הקברות היהודי הקדום בקהיר'. ספונות א (תשי"ז): ז-כד.

Benayahu, Meir. 1984.
'עסקי ספרים בין קנדיאה למצרים (תעודות מהגניזה)'. בתוך יד להימן: קובץ מחקרים לזכר א"מ הברמן, צבי מלאכי (עורך), 255–266. לוד: מכון הברמן למחקרי ספרות. תשמ"ד.

Berkey, Jonathan P. 2004. 'The Muḥtasibs of Cairo under the Mamluks: Toward an Understanding of an Islamic Institution'. In *The Mamluks in Egyptian and Syrian Politics and Society*, edited by Amalia Levanoni and Michael Winter, 245–76. Leiden: Brill.

Blau, Joshua. 1980a.
'הערות טקסטואליות לספרו של משה גיל על מסמכי הקדש מגניזת קהיר'. תרביץ מט (תש"ם): 207–217.

———. 1980b.
דקדוק הערבית־היהודית של ימי הביניים. ירושלים: מאגנס. תש"ם.

———. 1981. *The Emergence and Linguistic Background of Judaeo-Arabic*. 2nd ed. Oxford: Oxford University Press.

———. 1988. *Studies in Middle Arabic and its Judaeo-Arabic Variety*. Jerusalem: Magnes Press.

———. 2006. *A Dictionary of Mediaeval Judaeo-Arabic Texts*. Jerusalem: The Academy of the Hebrew Language.

Bosworth, Clifford E. 1972. 'Christian and Jewish Religious Dignitaries in Mamlūk Egypt and Syria: Qalqashandī's Information on their Hierarchy, Titulature, and Appointment'. *International Journal of Middle East Studies* 3: 59–74, 199–216.

Braslavi [Braslavski], Joseph. 1954.
'קטעי גניזה על רבת עמון ומעון(?) מן המאות הי"א–הי"ג'. ארץ ישראל ג (תשי"ד): 207–209.

Brinner, William M. 1999. 'A Fifteenth-Century Karaite–Rabbanite Dispute in Cairo'. In *The Majlis: Interreligious Encounters in Medieval Islam*, edited by Hava Lazarus-Yafeh, Mark R. Cohen, Sasson Somekh, and Sidney H. Griffith, 184–96. Wiesbaden: Harrassowitz.

Brown, Francis, Samuel R. Driver, and Charles A. Briggs. 1953. *A Hebrew and English Lexicon of the Old Testament*. Oxford: Clarendon Press.

Cahen, Claude. 1970. 'Quelques mots sur le déclin commercial du monde musulman à la fin du Moyen Âge'. In *The Economic History of the Middle East*, edited by Michael A. Cook, 31–36. London: Oxford University Press.

Chiesa, Bruno. 2008. 'Tanchum ben Yosef ha-Yerushalmi (m. 1291) e una insospettata fonte caraita'. In *Il mio cuore è a Oriente: studi di linguistica storica, filologia e cultura ebraica dedicati a Maria Luisa Mayer Modena*, edited by Francesco Aspesi, Vermondo Brugnatelli, Anna Linda Callow, and Claudia Rosenzweig, 341–48. Milano: Cisalpino.

Chojnacki, Stanley. 1999. 'From Trousseau to Groom Gift'. In *Medieval and Renaissance Venice*, edited by Ellen E. Kittell and Thomas F. Madden, 141–65. Urbana: University of Illinois Press.

Christ, Georg. 2012. *Trading Conflicts: Venetian Merchants and Mamlūk Officials in Late Medieval Alexandria*. Leiden: Brill.

Christie, Niall. 2014. *Muslims and Crusaders: Christianity's Wars in the Middle East, 1095–1382, from the Islamic Sources*. New York: Routledge.

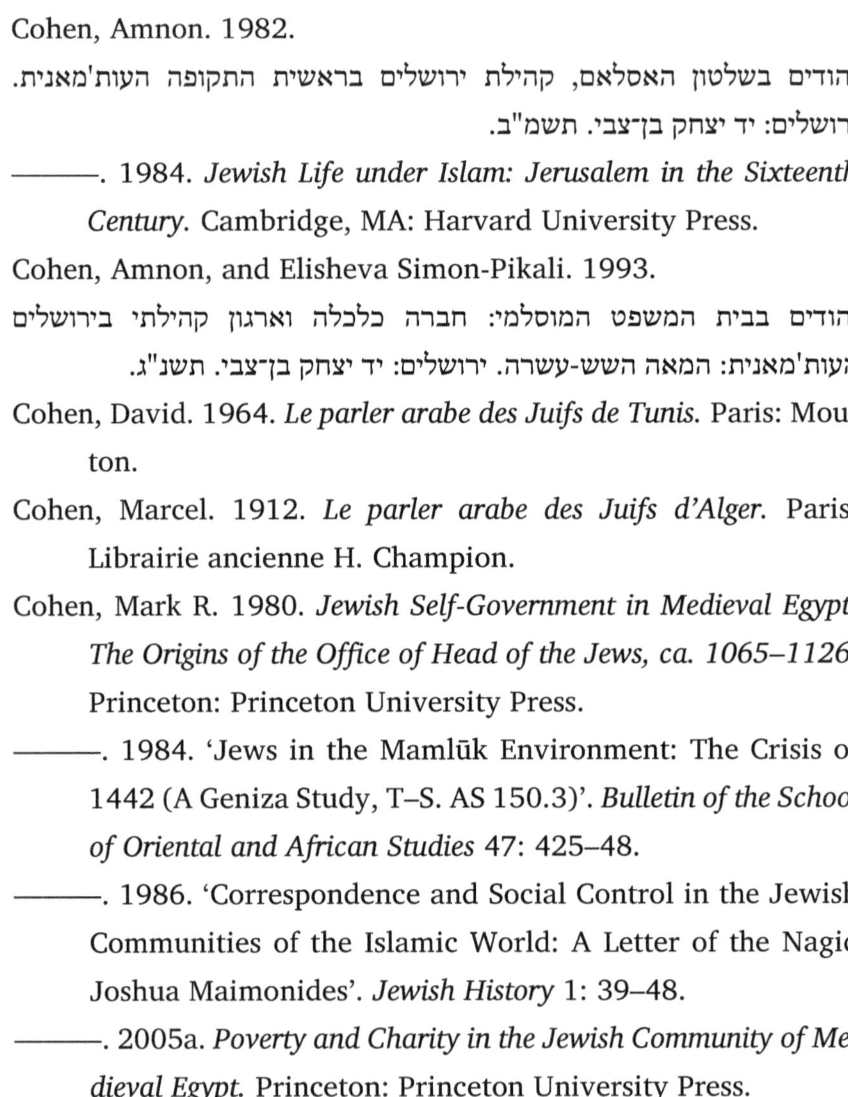

Cohen, Amnon. 1982.

יהודים בשלטון האסלאם, קהילת ירושלים בראשית התקופה העות'מאנית. ירושלים: יד יצחק בן־צבי. תשמ"ב.

———. 1984. *Jewish Life under Islam: Jerusalem in the Sixteenth Century.* Cambridge, MA: Harvard University Press.

Cohen, Amnon, and Elisheva Simon-Pikali. 1993.

יהודים בבית המשפט המוסלמי: חברה כלכלה וארגון קהילתי בירושלים העות'מאנית: המאה השש-עשרה. ירושלים: יד יצחק בן־צבי. תשנ"ג.

Cohen, David. 1964. *Le parler arabe des Juifs de Tunis.* Paris: Mouton.

Cohen, Marcel. 1912. *Le parler arabe des Juifs d’Alger.* Paris: Librairie ancienne H. Champion.

Cohen, Mark R. 1980. *Jewish Self-Government in Medieval Egypt: The Origins of the Office of Head of the Jews, ca. 1065–1126.* Princeton: Princeton University Press.

———. 1984. ‘Jews in the Mamlūk Environment: The Crisis of 1442 (A Geniza Study, T–S. AS 150.3)’. *Bulletin of the School of Oriental and African Studies* 47: 425–48.

———. 1986. ‘Correspondence and Social Control in the Jewish Communities of the Islamic World: A Letter of the Nagid Joshua Maimonides’. *Jewish History* 1: 39–48.

———. 2005a. *Poverty and Charity in the Jewish Community of Medieval Egypt.* Princeton: Princeton University Press.

———. 2005b. *The Voice of the Poor in the Middle Ages: An Anthology of Documents from the Cairo Geniza.* Princeton: Princeton University Press.

———. 2017. *Maimonides and the Merchants: Jewish Law and Society in the Medieval Islamic World.* Philadelphia: University of Pennsylvania Press.

Cuffel, Alexandra. 1999. 'Call and Response: European Jewish emigration to Egypt and Palestine in the Middle Ages'. *Jewish Quarterly Review* 90 (1–2): 61–102.

Darrāj, Aḥmad. 1963. 'Les relations commerciale entre l'État mamlouk et la France'. *Majallat Kullīyat al-Ādāb, Jāmiʿat al-Iskandarīyah* 25 (2): 1–21.

Dauverd, Céline. 2006. 'Genoese and Catalans: Trade Diaspora in Early Modern Sicily'. *Mediterranean Studies* 15: 42–61.

David, Abraham. 1972.

'לסיומה של הנגידות במצרים ולתולדותיו של אברהם די קאשטרו'. תרביץ מא (תשל"ב): 325–337.

———. 1979.

'המשמעות ההיסטורית של הזקנים בירושלים בדברי רבינו עובדיה מברטנורא'. בתוך פרקים בתולדות ירושלים בימי הביניים, בנימין זאב קדר וצבי ברס (עורכים), 221–243. ירושלים: יד יצחק בן־צבי. תשל"ט.

———. 1980.

'"וויצו נגיד" בהנהגה היהודית בירושלים במאה הט"ו ובראשית המאה הט"ז'. ציון מה (תש"ם): 327–331.

———. 1987.

'לתולדות חכמים בירושלים במאה השש-עשרה (לאור מסמכים חדשים מן הגניזה הקאהירית)'. שלם ה (תשמ"ז): 229–249.

———. 1988a.

'לתולדות בני משפחת שולאל במצרים וארץ-ישראל בסוף התקופה הממלוכית וראשית התקופה העות'מאנית, לאור מסמכים חדשים מן הגניזה'. בתוך גלות אחר גולה, מחקרים בתולדות עם ישראל מוגשים לפרופסור חיים ביינארט, אהרן

מירסקי, אברהם גרוסמן ויוסף קפלן (עורכים), 374–414. ירושלים: מכון בן־צבי. תשמ"ח.

———. 1988b.

'יישובי היהודים במאות ה־16–ה־17'. בתוך תולדות יהודי מצרים בתקופה העות'מאנית (1517–1914), ייעקב מ' לנדאו (עורך), 13–26. ירושלים: משגב ירושלים. תשמ"ח.

———. 1990–1991.

'לתולדותיו של ר' אלעזר בן החסיד ר' מתתיה מחכמי ארץ־ישראל(?) במאה הי"ג'. קרית ספר סג (תש"ן–תשנ"א): 996–998.

———. 1991.

'לתולדותיו של אברהם תלמיד הספרדי מנכבדי קהילת יהודי מצרים (לאור מסמכים חדשים מן הגניזה)'. בתוך מחקרים בספרות עם ישראל ובתרבות תימן: ספר היובל לפרופ' יהודה רצהבי, יהודית דישון ואפרים חזן (עורכים), 221–227. רמת־גן: הוצאת אוניברסיטת בר-אילן. תשנ"א.

———. 1999.

'מעורבותם של אחרוני הנגידים במצרים בענייני הקהילה היהודית בארץ ישראל'. תעודה טו (תשנ"ט): 293–332.

———. 2011. ‘The Role of Egyptian Jews in Sixteenth-Century International Trade with Europe: A Chapter in Social-Economic Integration in the Middle East’. In *“From a Sacred Source”: Genizah Studies in Honour of Professor Stefan C. Reif*, edited by Ben Outhwaite and Siam Bhayro, 99–126. Leiden: Brill.

———. 2013. *Jewish Settlement in Eretz ha-Zvi: Texts and Studies on Late Medieval Jewish History in the Land of Israel.* Jerusalem: Rubin Mass.

———. 2016.
חברה יהודית ים-תיכונית בשלהי ימי הביניים: לאור מסמכי גניזת קהיר. ירושלים וניו יורק: בית המדרש לרבנים באמריקה. תשע"ו.

Dishon, Judith. 2005.
ספר ערוגות הבשמים ליוסף בן תנחום הירושלמי. באר-שבע: אוניברסיטת בן-גוריון בנגב. תשס"ה.

Dols, Michael W. 1977. *The Black Death in the Middle East*. Princeton: Princeton University Press.

———. 1981. 'The General Mortality of the Black Death in the Mamluk Empire'. In *The Islamic Middle East, 700–1900*, edited by Abraham L. Udovitch, 397–428. Princeton: Darwin.

Dozy, Reinhart. 1881. *Supplément aux dictionnaires arabes*. Leiden: Brill.

Edbury, Peter W. 1991. *The Kingdom of Cyprus and the Crusades, 1191–1374*. Cambridge: Cambridge University Press.

EI[2] = Bearman, P. J., et al. 1960–2004. *The Encyclopaedia of Islam*. 2nd ed. Leiden: Brill.

el-Leithy, Tamer. 2005. 'Coptic Culture and Conversion in Medieval Cairo, 1293–1524 A.D.'. PhD diss., Princeton University.

Elizur, Shulamit. 2008.
'הפיוטים במחזור ארם צובה'. בתוך מחזור ארם צובה, כרך מבואות, מאיר בניהו, יונה פרנקל ושולמית אליצור (עורכים), 35–117. ירושלים: יד הרב נסים. תשס"ח.

Esposito, Mario. 1960. *Itinerarium Symonis Semeonis Ab Hybernia Ad Terram Sanctam*. Dublin: The Dublin Institute for Advanced Studies.

Fargeon, Maurice. 1938. *Les juifs en Egypte: depuis les origines jusqu'à ce jour.* Cairo: P. Barbey.

Fenton, Paul B. 1984. 'The Literary Legacy of David ben Joshua, Last of the Maimonidean Nĕgīdim'. *Jewish Quarterly Review* 75: 1–56.

———. 1987. *Obadiah et David Maïmonide: Deux traités de mystique juive*. Lagrasse: Verdier.

———. 1991. 'The Literary Legacy of Maimonides' Descendants'. In *Sobre la vida y obra de Maimonides*, edited by Jesús Peláez, 149–56. Cordoba: Editiones el Almendro.

———. 2000.

'הפירוש הערבי של ר' דוד בן יהושע מימוני על משנה תורה לרמב"ם'. בתוך מסורת ושינוי בתרבות הערבית־היהודית בימי הביניים, יהושע בלאו ודוד דורון (עורכים), 145–160. רמת־גן: אוניברסיטת בר־אילן. תש"ס.

———. 2003.

'מורשתם הספרותית של צאצאי הרמב"ם'. פעמים 97 (תשס"ד): 5–25.

———. 2006. 'A Mystical Commentary on the Song of Songs in the Hand of David Maimonides II'. In *Esoteric and Exoteric Aspects in Judeo-Arabic Culture*, edited by Benjamin Hary and Haggai Ben-Shammai, 19–53. Leiden: Brill.

Ferrer, Maria Teresa. 2012. 'Catalan Commerce in the Late Middle Ages'. *Catalan Historical Review* 5: 29–65.

Fischer, Wolfdietrich. 2002. *Grammar of Classical Arabic*. New Haven: Yale University Press.

Fleischer, Ezra. 1968.

'ראש ראשי חדשים'. תרביץ לז (תשכ"ח): 265–278.

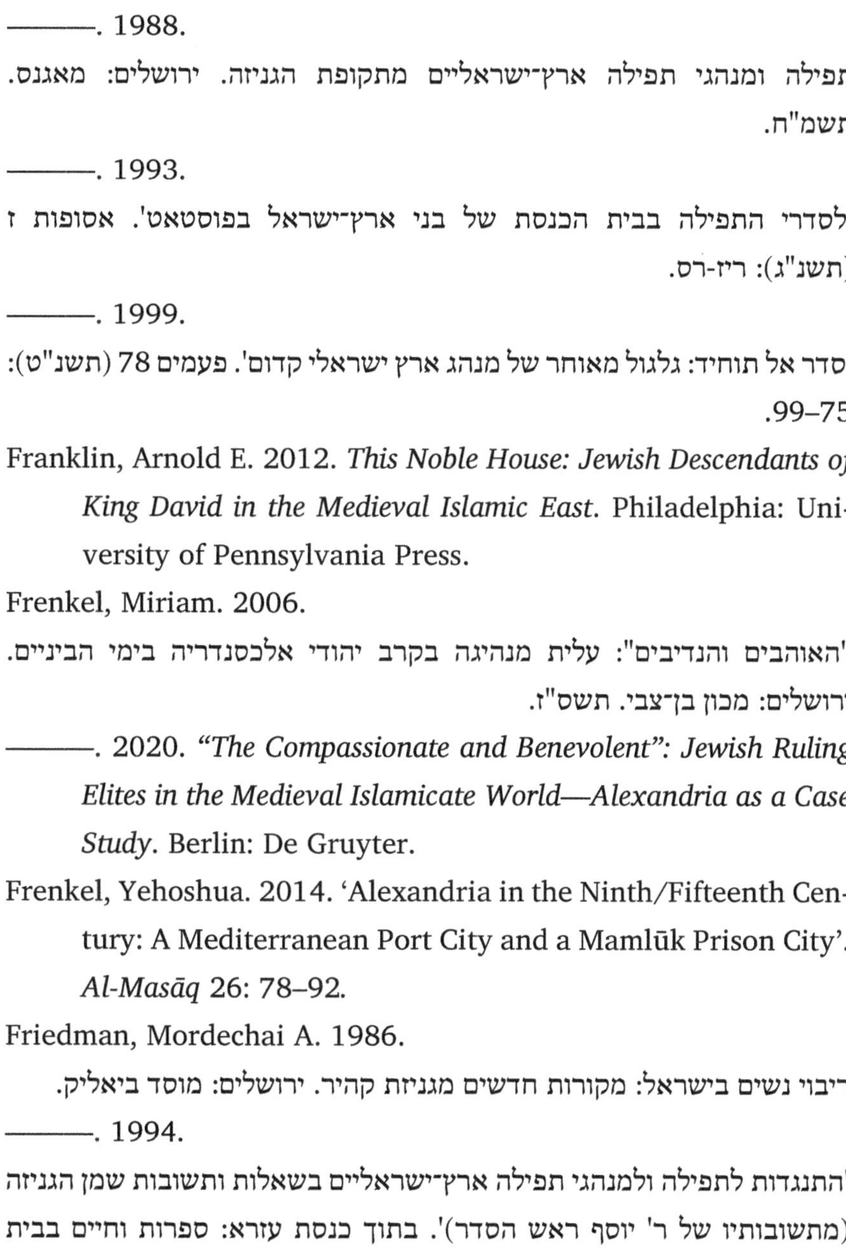

———. 1988.

תפילה ומנהגי תפילה ארץ־ישראליים מתקופת הגניזה. ירושלים: מאגנס. תשמ"ח.

———. 1993.

'לסדרי התפילה בבית הכנסת של בני ארץ־ישראל בפוסטאט'. אסופות ז (תשנ"ג): ריז-רס.

———. 1999.

'סדר אל תוחיד: גלגול מאוחר של מנהג ארץ ישראלי קדום'. פעמים 78 (תשנ"ט): 75–99.

Franklin, Arnold E. 2012. *This Noble House: Jewish Descendants of King David in the Medieval Islamic East*. Philadelphia: University of Pennsylvania Press.

Frenkel, Miriam. 2006.

"האוהבים והנדיבים": עלית מנהיגה בקרב יהודי אלכסנדריה בימי הביניים. ירושלים: מכון בן־צבי. תשס"ז.

———. 2020. *"The Compassionate and Benevolent": Jewish Ruling Elites in the Medieval Islamicate World—Alexandria as a Case Study*. Berlin: De Gruyter.

Frenkel, Yehoshua. 2014. 'Alexandria in the Ninth/Fifteenth Century: A Mediterranean Port City and a Mamlūk Prison City'. *Al-Masāq* 26: 78–92.

Friedman, Mordechai A. 1986.

ריבוי נשים בישראל: מקורות חדשים מגניזת קהיר. ירושלים: מוסד ביאליק.

———. 1994.

'התנגדות לתפילה ולמנהגי תפילה ארץ־ישראליים בשאלות ותשובות שמן הגניזה (מתשובותיו של ר' יוסף ראש הסדר)'. בתוך כנסת עזרא: ספרות וחיים בבית הכנסת, אסופת מאמרים מוגשת לעזרא פליישר, שולמית אליצור, משה דוד הר,

אביגדור שנאן וגרשון שקד (עורכים), 69–102. ירושלים: יד יצחק בן־צבי ומכון בן־צבי. תשנ"ה.

———. 1996.

'מחלוקת לשם שמים: עיונים בפולמוס התפילה של ר' אברהם בן הרמב"ם ובני דורו'. תעודה י (תשנ"ו): 245–298.

———. 1999.

'זעקת שבר על ביטול אמירת הפיוטים: בקשה לפנות לסולטן'. פעמים 78 (תשנ"ט): 128–147.

———. 2005.

'הרמב"ם, זוטא והמוקדמים: סיפורם של שלושה חרמות'.ציון ע (תשס"ה): 473–527.

———. 2016a.

'תלונה לסֻלטאן על ר' אברהם בן הרמב"ם'. ציון פא (תשע"ו): 335–390.

———. 2016b.

מילון הערבית־היהודית מימי הביניים לתעודות הגניזה של ספר הודו ולטקסטים אחרים. ירושלים: מכון בן־צבי, ירושלים. תשע"ו.

———. 2023.

הרמב"ם וגניזת קהיר. ירושלים: האקדמיה הלאומית הישראלית למדעים. תשפ"ד.

Gil, Moshe. 1976. *Documents of the Jewish Pious Foundations from the Cairo Geniza*. Leiden: Brill.

———. 1979.

'מגילת אביתר – מקור לתולדות מאבקיה של ישיבת ירושלים במחצית השנייה של המאה הי"א, קריאה חדשה של המגילה'. בתוך פרקים בתולדות ירושלים בימי הביניים, בנימין זאב קדר וצבי ברס (עורכים), 39–106. ירושלים: יד יצחק בן־צבי. תשל"ט.

———. 1992. *A History of Palestine, 634–1099*. Cambridge: Cambridge University Press.

———. 1997.

במלכות ישמעאל בתקופת הגאונים. תל-אביב: אוניברסיטת תל-אביב. 1997.

———. 2004. *Jews in Islamic Countries in the Middle Ages*. Leiden: Brill.

Gil, Moshe, and Ezra Fleischer. 2001.

יהודה הלוי ובני חוגו: 55 תעודות מן הגניזה. ירושלים: האיגוד העולמי למדעי היהדות. תשס"א.

Glick, Shmuel, et al. 2014.

שרידי תשובות מחכמי האימפריה העות'מאנית, מגניזת קהיר ומכתבי יד שבאוספי הספריות שבאוניברסיטת קמברידג', ג. ירושלים: מכון שוקן. תשע"ד.

Goitein, Shlomo Dov. 1948–1949.

'ספרו של אבן עובייה על הריסת בית הכנסת היהודי בירושלים בשנת 1474'. ציון יג–יד (תש"ח–תש"ט): 18–32.

———. 1953. ‘A Jewish Addict to Sufism in the Time of the Nagid David II Maimonides’. *Jewish Quarterly Review* 44: 37–49.

———. 1960. ‘The Documents of the Cairo Geniza as a Source for Mediterranean Social History’. *Journal of the American Oriental Society* 80 (2): 91–100.

——— 1962a. ‘The Title and Office of the Nagid: A Re-examination’. *Jewish Quarterly Review* 53: 93–119.

———. 1962b.

סדרי חינוך בתקופת הגאונים ובית הרמב"ם: מקורות חדשים מן הגניזה. ירושלים: מכון בן־צבי. תשכ"ב.

———. 1965.

'מכתב אל הרמב"ם בענייני הקדשות וידיעות חדשות על צאצאיו הנגידים'. תרביץ לד (תשכ"ה): 232–256.

———. 1971. *A Mediterranean Society*. Vol. 2, *The Community*. Berkeley: University of California Press.

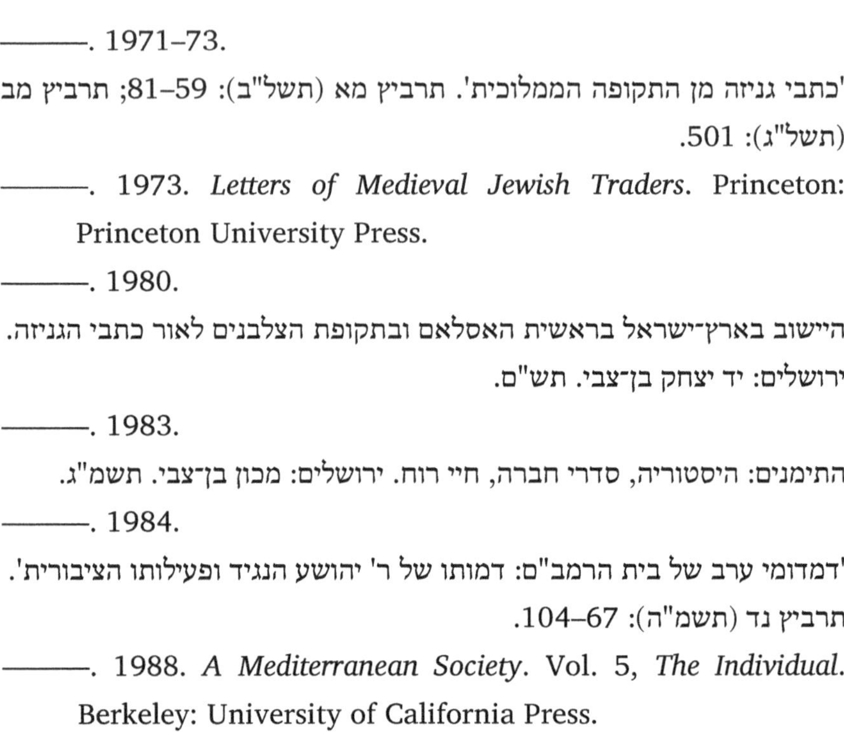

———. 1971–73.

'כתבי גניזה מן התקופה הממלוכית'. תרביץ מא (תשל"ב): 59–81; תרביץ מב (תשל"ג): 501.

———. 1973. *Letters of Medieval Jewish Traders*. Princeton: Princeton University Press.

———. 1980.

היישוב בארץ־ישראל בראשית האסלאם ובתקופת הצלבנים לאור כתבי הגניזה. ירושלים: יד יצחק בן־צבי. תש"ם.

———. 1983.

התימנים: היסטוריה, סדרי חברה, חיי רוח. ירושלים: מכון בן־צבי. תשמ"ג.

———. 1984.

'דמדומי ערב של בית הרמב"ם: דמותו של ר' יהושע הנגיד ופעילותו הציבורית'. תרביץ נד (תשמ"ה): 67–104.

———. 1988. *A Mediterranean Society*. Vol. 5, *The Individual*. Berkeley: University of California Press.

Goitein, Shlomo Dov and Mordechai A. Friedman. 2013.

ספר הודו ד (ב): חלפון הסוחר המשכיל והנוסע הגדול – תעודות מגניזת קהיר. ירושלים: מכון בן־צבי. תשע"ג.

Golb, Norman. 1965. 'The Topography of the Jews of Medieval Egypt I'. *Journal of Near Eastern Studies* 24: 251–71.

———. 1974. 'The Topography of the Jews of Medieval Egypt II'. *Journal of Near Eastern Studies* 33: 116–49.

Goldman, Israel M. 1970. *The Life and Times of Rabbi David Ibn Abi Zimra*. New York: Jewish Theological Seminary of America.

Granat, Yehoshua. 2001. 'Intertextual Polyphony: Scriptural Presence(s) in a Piyyutim Cycle by Yoseph Ibn Abitur'. *Zutot* 1: 64–76.

———. 2018.
'בקול פעמון ורימון לנֹא אמון: הגעתו של רבי יהודה הלוי לאלכסנדריה בראי שיר 'חדש' לאהרן אבן אלעמאני'. תרביץ פה (תשע"ח): 657–681.
Gottheil, Richard J. H. 1907. 'An Eleventh-Century Document Concerning a Cairo Synagogue'. *Jewish Quarterly Review (Old Series)* 19: 527–39.
Hacker, Joseph R. 1980.
'הנגידות בצפון-אפריקה בסוף המאה החמש-עשרה'. ציון מה (תש"ם): 119–132.
———. 1981.
'זיקתם ועלייתם של יהודי ספרד לארץ ישראל, 1391–1492'. קתדרה 36 (תשמ"א): 3–34.
———. 1984.
'"הרבנות הראשית" באימפריה העות'מאנית במאות הט"ו והט"ז'. ציון מט (תשמ"ד): 225–255.
———. 1985.
'ר' אליה מלה-מאסה בירושלים'. ציון נ (תשמ"ה): 241–263.
———. 1994. 'Jewish Autonomy in the Ottoman Empire: Its Scope and Limits—Jewish Courts from the Sixteenth to the Eighteenth Centuries'. In *The Jews of the Ottoman Empire*, edited by Avigdor Levi, 153–202. Princeton: Darwin.
———. 2000.
'יהודים מגרבים במצרים ובירושלים בסוף התקופה הממלוכית'. בתוך עטרה לחיים, מחקרים בספרות התלמודית והרבנית לכבוד פרופסור חיים זלמן דימיטרובסקי, דניאל בויארין ואחרים (עורכים), 573–603. ירושלים: מאגנס. תש"ס.

———. 2010.

'ה"מדרש" הספרדי – ספריה ציבורית יהודית'. בתוך ראשונים ואחרונים: מחקרים בתולדות ישראל מוגשים לאברהם גרוסמן, יוסף הקר ויוסף קפלן (עורכים), 263–292. ירושלים: מרכז זלמן שז"ר. תש"ע.

———. 2011.

'לדמותה של הנהגת קהל המוסתערבים בקהיר בסוף המאה השש-עשרה'. בתוך לא יסור שבט מיהודה: הנהגה, רבנות וקהילה בתולדות ישראל, מחקרים מוגשים לפרופ' שמעון שוורצפוקס, יוסף הקר וירון הראל (עורכים), 89–100. ירושלים: מוסד ביאליק. תשע"א.

Hartom, Menachem E., and Abraham David (eds). 1997.

מאיטליה לירושלים, איגרותיו של ר' עובדיה מברטנורא מארץ ישראל. רמת־גן: המחלקה ללימודי א"י, אוניברסיטת בר־אילן. תשנ"ז.

Hary, Benjamin. 1992. *Multiglossia in Judaeo-Arabic*. Leiden: Brill.

———. 1994. ‘Linguistic Notes on an Egyptian Judaeo-Arabic Passover Haggadah and the Study of the Egyptian *šarḥ*’. In *Actes des Premières journées internationales de diactologie arabe de Paris,* edited by Dominique Caubet and Martine Vanhove, 375–88. Paris: Inalco.

Herman, Arthur. 1997. *The Idea of Decline in Western History*. New York: The Free Press.

Herman, Geoffrey. 2012. *A Prince without a Kingdom: the Exilarch in the Sasanian Era*. Tübingen: Mohr Siebeck.

Hirschberg, Haim Z. 1974. ‘The Agreement between the Mustaʿribs and the Maghribis in Cairo, 1527’. In *Salo Wittmayer Baron Jubilee Volume,* edited by Saul Lieberman, 577–90. Jerusalem: American Academy for Jewish Research.

Hirschfeld, Hartwig. 1906. 'A Karaite Conversion Story'. In *Jews College Jubilee Volume: Comprising a History of the College by the Rev. Isidore Harris, and Essays by Teachers and Former Students of the Institution*, 81–100. London: Luzak and Co.

Hirshman, Marc (Menahem) (ed.). 2017.
מדרש קהלת רבה א-ו. ירושלים: מכון שכטר. תשע"ז.

Hofer, Nathan. 2017. 'The Ideology of Decline and the Jews of Ayyubid and Mamlūk Syria'. In *Muslim–Jewish Relations in the Middle Islamic Period: Jews in the Ayyubid and Mamlūk Sultanates (1171–1517)*, edited by Stephan Conermann, 95–120. Bonn: Bonn University Press.

Horbury, William, and David Noy. 1992. *Jewish Inscriptions of Graeco-Roman Egypt: With an Index of the Jewish Inscriptions of Egypt and Cyrenaica*. Cambridge: Cambridge University Press.

Huss, Boaz. 2016. *The Zohar: Reception and Impact.* Oxford and Portland, OR: The Littman Library of Jewish Civilization.

Ilan, Nahem. 2006. 'Between Halakhic Codification and Ethical Commentary: Rabbi Israel Israeli of Toledo on Intention in Prayer'. In *Esoteric and Exoteric Aspects in Judeo-Arabic Culture*, edited by Benjamin Hary and Haggai Ben-Shammai, 131–73. Leiden: Brill.

Imamuddin, S. M. 1980. 'Maritime Trade under the Mamluks of Egypt (644–923/1250–1517)'. *Hamdard Islamicus* 3 (4): 67–77.

Irwin, Robert. 1986. *The Middle East in the Middle Ages: The Early Mamluk Sultanate, 1250–1382*. Carbondale: Southern Illinois University Press.

Jacoby, David. 1987. 'Venice and Venetian Jews in the Eastern Mediterranean'. In *Gli Ebrei e Venezia (secoli XIV–XVIII)*, edited by Gaetano Cozzi, 29–58. Milano: Edizione di Comunità.

———. 1999. 'Cretan Cheese: A Neglected Aspect of Venetian Medieval Trade'. In *Medieval and Renaissance Venice*, edited by Ellen E. Kittel and Thomas F. Madden, 49–68. Urbana: University of Illinois Press.

Kalmin, Richard L. 2014. 'Zechariah and the Bubbling Blood: An Ancient Tradition in Jewish, Christian, and Muslim Literature'. In *Jews, Christians, and Zoroastrians: Religious Dynamics in a Sasanian Context*, edited by Geoffrey Herman, 203–51. Piscataway, NJ: Gorgias Press.

Kanaforgel, Ephraim. 1986. 'The *ʿAliyah* of "Three Hundred Rabbis" in 1211: Tosafist Attitudes toward Settling in the Land of Israel'. *Jewish Quarterly Review* 76: 191–215.

Kazimirski, A. de Biberstein. 1860. *Dictionnaire Arabe–Français*. Paris: Maisonneuve.

Kiperwasser, Reuven. 2005.

'מדרשי קהלת: התהוות ועריכה'. עבודת דוקטור, אוניברסיטת בר־אילן. תשס"ה.

———. 2007. 'Structure and Form in Kohelet Rabbah as Evidence of its Redaction'. *Journal of Jewish Studies* 58: 283–302.

Khan, Geoffrey. 1991.

'בחינה של הערבית־היהודית בתעודות הגניזה המאוחרות והשוואתה עם הערבית־היהודית הקלאסית'. ספונות כ (תשנ"א): 223–234.

———. 1992. 'Notes on the Grammar of a Late Judaeo-Arabic Text'. *Jerusalem Studies in Arabic and Islam* 15: 220–39.

———. 2006. 'A Judaeo-Arabic Commercial Letter from Early Nineteenth Century Egypt'. *Ginzei Qedem* 2: 37*–59*.

———. 2013. 'A Judaeo-Arabic Document from Ottoman Egypt in the Rylands Genizah Collection'. In *From Cairo to Manchester: Studies in the Rylands Genizah Fragments*, edited by Renate Smithuis and Phillip S. Alexander, 233–48. Oxford: Oxford University Press.

Koehler, Ludwig, and Baumgartner, Walter. 1995. *The Hebrew and Aramaic Lexicon of the Old Testament*. 3rd ed. Vol. 2. Leiden: Brill.

Krauss, Samuel, 1928.

'בתי כנסיות עתיקים בארץ־ישראל ובארצות הקדם'. ירושלים, קובץ החברה העברית לחקירת ארץ־ישראל ועתיקותיה ב (תרפ"ח): רכא-רמט.

Labib, Subhi Y. 1978. 'al–Iskandariyya'. In *EI*², 132–37.

Lane, Edward William, and Stanley Lane-Poole. 1863–1893. *An Arabic–English Lexicon*. London: Williams and Norgate.

Leibson, Gideon. 1975.

'על מה מנדין (עילות הנידוי בארץ־ישראל ובבבל בתקופת המשנה והתלמוד)'. שנתון המשפט העברי ב (תשל"ה): 292–342.

Lev, Efraim. 2002. 'Trade of Medical Substances in the Medieval and Ottoman Levant (Bilad al-Sham)'. In *Towns and Material Culture in the Medieval Middle East*, edited by Yaacov Lev, 159–83. Leiden: Brill.

Lieberman, Chaim. 1984.

אהל רח"ל, ג. ניו יורק: הוצאת המחבר. תשמ"ד.

Liebes, Yehuda. 1993. 'How the *Zohar* was Written'. In *Studies in the Zohar*, 85–138, 194–227. Albany: State University of New York Press.

Little, Donald P. 1976. 'Coptic Conversion to Islam under the Baḥrī Mamlūks, 692–755/1293–1354'. *Bulletin of the School of Oriental and African Studies* 39: 552–69.

Luz, Nimrod. 2004.

'הזירה הציבורית בירושלים הממלוכית והשתקפותה בפרשת בית הכנסת היהודי'. המזרח החדש מד (תשס"ד): 127–143.

———. 2014. *The Mamlūk City in the Middle East: History, Culture, and the Urban Landscape*. Cambridge: Cambridge University Press.

Mann, Jacob. 1920. *The Jews in Egypt and in Palestine under the Fatimid Caliphs*. Vol. 1. London: Oxford University Press.

———. 1926. 'A Second Supplement to the Jews in Egypt and In Palestine Under the Fāṭimid Caliphs'. *Hebrew Union College Annual* 3: 257–308.

———. 1931. *Texts and Studies in Jewish History and Literature*. Vol. 1. Cincinnati: Hebrew Union College Press.

———. 1935. *Texts and Studies in Jewish History and Literature*. Vol. 2. Cincinnati: Hebrew Union College Press.

Mayer, Leo A. 1938.

'עמדת היהודים בימי הממלוכים'. בתוך ספר מאגנס, קובץ מחקרים מאת אנשי האוניברסיטה העברית, י"נ אפשטיין ואחרים (עורכים), 161–167. ירושלים: האוניברסיטה העברית. תרצ"ח.

Mazor, Amir. 2001. 'The Jews in Medieval Egypt under the Mamlūks (1250–1517)'. In *The Jews in Medieval Egypt*, edited by Miriam Frenkel, 244–68. Boston: Brill.

Meloy, John L. 2003. 'Imperial Strategy and Political Exigency: The Red Sea Spice Trade and the Mamluk Sultanate in the

Fifteenth Century'. *Journal of the American Oriental Society* 123 (1): 1–19.

Meroz, Ronit. 2007. 'The Path of Silence: An Unknown Story from a Zohar Manuscript'. *European Journal of Jewish Studies* 1 (2): 319–42.

———. 2018.
הביוגרפיה הרוחנית של רבי שמעון בר יוחאי: דיון ביסודותיו הטקסטואליים של הזוהר. ירושלים: ביאליק. תשע"ח.

Modrzejewski, Joseph. 1995. *The Jews of Egypt: from Rameses II to Emperor Hadrian*. Philadelphia: Jewish Publication Society.

Müller-Wiener, Martina. 1992. *Eine Stadtgeschichte Alexandrias von 564/1169 bis in die Mitte des 9./15. Jahrhunderts: Verwaltung und innerstädtische Organisationsformen*. Berlin: K. Schwarz.

Nave, Pnina. 1970. 'The Works of Joseph ben Tanhum of Jerusalem'. *Studies in Bibliography and Booklore* 9: 57–75.

Neubauer, Adolf. 1886. *Catalogue of the Hebrew Manuscripts in the Bodleian Library*. Vol. 1. Oxford: Clarendon.

Neusner, Jacob. 1969. *A History of the Jews in Babylonia*. Part 1, *The Parthian Period*. Leiden: Brill.

Oron, Michal. 1980.
'ה'פליאה' ו'הקנה': יסודות הקבלה שבהם, עמדתם הדתית חברתית ודרך עצובם הספרותית'. עבודת דוקטור, האוניברסיטה העברית, ירושלים. תש"ם.

———. 2014.
'הספרות הפרשנית לעשרת הספירות'. בתוך אסופה ליוסף: קובץ מחקרים, שי ליוסף הקר, ירון בן-נאה, משה אידל, ג'רמי כהן ויוסף קפלן (עורכים), 212–229. ירושלים: מרכז זלמן שז"ר. תשע"ד.

Parkes, Malcolm. 1973. 'The Literacy of the Laity'. In *The Mediaeval World*, edited by David Daiches and Anthony Thorlby, 555–77. London: Aldus Books.

Pedani Fabris, Maria Pia. 2002. 'Bahr-i Mamluk-Venetian Commercial Agreements'. In *The Turks*, edited by Hasan Celâl Güzel, C. Cem Oğuz, and Osman Karatay, 298–305. Ankara: Yeni Türkiye Publications.

Pely, Hagai. 2008.
'הקנה והפליאה: הלכה ומטא־הלכה'. עבודת מ"א, האוניברסיטה העברית, ירושלים. תשס"ח.

Polliack, Meira. 1997. *The Karaite Tradition of the Arabic Bible Translation: A Linguistic and Exegetical Study of the Karaite Translations of the Pentateuch from the Tenth to the Eleventh Centuries CE*. Leiden: Brill.

Reiner, Elchanan. 1988.
'עלייה ועלייה לרגל לארץ ישראל, 1099–1517'. עבודת דוקטור, האוניברסיטה העברית, ירושלים. תשמ"ח.

———. 1992.
'הנהגת הקהילה בירושלים בשלהי התקופה הממלוכית; תעודות ובירורים בשולי "פרשת הזקנים"'. שלם ו (תשנ"ב): 23–81.

Richards, Donald S. 1972. 'Arabic Documents from the Karaite Community in Cairo'. *Journal of the Economic and Social History of the Orient* 15 (1972): 105–62.

Richler, Benjamin. 1981.
'מגנזי המכון לתצלומי כתבי היד העבריים של בית הספרים הלאומי והאוניברסיטאי'. קרית ספר נו (תשמ"א): 745–746.

Riegler, Michael. 2010.
'היהודים באיי אגן הים התיכון המזרחי כספקי ספרים: ידיעות מתוך קולופונים של כתבי יד עבריים מן המאות ה־13-ה־16'. עלי ספר כא (תש"ע): 75–90.
Rozen, Minna. 1981.
'מעמד המוסתערבים והיחסים בין העדות ביישוב היהודי בארץ ישראל משלהי המאה הט"ו עד שלהי המאה הי"ז [בעיקר בירושלים ובצפת]'. קתדרה 17 (תשמ"א): 73–101.
Russ-Fishbane, Elisha. 2015. *Judaism, Sufism, and the Pietists of Medieval Egypt: A Study of Abraham Maimonides and His Times*. Oxford: Oxford University Press.
Rustow, Marina. 2007. 'Karaites Real and Imagined: Three Cases of Jewish Heresy'. *Past and Present* 197: 35–74.
———. 2008. *Heresy and the Politics of Community: The Jews of the Fatimid Caliphate*. Ithaca: Cornell University Press.
Sandberg, Ruth Naomi. 1999. *Rabbinic Views of Qohelet*. Lewiston: Mellen Biblical Press.
Scheindlin, Raymond P. 2008. *The Song of the Distant Dove: Judah Halevi's Pilgrimage*. Oxford: Oxford University Press.
Schorreel, Thomas. 2011. 'An Edition and Translation of T-S Ar. 54.63 with a Grammatical Analysis of the Text'. MA thesis, University of Ghent. https://lib.ugent.be/fulltxt/RUG01/001/786/425/RUG01-001786425_2012_0001_AC.pdf (accessed 28 April 2025).
Schur, Nathan. 1992. *History of the Samaritans*. Frankfurt am Main: Peter Lang.
Schwarzfuchs, Simon. 1995. 'The Sicilian Jewish Communities in the Ottoman Empire'. *Italia Judaica* 5: 397–411.

Sela, Shulamit. 1994. ‘The Head of the Rabbanite, Karaite and Samaritan Jews: On the History of a Title’. *Bulletin of the School of Oriental and African Studies* 57: 255–67.

Sennoune, Oueded. 2004. ‘Fondouks, khans et wakalas à Alexandrie à travers les récits de voyageurs’. *Annales islamologiques/Ḥawlīyāt Islāmīyah* 38 (2): 453–89.

Shtober, Simon (ed.). 1994.
ספר דברי יוסף לר' יוסף ב"ר יצחק סמברי: אלף ומאה שנות תולדה יהודית בצל האסלאם. ירושלים: מכון בן־צבי. תשנ"ד.

Shtober, Simon. 2005. ‘The Establishment of the Riʾāsat al-Yahūd in Medieval Egypt as Portrayed in the Chronicle Divrey Yosef: Myth or History?’. *Revue des Études Juives* 164: 33–54.

Shy, Hadassa, 1997.
הדסה שי, 'תנחום בן יוסף הירושלמי'. בתוך פרקים בעברית לתקופותיה: אסופת זיכרון לשושנה בהט, משה בר אשר (עורך), 197–206. ירושלים: האקדמיה ללשון עברית. תשנ"ז.

Singer, Amy. 1994. *Palestinian Peasants and Ottoman Officials, Rural Administration Around Sixteenth-Century Jerusalem*. Cambridge: Cambridge University Press.

Sokoloff, Michael. 2002. *A Dictionary of Jewish Babylonian Aramaic of the Talmudic and Geonic Periods*. Ramat-Gan: Bar-Ilan University Press.

Spiro, Sokrates. 1895. *An Arabic–English Dictionary of the Colloquial Arabic of Egypt*. London: Quaritch.

Ta–Shema, Israel. 1980.
'היכן נתחברו ספרי הפליאה והקנה?'. בתוך פרקים בתולדות החברה היהודית בימי הביניים ובעת החדשה, מוקדשים לפרופסור יעקב כ"ץ במלאת לו שבעים

וחמש שנה, עמנואל אטקס ויוסף שלמון (עורכים), נו–סג. ירושלים: מאגנס. תש"ם.

———. 2010.
כנסת מחקרים: עיונים בספרות הרבנים בימי הביניים, ד: ארצות המזרח, פרובנס ומאסף. ירושלים: מוסד ביאליק. תש"ע.

Taragan, Bension. 1932. *Les communautés israélites d'Alexandrie: Aperçu historique depuis les temps des Ptolémées jusqu'à nos jours*. Alexandria: Les editions juives d'Egypte.

Tirosh-Becker, Ofra. 1990.
'הגלוסות הערביות שב"מקרי דרדקי" בנוסחו האיטלקי - מה טיבן?'. איטליה ט (תש"ן). לז–עז.

Toledano, Jacob M. 1907.
'לתולדות הנגידים בני שולאל במצרים ובארץ ישראל'. העולם א (תרס"ח), גליון מג: 519–520.

———. 1937–1938. 'בתי הכנסת העתיקים באלכסנדריה ובסביבתה'. *Hebrew Union College Annual* 12–13 (1937–1938): 701–14.

Valérian, Dominique. 2004. 'Le fondouk, instrument du contrôle sultanien sur les marchands étrangers dans les ports musulmans (XIIe-XVe siècles)?'. In *La mobilité des personnes en Méditerranée de l'antiquité à l'époque moderne: procédures de contrôle et documents d'identification*, edited by Claudia Moatti, 677–98, 741. Rome: École française de Rome.

———. 2005. 'Les marchands latins dans les ports musulmans méditerranéens: une minorité confinée dans des espaces communautaires?'. *Revue des mondes musulmans et de la Méditerranée* 107–10: 437–58.

Wagner, Esther-Miriam. 2010. *Linguistic Variety of Judaeo-Arabic in Letters from the Cairo Genizah*. Leiden: Brill.

———. 2017. 'The Socio-Linguistics of Judaeo-Arabic Mercantile Writing. In *Merchants of Innovation: The Languages of Traders*, edited by Esther-Miriam Wagner, Bettina Beinhoff, and Ben Outhwaite, 68–86. Berlin: De Gruyter–Mouton.

Wagner, Esther-Miriam, and Mohamed Ahmed. 2017. 'From Tuscany to Egypt: 18th c. Arabic Letters in the Prize Paper Collections'. *Journal of Semitic Studies* 62 (2): 389–412.

Wahrmund, Adolf. 1898. *Handwörterbuch der neu-arabischen und deutschen Sprache*. Giessen: J. Ricker'sche Verlags-Buchhandlung.

Wansbrough, John. 1965. 'Venice and Florence in the Mamluk Commercial Privileges'. *Bulletin of the School of Oriental and African Studies* 28 (3): 483–523.

Weinberger, Leon J. 1994. 'Moses Darī, Karite Poet and Physician'. *Jewish Quarterly Review* 84: 445–48.

———. 2000. *Jewish Poet in Muslim Egypt: Moses Darʿī's Hebrew Collection*. Leiden: Brill.

Wiet, Gaston. 1955. 'Les marchands d'épices sous les sultans mamlouks'. *Cahiers d'histoire égyptienne* 7: 81–147.

———. 1962. *La grande peste noire en Syrie et en Egypte*. Paris: G.-P. Maisonneuve et Larose.

Winter, Michael. 1983.

'יהודי מצרים בתקופה העות'מאנית לפי מקורות תורכיים וערביים'. פעמים 16 (תשמ"ג): 5–21.

Yaari, Abraham (ed.). 1948.

מסע משולם מוולטרה בארץ ישראל בשנת רמ"א (1481). ירושלים: מוסד ביאליק. תש"ט.

Yahalom, Joseph. 2008.

שירת חייו של רבי יהודה הלוי. ירושלים: מאגנס. תשס"ח.

Yeshaya, Joachim J.M.S. 2011. *Medieval Hebrew Poetry: The Secular Poetry of the Karaite Poet Moses ben Abraham Darʿī*. Brill: Leiden.

———. 2014. *Poetry and Memory in Karaite Prayer: The Liturgical Poetry of the Karaite Poet Moses ben Abraham Darʿī*. Brill: Leiden.

Zawanowska, Marzena. 2010. 'Moses ben Samuel of Damascus'. In *Encyclopedia of Jews in the Islamic World*, vol. 3, edited by Norman A. Stillman et al., 481–82. Leiden: Brill.

Zevin, Josef (ed.). 1983.

אנציקלופדיה תלמודית לעניני הלכה, כרך יז. ירושלים: יד הרב הרצוג. תשמ"ג.

TABLE OF ORIENTATION

Oxford

Bodl. MS Heb. c.	Document no.
72/1	W.1
72/2	P.9
72/3	W.1
72/4	W.2.a
72/5	W.2.b
72/6	W.6.a
72/7	W.6.a
72/8	W.6.c
72/9	W.6.b
72/10	P.5.a
72/11	P.4.a
72/12	P.4.b
72/13	P.4.c
72/14	P.5.b
72/14bis	C.1.d
72/15	P.4.d
72/16	P.2
72/17	C.2
72/18	P.6
72/19	P.3.a
72/20	P.3.b
72/21	C.1.a
72/22	P.3.c

Bodl. MS Heb. c.	Document no.
72/23	P.7
72/24	P.9
72/25	P.4.e
72/26	P.4.f
72/27	P.4.g
72/28	C.1.b
72/29	P.3.d
72/30	C.1.a
72/31	C.6
72/32	P.3.e
72/33	C.6
72/34	C.6
72/35	C.4
72/36	C.4
72/37	P.8
72/38	C.5
72/39	P.3.f
72/40	C.1.a
72/41	C.1.b
72/42	P.3.g
72/43	P.4.g
72/44	C.3
72/45	W.3
72/46	W.7
72/47	W.4
72/48	C.7
72/49	C.7

Bodl. MS Heb. c.	Document no.
72/50	P.3.h
72/51	W.5
72/52	W.5
72/53	C.1.c
72/54	P.11

New York, The Jewish Theological Seminary

ENA 4010.6	P.1
MS 2331, pp. 217b–218a	P.10

INDEX OF TEXTS

Hebrew Bible

Rabbinic Texts

Mishnah

Tosefta

Jerusalem Talmud

Babylonian Talmud

Other Works

INDEX OF NAMES

Personal Names

Place Names

GENERAL INDEX

About the Team

Alessandra Tosi and Geoffrey Khan were the managing editors for this book and provided quality control.

Anne Burberry and Paul Moore performed the copyediting of the book in Word.

The fonts used in this volume are Charis SIL, Scheherazade New and SBL Hebrew.

Annie Hine created all of the editions — paperback, hardback, and PDF. Conversion was performed with open source software freely available on our GitHub page at https://github.com/OpenBookPublishers.

Jeevanjot Kaur Nagpal designed the cover of this book. The cover was produced in InDesign using Fontin and Calibri fonts.

www.ingramcontent.com/pod-product-compliance
Lightning Source LLC
Chambersburg PA
CBHW061112100726
47911CB00013B/513

* 9 7 8 1 8 0 5 1 1 0 7 0 5 *